Praise for *The Political Brain*

★ ★ ★

"This is the most interesting, informative book on politics I've read in many years. . . . [Westen's] suggestions for what candidates should say—and should have said—should be read and studied by anyone who wants to understand modern American politics. This book is a handbook for how to talk about what really matters to you, written in just the way Westen says we should talk to voters—with vivid language, evocative imagery, and a sense of humor. It's also a good primer on why attacks can't go unanswered and how best to respond to them. If you want to know why candidates win or lose elections and what voters look for in a leader—whether you're an interested voter or a candidate for public office—you have to read this book."

— PRESIDENT BILL CLINTON

"This book could easily be titled *The Next Step*. Democrats have caught up with Republicans in being able to target voters and we're making rapid strides in rebuilding our party so we can talk to voters in fifty states. This book outlines a more intractable problem: How to actually talk to voters once we organize. Drew Westen is a must read and must hear for any Democrat who wants to win in Mississippi, Colorado, or rural Ohio. In 2006 we did win in those areas. In 2008 we will win the presidency if our candidate reads and acts on this book."

— HOWARD DEAN, chairman, Democratic Party

"*The Political Brain* is the most illuminating book on contemporary American politics I've ever read. By explaining how voters actually process information, Drew Westen lays bare the connection between politicaltechnique, political conviction, and the Democrats' habit of bungling winnable elections. If every leading Democratic politician reads this book, we could have a decent America back."

— ROBERT KUTTNER, cofounder and editor-in-chief,
The American Prospect

"In recent years, a small number of experts on language and rhetoric have been touted as the Democrats' savior. None of these panned out. . . . Many people are therefore skittish about anyone being heralded as the next source of advice. But Westen's analyses and suggestions speak precisely to Democrats' greatest tactical failures of the last quarter-century, and they do so without descending to the level of 'Mission Accomplished' banners and the 'death tax.' It will be fascinating to see how *The Political Brain* is received among the Democratic political professionals, who are for the most part insular and arrogant and have an explanation for everything. But Westen's explanations sound better than the ones that have long been circulating in Washington."

—MICHAEL TOMASKY, *The New York Review of Books*

"Why do most Americans agree with Democrats and vote for Republicans? Because Republicans know more about the human brain than their opponents do. In a delightful and insightful book, Westen uses the latest research in psychology and cognitive neuroscience to show how Republicans win by appealing to the heart while Democrats lose by appealing to the mind. This fascinating book will appeal to hearts and minds on both sides of the aisle. *The Political Brain* is scary and scary smart, serious and seriously funny. Machiavelli, move over, there's a new kid in town."

—DANIEL GILBERT, Harvard College Professor of Psychology, Harvard University, and author of *Stumbling on Happiness*

"In the last several months, [Westen] has gone from a politically inclined nobody to a hot ticket, presenting his ideas to presidential campaigns, political strategists, pollsters, consultants, and donors. In his work, they hope to find a grand unified theory of How Democrats Can Stop Blowing It." —*Los Angeles Times*

"*The Political Brain* . . . has catapulted the Emory University professor from the ivory tower to the political epicenter. And Democrats throughout the capital are listening to his prescriptions and adapting them for practical use." —*USA Today*

"[By a] psychologist with impressive research and clinical credentials. . . . No other book has so comprehensively linked psychological science with election-day choices. . . . He offers psychologically appealing and principled approaches that Democrats can take regarding divisive issues such as Iraq, abortion, gays, gun control, race relations, terrorism, and taxes. . . . Recommended for academic and public libraries."   *—Library Journal*

"A savvy, scary, partisan, provocative, take-no-prisoners-political primer, with cautionary tales drawn from the emotionally-challenged Michael Dukakis, Al Gore, and John Kerry campaigns, each of which snatched defeat from the jaws of victory. . . . His analysis of how and why political rhetoric stimulates voters' 'networks of association, bundles of thoughts, feelings, images, and ideas' will be instructive, if also infuriating, to political junkies, no matter what their partisan affiliation."
—The Baltimore Sun

"Exceptionally clear. . . . Democrats finally have a prophet who can lead them to the promised land of winning national elections, and his prescription is simple: Fight back, dadgummit."
—Sacramento Bee

"A recent book by Drew Westen, now being avidly read in Westminster, argues persuasively that voters, even the most analytical of them, think about politics with the touchy-feely part of their brains, rather than the rational."   *—The Sunday Times* (UK)

"Someone had to say it. . . . And Drew Westen, a clinical psychologist and political strategist from Emory University, has stepped up to the plate in *The Political Brain* to give a scathing, sobering diagnosis of what ails a political party whose beliefs are in line with the majority of Americans on almost every issue and yet fails to translate that alignment into sustainable electoral success. Armed with numerous studies on how the brain operates in that crucial interplay between emotion and reason that energizes voters, Westen has succeeded in penning a manifesto on behalf of bringing the passionate back into the narrative—and actions— of the Democratic Party."   —Susan Gardner, Dailykos.com

"Westen's book joins the ever-growing list of postmortems over why the Democrats lost their past two White House bids. But the author is no casual armchair pundit. He comes to the fray armed as a professor of psychology and psychiatry at Emory University who has used magnetic resonance imaging to understand how voters respond to partisan politics."   —Linda Kramer, *Politico.com*

The Political Brain

THE ROLE OF EMOTION IN DECIDING
THE FATE OF THE NATION

DREW WESTEN

PublicAffairs

New York

TO
Laura, Mackenzie, and Sarah

Library of Congress Cataloging-in-Publication Data

Westen, Drew, 1959-
    The political brain : the role of emotion in deciding the fate of the nation / Drew Westen.
    p. cm.
    ISBN-13: 978-1-58648-425-5
    ISBN-10: 1-58648-425-7
    1. Presidents—United States—Election—Psychological aspects. 2. Political campaigns—United States—Psychological aspects. 3. Voting—United States—Psychological aspects. 4. Political parties—United States—Platforms. 5. Political psychology. 6. Emotions—Political aspects. 7. United States—Politics and government—1989- 8. United States—Politics and government—1945-1989. I. Title.

JK528.W47 2007

324.973001'9—dc22

                                                                              2007011503

10 9 8 7 6 5 4 3

PB ISBN 978-1-58648-573-3

CONTENTS

★   ★   ★

INTRODUCTION

★　★　★

This book is aimed at readers interested in how the mind works, how the brain works, and what this means for why candidates win and lose elections. Its intended audience includes readers interested in politics, psychology, leadership, neuroscience, marketing, and law.

This book is likely to be of particular interest to the 50 million Democratic voters who can't figure out why their party has lost so many elections despite polls showing that the average voter agrees with Democratic positions on most policy issues, from protection of the earth to fairness to middle-class taxpayers who want nothing more than a better life for their children.

The central thesis of the book is that the vision of mind that has captured the imagination of philosophers, cognitive scientists, economists, and political scientists since the eighteenth century—a *dispassionate mind* that makes decisions by weighing the evidence and reasoning to the most valid conclusions—bears no relation to how the mind and brain actually work. When campaign strategists start from this vision of mind, their candidates typically lose.

If this book doesn't read like the typical book on politics or political strategy, it's because it asks a question seldom asked by political pundits or political scientists: How would candidates for public office run their campaigns if they started with an understanding of how the minds and brains of voters actually work?

The questions we ask invariably reflect our own background. I am a scientist who studies emotion and personality; the lead investigator in a team of neuroscientists who have been studying how the brain processes political and legal information; and a periodic contributor to public discourse on psychology and politics in print, television, and radio. For the last two decades, I have been advancing a view of the mind that differs substantially from the more dispassionate visions of the mind held by most cognitive psychologists, political scientists, and economists (which suggest that although we may cut a few cognitive corners here and there, we are largely rational actors, who make important decisions by weighing the evidence and calculating costs and benefits).[1]

I am also a practicing clinician, who has trained psychologists and psychiatrists for more than twenty years in how to understand the nuances of meaning in what people say, do, and feel. In working with patients, if you miss those nuances—if you misread what they may be trying to communicate, if you misjudge their character, if you don't notice when their emotions, gestures, or tone of voice don't fit what they're saying, if you don't catch the fleeting sadness or anger that lingers on their face for only a few milliseconds as they mention someone or something you might otherwise not know was important—you lose your patients. Or worse still, you don't.

In politics, if you misread these things, you lose elections.

The Partisan Brain

In the final, heated months of the 2004 presidential election, my colleagues Stephan Hamann, Clint Kilts, and I put together a research team to study what happens in the brain as political partisans—who constitute about 80 percent of the electorate—wrestle with new political information. We studied the brains of fifteen committed Democrats and fifteen confirmed Republicans.[2] (We would have studied voters without commitments to one party or candidate as well, but by the fall of 2004, finding people with intact brains who were not already leaning one way or the other would have been a daunting task.)

We scanned their brains for activity as they read a series of slides. Our goal was to present them with reasoning tasks that would lead a "dispassionate" observer to an obvious logical conclusion, but would be in direct conflict with the conclusion a partisan Democrat or Republican would *want* to reach about his party's candidate. In other words, our goal was to create a head-to-head conflict between the constraints on belief imposed by reason and evidence (data showing that the candidate had done something inconsistent, pandering, dishonest, slimy, or simply bad) and the constraints imposed by emotion (strong feelings toward the parties and the candidates). What we hoped to learn was how, in real time, the brain negotiates conflicts between data and desire.

Although we were in relatively uncharted territory, we came in with some strong hunches, which scientists like to dignify with the label *hypotheses*. Guiding all these hypotheses was our expectation that when data clashed with desire, the political brain would somehow "reason" its way to the desired conclusions.

We had four hypotheses.

First, we expected that threatening information—even if partisans didn't acknowledge it as threatening—would activate neural circuits shown in prior studies to be associated with negative emotional states.

Second, we expected to see activations in a part of the brain heavily involved in regulating emotions. Our hunch was that what passes for reasoning in politics is more often rationalization, motivated by efforts to reason to emotionally satisfying conclusions.

Third, we expected to see a brain in conflict—conflict between what a reasonable person could believe and what a partisan would want to believe. Thus, we predicted activations in a region known to be involved in monitoring and resolving conflicts.

Finally, we expected subjects to "reason with their gut" rather than to analyze the merits of the case. Thus, we didn't expect to see strong activations in parts of the brain that had "turned on" in every prior study of reasoning, even though we were presenting partisans with a reasoning task (to decide whether two statements about their candidate were consistent or inconsistent).

We presented partisans with six sets of statements involving clear inconsistencies by Kerry, six by Bush, and six by politically neutral male figures (e.g., Tom Hanks, William Styron). Although many of the statements and quotations were edited or fictionalized, we maximized their believability by embedding them in actual quotes or descriptions of actual events.

As partisans lay in the scanner, they viewed a series of slides.[3] The first slide in each set presented an *initial statement*, typically a quote from the candidate. The second slide provided a *contradictory statement*, also frequently taken from the candidate, which suggested a clear inconsistency that would be threatening to a partisan. Here is one of the contradictions we used to put the squeeze on the brains of partisan supporters of John Kerry:

Initial statement (Slide 1): During the first Gulf War, John Kerry wrote to a constituent: "Thank you for contacting me to express your opposition . . . I share your concerns. I voted in favor of a resolution that would have insisted that economic sanctions be given more time to work."

Contradiction (Slide 2): Seven days later, Kerry wrote to a different constituent, "Thank you for expressing your support for the Iraqi invasion of Kuwait. From the outset of the invasion, I have strongly and unequivocally supported President Bush's response to the crisis."

Without some kind of mitigating information, it would be difficult to argue that these two statements are not mutually contradictory (although, as we'll see, the human brain is a remarkable organ).

After partisans read the first two slides, which presented them with a clear contradiction, the third slide simply gave them some time to stew on it, asking them to consider whether the two statements were inconsistent. The fourth slide then asked them to rate the extent to which they agreed that the candidate's words and deeds were contradictory, from 1 (strongly disagree) to 4 (strongly agree).

Bush supporters faced similar dilemmas, such as the following:

Initial statement (Slide 1): "Having been here and seeing the care that these troops get is comforting for me and Laura. We are, should, and must provide the best care for anybody who is willing to put their life in harm's way for our country."—President Bush, 2003, visiting a Veterans Administration Hospital.

Contradiction (Slide 2): Mr. Bush's visit came on the same day that the Administration announced its immediate cutoff of VA hospital access to approximately 164,000 veterans.

For the politically neutral figures, the inconsistency was also real, but it was not threatening to partisans of one candidate or the other. Thus, it provided a useful comparison.

Our committed Democrats and Republicans were scanned in the run-up to one of the most polarized presidential races in recent history. So how did they respond?

They didn't disappoint us. They had no trouble seeing the contradictions for the opposition candidate, rating his inconsistencies close to a 4 on the four-point rating scale. For their own candidate, however, ratings averaged closer to 2, indicating minimal contradiction. Democrats responded to Kerry as Republicans responded to Bush. And as predicted, Democrats and Republicans showed no differences in their response to contradictions for the politically neutral figures.

Science is an untidy business, and you don't expect all your hypotheses to pan out. But in this case, we went four for four. The results showed that when partisans face threatening information, not only are they likely to "reason" to emotionally biased conclusions, but we can trace their neural footprints as they do it.

When confronted with potentially troubling political information, a network of neurons becomes active that produces distress. Whether this distress is conscious, unconscious, or some combination of the two we don't know.

The brain registers the conflict between data and desire and begins to search for ways to turn off the spigot of unpleasant emotion. We know that the brain largely succeeded in this effort, as partisans mostly denied that they had perceived any conflict between their candidate's words and deeds.

Not only did the brain manage to shut down distress through faulty reasoning, but it did so quickly—as best we could tell, usually before subjects even made it to the third slide. The neural circuits charged with regulation of emotional states seemed to recruit beliefs that eliminated the distress and conflict partisans had experienced when they confronted unpleasant realities. And this all seemed to happen with little involvement of the neural circuits normally involved in reasoning.

But the political brain also did something we *didn't* predict. Once partisans had found a way to reason to false conclusions, not only did neural circuits involved in negative emotions turn off, but circuits involved in positive emotions turned *on*. The partisan brain didn't seem satisfied in just feeling *better*. It worked overtime to feel *good*, activating reward circuits that give partisans a jolt of positive reinforcement for their biased reasoning. These reward circuits overlap substantially with those activated when drug addicts get their "fix," giving new meaning to the term *political junkie*.[4]

So what are the implications of this study?

One is pragmatic. If you're running a campaign, you shouldn't worry about offending the 30 percent of the population whose brains can't process information from your side of the aisle unless their lives depend on it (e.g., after an attack on the U.S. mainland). If you're a Republican, your focus should be on moving the 10 to 20 percent of the population with changeable minds to the right and bringing your unbending 30 percent to the polls. Republican strategists in fact have had no trouble branding Northern Californians and Northeasterners "latte-drinking liberals." They know their own party's kitchen doesn't have room for a latte maker, and that scalding the other side can bring a little froth to the mouths of their own voters.

The implications for Democrats should be equally clear: Stop worrying about offending those who consider Pat Robertson and Jerry Falwell moral leaders because *their minds won't bend to the left*. Indeed, the failure of the Democratic Party for much of the last decade to define itself in opposition to anyone or anything has created a Maxwell House Majority convinced that the only coffee the Democrats are capable of brewing is lukewarm and tepid—tested by pollsters to insure that it's not too hot or too strong—and served up with stale rhetoric. And they're right.

But if we take a step back, and place this study in the context of a growing body of research in psychology and political science, there's another message in these findings: *The political brain is an emotional brain*. It is not a dispassionate calculating machine, objectively searching for the right facts, figures, and policies to make a reasoned decision. The partisans in our study were, on average, bright, educated, and politically aware. They were not the voters who think "Alito" is an Italian pastry, the kind of voters who have raised so many alarm calls among political scientists and pundits.

And yet they thought with their guts.

Rational readers may take solace in noting that in American politics today, partisans are roughly equally split, with a little over a third of voters identifying themselves as Republican and roughly the same percent identifying themselves as Democrats. So they cancel each other out, leaving those in the center to swing elections based on more rational considerations.

But as it turns out, they think with their guts, too.

There is, however, a bright side to this story. Most of the time, emotions provide a reasonable compass for guiding behavior—including voting behavior—although the needle sometimes takes a couple of years to move. What led voters to demand a change of course on Iraq in November 2006 was not that they had new information. They had new emotions. The compass shifted from nationalistic pride and hope to anger, concern, and a rising crest of resignation. "Stay the course" made little sense in light of this emotional shift.

We can't change the structure of the political brain, which reflects millions of years of evolution. But we can change the way we appeal to it.

And that's what this book is about.

Part One

MIND, BRAIN, AND EMOTION IN POLITICS

chapter one

WINNING STATES OF MIND

Politics has always been as much about identity and community . . . as about the economy. Self-interest defined in purely
economic terms is an idea that reduces the Democratic Party to
little more than the human-resources department of American
politics, endlessly fussing over pensions and health-care plans
and whether or not you got your flu shot, rather than a party
concerned with the fundamental stuff of life: who we are, how
we organize our society, and what it means to be American at
this particular moment in history.

— GARANCE FRANKE-RUTA, *The American Prospect, 2004*[1]

W e have grown accustomed to thinking about politics in
terms of red states and blue states. But it's easy to forget
that the states that really determine elections are voters'
states of mind.

Although brain scanning studies sometimes create the impression
that thoughts or feelings come and go when one part of the brain
"turns on" or another "turns off," the reality is that our brains are vast
networks of neurons (nerve cells) that work together to generate our
experience of the world. Of particular importance are *networks of associations*, bundles of thoughts, feelings, images, and ideas that have become connected over time.

3

If you start with networks, you think very differently about politics.

Just how important networks are in understanding why candidates win and lose can be seen by contrasting two political advertisements, the first from Bill Clinton's campaign for the presidency in 1992, and the second from John Kerry's in 2004. Both men were running against an increasingly unpopular incumbent named Bush. Both ads were, for each man, his chance to introduce himself to the general electorate following the Democratic primary campaign and to tell the story he wanted to tell about himself to the American people. And both were a microcosm of the entire campaign.

The two ads seem very similar in their "surface structure." But looks can be deceiving. A clinical "dissection" of these ads makes clear that they couldn't have been more different in the networks they activated and the emotions they elicited.

Clinton's ad was deceptively simple, narrated exclusively (and with exquisitely moving emotion) by the young Arkansas governor. In the background was music evocative of small-town America, along with images and video clips that underscored the message. (Here and throughout the book, I describe relevant visual images or sounds in brackets.)

BILL CLINTON: I was born in a little town called Hope, Arkansas [image of a small-town train station, with the name HOPE on a small white sign against a brick background], three months after my father died. I remember that old two-story house where I lived with my grandparents. They had very limited incomes. It was in 1963 [video clip of John F. Kennedy, looking presidential, coming up to a podium] that I went to Washington and met President Kennedy at the Boy's Nation Program [video of the young Clinton and the youthful President Kennedy shaking hands]. And I remember [living room video of a now-adult Clinton, starry eyed and nostalgic thinking about the encounter with a man who was obviously his hero] just, uh, thinking what an incredible country this was, that somebody like me, you know, who had no money or anything, would be given the opportunity to meet the President [photo of their hands clasped, slowly and gradually expanding to show the connection between the two men]. That's when I decided I could really do public service because I cared so much about people. I worked my way through law school with part time jobs—anything I could find. After I graduated, I really didn't care about making a lot of money [photos of poor and working-class houses in Arkansas]. I just wanted to go home and see if I could make a difference [photo of the young governor-elect raising his right hand to take the oath of office as governor of Arkansas]. We've worked hard in education and health care [video clips of Clinton with children in a classroom, being hugged by a woman in her seventies or eighties, and talking with workers] to create jobs, and we've made real progress [photo of the governor hard at work late at night in his office]. Now it's exhilarating to me to think that as president I could help to change all our people's lives for the better [video of Clinton obviously at ease with a smiling young girl in his arms] and bring hope back to the American dream.[2]

If you dissect this ad, you can readily see why it was one of the most effective television commercials in the history of American politics. Bill Clinton never shied away from policy debates, but this ad was not about policy. Its sole purpose was to begin creating a set of positive associations to him and narrative about the Man from Hope—framed, from start to finish, in terms of hope and the American dream.

In his first sentence, Clinton vividly conveyed where he was coming from, literally and metaphorically—from a place of Hope. But he was not content to do this just with words. The ad created in viewers a vivid, multisensory network of associations—associations not just to the word *hope* but to the image of Hope in small-town America in an era gone by, captured by the image of the train station, and the *sound* of hope, captured in his voice. Clinton told his own life story, but he told it as a parable of what anyone can accomplish if just given the chance. He tied the theme of hope to the well-established theme of the American dream, presenting himself not as a man of privilege descending (or condescending) to help those less fortunate but as someone no different from anyone else who grew up on Main Street in any town—indeed, as someone who had suffered more adversity than most, having been born after his own father's death.

The "story line" of the narrative might be summarized in three simple sentences: "Through hard work, caring, and determination, I know what it's like to live the American dream. In my home state, I've done everything possible to help others realize that dream. And as your president, I'll do everything I can to help people all over this country realize their dreams like I've done in Arkansas." In the closing line, he tied these twin themes—hope and the American dream—together, describing his desire to bring "hope back to the American dream." The theme of hope was reinforced by the final image of a young child, representing our collective hope for the future, and the hope of every parent. Although you can't get much more "hopeful" than that, the final line of the ad actually included a subtle allusion to the Bush economy (bring hope *back* to the American dream, implying that it had been lost), with an implicit negative message most voters would likely register only unconsciously.

The association to President Kennedy was instrumental to the emotional appeal of the ad. Kennedy was an American icon, whose brief tenure in the White House is widely remembered as a time in which America's hopes soared along with its space program. Careful dissection of the *sequence* of visual images shows how brilliantly the ad was crafted.

The sequence began with Kennedy by himself, looking young, vibrant, serious, and presidential—precisely the features the Clinton campaign wanted to associate with Clinton. Then came the video of a young Bill Clinton shaking hands with Kennedy, dramatically bringing the theme of the American dream to viewers' eyes—a poor boy from Arkansas without a father finding himself in the presence of his hero—while creating a sense of something uncanny, of "fate," of the chance meeting of once and future presidents that seemed too accidental not to be preordained. Then came a still photo of their hands tightly clasped, emphasizing the connection between the two men. This image lasted far longer than any other in the ad and gradually expanded until the two hands panned out into an image of the two recognizable figures.

Clearly, a central goal of the ad was to establish Clinton as *presidential*, particularly in light of the rumors about his sexual escapades during the bruising primary season (which may actually have been turned to his advantage through the associations to the handsome Kennedy, who himself was associated with tales of infidelities but was nonetheless revered). In a race against an incumbent president, who needed only to stand in front of a podium with the seal of the presidency to appear presidential, the Clinton ad seized every opportunity to show what Bill Clinton would look like as president, with the image of his raising his right hand to accept the oath of office (as governor of Arkansas, but from a visual point of view, literally showing what Clinton would look like in his swearing in ceremony as president) followed by a photo of him working tirelessly at his desk, signing bills (itself reminiscent of photos of Kennedy).

I do not know how much of this was consciously intended by Clinton and his consultants. I suspect that much of it was, although some of the emotional overtones and sequencing of images might well have simply reflected Clinton's extraordinary emotional intelligence and gut-level, implicit political horse sense.*

But I *can* say with confidence that political strategists who cannot either construct or "dissect" the emotional structure of an ad like this present a far greater danger to the Democratic Party and its values than all of President Bush's appointees to the federal bench.

Because ultimately, they are the ones who put them there.

Like Clinton's "Hope" ad, the first television advertisement run by the Kerry campaign in the general election, in early May 2004, attempted to begin painting a picture—to tell a story—about John Kerry, the man and potential president:

JOHN KERRY [patriotic music, with prominent brass]: I was born in Fitzsimmons Army Hospital in Colorado [initial video of

---

*Here and elsewhere, I describe the candidate as the author of a strategy or appeal, recognizing, of course, that much of the time strategies reflect the joint efforts of candidates and their campaign teams.

candidate speaking, which returns throughout the ad]. My dad was serving in the Army Air Corps. Both of my parents taught me about public service [photos of the candidate's parents]. I enlisted because I believed in service to country [photo of the young solider with his comrades in arms]. I thought it was important if you had a lot of privileges as I had had, to go to a great university like Yale, to give something back to your country [video footage of a soldier, presumably Kerry, walking in the jungles of Vietnam].

DEL SANDUSKY: The decisions that he made saved our lives.

JIM RASSMAN: When he pulled me out of the river, he risked his life to save mine.

ANNOUNCER: For more than thirty years, John Kerry has served America [photo of Kerry talking on the phone, with glasses hanging off his face].

VANESSA KERRY: If you look at my father's time in service to this country, whether it's as a veteran [photo of war service], prosecutor [photo of Kerry pointing toward a window in setting that looks like a courtroom, which zooms quickly in to Kerry], or senator, he has shown an ability to fight for things that matter.

TERESA HEINZ-KERRY: John is the face of someone who's hopeful [photo of the two, possibly as newlyweds, with Kerry smiling broadly], who's generous of spirit and of heart.

JOHN KERRY: We're a country of optimists. We're the can-do people. And we just need to believe in ourselves again [video of Kerry speaking again, followed by video of profile of Kerry waving in some political event].

ANNOUNCER: A lifetime of service and strength. John Kerry for President.[3]

On the surface, the differences between this ad and Clinton's may be difficult to detect. Both begin with the candidate using his birthplace to drive home a central theme. For Kerry, the central theme was that he was born and bred in uniform, a theme central to a campaign trying to unseat an incumbent widely seen as a strong leader in a perpetual "war on terror."

The ad began with moving, patriotic music that played throughout, with an emphasis on muted brass tones, congruent with the military theme, and conveying both strength and majesty—precisely the tone he needed to convey. The most moving moments of the ad came as Kerry's fellow soldiers told, with genuine emotion in their voices, how he had saved their lives.

But that is where the similarity with the Clinton ad ends.

After Kerry's opening paragraph, in which he told the American people in his own words who he was and what he wanted them to know about him, the rest of the ad didn't matter. Kerry had already spent his first millions of campaign dollars telling the story *George W. Bush* wanted to tell about him, beginning to weave precisely the web of emotional associations in which the Bush campaign hoped to ensnare him: that he was not only *privileged* (a word Kerry, who was married to an heiress, introduced himself) but a Northeastern liberal intellectual.

The fact that he was from Massachusetts was well-known—the Republicans were already emphasizing that he was "Ted Kennedy's junior senator"—and the phrase "Massachusetts liberal" had become so successfully branded by the Republicans by 1988 in the Bush–Dukakis campaign that either word could readily evoke the other. When Kerry added the reference to Yale, he fully activated the primary network that the conservative movement has worked for so many years to stamp into the American psyche to galvanize disdain and resentment toward Democrats: the *liberal elite*. Put together Massachusetts, liberal senator, and Yale, and you have virtually the whole network activated. The only thing missing is a windsurfing outfit.

That came later.

Whatever its intended goal, that first paragraph of the Kerry ad served to convey one primary message that would stick in the neural networks of voters for the remainder of the election: *This guy isn't like me*. Indeed, when I saw this ad for the first time, I asked my wife, in disbelief, "Did that ad end with 'I'm John Kerry, and I approve this ad' or with 'I'm George Bush, and I approve this ad'?"

Just four years earlier, the American electorate (with, to be fair, the help of a little creative lawyering) had placed into the highest position in the land the most anti-intellectual president in more than 150 years. The Bush campaign certainly understood what "average folks" think about intellectuals. Consider what I believe is the only reference George W. Bush ever made in two runs for the White House to his own privileged educational pedigree (Yale, Harvard Business School). The reference came in a commencement address at Yale in May 2001:

> Most important, congratulations to the class of 2001. (Applause.) To those of you who received honors, awards, and distinctions, I say, well done. And to the C students—(applause)—I say, you, too, can be President of the United States. (Laughter and applause.) A Yale degree is worth a lot, as I often remind Dick Cheney—(laughter)—who studied here, but left a little early. So now we know—if you graduate from Yale, you become president. If you drop out, you get to be vice president. (Laughter.)[4]

Bill Clinton, one of the most intellectual men ever to inhabit the West Wing, never mentioned in his ad *which* law school he worked his way through. (For the record, it was the alma mater shared by Kerry and Bush.) Nor did he mention that his tenure in New Haven came on the heels of two years at Oxford as a Rhodes Scholar.

Kerry's reference to Yale raises a profound psychological question. What implicit assumptions about mind, brain, and political persuasion did the strategists and consultants who crafted that ad—or who saw it but failed to wave a bright red flag before it aired—share that would lead them to make such an extraordinary mistake?

The references to Yale and privilege were the most glaring mistakes in that ad, but they were not the only ones. Perhaps most importantly, the ad did not, like Clinton's, tell a coherent story. Try to summarize it using the narrative structure of a good storyteller, and you'll see the problem.

In fact, it told two stories. The second had nothing to do with the first, and seemed like it had come straight from the head of a consultant rather from the heart of the candidate.

The first story, "John Kerry was born on a military base, served his country heroically because he believed it was his duty, fought bad guys as a prosecutor, and would be a strong commander in chief," was clear and effective. Then the ad introduced two related themes, using words associatively linked to military strength (*service* and *fighting*) that created two distracting subplots, one about a lifetime of service (not the same thing as being heroic in the face of attack) and the other about fighting for things that matter (I suspect intended to smuggle in a populist theme under the banner of strength). Whereas the Clinton ad wove together and created an emotionally powerful network, the subthemes in the Kerry ad drew on existing associative links (the words *military, service*, and *fighting*) but actually took them in diverging directions, essentially *dismantling* a network whose activation was the central goal of the ad.

Two-thirds of the way through the commercial, the plot shifted, with Teresa Heinz-Kerry introducing the theme of optimism. The insertion of this non sequitur no doubt reflected his consultants' belief that optimism is a "winner" for presidential candidates. But if changing narrative horses in midstream were not enough, Mrs. Kerry introduced it with an incongruent facial expression—a mixture of serious and dour—that undercut the words. Then the senator reiterated the theme, with his facial expression similarly discordant from the language. His face was flat and impassive—no smile, no twinkle, nothing to engender feelings of excitement, national pride, or hope. The optimism theme seemed grafted onto both the message and the candidate.

Finally, the use of imagery in the Kerry ad stands in stark contrast to its effective use in the Clinton ad. The scenes of Vietnam, and particularly the faces and intonation of the men who served with Kerry, painted a clear and moving portrait of Kerry as a man and a potential leader. But after that, it seemed as if someone had just hastily rummaged through the Kerry family scrapbook. The photo of Kerry "serving" conveyed nothing about him, other than perhaps that he needed bifocals. The image used to illustrate his service as a prosecutor and then as a senator was difficult even to decipher. After watching the video multiple times, I realized he was in a courtroom pointing at a defendant. However, for the first several viewings, I couldn't tell where he was standing and what he was pointing at (eerily foreshadowing the campaign George W. Bush would so successfully run against him). It looked, at first inspection, as if he were pointing at something outside the window because the camera moved too quickly from the full photo, which showed the heads of jurors in a courtroom at the bottom of the screen, to Kerry pointing toward a prominent leaded-glass window (because the defendant had been cropped out of the picture). Even the candidate's final, arm-waving profile at the end seemed tepid, conveying weakness rather than strength.

The difference between the Clinton ad and the Kerry ad—like the difference between the Clinton campaign and virtually every other Democratic presidential campaign of the last three decades—reflects the difference between understanding and misunderstanding mind, brain, and emotion in American politics. If you think the failure to tell a coherent story, or to illustrate your words with evocative images, is just the "window dressing" of a campaign and makes little difference in the success or failure of a candidacy, you're missing something very important about the political brain:

*Political persuasion is about networks and narratives.**

Getting Our Thoughts and Feelings in Order

MODERATOR: Do you believe in general terms that gays and lesbians should have the same rights as other Americans?

---

*The same is true of virtually every other form of persuasion, from marketing products to managing people.

BUSH: Yes. I don't think they ought to have special rights, but I think they ought to have the same rights.

GORE: Well, there's a law pending called the Employment Non-Discrimination Act. I strongly support it. What it says is that gays and lesbians can't be fired from their job because they're gay or lesbian. And it would be a federal law preventing that. Now, I wonder if the—it's been blocked by the opponents in the majority in the Congress. I wonder if the Governor would lend his support to that law.

MODERATOR: Governor?

BUSH: Well, I have no idea. I mean, he can throw out all kinds— I don't know the particulars of this law. I will tell you I'm the kind of person, I don't hire or fire somebody based upon their sexual orientation. As a matter of fact, I would like to take the issue a little further. I don't really think it's any of my—you know, any of my concerns what—how you conduct your sex life. And I think that's a private matter. And I think that's the way it ought to be. But I'm going to be respectful for people, I'll tolerate people, and I support equal rights but not special rights for people. (Second Presidential Debate between Vice President Al Gore and Governor George Bush, October 3, 2000)[5]

Republican strategists have recognized since the days of Richard Nixon that the road to victory is paved with emotional intentions. Richard Wirthlin, an economics professor who engineered Ronald Reagan's successful campaigns of 1980 and 1984, realized that all the dispassionate economic assumptions he'd always believed about how people make decisions didn't apply when people cast their ballots for Reagan.[6] As he discovered, people were drawn to Reagan because they *identified* with him, liked his emphasis on values over policy, trusted him, and found him authentic in his beliefs. It didn't matter that they disagreed with most of his policy positions. Since Lyndon Johnson's victory in 1964, Republicans have seen only two Democrats elected to the White House, and both of those Democrats offered compelling emotional messages: Jimmy Carter promised to restore faith in government after Watergate, and Bill Clinton promised to restore hope to the American dream.

In the interchange between Vice President Gore and then-Governor Bush, Gore caught an inconsistency between Bush's statement and the Republican position on the issue of gay rights. He then artfully challenged the governor either to support a tolerant stance that would have antagonized Bush's fundamentalist base or to present himself as both a bigot and a hypocrite, having just stated that he was for equal rights.

Bush dodged the bullet. He played implicitly on the theme of the Washington outsider, essentially saying, "Aw, shucks, I don't keep track of all them bills they're always passing up there in Warshington." He then turned a potential discussion of the intolerance of his party's position into a discussion of the goodness of his heart and presented himself as a fair and compassionate person. Finally, he repeated a phrase, "special rights," that implied that gays were asking for something *more* than the average person, not just parity. In so doing, he activated a sense of *unfairness* in what gays and lesbians were asking for and hence allowed people to feel righteous—and self-righteous—in refusing to support the "unequal treatment" of a particular minority group. The use of "special rights" also elicited associations—largely unconscious, and hence all the more powerful because their effects were largely sub rosa—of affirmative action, a hot-button issue for many of the same people whose gut-level discomfort with homosexuality was the target of his communication.

The appeal of Bush's response was not in its logical structure but in its emotional structure. One may certainly question the ethics of this subterfuge. My goal in this book is not to advocate that Democrats emulate the ethics of Karl Rove. But there is no relation between the extent to which an appeal is rational or emotional and the extent to which it is ethical or unethical. *Every* appeal is ultimately an emotional appeal to voters' interests—what's good for them and their families—or their values—what matters to them morally. The question that decides elections is whether the appeal is a weak one or a strong one.

In the exchange with Gore, Bush had made an emotional appeal that resonated with a significant sector of the population. The only response that could have countered its impact was *an equally compelling emotional appeal*—particularly a moral appeal—to many of the same voters whose emotions were activated by the phrase, "special rights" (a phrase that had been well honed and market-tested). Because intolerance toward gays and lesbians is often justified on religious grounds, Gore might well have used a religious idiom in response, such as the following:

> Governor, no one is suggesting we give *special* rights to anyone, only that we treat *all* Americans as equal under the law—that we treat *all* Americans as God's children. It's about loving your neighbor, and recognizing that none of us—not me, and not you—is in the position to cast the first stone.

And if Gore wanted to see the interchange replayed a hundred times on cable—and to demonstrate his own affability (something he desperately needed to do)—he might have added, "But don't worry, Governor, lovin' your neighbor doesn't mean you have to kiss 'em."

Republicans understand what the philosopher David Hume recognized three centuries ago: that reason is a slave to emotion, not the other way around. With the exception of the Clinton era, Democratic strategists for the last three decades have instead clung tenaciously to the dispassionate view of the mind and to the campaign strategy that logically follows from it, namely one that focuses on facts, figures, policy statements, costs and benefits, and appeals to intellect and expertise.

They do so, I believe, because of an *irrational emotional commitment to rationality*—one that renders them, ironically, impervious to both scientific evidence on how the political mind and brain work and to an accurate diagnosis of why their campaigns repeatedly fail.

Paradoxically, this irrational commitment to rationality has rendered Democrats less, rather than more, likely to speak the truth. If you think about voters as calculating machines who add up the utility of your positions on "the issues," you will invariably find yourself scouring the polls for your principles. And as soon as voters perceive you as turning to opinion polls instead of your internal polls—your emotions, and particularly your moral emotions—they will see you as weak, waffling, pandering, and unprincipled.

And they will be right.

Careful attention to policy is the stuff of good governance. And under the right circumstances, even voters without much interest in politics—who are usually the voters most up for grabs in an election—will think about what they've heard, consider the differences between two principles or positions, and deliberate—if only long enough to draw an emotional conclusion (e.g., "I just don't like that guy").

But the "right circumstances" are always emotional. Behind every reasoned decision is a reason for deciding. We do not pay attention to arguments unless they engender our interest, enthusiasm, fear, anger, or contempt. We are not *moved* by leaders with whom we do not feel an emotional resonance. We do not find policies worth debating if they don't touch on the emotional implications for ourselves, our families, or things we hold dear. From the standpoint of research in neuroscience, the more purely "rational" an appeal, the less it is likely to activate the emotion circuits that regulate voting behavior.

"Reasonable" actions almost always require the integration of thought and emotion,[7] and the most powerful campaign advertisements, the most effective speeches, and the most effective moments in debates all combine emotion and cognition. But they do so in a very particular way, and in a very particular sequence. Usually they lead with something emotionally compelling—a moral issue facing the country, the personal history of the candidate, a story about a person the candidate has met on the campaign trail, an injustice that cries out to be rectified. They then follow with a contrast between the two candidates or parties, creating emotional resonance with one and dissonance with the other. Only *then*—once people are engaged emotionally and made aware of the choices confronting them—do they describe how they might fix the problem. And they usually "conclude the argument" with a return to emotion.

In the chapters that follow, I contrast the dispassionate and passionate visions of the mind, describe their manifestations in American politics, and provide a blueprint for running emotionally compelling campaigns. Part I describes how the political mind and brain actually work. Part II provides principles for running an emotionally compelling campaign based on the best available science and a "clinical" dissection of campaign speeches, inaugural addresses, presidential debates, stump speeches, radio addresses, and television commercials. These chapters also focus on several issues that have left Democrats tongue-tied for much of three decades—most importantly, abortion, guns, race, taxes, national security, and gay marriage—and show how a different understanding of mind and brain leads to a very different way of talking with voters about them.

There Is a Better Way

This book is about the science and practice of persuasion in American politics, not about my own political persuasion. However, I had a choice to make in how to write it. I could have written it as a twenty-first-century scientific advisor to the prince, whether the prince happens to be garbed in red or blue. And in one sense, by laying out a vision of mind and brain and principles for campaign strategy that flow from it, I am stepping into some large, if not altogether savory, sixteenth-century Italian shoes.

But the timing, if not the content, of this book is neither accidental nor apolitical. When I began writing this book, we had been living for several years in a one-party state. As I write these words today, the Democratic Party is enjoying a renewed vitality, having regained both houses of Congress in the November 2006 midterm elections. The obvious question is the extent to which the election of 2006 reflects changes in political strategy, a realignment of the electorate, or the fact that Democrats were running against a spectacularly unpopular president, a war opposed by two-thirds of the country, and a party that had staked its claims on morality while its members were dropping like flies because of moral indiscretions, culminating in the revelation, just before the election, that the congressman chairing the House committee charged with doing something about pedophilia was doing a little too much about it on his own time.

There is no question that Democrats made better campaign decisions in 2006 than they had made in 2000, 2002, and 2004. A conspicuous example was the directive by Democratic campaign leaders in the House and Senate that their candidates were no longer going to take attacks on the chin and were instead going to respond forcefully and immediately. And by the fall of 2006, when Democrats could smell red meat on Iraq, they found their voice, overcoming the deadly laryngitis that had infected the party since September 11, 2001.

In an interview of *Meet the Press*, rising Democratic superstar (and now Senator) Claire McCaskill had this exchange with Tim Russert, in which she combined bluntness, folksiness, and a powerfully evocative metaphor:

> MR. RUSSERT: Ms. McCaskill, you said this. "We should redeploy our troops strategically within the region over a two-year time frame." What does that mean?
>
> MS. McCASKILL: . . . [Y]ou know, as a daughter of rural Missouri, we have a saying, "If you're in a hole, you need to quit digging."[8]

On a range of issues, Democrats began to use phrases and imagery that translated the Democratic litany of issues that had shown little traction earlier in the campaign into the language of values and emotion. Soon-to-be Speaker of the House Nancy Pelosi described the Republicans' refusal to raise the minimum wage in ten years as "immoral," declared that "We want to send our energy money to the Midwest, not the Middle East,"[9] and proclaimed on the eve of the election that the only way to end the culture of corruption in Congress was to "drain the swamp."

Clearly, something very different was happening on the left side of the aisle in the fall of 2006 than had been the case for the last six years, culminating in Virginia Senator Jim Webb's blistering response to the president's surreally upbeat State of the Union message in January of 2007. Webb began by sounding a populist theme with just the kinds of words that would—and should—make the average voter angry:

When one looks at the health of our economy, it's almost as if we are living in two different countries. Some say that things have never been better. The stock market is at an all-time high, and so are corporate profits. But these benefits are not being fairly shared. When I graduated from college, the average corporate CEO made 20 times what the average worker did; today, it's nearly 400 times. In other words, it takes the average worker more than a year to make the money that his or her boss makes in one day.

He went on to describe his own family's long history of military service, including his own son's boots on the ground in Iraq, and immediately disarmed any attempt to represent him as the spokesperson for a party that doesn't "support our troops":

Like so many other Americans, today and throughout our history, we serve and have served . . . because we love our country. On the political issues—those matters of war and peace, and in some cases of life and death—we trusted the judgment of our national leaders. We hoped that they would be right, that they would measure with accuracy the value of our lives against the enormity of the national interest that might call upon us to go into harm's way.

We owed them our loyalty, as Americans, and we gave it. But they owed us—sound judgment, clear thinking, concern for our welfare, a guarantee that the threat to our country was equal to the price we might be called upon to pay in defending it.

The president took us into this war recklessly. He disregarded warnings from the national security adviser during the first Gulf War, the chief of staff of the army, two former commanding generals of the Central Command, whose jurisdiction includes Iraq, the director of operations on the Joint Chiefs of Staff, and many, many others with great integrity and long experience in national security affairs. We are now, as a nation, held hostage to the predictable—and predicted—disarray that has followed.[10]

Clearly this was the face of a very different Democratic Party.

Yet when a CNN poll taken shortly after the election asked voters what they made of the Democrats' extraordinary reversal of fortune on Election Day, 64 percent described it as a rejection of the Republicans, 27 percent as a mandate for Democrats, and less than half that number—13 percent—as a reflection of support for Democratic programs.[11]

The problems that inspired me to write this book are systemic, not transient, reflected in forty years of electoral history. The same problems were apparent even in January 2006, at the start of what turned out to be a transformative election year. Despite all the trenchant post-mortems of the Kerry campaign and a spate of wonderfully insightful books about the State of the Party,[12] the Democratic response to the president's State of the Union address provides a sobering contrast to the one delivered just a year later, showing how little party strategists had learned from the debacles of the prior three elections.

Against a formidable opponent, the Democratic Party put up a fresh, earnest, but mild mannered political newcomer, and armed him with a tepid refrain with all the emotional appeal of flat soda mixed with backwash: "There *is* a better way."

Against a president in a dark suit and power tie, with a dark and powerful message about evil lurking in the dark—delivering his message in a weighty setting, before the U.S. Congress—they chose a fireside setting and a matching sartorial selection with all the gravitas of *Mr. Rogers' Neighborhood.*

Against a president who flaunted a law against wiretapping without judicial authority and began his speech with a moving tribute to Coretta Scott King, they neglected to mention the wiretaps against *Dr. Martin Luther King* that had in part inspired the law the president was breaking—or the president's decision to take a week of vacation and fundraising trips as poor black people watched their homes swept away by Hurricane Katrina—or the tens of thousands of African Americans his brother had kept from the polls in Florida in 2000 with his infamous "felons list"—or the thousands of African Americans in Ohio in 2004 who had been forced to choose between exercising the right to vote, for which Dr. King had given his life, and their need to go home to take care of their children after six hours in line without adequate polling booths.

In arguably one of the most disastrous years of any presidency in modern American history—the response to Katrina, the election of Hamas in Palestine, the election of Shiite clerics in Iraq, 2,500 American soldiers dead in Iraq and counting, the indictment of the vice president's closest advisor—the most trenchant emotional chorus the Democratic Party could muster was "There *is* a better way."

Republicans would never have sent out a rookie to guard Bill Clinton. They would never have tried to "market" a slogan without vetting it for its emotional power by people who understand the power of emotion. And if an incumbent Democratic president had *ever* had a year like Bush did in 2005, the Republicans would have come out with their unregulated guns a'blazin'.

It's easy to forget history, even recent history. The Iraq War was the ticket to Democratic success in 2006, but it didn't start out that way. When now-Congressman Joe Sestak announced he was running for Congress in Pennsylvania in early 2006, he was told by leading Democratic strategists not to talk about pulling troops out of Iraq because doing so might encourage the image of Democrats as weak on national security."[13] Sestak, a retired vice admiral in the Navy, ignored their advice and won his bid against a twenty-year Republican incumbent.

The advice Sestak received was standard Democratic fare. Democrats didn't begin to speak with even a half-dozen voices (let alone one) on Iraq until late August, just three months before the election. At the end of July 2006, polls showed the electorate, including Independents, split down the middle on Iraq.[14] Less than three weeks later, the tide had begun to turn, as the majority now believed the war was a mistake. As journalists and Democratic candidates began challenging Republican statements about Iraq as part of the "global war on terror," the majority of Americans started to perceive the war in Iraq as a hindrance to antiterrorist efforts—a view that had been held only by a small minority since 2002.[15] By the time of the election, the war was deeply unpopular, and the vast majority of Independents had swung to the left.

What happened in the three short months from the end of July to the beginning of November?

What should have happened in 2002.

The political scientist John Zaller[16] has shown that public opinion follows the lead of party leaders and pundits, with partisans turning to their own leaders for cues on what to think and feel about the central questions of the day where there is no obvious consensus. When "opinion makers" on their side of the aisle are silent, when only a handful of them are breaking with the current consensus, or when they speak with multiple, inconsistent voices, most people stick with the consensus view. Until August 2006, the consensus remained as it had been since 2002, that Iraq was part of the "war on terror."

The situation in early 2006, when Democratic strategists were advising candidates to go light on criticism of the president and the war, was not an anomaly. In 2002, as the Maryland sniper terrorized the nation's capital on the eve of the midterm election, Democrats didn't utter a word about guns. Poll numbers showed that two-third of Americans supported stricter gun laws even before the Maryland sniper began his rampage. Yet party strategists were afraid Democrats would get branded as "anti-gun," so they advocated silence instead of branding *Republicans* and the National Rifle Association as extremists who can't tell the difference between a hunting rifle and an M–16. The same scenario recurred four years later, as multiple fatal school shootings occurred just weeks before the midterm election of 2006.

This book offers a diagnosis of why the party of McGovern, Dukakis, Mondale, Gore, and Kerry has had trouble doing better than "There *is* a better way."

If my words seem harsh to the Democratic ear, it is not out of disrespect. It is out of respect for the values of the Democratic Party, and for the tens of millions of Americans both on the left and in the center of the political spectrum who cherish many of those values and want to see them reflected in their government. But these values won't be reflected if Democrats continue to make their best appeals to the electorate only when the other side is so bad that people have no choice but to slouch toward Massachusetts. And they won't be reflected if they continue to offer voters the choice between the Grand Old Party that competes in the marketplace of emotions and the Bland Old Party that has bet the farm on the marketplace of ideas—and as a result has too often found itself with little but the donkey and the dung.

chapter two

RATIONAL MINDS,
IRRATIONAL CAMPAIGNS

★   ★   ★

When the eloquent Adlai Stevenson was running for president against Dwight Eisenhower, a woman gushed to the Democratic candidate after a rally, "Every thinking person will be voting for you." Stevenson supposedly replied: "Madam, that is not enough. I need a majority."[1]

The founding fathers, many of the great seventeenth and eighteenth century philosophers whose ideas shaped their thinking (and ultimately the U.S. Constitution), and two hundred years of political scientists, economists, and cognitive scientists have held to some version of a *dispassionate* vision of the mind. According to this view, people make decisions by weighing the available evidence and reaching conclusions that make the most sense of the data, as long as they have a minimum of time and interest. Many have argued that this is the way the mind works. The vast majority have argued that this is the way it *should* work if people are behaving rationally.[2]

This view of the mind is not one to be dismissed lightly. It is a vision that ushered in the Age of Reason and was intimately related to the rise of democracy, freedom from religious authority, and development of the scientific method. By turning to reason, philosophers could argue against the absolute authority of monarchy, usually justified by appeals to divinity, tradition, or assumptions about the natural order of things.

This was the approach taken by the social contract philosophers who influenced the framing of the American Constitution. The common denominator of the social contract theorists (and their modern-day descendants, notably the philosopher John Rawls) was that people came together to create a state and govern themselves through rational autonomous choice.

Although these philosophers generally agreed that reason is the basis of democracy, they differed in the extent to which they allowed a place for emotion at the table of the republic. Thomas Hobbes, whose *Leviathan* ushered in the age of social contract theories, argued that people enter into a social contract—an agreement to submit to laws and join civilized society—because they seek pleasure and avoid pain. Ultimately, however, he presumed that giving up the liberty to do as one pleases makes rational sense when compared with the "war of all against all" that constitutes the "state of nature" prior to the social contract, in which life is "nasty, brutish, and short."[3]

The framers of the U.S. Constitution themselves were of many minds about emotion, although in general, in keeping with more than 2000 years of Western philosophy since Plato, they feared the distorting influence of emotion on the rational thought necessary for good decisions in a democracy.[4] Plato argued that when reason and passion collide, the proper place for passion is in the back seat. In the *Federalist Papers*, the framers of American democracy made clear, like both Plato and the social contract philosophers, that only through reason can people set aside their self-interested and parochial desires to make decisions in the common interest. Passions can lead to rapid, poorly thought-out, self-interested acts, or to the psychology of the mob, inflamed by the emotion of the moment and capable of turning on anyone in its path.[5]

Inventing the Calculator

In one version or another, the vision of an ideally dispassionate electorate has dominated political science as well as political philosophy.

Political scientists have expressed concerns since the origins of their discipline—and particularly since the advent of modern polling in the 1940s—about the "irrationality" of the American electorate. Walter Lippmann used the term *public opinion* in 1922 to describe the morass of beliefs (about what is happening in the economy, what is going on in the world, and what policies might make things better) held by a population that generally lacks the firsthand experience and expertise to know what is truly going on. For eighty years, political scientists have echoed his concerns, focusing on the way American voters are vulnerable to all manner of irrational appeals[6] and seem more likely to attach a sense of duty to showing up at the polls than to knowing who and what, exactly, they are voting for.

In actuality, the American public at the dawn of our democracy was even less issue-oriented than the public today, largely pledging its political allegiance to the men who had fought the Revolutionary War until their generation died out in the early to mid-1800s, and then voting primarily based on their habitual allegiance to one or another political party for decades thereafter.[7] As we shall see, allegiance to party—a largely emotional allegiance[8]—remains the central determinant of voting behavior today. The same is true in most stable Western democracies, where political affiliation tends to be handed from generation to generation like a family heirloom.

With the advent of modern polling, U.S. politicians have had at their disposal constant information on public opinion—on where it is and where it seems to be going—that has been a constant source of both angst and ambivalence to political campaigns. On the one hand, in a representative democracy or a republic such as our own, representatives are supposed to *represent* their constituents—and hence to attend to their opinions. On the other hand, leaders have access to information not available to the average citizen and expertise that comes from governing. Thus, they are supposed to *lead*—including staying one step ahead of, and helping to shape, public opinion.

The problem, according to most accounts, is that public opinion largely reflects efforts at manipulation by special interests and political elites, often filtered through a media that only sometimes serves as the

"Fourth Estate" envisioned by the founders. George Marcus, a political scientist who has challenged the traditional understanding of reason and emotion in politics, has eloquently described the prescriptions typically offered by scholars of American electoral politics:

> Most of the current proposals for reform . . . minimize the evocation of passion and enhance the function of rationality. The effort has been to encourage the dispassionate citizen: a citizen who will watch reasoned debates, read detailed issue position papers, read newspapers to get thoroughly informed about the facts underlying the many public policy issues; a citizen who will be less inclined to vote as he or she has voted in the past and more inclined to "weigh the issues" . . . ; a citizen who will be less responsive to the attractiveness and appeal of candidates and guided more by their programs; a citizen who will be less distracted by matters of public performance, the gaffes or slips of the tongue, and more mindful of the candidate's record of public service. All in all, what is called for is a citizen more serious, more reasoning, and less passionate.[9]

Such prescriptions are not entirely without merit. The problems they attempt to address have been amplified in the era of cable television, when the media increasingly mix information with entertainment (sex scandals are much more entertaining than war scandals) and when public disinterest in "issues" leads to less issue-oriented programming (because "issue" programming is less profitable), creating a vicious circle in which increasingly ill-informed voters prefer increasingly ill-informing programs (whatever happened to Chandra, Laci, the runaway bride, and Natalie?). The problem is further compounded when media executives follow precisely the same polls as politicians and use them to "spin" their news in a way more likely to appeal to a larger segment of the population, as when CNN veered sharply to the right during the 2004 presidential campaign as it watched its market share erode in favor of the more conservative Fox Network.

However, these maneuvers seriously understate the complex relations between thought and feeling in mind and brain—and by extension in state and nation.

Neither the social contract philosophers nor their dispassionate modern-day heirs in political science ever wrestled adequately with the fact that people all start out with strong emotional commitments to communities, tribes, sects, or nations that raise the question, "Whose interests should the rational actor pursue—his own, his immediate family, his extended family, his tribe, his religious sect, his state, or his nation?" This has been one of the great sticking points—and one of the great unknowns—in the attempt to extend democracy to peoples who do not start with the Western assumption of autonomous individuals, who may instead put what the anthropologist Clifford Geertz[10] called "primordial sentiments" toward tribal or religious communities above all others. There is nothing to protect a minority group in a democracy if people enter into the social contract without the peculiarly Western, individualistic assumptions embodied in our Declaration of Independence that were themselves the product of centuries of intellectual history: that all men (and ultimately women and blacks) are created equal, endowed with certain inalienable rights.

The vision of the dispassionate mind of the political scientist is remarkably consistent with the vision of the decision theorist and cognitive scientist. Indeed, it is no accident that when Howard Gardner published his landmark book, *The Mind's New Science*,[11] the word *emotion* did not appear in the index. Across a number of fields—cognitive science, psychology, and business, as well as political science and economics—the most widely held models of judgment and decision making are "bounded rationality" models. These models suggest that we are essentially reasonable animals, give or take a few shortcuts our minds take to make rapid judgments when we have neither the time nor interest to deliberate over which brand of olive oil to grab off the shelf—or which lever to pull in the ballot box if we are not terribly informed or interested in politics.*

Contemporary models of decision making are derived from rational decision theories that focus on the processes by which people

---

*My apologies to decision theorists who may find this characterization too categorical, particularly in light of discussions of heuristics involving emotion. A close reading of reviews of judgment and decision making in the *Annual Review of Psychology*, however, turns up remarkably few references to emotion.

weigh the pros and cons of various options and draw conclusions designed to maximize their expected utility. According to these models, when people make decisions, they consider the utility to them of different aspects of each option and the likelihood of obtaining them.[12] A rational actor compares each potential option on its *expected utility* by adding up the costs and benefits of each option, weighing in their probabilities.

So how might such models work in practice, particularly in electoral politics?

It's 2004, and a fifty-two-year-old coal miner in rural Pennsylvania has to decide whether to vote for George W. Bush or John Kerry. According to rational decision models, he makes (and should make) his choice as follows.

First, he selects the issues that affect him most and weighs their importance, from least to most important. Let's say these issues include safe working conditions at the mine, job security, the solvency of Social Security and his pension plan, safety from terrorist attacks, and safety from violent crime. Given that he lives in rural Pennsylvania, he doesn't need to worry much about terrorist attacks or violent crime from inner-city gang members. The probability of such events is small enough that he might give each one a low importance rating, perhaps a 1 on a scale from 1 to 5. On the other hand, given his occupation and his age, if he is rational, he should heavily weigh safety conditions at the mine, job security, and his retirement security, giving these issues each an importance rating of, say, 5.

He then assigns a *utility value* for each candidate on each issue. Let's say Kerry receives a score of +3 for each of the economic and occupational issues, whereas Bush receives −3 on each of these issues, given his prior voting record. But Bush is tough on terror and crime, so he gets +3 on the final two issues, whereas Kerry seems to be windsurfing through life and hence earns a −2 on each.

The next step is to multiply the two sets of numbers, producing a combined index of the importance of each issue and the likely utility of a vote for the candidate. Finally, to decide which way to cast his vote, the miner adds up the totals for each candidate to see who scores best for him across the issues that matter.

If our coal miner has even a napkin on which to scribble a few numbers, his decision should be clear. Kerry's score for the three most important issues totals 45, minus 4 points for his disutility on terror and crime, earning him a total expected utility of 41. Bush, on the other hand, racks up 6 points for his toughness but loses 45 for his record on worker safety, the economy, and Social Security, producing an expected utility of −39. The contest isn't even close, with an 80-point spread between the two candidates.

Kerry's problem, however, is that he never met a coal miner, or any other voter for that matter, who actually makes decisions this way. Nor have I. The only people who think like this on important issues—whether choosing a spouse or a president—have serious brain damage or psychopathology. In *Descartes' Error*, the neurologist Antonio Damasio[13] describes patients with damage to regions of the frontal lobes involved in emotional decision making (and particularly in linking thought and feeling) who look very much like this. In one case, a patient spent over thirty minutes trying to decide which date and time would be optimal for their next appointment. Without an emotional signal to say "this isn't worth debating anymore," he continued to weigh the utility of every possible alternative.

Yet not only do most decision theories assume this kind of decision making on issues of importance to people. *So does much of contemporary Democratic campaign strategy.* We can hear the whirring of the dispassionate mind in the following exchange on Medicare that occurred during the first presidential debate between Al Gore and George W. Bush in 2000:

> GORE: . . . Under the Governor's plan, if you kept the same fee for service that you have now under Medicare, your premiums would go up by between 18% and 47%, and that is the study of the Congressional plan that he's modeled his proposal on by the Medicare actuaries. Let me give you one quick example. There is a man here tonight named George McKinney from Milwaukee. He's 70 years old, has high blood pressure, his wife has heart trouble. They have an income of $25,000 a year. They can't pay for their prescription drugs. They're some of the ones that go to

Canada regularly in order to get their prescription drugs. Under my plan, half of their costs would be paid right away. Under Governor Bush's plan, they would get not one penny for four to five years and then they would be forced to go into an HMO or to an insurance company and ask them for coverage, but there would be no limit on the premiums or the deductibles or any of the terms and conditions.

BUSH: I cannot let this go by, the old-style Washington politics, if we're going to scare you in the voting booth. Under my plan the man gets immediate help with prescription drugs. It's called Immediate Helping Hand. Instead of squabbling and finger pointing, he gets immediate help. Let me say something.

MODERATOR (Jim Lehrer, PBS): You're—

GORE: They get $25,000 a year income; that makes them ineligible.

BUSH: Look, this is a man who has great numbers. He talks about numbers. I'm beginning to think not only did he invent the Internet, but he invented the calculator. It's fuzzy math. (First presidential debate between Vice President Al Gore and Governor George Bush, October 3, 2000)[14]

Now let's take a "clinical" look at this interchange. Note the *expected utility model* underlying Gore's approach. He saw his job as to convince the average senior citizen or aging worker—someone not unlike our hypothetical Pennsylvania coal miner—that Bush's plan would have a lower utility value than his own. Now there's nothing wrong with comparing and contrasting plans, although Gore's appeal would have been far more effective if he had simply reversed the order, reeling voters in with a personal story and *then* hooking them with a contrast between his plan and Bush's. And from the standpoint of the dispassionate mind, Bush clearly had few answers to Gore's charges, other than to play the Washington outsider and mumble some platitudes about helping hands.

After eight years as vice president and months campaigning against George W. Bush, Gore clearly knew everything he needed to know about every "issue" in the campaign. The last thing he needed was a debate coach to quiz him on facts and figures. Yet precisely this kind of debate preparation set him up for the most memorable (and, for Gore, the most destructive) moment of the debate: Bush's line about Gore claiming to invent the calculator. Bush delivered this barbed one-liner with an affable style that stood in stark juxtaposition to Gore's nonverbal dismissiveness of Bush's arguments (and, by extension, of his intellect).[15] The line was unfair, but the Gore team handed it to him, by attending to the facts and figures rather than to the *stories* Bush had been telling the public about Gore. Instead of getting voters to *feel* the difference between his concern for the welfare of seniors struggling to pay their medical bills and Bush's, Gore went to a level of numerical precision—premised on a model of expected utility, giving them every number they needed to make the appropriate calculations—that played right into Bush's strategy of portraying Gore as an emotionless policy wonk, "not a regular guy, like us."

Gore's statement, "your premiums would go up by between 18% and 47%, and that is the study of the congressional plan that he's modeled his proposal on by the Medicare actuaries," may well have been accurate, and it was surely convincing to his debate "prep" coach, Bob Shrum, who was a master debater at Georgetown and must have clenched his fist with delight and shouted "yes!" when he heard the figures roll off Gore's tongue. In fact, following the debate, while media pundits were concluding decisively on television that the debate had been a disaster for Gore, Shrum and his colleagues were celebrating, convinced that their fighter had put his opponent on the mat multiple times.[16]

In rational terms, Gore *had* given Bush a beating. But in emotional terms, both the presentation of exact numbers (as opposed to "your premiums would go up by about a third") and the mention of "actuaries" undercut the story Gore most needed to tell the American people: that he *cared about* that seventy-year-old man, and he would *do* something about it. Instead, his exacting reference to numbers and actuaries reinforced the story George W. Bush wanted to tell about him: "Look,

I'm like you, I don't care about all this fancy math. I care about people. They're just statistics to him."[17]

In that single line about inventing the calculator, Bush killed three birds with one stone. He established himself as a guy with a sense of humor who would likely be fun to have around for the next four years. He reiterated themes about Gore's hubris and lack of trustworthiness that struck at the heart of his character. And most importantly, he disarmed Gore for the remaining debates—and the rest of the election—of the *value of data*. From that point forward, all reference to numbers was just "fuzzy math."

It didn't help, of course, that the media did their postmodernism routine, turning Gore's claims about Bush's Medicare plan and tax cuts, which both turned out to be true, into a he said/she said contest of competing claims to a truth that somehow couldn't be adjudicated.[18] But it's the job of a campaign to get the media to convey its message rather than the opponent's message, and in the last thirty years, with the exception of the Clinton years, Republicans have consistently outflanked Democrats in these maneuvers, using the same emotional skill they have demonstrated with the electorate.

So now let's return to our hypothetical Pennsylvania coal miner, who was likely a Democrat in the 1970s, a Reagan Democrat in the 1980s, and considered himself an Independent with Republican leanings in 2004. If public opinion polls provide any indication, he was *not* likely to place more weight on the issues that actually affect his life than on concerns about terrorism and violent crime that were of far less immediate relevance to his own and his family's safety. And, with the right priming, he was likely to place a heavy weight on homosexuals getting married in San Francisco and Massachusetts.

With this emotional calculus, our rational decision maker enthusiastically cast his ballot for Bush in 2004. And in fact, extrapolating from the 2004 exit polls, he had a 55% to 60% likelihood of voting doing so, as long as he wasn't a union member. Like his fellow Pennsylvanians, he also probably rated terrorism as the most important issue on his mind as he cast his ballot.[19]

Now to be fair, bounded rationality models are more sophisticated than the kind of classical utility models I have described.[20]

Their rationality is *not* boundless. They recognize the existence of cognitive shortcuts (called heuristics) and other cognitive biases that can lead a rational mind astray (biases whose discovery led to the Nobel Prize for psychologist Daniel Kahneman).[21] For example, people are prone to the *availability bias*, by which they may overestimate the frequency (or danger) of an event on the basis of how readily it comes to mind (i.e., on how available it is to their consciousness).[22] Thus, after the United States was attacked on September 11, and after repeated televised terror alerts, a voter was likely to weight the likelihood of a terrorist attack as higher than a car accident, even though tenfold more people died in car accidents in 2001 than in the Twin Towers.[23]

Bounded rationality models are a vast improvement over eighteenth century notions of rationality, but they actually don't help us much with our Pennsylvania coal miner. The availability bias might explain why he placed so much emphasis on the possibility of terrorist attacks. But it doesn't explain why terrorism was more available to his consciousness than to the consciousness of the average urban New Yorker, who, realistically, had much more to fear from al Qaeda but voted for John Kerry. And it doesn't explain why recent mine disasters, which should be particularly available to the consciousness of a miner in a neighboring state, seemed to loom less large than the specter of two men kissing on the courthouse steps in San Francisco.

The Marketplace of Emotions

The view of democracy that naturally flows from the dispassionate view of the mind is of a *marketplace of ideas*. Parties and politicians who want to convince others of their point of view lay out the data, make their best case, and leave it to the electorate to weigh the arguments and exercise their capacity to reason. To the Western ear, and particularly to the American ear, this view of mind and politics seems eminently "reasonable."

But this view of mind and brain couldn't be further from the truth. In politics, when reason and emotion collide, emotion invariably wins. Although the marketplace of ideas is a great place to shop for policies, the marketplace that matters most in American politics is the *market-place of emotions*.

Republicans have a keen eye for markets, and they have a near-monopoly in the marketplace of emotions. They have kept government off our backs, torn down that wall, saved the flag, left no child behind, protected life, kept our marriages sacred, restored integrity to the Oval Office, spread democracy to the Middle East, and fought an unrelenting war on terror. The Democrats, in contrast, have continued to place their stock in the marketplace of ideas. And in so doing, they have been trading in the wrong futures.

I have it on good authority (i.e., off the record) that leading conservatives have chortled with joy (usually accompanied by astonishment) as they watched their Democratic counterparts campaign by reciting their best facts and figures, as if they were trying to prevail in a high school debate tournament. They must have heaved a huge sigh of relief (but not on the air) when Al Gore ran for president pretending that he had not co-presided over one of the most prosperous periods in modern American history. One can only imagine the relief of the Bush campaign in 2004 when no one thought to pull out the classic television footage of a smiling Secretary of Defense Dick Cheney shaking hands in the 1980s with an equally charming Saddam Hussein, with the narration, "Why was Vice President Cheney so sure Saddam had weapons of mass destruction? Because he sold them to him." And they must certainly have appreciated the Kerry campaign's failure to juxtapose footage of Governor Bush running for his first term as president with his arm around his biggest campaign contributor, Ken Lay, promising to "run this country like a CEO runs a company."

These failures are systematic, not incidental. There is no doubt that institutional factors play a key role in the difficulty Democrats have had, particularly in presidential politics. Since John F. Kennedy, in the last forty-five years, the three Democrats who have ascended to the presidency (Lyndon Johnson, Jimmy Carter, and Bill Clinton) have shared one characteristic: They were from the South. Indeed, virtually every political consultant who has led his candidate into the White House in the last three decades on *both* sides of the aisle—Roger Ailes (who later started Fox News), Lee Atwater, Hamilton Jordan, Patrick Caddell, James Carville, Paul Begala, and Karl Rove—have hailed from the South. Given the strength of John Edwards' resurgence in the 2004 primaries after Super Tuesday in 2004—despite the fact that voting for Edwards was by that point a lost cause since John Kerry had already just about wrapped up enough delegates to win the nomination—it takes little stretch of the imagination to suggest that had the first Democratic primaries been held in Georgia and Florida, we might today be writing about the prospects for reelection of President Edwards.

But institutional factors are only part of the problem. Since Franklin Roosevelt more than sixty years ago, only one Republican incumbent has *failed* in his bid for re-election to the Presidency, whereas only one Democrat has *succeeded*. These are astounding figures given that when the electorate hasn't been evenly split in party identification during those years, Democrats have generally outnumbered Republicans.

What Franklin Roosevelt and Bill Clinton shared was not only the keen intellect so valued by those of us to the left of center but something deeply valued by people in the heartland: an understanding of what they were feeling. When Roosevelt assured Americans that they had nothing to fear but fear itself; when he engaged them in heart-to-heart conversations in their own homes in his fireside chats; when he confidently responded with innovative programs and offered people a "New Deal" in a terrible time of depression and desperation, he was reading the emotional pulse of the American people.

The following passage from his second fireside chat was delivered less than three months into his presidency, on May 7, 1933, as he was engaged in the most radical legislative agenda in the history of the nation:

> Two months ago we were facing serious problems. The country was dying by inches. It was dying because trade and commerce had declined to dangerously low levels; prices for basic commodities were such as to destroy the value of the assets of national institutions such as banks, savings banks, insurance

companies, and others. These institution . . . were foreclosing mortgages, calling loans, refusing credit. . . . We were faced by a condition and not a theory.[24]

In this one paragraph, we can see the opening act of a narrative structure that would frame not only this particular (and crucial) fireside chat but the story of his presidency. He began with a diagnosis. He made clear that he understood that this was "a condition and not a theory," that these were real people's lives he was talking about. He then continued, using a familiar narrative construction with tremendous emotional power, describing two alternatives, one that had already led to ruin, and the other that would require a leap of faith in a time of hopelessness:

> There were just two alternatives: The first was to allow the fore-closures to continue, credit to be withheld and money to go into hiding. . . . It is easy to see that the result of this course would have not only economic effects of a very serious nature but social results that might bring incalculable harm. Even before I was inaugurated I came to the conclusion that such a policy was too much to ask the American people to bear. It involved not only a further loss of homes, farms, savings and wages but also a loss of spiritual values—the loss of that sense of security for the present and the future so necessary to the peace and contentment of the individual and of his family. When you destroy these things you will find it difficult to establish confidence of any sort in the future. It was clear that mere appeals from Washington for confidence and the mere lending of more money to shaky institutions could not stop this downward course. A prompt program applied as quickly as possible seemed to me not only justified but imperative to our national security.

In this passage, Roosevelt was elaborating his narrative emotionally, leading the listener from the hopeless state of economic affairs with which he began his presidency, to the alternatives facing the country, to the dire consequences of failing to take bold and decisive action. He reassured his listeners that in taking a leap of faith with him they were not plunging into the abyss with a man who lacked either the courage or the knowledge to lead, liberally mixing occasional phrases that most Americans could not exactly understand (e.g., "forcing liquidation") that conveyed his command of the issues with emotionally charged phrases that conveyed that he *understood where they lived*.

After next outlining one piece of bold legislation after another, sharing the credit for these legislative achievements with the Congress and members of both parties, Roosevelt continued, in a spirit of honesty and humility that today seems like a distant memory in American political-speak:

> Today we have reason to believe that things are a little better than they were two months ago. Industry has picked up, railroads are carrying more freight, farm prices are better, but I am not going to indulge in issuing proclamations of overenthusiastic assurance. We cannot bally-ho ourselves back to prosperity. I am going to be honest at all times with the people of the country. . . . I know that the people of this country will understand this and will also understand the spirit in which we are undertaking this policy. I do not deny that we may make mistakes of procedure as we carry out the policy. I have no expectation of making a hit every time I come to bat. What I seek is the highest possible batting average, not only for myself but for the team. Theodore Roosevelt once said to me: "If I can be right 75 percent of the time I shall come up to the fullest measure of my hopes."

And ultimately, he concluded his address to the hearts and minds of the American people on a note of confidence, determination, and shared mission:

> To you, the people of this country, all of us, the Members of the Congress and the members of this Administration, owe a profound debt of gratitude. Throughout the Depression you have been patient. You have granted us wide powers, you have encouraged us

with a wide-spread approval of our purposes. Every ounce of strength and every resource at our command we have devoted to the end of justifying your confidence. We are encouraged to believe that a wise and sensible beginning has been made. In the present spirit of mutual confidence and mutual encouragement we go forward.

Fast-forward a half century, and we see Bill Clinton listening to people in unstaged town hall meetings, his eyes always locking with theirs. Like Roosevelt, he understood the power of a one-two punch in politics: following an emotional appeal that draws his audience in with some specifics about what exactly he is going to do to make their lives better.

The second debate of the presidential election of 1992 had a town hall format that showcased a spry, young, emotional heavyweight (Clinton) against an aging, badly mismatched welterweight (George H. Bush) on a canvas that could not have been better suited for the younger, quicker, more emotionally powerful man. An audience member posed a question to President Bush about the national debt that was essentially about how he could understand the plight of people in the midst of a recession when he was not personally feeling it.

BUSH: Well, listen, you ought to be in the White House for a day and hear what I hear and see what I see and read the mail I read and touch the people that I touch from time to time. I was in the Lomax AME Church. It's a black church just outside of Washington, DC. And I read in the bulletin about teenage pregnancies, about the difficulties that families are having to make ends meet. I talk to parents. I mean, you've got to care. Everybody cares if people aren't doing well.

But I don't think it's fair to say, you haven't had cancer. Therefore, you don't know what it's like. I don't think it's fair to say, you know, whatever it is, that if you haven't been hit by it personally. . . . But I think in terms of the recession, of course you feel it when you're president of the U.S. And that's why I'm trying to do something about it by stimulating the export, vesting more, better education systems.

Thank you. I'm glad you clarified it.

Bush's response was probably a turning point in the election, confirming the average voter's worst fears about their president as someone who had no idea what they were feeling. It was strangely egocentric for a man not generally characterized by egocentrism (focusing on *his* discomforts as president), likely reflecting his defensiveness in the face of an "in your face" question. Bush tried (no doubt advised by his consultants to take a leaf from the Reagan playbook) to use a human example, an encounter at an AME church. But he *forgot to include the human part.* He didn't mention any of the nameless, faceless people he had met. He seemed more interested in reading their bulletins. He obviously had been advised to use emotionally evocative phrases such as "the people that I touch," but they were not in his vernacular, and he immediately spoiled them with phrases such as "from time to time" that only reinforced a sense of his fleeting contact with everyday Americans.

Clinton seized on the opportunity, first expressing an interest in the *questioner's* experience, asking what *her* experience had been. He then described precisely how he knew what the recession felt like, artfully overcoming the same potential challenge leveled against President Bush (that he had easily weathered tough times in his own Arkansas White House). Once he had established an emotional connection with the questioner—and with similar "questioners" throughout all around the country—he gave his listeners a diagnosis and a dose of policy—ascribing the recession to a failed economic theory that had guided the last twelve years of Republican policy—and made clear that he would follow a different approach.

CLINTON: Well, I've been governor of a small state for twelve years. I'll tell you how it's affected me. Every year Congress and the president sign laws that make us do more things and gives us less money to do it with. I see people in my state, middle class people—their taxes have gone up in Washington and their services have gone down while the wealthy have gotten tax cuts.

I have seen what's happened in this last four years when—in my state, when people lose their jobs there's a good chance I'll know them by their names. When a factory closes, I know the people who ran it. When the businesses go bankrupt, I know them.

And I've been out here for thirteen months meeting in meetings just like this ever since October, with people like you all over America, people that have lost their jobs, lost their livelihood, lost their health insurance.

What I want you to understand is the national debt is not the only cause of that. It is because America has not invested in its people. It is because we have not grown. It is because we've had twelve years of trickle down economics. We've gone from first to twelfth in the world in wages. We've had four years where we've produced no private sector jobs. Most people are working harder for less money than they were making ten years ago.

It is because we are in the grip of a failed economic theory. And this decision you're about to make better be about what kind of economic theory you want, not just people saying I'm going to go fix it but what are we going to do? I think what we have to do is invest in American jobs, American education, control American health care costs, and bring the American people together again.

QUESTIONER [spoken with genuine appreciation]: *Thank you.*[25]

The ability to speak to people's concerns at an emotional level was characteristic of Clinton's campaigns and governance. During the New Hampshire primary, with news stories swirling about Jennifer Flowers and other less-than-perfumed daisies that could readily have derailed his campaign, Clinton responded in an interview on *60 Minutes* with his wife by his side. He made a simple statement that allowed millions of viewers to respect his admission of the human frailty shared with half of them, and to share his wife's forgiveness: "I have acknowledged causing pain in my marriage. I think most Americans who are watching this tonight, they'll know what we're saying, they'll get it, and they'll feel we have been more than candid." Whether planned or unplanned, I don't think it was accidental that he used the word *we* rather than the more logical *I*. Doing so signaled that this was an issue shared with his wife and, most importantly, that this was an issue *between him and her* within the privacy of their marriage and not between him and the American people. The issue died.

This level of emotional intelligence is unusual in American politics (and among the population, where emotional intelligence, like all forms of intelligence, is distributed along a bell-shaped curve, with most people squarely in the middle). Among twentieth-century presidents, Franklin Roosevelt and Bill Clinton were probably rivaled in this respect only by Teddy Roosevelt and Ronald Reagan. But with the exception of the Clinton years, what has differentiated Republican candidates and strategists in the last thirty years from their Democratic counterparts is whether they drew their inspiration from the marketing team or the debate team.

When the younger Bush's pollsters detected in early 2000 that his infamous smirk was creating "the wrong impression," they rapidly coached him on how to reflect gravitas instead of hubris. As it turns out, voters were not being "irrational" in their initial negative "take" on Bush's facial movements. They were detecting what turned out to be perhaps the central character defect that colored his presidency, a pathological certainty and smugness without regard to the facts. No one appears to have systematically coached Dukakis on the wooden use of his hands, Gore on the hints of condescension in his demeanor, or Kerry on the emotional messages conveyed by his periodic lack of vocal intonation or facial movement. What candidates' faces, tone of voice, and gestures often reveal are aspects of their character to which voters respond—and to which they sometimes *should* respond because they may provide a window into the soul of a person who can only be seen through a television glass darkly.

The failure of Democratic political consultants and campaign managers to attend to these signals reflects the overvaluation of reason and undervaluation of emotion characteristic of Democratic campaigns over several decades. Although many Democrats have come to associate emotional appeals with demagoguery, as the illustrations in this chapter from the only two Democrats in the last eighty years to win reelection to the presidency make clear, emotionally compelling appeals need not be appeals to people's fears and prejudices. They can just as easily be appeals to their hopes and dreams, their sense of shared fate or purpose, their better angels, or their sense that there might be someone who genuinely cares about their welfare and has what it takes to help restore it.

Indeed, implicit in most of the dispassionate "issue appeals" of Democratic candidates over the last several decades is the same *moral compass* that guides most Americans: the conviction that everyone who works hard should earn a livable wage and should be able to take his or her sick child to a doctor; that people who get the most benefit from living in this country should pay the most for what America has given them; that workers should be safe on their jobs from foreseeable dangers; that we should take care of the environment so that we don't drown the living or poison the unborn; that a great and wealthy nation does everything it can to fight poverty within its borders; and that tolerance is a virtue not a sign of moral weakness or uncertainty.

It's the job of a candidate to get people to feel these things during an election. And it's the job of a genuine leader to get them energized by these feelings when the election is over and it's time to govern.

The paradox of American politics is that when it comes to winning hearts and minds, the party that views itself as the one with the heart (for the middle class, the poor, and the disenfranchised) continues to appeal exclusively to the mind. True to the liberal philosophers of the seventeenth and eighteenth centuries (who by today's standards would be far to the right of, say, Pat Buchanan—even *he* would let his wife vote, and probably black people), contemporary "liberals" believe that the way to voters' hearts is through their brains.

But they are appealing to the wrong part of the brain.

chapter three

THE EVOLUTION OF THE
PASSIONATE BRAIN

★　　★　　★

O n March, 7, 1965, Dr. Martin Luther King organized a march in Selma, Alabama. The Civil Rights Act of 1964 had attempted to protect those rights. But officials all over the South circumvented it. Mississippi, for example, registered only 6% of its black voters. The march from Selma to Montgomery—the first of three King was to organize that month—made it only six blocks from the steps of the humble church from which it began. An entire nation watched in horror—and in real time, as ABC, ironically, had to interrupt its showing of *Judgment at Nuremberg* to reveal America's own day of judgment—as the local police and a "deputized" lynch mob descended on the peaceful marchers with batons, tear gas, bullwhips, and rubber tubing wrapped in barbed wire. The next day, people from all over the nation began flooding south to march with Dr. King.[1]

A week later, on March 15, 1965, President Johnson delivered an address before the Congress, demanding the passage of legislation that would truly put an end to the disenfranchisement of African Americans:

At times history and fate meet at a single time in a single place
to shape a turning point in man's unending search for freedom.

45

So it was at Lexington and Concord. So it was a century ago at Appomattox. So it was last week in Selma, Alabama.

There, long-suffering men and women peacefully protested the denial of their rights as Americans. Many were brutally assaulted. One good man, a man of God, was killed.

. . . [R]arely in any time does an issue lay bare the secret heart of America itself. Rarely are we met with a challenge, not to our growth or abundance, our welfare or our security, but rather to the values and the purposes and the meaning of our beloved Nation.

Having laid out the significance of this moment and placed it in the context of moments whose significance his countrymen understood, he continued:

The issue of equal rights for American Negroes is such an issue. And should we defeat every enemy, should we double our wealth and conquer the stars, and still be unequal to this issue, then we will have failed as a people and as a nation.

For with a country as with a person, "What is a man profited, if he shall gain the whole world, and lose his own soul?"

There is no Negro problem. There is no Southern problem. There is no Northern problem. There is only an American problem. And we are met here tonight as Americans—not as Democrats or Republicans—we are met here as Americans to solve that problem.[2]

Following this direct, elegant introduction, Johnson continued, drawing on the ideals of the nation's founders—some of whom owned slaves, and all of whom ultimately had little choice but to collude in slavery in exchange for creation of the union—to honor the *spirit* of the values enshrined in the document they created:

This was the first nation in the history of the world to be founded with a purpose. The great phrases of that purpose still sound in every American heart, North and South: "All men are created equal"—"government by consent of the governed"—"give me liberty or give me death." Well, those are not just clever words, or those are not just empty theories. In their name Americans have fought and died for two centuries, and tonight around the world they stand there as guardians of our liberty, risking their lives.

Those words are a promise to every citizen that he shall share in the dignity of man. . . . To apply any other test—to deny a man his hopes because of his color or race, his religion or the place of his birth—is not only to do injustice, it is to deny America and to dishonor the dead who gave their lives for American freedom.

Johnson did not rest his assertion that every American deserved the right to vote on principles of reason. He made clear that what he was asserting was not subject to argument. It was *beyond reason*. Reason, he noted, had been artfully employed to *derail* justice at the polls:

Many of the issues of civil rights are very complex and most difficult. But about this there can and should be no argument. Every American citizen must have an equal right to vote. There is no reason which can excuse the denial of that right. There is no duty which weighs more heavily on us than the duty we have to ensure that right. Yet the harsh fact is that in many places in this country, men and women are kept from voting simply because they are Negroes.

Every device of which human ingenuity is capable has been used to deny this right.

The president then went on to describe the bill he was proposing. He challenged the Congress to pass it, and he threw down the gauntlet to southern officials who might try yet again to circumvent it:

To those who seek to avoid action by their National Government in their own communities; who want to and who seek to maintain purely local control over elections, the answer is simple:

> Open your polling places to all your people. Allow men and women to register and vote whatever the color of their skin. Extend the rights of citizenship to every citizen of this land.

Knowing he had to overcome deeply felt sources of emotional resistance, he empathized with his southern listeners as one of them, and then told the story of a moment in his own history whose haunting imagery no one who heard the speech—or who reads it now—could ever forget:

> My first job after college was as a teacher in Cotulla, Texas, in a small Mexican-American school. Few of them could speak English, and I couldn't speak much Spanish. My students were poor and they often came to class without breakfast, hungry. They knew even in their youth the pain of prejudice. They never seemed to know why people disliked them. But they knew it was so, because I saw it in their eyes. I often walked home late in the afternoon, after the classes were finished, wishing there was more that I could do. But all I knew was to teach them the little that I knew, hoping that it might help them against the hardships that lay ahead.
>
> Somehow you never forget what poverty and hatred can do when you see its scars on the hopeful face of a young child.
>
> I never thought then, in 1928, that I would be standing here in 1965. It never even occurred to me in my fondest dreams that I might have the chance to help the sons and daughters of those students and to help people like them all over this country.
>
> But now I do have that chance—and I'll let you in on a secret—*I mean to use it.*
>
> And I hope that you will use it with me.

The Voting Rights Act of 1965 passed that August. It had the effect Johnson intended, as most southern officials read the writing on the wall, and the others watched as the federal government came into their jurisdictions to read it to them.

Johnson knew as he delivered this speech that he was not acting in his own—or his party's—"rational self-interest." He knew he was alienating an entire region of the country that had been largely united in its hatred for the Republican Party since Abraham Lincoln signed the Emancipation Proclamation a century before. Johnson reportedly told an aid, prophetically, as he laid down his pen after signing the Civil Rights Act the previous year, "We have lost the South for a generation."[3]

The only error in his judgment was that he underestimated the number of generations.

So why did he do it? Johnson was a complicated man, as his biographers attest, but he knew in his gut that this was the right thing to do. The stirrings in his gut were not the stirrings of reason. They were the emotions he experienced as he saw the faces of those Mexican-American children in 1928. They were the emotions he, like millions of his fellow Americans, felt a week earlier when they watched the events of Bloody Sunday unfold before their eyes. They were feelings of compassion, disgust, sadness, empathic fear and pain, righteous indignation, and rage.

In 1965, these were the moral emotions that transcended reason. These were the emotions that moved a nation.

Johnson's speech to the Congress and the American people in March 1965 not only stirred them to *feel* but spurred them to *act*. A more purely "rational" appeal would have been *irrational* in light of Johnson's goals.

Sometimes you have to work with the brain you have, not the brain you might have wished you had. And the brain Johnson—like the rest of us—had to work with was an emotional brain, a masterpiece of nature that is guided by an emotional compass and was crafted by millions of years of evolution.

From an evolutionary standpoint, emotional reactions generally "work." We feel scared or angry when someone attacks us or our family. We feel pride toward our children when they show character traits or abilities we admire or have worked to instill. We feel gratitude when someone helps us. We feel admiration when someone shows courage or altruism. We feel guilt when we have wronged another person.

All these emotions motivate us to behave in ways that are ultimately in our interest and the interest of those within our sphere of care or concern. They lead us to protect ourselves and our family, to nurture our children, to reward others who are generous or honorable, and to repair relationships we have damaged. Emotions provide a compass for guiding our attention and behavior.

Emotional reactions are not infallible. They play an important role in most of the psychological problems that lead people to seek treatment (or that lead their spouses, families, or coworkers to wish they did). They can motivate the worst in human nature, when people come to associate entire classes of people with emotions such as rage, contempt, and disgust. And as we have seen, emotions can distort the way we reason.

The implications of a passionate mind and brain for contemporary American politics are considerable. To understand our politics, one must appreciate why our brains work the way they do.

Evolving Emotions

An evolutionary history of the human brain remains something of an unfinished detective story. We have the outlines of a plot but lots of clues missing.[4] One thing, however, seems certain: nature did not start with a blueprint. Rather, natural selection—the process through which nature weeds out mutations that render organisms poorly adapted to their environment and selectively retains those that confer adaptive advantages—worked in fits and starts over millions of years.

Its creation was an elegant patchwork of circuits, one grafted onto the next, as the edifice grew larger and more complex. At every evolutionary juncture—as when the simplest vertebrates (animals with spinal cords) began to evolve the neural machinery that increased their ability to grasp the world around them—nature had to work with the structures already in place, without the luxury of redesigning the system from the bottom up.

The human central nervous system (which consists of the brain and the spinal cord) is essentially a living fossil record of its own history. The further down you go (almost literally, from the upper layers of the brain to the spinal cord), the more you see ancient structures that evolved hundreds of millions of years ago and continue to be shared by our vertebrate cousins. Most of us would be truly embarrassed if we realized the extent to which the more primitive structures of our brains, particularly the structures that regulate basic motives such as sex and hunger, resemble those of a sheep.

The differences between the human brain and the brains of our primitive ancestors (and many contemporary animals) lie mostly in addition to the original brain structures, which continue to guide emotion, motivation, and learning. This fact led Charles Darwin to place some species on our family tree whom we might consider rather poor relations. It led Sigmund Freud, a neurologist by training, to view our extraordinary capacities to love, create, and understand ourselves and the universe as a thin veneer—as we will see, only a few millimeters thick—over primitive structures that motivate our most extraordinary achievements and our most "inhuman"—that is, distinctively human—atrocities.

Feeling and thinking evolved together, and nature "designed" them to work together. Anxiety would have been of little use to our distant ancestors had it not co-evolved with the capacity to distinguish stimuli in the environment likely to evoke it. (That would surely have been a cruel trick of nature, akin to the experience of many people suffering with Generalized Anxiety Disorder, who are beset by constant signals of anxiety, often without any clear sense of what causes it.) Similarly, the capacity to recognize whether an object in the environment is a banana or a snake would have been little use to our ancestors if they lacked the feelings that would impel them to eat it or run from it. People whose memory systems remain intact but who suffer damage (e.g., by accident or stroke) to neural systems that attach emotional meaning to things or people provide living examples of what happens when reason is divorced from emotion. Such individuals can "know" that something is dangerous, and can even calculate the probability of danger, but they can't stop themselves from approaching it when enticed.[5]

Emotions not only provide much of the "fuel" that fires up our engines. They also provide most of the brake fluid.

We know something about how simple organisms learn to connect painful stimulation (the rudiments of feelings) with experience (the rudiments of knowledge) from the work of Eric Kandel and his colleagues. Kandel won a Nobel Prize studying how neurons change as the lowly marine snail, Aplysia, learns to associate stimuli with feelings and self-protective reflexes. This simple organism is an ideal research subject because, unlike humans, it has a small number of large neurons. Thus, researchers can actually *see* how neurons are communicating—they can measure the "chemistry" between them—as Aplysia learns to associate stimuli in its environment with the sluggish equivalent of pain.

When Aplysia repeatedly experiences a painful experience, such as shock in the presence of a previously innocuous stimulus (e.g., a benign-looking live wire), changes occur in both the neuron that detects the stimulus and the neuron adjacent to it that allows the organism to recoil. The more times the stimulus occurs along with the shock, the more readily the two neurons communicate, so that activation of one "turns on" the other. Over the long-term, the neuron that registers the shock actually "reaches out" to the neuron that controls recoiling, sprouting more connections to it. In this way, remarkably, the structure of nature—the regularity with which one stimulus predicts another—is recorded in the structure of the snail's nervous system.

Similar processes occur in just the same way when humans form associations (e.g., between a candidate and a feeling, such as hope or disgust), except that these processes involve hundreds of thousands or millions of neurons rather than two or three. During the 2004 election, my colleagues and I studied what happens in the brain as partisans view brief images of their own presidential and vice presidential candidates versus the opposition candidates. When viewing their own party's candidates, the most salient activations were in the very front of the brain, a part of the frontal lobes called the "frontal pole," shown in prior studies to become particularly active when people see or think about something related to themselves. In other words, our party's candidates tend to activate *identification* with them, a point of substantial importance for anyone crafting an emotionally compelling campaign.

In contrast, when briefly viewing images of the opposing candidate, circuits involved in negative emotional reactions became active.

Moving from snails and slugs to the primitive vertebrates a little higher up on our family tree, we see an evolution that mirrors in some respects the evolution of the American political system, from a loose confederation of states to a more centralized, federal system. The behaviors of the earliest vertebrate precursors were likely controlled at the "local" level, at particular points along the body, as stimuli impinging at one place or another led these animals to swish one direction or another. (These were the original flip-floppers.)

After a few million years of evolutionary work, the front end of the spinal cord began to take on some "federal" functions, leading what was no longer a loose confederation of neurons. This end of the spinal cord presumably developed because our early ancestors moved forward head first (which is why our brains are in our heads instead of our feet).

As animals, and particularly mammals, evolved, they developed a *brainstem*, or primitive brain. This primitive brain still exists in modern humans, although it is covered by thick layers of neural tissue. One section of the primitive brainstem was specialized for sensation at a very immediate level (smell and taste), whereas another section, a little lower down, was specialized for sensation at a distance (vision and hearing).[6]

Primitive feeling and thinking (sensation and perception) were always linked. Smell and taste not only convey *information* about what is in front of our noses or in our mouths but inherently arouse *feelings*. Something smells fresh or rotten, tastes good or bad, resembles something that has previously led to satisfaction or nausea—and these feelings motivate action, whether approach or avoidance.

Smells and tastes are readily associated with feelings (e.g., nausea, disgust). Forty years ago, psychologists discovered that if rats were exposed simultaneously to a taste, a sound, and a sight just before experiencing a blast of radiation that made them nauseous, they would subsequently avoid the taste, not the sound or sight.[7] That is, they would form an association between the feeling and the taste and ignore their other senses. From an evolutionary standpoint, this makes good sense, given that smell and taste are our two most reliable senses for detecting substances likely to make us ill. It is no accident that even today we convey certain feelings in the language of smell and taste, as when we say that something "smells fishy" or that an incident "left a bad taste in my mouth."*

Sights and sounds are not as invariably emotion-laden as smell and taste, but they often elicit feelings and are readily associated with them.[8] Most acquire their capacity to generate emotion through experience. In humans, sight and sound allow us to detect dangers at a distance, to see or hear our children wandering off, to spot food or potential mates, or to associate symbols with feelings (e.g., the flag). They also allow children as young as nine months old to scrutinize their parents' facial expressions in response to an approaching person or object and to respond with similar fear or excitement even before parents exclaim, "Look, it's grandpa!" or "Don't touch that, it's hot!"

The readily formed links between feeling-states and sensory experiences are of tremendous relevance to the emotional appeal of political campaign ads. The political scientist Ted Brader has shown in a series of experiments that something as subtle as varying the musical score in a political ad can alter its power to persuade.[9] Although largely ignored until very recently by political scientists, the power of music in political advertising would likely come as no surprise to marketers, who have used music and jingles since the beginning of radio advertisements. Many of the campaign ads that aired in the early years of television, from 1952 through 1960, had the distinct feel of Brylcreem commercials, and Republicans, unlike Democrats, have tended to maintain productive links between Madison Avenue and Pennsylvania Avenue. The power of music would also come as no surprise to movie produc-

---

*Interestingly, birds, who swoop down to eat their prey—and hence already have a toxic insect in their mouths before they can taste or smell it—show exactly the opposite pattern. They are genetically prepared to associate nausea with a visual configuration (e.g., the pattern of a butterfly's wings) rather than with a taste or smell. Perhaps if we could understand the chirpings of birds, we would hear them describe their sleazier flock-mates with comments like, "He looks a little paisley, if you ask me."

ers, who rarely create a movie without a "score," even though—or, more accurately, precisely because—the music in the background tends to work its effects outside of awareness.

In 1964, Lyndon Johnson ran what became known as the "Daisy" ad against conservative Senator Barry Goldwater, an ad that exemplifies the power of sounds and images in eliciting political emotions. Although the ad played only once, it received tremendous media attention and raised questions about what crosses the line in political advertising.

The context for the ad is not inconsequential to evaluating its ethics. It came at the height of the Cold War, just a year after the Cuban Missile Crisis, when the United States and the Soviet Union came within hours of mutual annihilation. Although the ad never mentioned Goldwater by name, it was designed to activate and amplify fears that Goldwater, an avid hawk who had made intemperate statements about the use of nuclear weapons, was too dangerous to be trusted with the bomb.

The text of the sixty-second ad itself was simple and sparse, but the combination of sounds and images conveyed a powerful and frightening message:

SMALL CHILD [birds chirping in the background, the camera pans in for four seconds on a little girl, plucking the pedals slowly off a daisy, in a sweet, high, and innocent voice]: One, two, three, four, five, seven, six, six, eight, nine, nine. . .

MAN: [suddenly a loud, reverberating voice begins a countdown, loud enough to be startling after the soft tones of the little girl's voice] Ten, nine, eight [the camera progressively zooms in on the face of the little girl as she looks up toward the sky, as if she is hearing the countdown or seeing something far away in the sky that she doesn't understand], seven, six, five, four [the camera continues to pan in closer and closer, until by the count of zero all that can be seen is the black pupil of her eye], three, two, one, zero [replacing the blackness of her pupil, as if both in her eye and obliterating it, is a video clip of an atomic bomb detonating, with accompanying sound].

JOHNSON: These are the stakes [the mushroom cloud video continues for over ten seconds, showing the combination of fire against the darkness, until Johnson's voice is no longer heard]: To make a world in which all of God's children can live, or to go into the darkness. We must either love each other, or we must die.

ANNOUNCER: Vote for President Johnson on November 3rd. The stakes are too high for you to stay home [the screen simply reads, "Vote for President Johnson on November 3rd," in white letters against a black background"].[10]

No one who saw that ad could ever forget it. Beginning with birds chirping, it reminds viewers of the sounds of life: the image of the little girl and the sound of her voice are "natural symbols" that evoke positive feelings, rendering all the more emotionally vivid the possibility of the destruction the viewer sees through her eyes. The announcer's voice—both in its volume and content (a countdown, in an era in which signs denoting fallout shelters were everywhere, and schools held nuclear disaster drills)—is startling, reorienting even the most uninterested listener to what is happening on the screen. Johnson's booming voice, preaching a message of love and ending startlingly with an apocalyptic warning of death, provides a stark and unsettling contrast to the images on the screen.

Although this was a "risky" ad, in the sense that it could have led voters to see Johnson as fear-mongering rather than raising their consciousness, its producers made three decisions that rendered this less likely. First, they avoided showing Johnson's face as listeners heard his words, effectively avoiding the potential inadvertent association of the fear he was activating with him rather than his opponent. Second, his own words invoked God and love, even though they ended with a frightening warning. It is difficult to see this as a "hateful" message. Indeed, although this is a classic "negative ad," central to its power is a message designed to resonate with people's love of their children, families, and God. Third, Johnson never mentioned Goldwater. The comparison he was drawing was clear, but it was implicit, essentially saying to voters, "With stakes this high, do you really want to take a risk?"

This third feature did not deflect overt criticism of the ad, which never ran again. But the gestalt of the short film—the mood it created, reinforcing preexisting doubts about Goldwater's temperament as the man with his finger on the button—rendered it highly effective, particularly as viewers watched it replayed in televised discussions.

The Thin Veneer of Reason

Precisely when emotions as we understand them in humans emerged is unclear. Nevertheless, it is clear that "feelings" are millions of years older than the kind of conscious thought processes we call "reason," and they have been guiding behavior for far longer.

To appreciate fully the power of the Daisy ad, you have to have a cerebrum, the next junction on our whistle-stop evolutionary journey through the emotional heartland. The cerebrum evolved neural pathways that continue to play an important role in our ability to associate behaviors with painful or pleasurable consequences. These pathways allow rats to learn to avoid electric shocks or press a bar to get morphine injections.[11] Further evolution led to structures higher up that are crucial to our experience of emotion. The structure that has received the most attention, including popular attention through the work of the neuroscientist Joseph LeDoux, is the *amygdala*. The amygdala is involved in many emotional processes, from identifying and responding to emotional expressions in others, to attaching emotional significance to events, to creating the intensity of emotional experience, to generating and linking feelings of fear to experiences.[12]

Researchers first began to understand the functions of the amygdala decades ago, when they found that destroying a region of the brain in monkeys that later turned out to include the amygdala produced a peculiar syndrome.[13] The monkeys no longer seemed to understand the emotional significance of objects in their environment, even though they had no trouble recognizing, identifying, or remembering them. They would eat feces or other inedible objects that normally elicited disgust or indifference, and they were no longer afraid of things that had previously led to fear. With "reason" intact but emotion incapacitated, these monkeys were generally unable to use their emotions to guide their behavior.

The amygdala can respond to stimuli even when the person has no awareness of having seen them. Presenting a threatening stimulus subliminally (i.e., so quickly that the person cannot report seeing it) can lead to activation of the amygdala, suggesting an emotion system that is constantly processing emotionally relevant information faster than we can consciously register it.[14]

The fact that people can register emotional experiences outside of awareness has important implications for understanding the way candidates appeal to voters. The clearest example was an ad run in 2000 by the Republican National Committee for George W. Bush against Al Gore. The ad was ostensibly about Al Gore's prescription drug plan for seniors, but toward the end of the ad, whose theme was "The Gore prescription plan: Bureaucrats decide," the word *RATS* appeared in large, bold letters for a fraction of a second while the narrator uttered the phrase, "Bureaucrats decide."

At the time, the Bush campaign quickly dismissed the idea that a "subliminable" appeal, as then-Governor Bush called it, could have any effect. They claimed that the ad's producer must have inadvertently botched the hyphenation of *BUREAUCRATS*, putting *BUREAUC* and *RATS* in different frames. In any case, they argued, with the support of a host of advertising executives who appeared on television, comparing the belief in subliminal appeals to, among other things, alien abduction, appeals of this sort don't work.

However, my colleague Joel Weinberger and I weren't so sure.[15] We ran an experiment on the Internet in which we subliminally flashed the word *RATS* before a photo of an anonymous candidate and then asked subjects to make a series of ratings about the candidate (e.g., "he seems honest," "something about him makes me feel disgusted"). We compared the ratings of subjects exposed to subliminal *RATS* to those who saw a different subliminal stimulus, such as *STAR* (*RATS* spelled backwards).

Subliminal *RATS* *did* affect voters' perceptions of the "candidate," leading to significantly more negative ratings of him. Although we were at the time agnostic as to whether the intrusion of *RATS* into the ad was intentional, it seemed unlikely that the word *RATS* had accidentally found its way into an ad that cost millions of dollars to produce and air. My own agnosticism subsequently disappeared when I learned recently that the ad's producer was a protégé of Lee Atwater, who taught seminars on "dirty tricks" with Karl Rove before the two hit the presidential jackpot with the George H. W. Bush and George W. Bush, respectively.

Unconsciously manipulating people's emotional associations through the use of subliminal stimuli is clearly unethical, although oddly, Democrats never thought to turn to experts in subliminal processes in either 2000 or in 2006, when a Rove protégé used the same strategy in a Senate race in Tennessee. Subliminal appeals, however, only represent the extreme end of a continuum of unconscious efforts at persuasion. The further we move from that extreme, the harder it is to distinguish appeals that are unethical from those that are simply effective.

From an ethical standpoint, the situation is more ambiguous when the stimulus is *technically* conscious but *functionally* unconscious or "implicit" (i.e., processed consciously minimally if at all). In 2000, then-candidate George W. Bush began the practice of speaking in front of a screen with the theme of his talk written all over it (e.g., "Spreading Freedom"). Although the words are not subliminal, if they are noticed consciously, they tend to draw nothing but an initial, fleeting glance. Their impact is thus largely registered peripherally, outside conscious awareness, as viewers turn their attention to the president's face, words, intonation, and gestures. Nevertheless, it is difficult to classify stimuli available to consciousness that are not deliberately misleading as unethical.

Many of the visual and auditory components of political ads (e.g., the music playing in the background, which is often noticeable only if viewers deliberately direct their attention to it[16]) may similarly become functionally subliminal for viewers who are "channel surfing." And as it turns out, the Bush campaign team always paid exquisite attention to the way it framed its messages so that they would have their maximum effect even when people were not paying attention.[17] This is probably better characterized as effective marketing than subliminal manipulation, although the two are difficult to distinguish at their borders.

Emotion Gets Cerebral

The final stop on our tour of the emotional brain is the many-layered surface of the cerebrum, the cerebral *cortex*, which constitutes about 80 percent of the mass of our brains.[18] Generalizations about neural structures are always overgeneralizations. No single structure has one function, and the more neuroscientists study the brain, the more we recognize that every mental act of any consequence occurs through the activation and coordination of circuits throughout the brain, from the more primitive circuits of the brainstem to the most recently evolved circuits of the frontal lobes. Nevertheless, different structures and circuits do serve different functions, and I will attempt to describe some of them briefly in ways that do minimal disservice to nature's extraordinary wiring diagram.

Broadly speaking, the further toward the back of the head one moves, the more the cortex is doing the yeoman's work of sensation and perception, and the further one moves toward the front, the more the brain is trying to interpret the signals.[19] To understand reason, emotion, and the complex interplay between them, we have to move to the front of the brain, to the part of the cortex that begins behind the eyes and runs to the top of the head and back a couple of inches. This region of the frontal lobes is known as the *prefrontal cortex*.

Roughly speaking, two broad regions of the prefrontal cortex are worth distinguishing. Toward the top and sides of the frontal lobes is the *dorsolateral prefrontal cortex*. (In brainspeak, *dorsal* means toward the top, and *lateral* means to the sides; the dorsolateral prefrontal cortex is thus toward the top and sides of the frontal lobes.) This part of the brain is always active when people are making conscious choices. Our ability to hold information consciously in mind (e.g., remembering a phone number when walking from the phone book to the phone, something I fondly remember once having had the capacity to do) and to weigh costs, benefits, and probabilities is "orchestrated" by the dorsolateral prefrontal cortex. (I say "orchestrated" because it's important to remember that virtually every mental act is a symphony, with each activated "section" contributing its own tone and timbre.)

For simplicity, I'll refer to this part of the brain as the *frontal reasoning circuits* because it is always "turned on" when people are consciously thinking and weighing evidence. This is the part of the brain to which Democrats traditionally target their appeals. Unfortunately, as we saw in the study that opened this book, that's probably not a good idea, since this part of the brain isn't typically open for business when partisans are thinking about things that matter to them. Nor, as we'll see, is it likely the busiest bee in the neural bonnet of Independents, either.

The other region of the prefrontal cortex, peering out from behind the eyes and extending about halfway up the forehead, is the *ventromedial prefrontal cortex* (*ventral* meaning toward the bottom of the brain, and *medial* meaning toward the middle). The ventromedial prefrontal cortex is involved in emotional experience, social and emotional intelligence, and moral functioning. It also plays a crucial role in linking thought and emotion, particularly in using emotional reactions to guide decision making. Not surprisingly, this region has dense neural connections with cerebral structures below the cortex involved in generating emotional states, such as the amygdala, which allows it both to *register* feelings and to *regulate* them (i.e., to try to bring them under control). For simplicity, I'll refer to this part of the brain as the *frontal emotion circuits* because it tends to be active whenever the brain is wrestling with emotional issues.

It is tempting to map our current political topography onto these two regions of the prefrontal cortex, with Democrats consistently appealing to the "blue brain" on the coasts of the cortex and Republicans appealing more effectively to the "red brain" in the middle. Patients with damage to the frontal emotion circuits often seem cognitively intact—to have the faculties of reason. Like ideal Democratic voters, they can solve problems and recall events from the recent and distant past. However, they may have difficulty controlling their impulses or regulating their moods, either showing intense or rapidly changing emotions, or experiencing minimal emotion where emotional reactions would be normal. They may also display socially inappropriate behavior or minimal guilt for harm caused to others.

A famous early report of damage to this neural region was the case of a construction worker named Phineas Gage. In 1848, an explosion sent a metal bar of more than an inch in diameter through Gage's forehead between his eyes. Remarkably, he walked away from the incident. However, over time, his friends complained that he was "no longer Gage." Previously known as a decent, conscientious man, Gage was described following the accident as childish and irreverent, for example, using profanity in polite company. He was unable to control his impulses and was constantly devising plans that he would abandon within moments.[20] According to his doctor, the accident disrupted the balance between Gage's intellect and his "animal propensities."

The neurologist Antonio Damasio has studied many such patients using a variety of procedures.[21] He describes a patient who came in for testing on a winter day when icy roads were causing many accidents. Damasio asked him if he had had any trouble driving in. The patient responded, casually, that it was no different than usual, except that he had had to take proper procedures to avoid skidding. The patient mentioned that on one especially icy patch, the car ahead of him had spun around and skidded off the road. Unperturbed, the patient simply drove through the same patch with no particular concern. This example illustrates just how "unreasonably" people might behave if guided only by reason.[22]

Although Western philosophy and culture have a history of viewing reason and emotion as opposing forces, what becomes clear from understanding their evolution is how intimately they typically work together. It is difficult to think about virtually anything or anyone that matters to us without experiencing a corresponding emotional response. The fact that someone or something holds any significance to us at all means that it has *emotional associations* that generally become active along with any thoughts of it, whether or not we are aware of them.

The capacity for rational judgment evolved to augment, not replace, evolutionarily older motivational systems. The emotional systems of simpler organisms are "decision-making" systems that initiate approach, avoidance, fight, or flight. The neural circuits activated during complex human decision making do not function independently of these more primitive systems. Freud analogized reason to a hapless rider on a horse, who does his best to channel and control the large beast—pulling it this way and tugging it that way—but ultimately, the power resides in the horse, not the rider. The rider could always get off, but he wouldn't get very far on foot.

And so it is with reason and passion. Reason can prod, regulate, and offer direction, but on its own it is pedestrian.

When reason and emotion become disconnected, the result is often disaster. Sometimes that disaster may take the form of a neurology patient who, like those described by Damasio, can't use emotion to stay out of harm's way. Sometimes it takes the form of a psychopath, a person who experiences little or no remorse, empathy, or concern for others, who may *know* he is breaking laws or causing others pain, but doesn't *care*.

At other times, that disaster may take the form of a Democratic political campaign.

Injustice of the Soul

The first great political theorist, Plato, was an ardent admirer of reason. Yet he recognized that reason and passion each had its proper place in mind and state. When one or the other consistently takes control in an individual, Plato asserted, the result is "injustice of the soul." The same imbalance between reason and passion can lead, he argued, to injustice in the state.

Both the Republicans and the Democrats today could probably learn from Plato, as one party has the illusion that appeals to emotion are sufficient not only for electoral victory but for good governance, and the other has the illusion that appeals to reason are sufficient for both. Unfortunately, the "injustices of the soul" that afflict each party sometimes work together to inflict an injustice on the state.

From September 21 to October 4, 1988, a political action committee with close ties to the campaign of then-Vice President George H. Bush ran the infamous "Willie Horton" ad against Democratic presidential contender Governor Michael Dukakis. The ad ostensibly criticized Dukakis for his prison furlough plan in Massachusetts, but its emotional overtones were far more significant than its explicit melody:

ANNOUNCER: Bush and Dukakis on crime [Bush's face in photo on the left, with a look of resolve, if not anger, on his face; Dukakis's face in photo on the right, looking soft and confused; the title below reads "Bush and Dukakis on Crime"]. [Bush photo moves to center of screen, with the large title below it, "Supports Death Penalty"] Bush supports the death penalty for first degree murderers. [New photo of Dukakis appears in the center of screen, looking goofy, obviously captured between facial expressions, with the title, "Opposes Death Penalty"] Dukakis not only opposes the death penalty [new title appears, "Allowed Murderers to Have Weekend Passes"], he allowed first degree murderers to have weekend passes from prison. [Mug shot of a black man, with dark skin and facial hair, appears in the center of the screen by itself for half a second, followed by the title below it, "Willie Horton"] One was Willie Horton, who murdered a boy in a robbery, stabbing him nineteen times. Despite a life sentence [image of a black man, presumably Horton, with a thick "Afro," accompanied by a police officer; the black man appears to be sneering at the officer as the officer stares straight ahead, apparently taking him to prison; a "one way" sign is visible in the background], Horton received ten weekend passes from prison [below the image appears the title, "Horton received 10 Weekend Passes From Prison"]. Horton fled [image of Horton and the policemen remains, as the title disappears, to be replaced by the title "Kidnapping"], kidnapped a young couple [followed by the word "Stabbing" below "Kidnapping"], stabbing the man and [the word "Raping" appears below Horton's other two heinous acts], repeatedly raping his girlfriend [befuddled image of Dukakis again appears alone in center of screen, replacing Horton]. Weekend prison passes [title appears below Dukakis: "Weekend Prison Passes"]. Dukakis on crime [second title appears below Dukakis: "Dukakis on Crime"].[23]

The Willie Horton ad was surely one of the low points in American electoral history.[24] The Bush campaign itself could not have risked running the ad, as it was too likely to backfire if attributed to the candidate. Thus, an "independent" political action committee took responsibility for it.

As it turned out, however, the Willie Horton ad was just the first half of a one-two combination carrying a powerful punch, with the explicit message, "Dukakis is soft on crime" and the implicit message, "Dukakis lets scary black men endanger your safety." The day after the Horton ad stopped running, the "official" Bush campaign began running its own ad, "Revolving Door," with the same explicit message but without any mention of Horton. The Willie Horton ad was crafted by a close colleague of media consultant, Rogers Ailes, who developed the "Revolving Door" ad that immediately followed it.[25]

The Willie Horton ad was well attuned to the primate brain, and particularly to the amygdala, which is highly responsive to both facial expressions and to fear-evoking stimuli. The ad was packed with both. The producers chose photos of Dukakis with unnatural facial expressions and contrasted them with images of a tough, resolute-looking Bush. Leaving nothing to chance, it reinforced every spoken word with a corresponding image—a threatening photo, a title describing a heinous act, or both together.

The mug shot of Horton was obviously the most emotionally powerful image in the ad, playing on every white person's fears of the dangerous, lawless, violent, dark black male. Research shows that even *subliminal* presentation of black faces activates the amygdala in whites, and implicit racial appeals are more effective than explicit ones because they don't raise people's conscious attitudes toward racism.[26] The Bush team chose its photos—and its subject, a brutal and, coincidentally, very black, criminal—well. Recent findings suggest that the more "Afrocentric" the features of a convicted criminal (the darker the skin, the more African the features—as in Horton's "Afro" haircut), the tougher the sentence he tends to receive in American courts.[27]

But the Bush team left nothing to chance in activating racial stereotypes designed to elicit fear. As far as anyone knows, the convict, William Horton, actually never went by the name "Willie."[28] Using a black name was just a helpful contrivance in activating the right mental associations. (Another Bush, Jeb, later used the ability to distinguish black from white and Latino names in a different way, to create a "felons" list of everyone in the state of Florida with names like "Willie" who shared the name of anyone who had committed a felony, disqualifying tens of thousands of African American voters in his brother's race for the White House in 2000.)

The "official" Bush ad came right on the heels of the "unofficial" ad that had laid down the neural tracks for it. The "Revolving Door" ad told a very coherent, and very disturbing, story about what voters could expect if the liberal governor from Massachusetts were to be set loose, like Willie Horton, on an unsuspecting American public:

ANNOUNCER: [movie clip of guard climbing a spiral staircase up a tall, daunting guard tower, as ominous sounds and music begin in the background] As Governor Michael Dukakis vetoed mandatory sentences for drug dealers [scene pans outward to show an enormous guard tower, which the guard is still only halfway up, as the image fades to the next scene] he vetoed the death penalty [photo of a prison guard walking slowly, gun in hand, watching inmates in the distance, which fades into the next image of bars]. His revolving door prison policy gave weekend furloughs to first degree murderers not eligible for parole [photo of a revolving door made of bars; a thick black horizontal band then appears toward the bottom of the screen, with the words "268 Escaped" in white]. While out, many committed other crimes [camera pans out, showing a line of convicts that looks like it extends far into the distance, with prisoners coming and going through the revolving door] like kidnapping and rape [the black band reappears at the bottom of the screen with the words in white, "Many are still at large"], and many are still at large. Now Michael Dukakis says he wants to do for America what he's done for Massachusetts [scene fades to the tall guard tower again, with a guard stationed like a sentinel atop a nearby prison building]. America can't afford that risk.[29]

The symbolism in this second ad was powerful. Throughout, the listener hears the sound of increasingly loud, shuffling feet, keeping time like a metronome, as prisoners, *en masse*, pass through the revolving door. The ad begins and ends with a spiral staircase, with a Sisyphean guard trying to climb to the top of the tower to keep his eye on killers and rapists perpetually beyond his vista. As the narrator tells a grim, damning story of Dukakis's indifference to the plight of an innocent public, the photo of a prison guard patrolling alertly, rifle in arms, fades into the image of the bars on the revolving door, creating momentarily an image of a guard *on the inside* looking wistfully at dangerous prisoners *on the outside*. Visually, for a split second, the scene reinforces what the narrator is conveying in words: that the convicts are on the *wrong side of the bars*. The narrative itself is exquisitely constructed, augmented with occasional words in print for effect, capturing the viewer's attention and peppering the ad with messages designed to make even the most casual viewer get up from the sofa to go lock the doors (e.g., *Many are still at large*).

The framers of these ads clearly committed what Plato would call an "injustice of the soul" that was simultaneously an "injustice of the state." The first ad blatantly played on people's racial fears and prejudices, whereas the second, which alone would simply have been emotionally powerful, capitalized on the associations created by the first and the enormous media attention it attracted, including heart-wrenching testimonials (paid for by the GOP) from Horton's victims, who directly blamed Dukakis and Horton in a single breath. This orchestrated campaign was highly effective. Survey data following the same potential voters over time from January to October of 1988 showed that anxiety about a possible Dukakis presidency skyrocketed in October, while enthusiasm toward him dropped precipitously.[30]

The goal of the Willie Horton ad was to activate fear and loathing, and it succeeded. But it did so with the complicity of the Dukakis campaign, whose soul suffered the opposite injustice, by failing to understand its emotional significance. The Bush campaign was successful in activating the public amygdala because the Dukakis campaign had undergone a radical amygdalectomy and hence never registered the danger.

As was characteristic of the Dukakis campaign, the response to an emotional attack was a combination of appeals to reason (explanations of the furlough program) and a deafening, seemingly insouciant silence, as Willie Horton's stab wounds to the candidate's heart increasingly infected popular sentiment. Dukakis largely proceeded with business as usual, pressing ahead with themes of "good jobs and good wages,"[31] as if he had not just been the victim of a brutal political mugging himself.

When hit with a dangerous emotional punch in politics—particularly a low blow, such as this one—the only appropriate response is an equally powerful emotional counterpunch. As soon as the Willie Horton ad aired, Dukakis should have dealt Bush swift and immediate justice.

Perhaps the most powerful way to do so would have been to bring up Bush's own record on civil rights, which was not pretty. Bush had run a Texas Senate campaign in 1964 opposing the Civil Rights Act.[32] All Dukakis needed to do was to link this *overtly* racist stance in 1964 with the *covertly* racist Willie Horton ad twenty-four years later. He could then have demanded that Bush apologize to the American people for yet another Republican effort to divide the nation along racial lines, placing Bush on the defensive, in the uncomfortable position of having to explain a stance he took two decades earlier that no one in 1988 any longer believed was morally defensible. In any case, it would have prevented Bush from running the Revolving Door ad, and hence cauterized Dukakis's wound, if not given him a necessary heart implant.

But instead of going on the attack, Dukakis mortally stabbed himself while the Revolving Door was still swinging.

chapter four

THE EMOTIONS BEHIND
THE CURTAIN

★   ★   ★

BERNARD SHAW (MODERATOR): Governor, if Kitty Dukakis
were raped and murdered, would you favor an irrevocable
death penalty for the killer?

DUKAKIS: No, I don't, Bernard. And I think you know that I've
opposed the death penalty during all of my life. I don't see any
evidence that it's a deterrent, and I think there are better and
more effective ways to deal with violent crime.[1]

Although the debate continued for another eighty-nine minutes, it was over by the end of the first. And so was the presidential election of 1988. Dukakis had begun the general
election nearly 20 points ahead in the polls. Despite his commanding
lead and his commanding intellect, he lost, because he didn't understand the question.

On the face of it, Shaw asked the governor a direct question, and
Dukakis gave him a direct answer. But he answered the wrong question. The question was not the pragmatic, utilitarian one Dukakis
heard ("Is the death penalty a useful deterrent?"). Dukakis answered
in the language of rational utility: "I don't see any evidence that it's a

deterrent, and I think there are better and more effective ways to deal with violent crime."

But what the average listener heard was his answer to three very different questions: "Are you a man?" "Do you have a heart?" and "Are we similar enough that I could trust you to represent me and my values as president?"

For most Americans, the answer to all three questions was no.

What the American people needed to hear from Dukakis was that he understood that this was a *moral* question. And although I'm sure his personal opposition to the death penalty *did* reflect a moral position, his answer didn't.

So if we dispense with the dispassionate vision of the mind, what is the alternative? A passionate vision of mind, brain, and emotion, which stands on the shoulders of three intellectual giants: Charles Darwin, B. F. Skinner, and Sigmund Freud.[2]

Two Siblings Are Worth Eight Cousins

Darwin[3] argued that emotions, like most characteristics seen across animal species, serve an adaptive function. The function he emphasized involved communication: animals, including humans, signal their readiness to fight, run, or attend to each other's needs through a variety of postural, facial, and other nonverbal communications. A baby's cry and a dog's raised hackles send signals to other members of the species, just as bared teeth display anger.

Many of these signals are similar across species, suggesting their common evolution (e.g., the baring of the teeth, an angry prelude to aggression not only in humans but in other species). Darwin argued that the ability to send and receive emotional signals regulates social behavior and increases the individual's chances of survival. And it turns out that many emotional expressions (e.g., fear, anger, happiness) are wired into the brain and face, allowing people from widely disparate cultures to recognize them.

As subsequent theorists have emphasized, however, emotion serves another purpose: it is one of the most potent sources of motivation that drives human behavior.[4]

It is no accident that the words *motivation* and *emotion* share the same Latin root, *movere,* which means *to move.* When parents hear the cry of their baby, they feel distress, which leads them to provide nurturance without which the baby would not survive. That our brains respond to the auditory frequency of an infant's cry, or that we tend to experience soft, warm, cuddly things—particularly those with oversized heads—as "cute," is no accident of nature. It is a *work* of nature.

Emotions channel behavior in directions that maximize our survival, reproduction, and care for the welfare of others in whom we are emotionally invested. Evolutionary biologists and psychologists since Darwin have come to recognize that nature selects genes that contribute to an animal's capacity to survive and produce viable offspring, or what scientists call, in the unromantic language of biology, "reproductive success." Natural selection also favors animals that care for close relatives, which evolutionary scientists call "inclusive fitness" (because it includes the "fitness" of others who share their genes). To boil it down to its essence: blood is thicker than water.

The reasons are strictly mathematical.

Imagine you are sailing with your brother or sister and with your cousin, and the ship capsizes. Neither your sibling nor your cousin can swim. They are both screaming and flailing helplessly, begging you to save them, but you can save only one. Toward whom will you swim?

Most readers, after perhaps a brief, gleeful flicker of sibling rivalry, will opt for the sibling. In so doing, they will optimize their inclusive fitness because first-degree relatives (siblings and parents) share much more genetic material than more distant relatives. Aside from the genes all humans share in common (most of which we also share with chimpanzees), siblings share half of their genes, whereas cousins share only one-eighth. In crass evolutionary terms, two siblings are worth eight cousins. Natural selection has favored the neural mechanisms—emotional mechanisms—that make this preference feel natural.

At this point, the reader might object that the real reason for saving your sibling over your cousin is that you know your sibling better.

You grew up together, and you have more bonds of affection. From an evolutionary view, however, childhood familiarity and bonds of affection are precisely the emotional mechanisms likely selected by nature to maximize inclusive fitness. When human genes were evolving, close relatives typically lived together. People who were familiar from childhood and who shared bonds of deep emotion were more often than not relatives. Humans who protected others based on familiarity and affection would be more prevalent in the gene pool thousands of years later because more of their genes would have survived.

The same kinds of explanations suggest why people seek power, wealth, and status. For example, human males, like males of many species, get a surge of pleasure from status and prestige, and they become angry when their status is challenged and depressed when they are deposed. During the same week, I happened to be reading the eminent primatologist Frans de Waal's description of a political coalition that deposed a powerful chimpanzee from his alpha male status and Haynes Johnson's depiction of Joseph McCarthy's slump into a near-catatonic depression after being disgraced and censured by the Senate following a long run as the nation's fiercest alpha male. The descriptions of the two males' behavior were uncannily similar (except that the ape did not have alcohol at his disposal).

These explanations make sense of why people look out for the interests of themselves and their kin. But why do people often show altruism toward others who are completely unrelated to them, such as saving a comrade in battle? The same reason other animals do: natural selection favors animals that practice *reciprocal altruism*, the tendency to help each other out, when the benefits of cooperation are likely to exceed the costs over time. Just as an individual bird might increase its danger by joining other members of its flock to swarm a predator that has just caught "one of its own," birds that evolved the tendency to swarm predators will be more likely to survive than winged Thoreaus wandering through the woods in solitary reverie. In humans, being part of a larger community confers so many advantages in terms of mutual protection, food gathering, culture, and mating that the emotions involved in friendship, sympathy, compassion, and even justice and injustice (the sense that others either are or are not pulling their weight) should be part of our evolutionary heritage.[5]

If natural selection favors animals that survive, reproduce, take care of their children and relatives, and behave like "good citizens" in their community, it follows that the emotions that have evolved over millions of years of evolutionary time are likely to serve those functions. In politics, this means that the themes at the heart of our evolutionary history—survival, reproduction, connection to kin, and connection to others—should be themes that resonate emotionally with the electorate. And campaign strategists would do well to think in evolutionary terms as they craft messages and select images, since nothing is as potent as a message about the welfare of our children, followed by our extended family, local community, and nation.

Paradoxically, the political strategists who really understand the evolution of emotion are the ones who don't believe in it. One of the most effective political commercials in American history was Ronald Reagan's "Morning in America." This was the first advertisement of his 1984 campaign for reelection, and set a generally positive, upbeat tone that he maintained throughout the campaign. Like many successful ads, it was simple, foreshadowing the central theme of his campaign: "Are you better off than you were four years ago?"

ANNOUNCER: [quiet symphonic music, accompanied by a video of boats pulling out of the harbor in the early morning, against a clean city skyline] It's morning again in America. Today, more men and women [video clip of a smiling businessman stepping out of a taxi on a New York street in the morning, followed briefly by the image of a busy street filled with people heading to work] will go to work than ever [video clip of farmer working the land on his tractor] before in our country's history [video clip of newspaper boy throwing papers from his bike in a suburb, as a smiling man in a tie walks along the sidewalk and waves as a car picks him up for work]. With interest rates at about half the record highs of 1980 [video of a station wagon pulling a small trailer in front of a white paneled home on a large lot], nearly

2,000 families today will buy new homes [video of a man and his young son, with a spring in their steps, carrying a rug into their new home, with a white picket fence increasingly perceptible at the bottom of the screen as the camera pans out, revealing other family members walking briskly and skipping behind them], more than at any time in the past four years. This afternoon [video of a grandmotherly woman with a corsage and a big smile of anticipation on her face, 6,500 young men and women will be married [the video continues, revealing that she is at her grand-daughter's wedding, followed by a close-up of the smiling face of the bride, dressed in traditional white with a conspicuous wed-ding veil], and with inflation at less than half of what it was just four years ago [the video continues, showing the couple embraced in their first kiss as husband and wife], they can look forward with confidence to the future [the scene moves to the couple exit-ing the church, as happy onlookers throw rice, followed by a big hug between the bride and her grandmother]. It's morning again in America [photo of a lit White House at dusk, gradually pan-ning out to show a more panoramic view] and under the leader-ship of President Reagan [video clip of a flag waving in the wind] our country is prouder [video of children looking upward rever-ently] and stronger [video of a man with a blue shirt and an in-signia on his left shoulder indicating that he is a law enforcement officer, pulling the ropes to raise an American flag] and better [video clip of an elderly man proudly raising the flag over his white home]. Why would we ever want to return to where we were [the screen is filled with an American flag waving in the wind] less than four short years ago [the screen reads, simply, PRESIDENT REAGAN, accompanied by a flag attached to a Reagan button by gold tassels]?[6]

This ad was masterfully crafted, focusing on the theme of morn-ing, symbolizing that America under Reagan's leadership was experi-encing a new day, much like the quiet, prosperous times of an era gone by. The ad has many features designed to evoke positive and hopeful feelings toward four more years with the grandfatherly Reagan at the helm, with its images of families, picket fences, weddings, closeness across the generations, and waving flags viewed with reverence by Americans of all ages—children, a policeman, and a man in his later years of life. It also emphasizes, without Reagan even speaking a word, that this man is *presidential* (and hence should remain president)—indeed, that he is himself a symbol of American pride—with the glowing image of the White House, the image of an American flag waving as the announcer utters the phrase "under the leadership of President Reagan," and with the simple message that lingers at the end of the commercial: "PRESIDENT REAGAN."

At the same time, the ad skillfully wove into its fabric of positivity a more subtle message that might be summarized as follows: "Don't let America fall back again into those dark days represented by my opponent, who was the vice president during the last administration and will drag America back down again." Note that the ad does not begin with the statement, "It's morning in America," although that is how the ad is usually remembered. Rather, "It's morning *again* in America" (emphasis added), meaning that the sun has finally risen after four dark nights of Carter-Mondale. The only time the announcer pauses in the entire ad is when he pronounces three words, each followed by videos with appropriate imagery: *prouder, stronger*, and *better*. Note the *er* at the end of each word, suggesting so subtly that most listeners would not even register consciously a scathing attack: that under Carter and Mondale, the nation was ashamed, weak, and worse. It then weaves together the comparisons implicit in the first sentence and in these three powerful words, asking, rhetorically, why anyone would want to go back into the dark of night.

The images are also filled with traditional American themes—work, family, simple living (represented by life on the farm), strength, and the innocence of children, brides, and green neighborhoods with white picket fences. The use of brightness, whiteness, and scenes of morning conveys a freshness and hope that are central to the emotional appeal of the ad. So, too, is the use of flags waving, which figured prominently in virtually all Reagan's ads throughout the campaign, conveying the theme of American strength and pride restored. This theme was particularly powerful emotionally after what many Americans experienced as their country's humiliation at the hands of a weak third-world nation (Iran, which held roughly seventy U.S. hostages for 444 days, releasing them moments after Reagan's inauguration).

Now, let's take a slightly different look at the storyline. Although traditionally described as Reagan's "Morning in America" commercial, it could just as easily be described as his "Evolution" ad.

The theme of the first part of the ad is the welfare of parents and their children (reproductive success). People are working. They have money in their pockets to take care of themselves and their families. No one is unhappy on the way to work, regardless of their station in life. They are all smiling, allowing the creators of the ad to make use of an inborn mechanism for communicating pleasure, security, and satisfaction. Not only are people working, but they have *homes*, nests to and from which their happy children are walking and skipping with a spring in their step, conveying their delight with universally understood gestures and posture.

The middle part speaks to kinship (inclusive fitness). It begins with a smiling grandmother, who is not only the first person we see at the wedding but the last person to hug the new bride as she leaves the church walkway on her way to her new life. The theme of marriage, replete with rice-throwing (a tradition that emerged as a fertility ritual), brings to mind the obvious next step in the life of this young couple, who will no doubt go on to have a white picket-fenced home of their own, as the circle of life is renewed.

The last part of the ad focuses on the ties that bind beyond kin, to community (reciprocal altruism). It is about national pride. Reagan's America stands together, with the flag, its symbol of our common fate and identity.

I present this alternative "reading" of "Morning in America" with tongue slightly in cheek—but only slightly. It is remarkable that the ad rests on the three central pillars of evolutionary psychology and, in so doing, evokes such powerful emotions.

But from an evolutionary standpoint, this is not so remarkable at all. Ultimately, survival, reproduction, care for our children, concerns for our extended families, and maintenance of broader ties that extend beyond the family and lead to our mutual protection are the stuff of life—and the stuff of emotional resonance. It is difficult to find an issue that has taken center stage in American politics in our lifetimes—economic security, reproductive rights, education, Social Security, states' rights, nationalism, and national security—that is not derivative of "issues" at the heart of our evolution.

And no one has ever provided such a powerful demonstration as Ronald Wilson Reagan.

Internal Checks and Balances

The second intellectual giant on whose shoulders we stand is B. F. Skinner. Skinner might seem an unlikely intellectual inspiration for a vision of a passionate mind and brain, given his attitude toward all three terms of the equation: mind, brain, and passion. Skinner was committed philosophically to a radical behaviorist worldview, in which the concept of mind had no place. For Skinner, scientists should only theorize about what they can observe. What psychological scientists can observe are what people and other animals do (their behavior) and what happens to them before or after they do it (environmental events, or stimuli). Skinner never studied the brain, an organ he preferred to treat as a black box (grayish, really). As for emotion, in his weaker moments he referred to it as a form of "private behavior" that could not be scientifically observed and, hence, lay outside the realm of science. In his more stridently behaviorist moments, he considered emotion epiphenomenal, a by-product of the interaction of animals with their environment that has little if any causal influence on their behavior.

So how might a thinker who didn't care much for reason *or* emotion (both of which he considered mentalistic constructs outside the purview of a scientific psychology) contribute to a passionate vision of the mind? If we strip Skinner of his philosophical baggage, we find a very different theory waiting in the wings.

Skinner's most important contribution to psychology was his description of the way humans and other animals learn by consequences, through reinforcement and punishment. Reinforcement increases the likelihood that a person (or animal) will behave in a particular way, and occurs when a behavior is associated with something rewarding (e.g., praise) or the removal of something aversive (e.g., nagging). Punishment occurs when a behavior is associated either with something aversive (e.g., an angry look) or with removal of something rewarding (e.g., "grounding" a teenager), making it is less likely to occur in the future. According to Skinner, much of what we do reflects these two simple principles.

Skinner was himself profoundly influenced by Darwin, and he hitched his wagon to Darwin's. He argued that the natural selection of *behavior* through reinforcement and punishment is a natural extension of the natural selection of organisms. In other words, nature selectively retains organisms that can learn, and reinforcement and punishment are the principle mechanisms by which organisms learn to adapt to their environment.

What Skinner left out, because he didn't want to talk about mental states, was that humans and other animals find experiences reinforcing or punishing because these experiences elicit *positive or negative feelings and emotions*.[7] Subsequent theorists, however, began to populate Skinner's black box with feelings.

The neuroscientist Jeffrey Gray[8] distinguished two neural systems involved in motivation and emotion in humans and other animals. The first, which he called the behavioral approach system, generates pleasurable emotional states and leads animals to approach stimuli associated with them. The second, which he called the behavioral inhibition system, generates anxiety and leads to avoidance of stimuli associated with it. The two systems differ not only in their neural circuitry but in the neurotransmitters (chemicals that allow communication between neurons) they use. Approach and positive emotion are related to dopamine (a neurotransmitter found in rewards circuits in the brain) and inhibition and avoidance are associated with norepinephrine (a close cousin of the hormone adrenalin, which can produce fear and anxiety).

Independently, researchers studying personality and emotion have come upon a similar distinction, between positive and negative emotion.[9] People who tend to experience one negative emotion, such as anxiety, also tend to experience others, such as sadness. Not only do these broad emotional clusters tend to emerge across cultures, but developmentally, they represent the first emotional discriminations children generally make (distinguishing things that feel good from those that feel bad).

When people describe their own personalities and emotional experience, two of the first dimensions on which they tend to describe themselves are positive and negative emotion. People who are particularly prone to negative emotion may organize their lives around preventing potentially unpleasant events from occurring, and may deprive themselves of pleasure as a byproduct of escaping anxiety or sadness. In contrast, people who are more driven by positive emotion tend to seek novel and exciting events, and may sometimes pay for it.

For most people, positive and negative emotion provide an internal set of checks and balances, leading them to pursue things they enjoy but putting on the brakes when they are about to get themselves into trouble. People who are too high on one and too low on the other are at risk for psychological problems. They may be vulnerable to depression and anxiety on the one hand or to excessive risk taking and antisocial behavior on the other.

The one emotion that doesn't neatly fit into this distinction is anger. Although it is often placed unceremoniously by psychologists in the "negative emotion" column, subjectively, anger can feel either pleasant or unpleasant, as anyone knows who has ever fantasized about revenge. Neuroscientists have identified a part of the brain that is specifically activated by feelings of "sweet revenge." And although anger can lead to avoidance or withdrawal, it can just as easily be an approach-oriented emotion, causing people to approach someone or something they intend to attack.[10]

In politics, much has been made of the distinction between positive and negative campaigning, which is another way of talking about appeals to positive versus negative emotions. Positive and negative emotions independently affect behavior, including voting behavior, and failing to shape and elicit negative associations to the opposition can be just as disastrous as failing to shape and elicit positive associations to your own candidate. Even Reagan's "Morning in America," a prototype of a positive campaign ad, included subtle but powerful negative allusions to Carter and Mondale.

Underground Emotions

Sigmund Freud—our third giant—had a complex relationship with emotion. His clinical hypotheses and case descriptions were replete with descriptions of the dynamics of emotion, and the treatments he spawned uniformly focus on the complicated ways people try to seek pleasure and deceive themselves to escape unpleasant feelings. Yet in much of his theorizing, he was wedded to a nineteenth-century concept of instinct or "drive" that obscured the central role of emotion in his own clinical work.

Early in his career, Freud proposed two instincts, which would be very familiar to contemporary evolutionary theorists—survival and sex—foreshadowing the concept of reproductive success. This is perhaps not surprising, given that Freud, like Skinner, was heavily influenced by Darwin's *Origin of Species*. Later, Freud came to view sex and aggression as the central instincts that motivate human behavior. This shift reflected both his clinical experience, in which he repeatedly observed that these seemed to be the two motives most likely to twist people into knots, and his witnessing of one world war and the beginnings of another. For Freud, the failure of modern culture to constrain naked aggression could only be explained by the triumph of biology, of nature over nurture.

Freud had some good reasons to fixate on instinct theory. As a neurologist, he understood well that the cerebral cortex that was responsible for the heights of human accomplishment evolved atop some very seedy structures, whose primitive demands it could only cover like cheap neural perfume. It is no accident that the guardians of public decency who decide what is "too much" for television and what rating to assign a movie use two criteria to make their determinations: how sexy it is, and how aggressive it is. Clearly, they did not arrive at these two criteria through a careful reading of the twenty-four volumes of Freud's collected works.

Further, if we strip males in particular of the inhibitions of conscience—either by blasting a hole through their frontal lobes around the eyeballs, or sending them off to war with even the slightest ambiguity about the rules of engagement—we always see the same things: rape, murder, and torture. We need look no further than Abu Ghraib to see naked (male) human instincts, shorn of the shackles of conscience. We have seen the same footprints in Uganda, Bosnia, Rwanda, Burundi, and Darfur.

Today, few scientists, and few theorists who have followed in Freud's footsteps, deny the imprint of biology on most of what we do. The tendency for children to develop attachments to their parents—and the corresponding agony parents feel at the thought of anything happening to their child—is every bit as genetically wired as the drives for food and sex we share with other animals. But what emotions can do that drives can't is to serve as multipurpose motivators, allowing us to attach motivational significance to almost anything.

Although Freud was devoted *emotionally* to his instinct theory, in his clinical theory and practice, he pointed the way toward a model of motivation that just happens to converge strongly with elements of the models we have yanked so mercilessly from the entrails of Darwin and Skinner.[11] What tends to "drive" people instead are their *wishes, fears,* and *values.* And emotion is central to all three.

A *wish* is simply a mental representation of a desired state of affairs, one that is associated with positive emotion. A *fear* is a representation of an unpleasant state of affairs associated with negative emotion, particularly anxiety.

Wishes and fears can be every bit as biologically driven as instincts. When our first daughter, Mackenzie, was about six months old, my wife and I decided to spend an evening at the theatre. A family friend, whose company Mackenzie had thoroughly enjoyed on a few occasions, came over to spend the evening with her. Mackenzie had never before experienced separation distress, but this night was different. The wailing began as soon as she realized we were really gone. And we had to return home at intermission, when we received a defeated call from our poor friend, accompanied by pitiful six-month-old sobbing in the background. Whereas a week before, we would have enjoyed Act II, we (and Mackenzie) were the victims of brain maturation.

So how do we understand this emergent fear? In the second half of the first year of life, as the amygdala and other neural structures come "online," children separated from their primary attachment figures begin to experience intense distress. This distress is as biologically "given" as the desire for water or food, although it presupposes that the child has experienced the environmental input the brain "expects" (e.g., stable caregivers).

Upon our return, Mackenzie was immediately soothed. And when our presence quelled her distress, her little brain created an association between our presence and soothing, which was very different from the association she had formed over the last excruciating hour or two between our absence and intense distress. That night, a wish and a corresponding fear were born.

Aside from wishes and fears, humans are also motivated by *values,* emotion-laden beliefs about how things *should* or *should not* be— morally, interpersonally, or aesthetically. Although we tend to view values as quintessentially cultural, many of the values that motivate people cross-culturally draw on biological proclivities just as wishes and fears do, such as moral injunctions against incest or the "family values" that, as we have seen, draw on our evolutionary heritage.

Freud argued, and considerable evidence now supports his view, that children develop values in part through *internalization*, first of the values of their parents and family and then of their broader society. The single best predictor of party affiliation—and of the broader value systems associated with it—is in fact the party affiliation of our parents.*

Most of our values are variations on the themes of the values of those who brought us up. When Mackenzie was three and one-half years old, she was attending preschool at the temple down the street.

---

*It is not, however, the only predictor. Politics can literally be in our genes. The extent to which people self-identify as conservative is about 40 percent genetic. We don't, of course, inherit the tendency to admire Rush Limbaugh or worry about the size of the deficit. But partisan leanings are related to personality traits such as conscientiousness and fearfulness, which are themselves in part genetic.

One evening, shortly before dinner, she asked, "Daddy, where is God?" Not being much of a theologian, I responded, "Well, no one is really sure, but most people think he's everywhere, watching over us." "Well," she said, with some irritation in her voice, "he must not be watching very well." Perplexed, I asked what she meant. "Because of *President Bush*," she responded emphatically, her disgust circuits obviously firing wildly. My wife flashed me a look of consternation, although I must admit having experienced considerable paternal pride at the thought processes that led her three-year-old mind to juxtapose the religious beliefs she was learning at preschool with the political biases she was internalizing at home. A couple years later, she made her daddy proud again, first asking, "Why does God let bad things happen?" and then pondering how God could let Bush be president.

I suspect in a different home, President Bush would not have provoked the centuries-old problem of theodicy in a five-year-old.

Freud's contributions to an understanding of the passionate mind do not, however, end with a somewhat emasculated version of his instinct theory. Several of his theories have stood the test of time, many of them recently reclaimed in one form or another by contemporary neuroscience.[12] Of particular relevance to understanding the political brain is the idea that much of our behavior reflects the activation of emotion-laden networks of association, and that much of this activation occurs outside of our awareness.

Freud and Skinner didn't agree on much, but what they did agree on was the importance of associations. Where Skinner had little interest in the "black box" between behavior and the environment, however, Freud recognized that the contents of that box are millions of networks of association—thoughts, memories, images, sounds, smells, and feelings that are linked to each other. These neural networks represent our knowledge and attitudes toward everyone and everything we encounter. Thus, my network of associations around John F. Kennedy includes knowledge about him, images of his face and speeches, recognition of the characteristic sound of his voice (including his patrician Massachusetts accent), feelings toward him, and my first political memory: seeing his flag-draped coffin on our black-and-white television set when I was four. When Freud developed his method of "free association" as a therapeutic tool (the encouragement to say "whatever comes to mind"), a primary aim was to try to map the structure of the associational networks underlying his patients' symptoms.

Cognitive neuroscientists have studied networks of association using some ingenious methods, relying on the fact that activating one part of a network tends to spread activation to other parts of the network. For example, an experimenter administers a spelling test, asking subjects to press a button as soon as they recognize whether a word is correctly spelled. Just before the spelling test, however, the researcher "primes" subjects with the word *dog*, by including it on a list of words they are asked to read or memorize.

When subjects take the spelling test, they press the button quickly when presented with *terrier* or *collie*. The reason is that "priming" them with *dog* activates a network of association that includes *terrier* and *collie*, placing the rest of that network in a state of latent activation. Although this network isn't conscious, its contents now have a greater propensity to *become* conscious because they already have more activation than usual.

Researchers can study the linkages *across* networks using similar methods. In one study, scientists presented subjects with word pairs to learn, including the pair, *ocean–moon*.[13] Later, when asked to name the first laundry detergent that came to mind, subjects previously exposed to *ocean–moon* were more likely to generate the name *Tide*.

Why? *Ocean* and *moon* are part of a network of associations that includes *tide*. *Tide* is also part of another network, of laundry detergents. By priming the first network, the researchers spread activation unconsciously to the word *tide*, which was then doubly activated, and hence readily recalled, when subjects were asked to name a laundry detergent.

Freud was particularly interested in *emotional* associations, the feelings attached to ideas and images. He was also interested in the way multiple networks activated simultaneously could together influence the way we think, feel, and behave.

A case in point is Freudian slips, in which a person means to say one thing but another active network interferes, leading to an elision of the two networks. A woman I knew was dating a much younger man, and her friends weren't being very supportive. When I asked her how *she* felt about the age difference, she replied, "Oh, it doesn't mother."

Obviously it did, as a network of association that included "old enough to be his mother" appeared to be active under the surface of consciousness, despite her protestations to the contrary. As a result, when she tried to produce a sentence that included a phonologically similar word (*matter*), *mother* was doubly activated by both its latent meaning in relation to her boyfriend and its sound (phonology). We now know that efforts to suppress thoughts like this actually increase their activation.[14]

Researchers have been able to *generate* slips of the tongue in the laboratory.[15] In one set of studies, researchers briefly presented a pair of words on a screen, rapidly followed, a fraction of a second later, by a second word pair. The goal of flashing the first word pair was to interfere with the second. For example, when the investigators flashed the words *angry insect* just prior to presenting the target word pair, *bad mug,* subjects were more likely to respond with *mad bug*, as the network about angry insects intersected with the sound of the word pair *bad mug.*

A central aspect of the art of political persuasion is creating, solidifying, and activating networks that create primarily positive feelings toward your candidate or party and negative feelings toward the opposition. The Republicans are tremendously adept at doing so, having spent billions of dollars over forty years on think tanks designed in part to hone the conservative message (i.e., shape associations to conservatism and its advocates) and to associate Democrats and liberals with taxing, spending, military weakness, special treatment of minority groups, low moral standards, and a host of other unsavory characteristics. And they have done so remarkably successfully, using procedures straight out of a textbook on associative networks.

One of the most paradoxical implications of Freud's theories was so paradoxical that he himself could not quite accept it, even though it was axiomatic to everything he wrote and did clinically: that emotional processes can be activated and shaped outside of awareness. We often think of emotions as involving a subjective (i.e., conscious) experience. Yet once we understand the logic of networks—how activation spreads from one part a network to everything it touches—what becomes clear is that most of the time *many* emotional processes are at a state of latent activation (i.e., are active unconsciously), and by the time we become conscious of an emotional response, we are likely to have been "chewing on it" outside of awareness for quite some time (in neural time, that is, which is usually milliseconds).

Some of the most instructive examples of unconscious emotional processes come from patients with brain damage. A famous case, known only by the initials H.M., suffered damage to his hippocampus, a part of the brain deep inside the cerebrum that is involved in memory. Each time he met Brenda Milner, the psychologist who studied him, he would politely respond that he was pleased to make her acquaintance, as he had no recollection of having met her before. Despite his amnesia, however, he was capable of forming emotional associations—he just didn't know why he was feeling what he was feeling. For example, following a visit to his mother in the hospital, H.M. could remember nothing of the visit, but afterwards he expressed a vague worry that something had happened to her.[16]

People don't have to be brain damaged to respond emotionally outside of awareness. The best evidence comes from research on subliminal stimulation, like our *RATS* study. Over sixty years ago scientists discovered that people can respond emotionally to the content of subliminal stimuli even though they have no idea what they have seen— and may have no awareness of the feeling even though it is oozing out of their pores. In one study, researchers paired particular nonsense syllables (e.g., *yot, tiv*) with a mild electric shock, creating an emotional association (anxiety) to those syllables. (They used nonsense syllables to be sure the stimuli would have no prior emotional associations.) They then presented the same syllables subliminally, intermixed with other nonsense syllabus that had not been paired with shock. Syllables previously associated with shock elicited an electrodermal response—sweat on the skin—indicative of anxious arousal, similar to what is assessed by a polygraph. Thus, although subjects couldn't consciously perceive them, the words associated with shock were eliciting anxiety.

Other studies have shown that people can *acquire* these kinds of emotional associations outside of awareness, becoming afraid of things they have never consciously seen.[17] Simply preceding an image of a person with a subliminal image of a happy or sad face can also alter the way the person is perceived. People are likely to find a person they have never seen unlikable, or to attribute to him negative qualities, if his image is preceded by an angry face.[18] Recent research has found that subliminal presentation of threatening stimuli activates the amygdala, eliciting fear responses of which the person may be entirely unaware.[19]

A Different Vision of Mind, Brain, and Emotion in Politics

The political implications of these findings could not be more profound. They suggest that the choice of words, images, sounds, music, backdrop, tone of voice, and a host of other factors is likely to be as significant to the electoral success of a campaign as its content. And they suggest the importance of paying close attention to the positive and negative images and emotions that are becoming associated with candidates in the minds of voters, whether or not they are aware of them.

Richard Nixon and his consultants understood the power of emotional associations as early as 1968, when they ran a disquieting ad in which no one uttered a word and not a single word of text appeared on the screen.[20] The ad simply created associations between a serene-looking Hubert Humphrey and pictures of mayhem at the bloody Democratic Convention in Chicago, riots on the streets, and death and destruction in Vietnam—images presented in such rapid succession that many could not be processed consciously.

The ad began with triumphant marching music, congruent with the innocuous still photos of Humphrey's nomination at the Democratic Convention. However, the music continued in the background throughout, often barely perceptible. The result was a dissonant, eerie juxtaposition of the music to the photos of chaos and carnage that flashed across the screen, creating the impression that Humphrey was impervious to the events that had transpired in the bloody months leading up to his nomination. During those months, Bobby Kennedy and Martin Luther King had both been assassinated, the streets were filled with rioters, and the Vietnam War raged on, with journalists and cameramen giving Americans a view of war "up close and personal."

Nixon's media consultants understood the utility of an ad that didn't speak a word to the dispassionate brain.

The vision of mind, brain, and emotion presented in this chapter and the last is very different from the vision that has dominated much of Western thinking about judgment, decision making, and political behavior over the last three centuries. Emotions provide a compass that leads us toward and away from things, people, or actions associated with positive or negative states. Organisms survived for millions of years without consciousness and without the faculty philosophers have extolled for 2,500 years as reason. They learned to avoid aversive stimuli and seek rewarding ones, and it is the ancestors of those primitive organisms—including ourselves—who survived, reproduced, and exist today. With the evolution of our most refined neural circuitry came not only our capacity for reason but also our capacity to be guided by rich, complex, emotional-laden networks, whose level of activation fluxes and flows outside of our awareness.

This, I believe, is the emotional legacy of Darwin, Skinner, and Freud. It is a deceptively simple legacy, supported by the best available science.

This simple reorientation toward mind, brain, and emotion suggests a very different way of thinking about electoral campaigns. You can slog it out for those few millimeters of cerebral turf that process facts, figures, and policy statements. Or you can take your campaign to the broader neural electorate, collecting delegates throughout the brain and targeting different emotional states with messages designed to maximize their appeal.

chapter five

SPECIAL INTERESTS IN MIND

★ ★ ★

The human understanding when it has once adopted an opinion
. . . draws all things else to support and agree with it. And though
there be a greater number and weight of instances to be found
on the other side, yet these it either neglects or despises . . . in
order that by this great and pernicious predetermination the authority of its former conclusions may remain inviolate.

— FRANCIS BACON, *Novum Organum, 1620*

O n January 20, 2005, President George W. Bush delivered his
second inaugural address. The theme was spreading liberty.
For many Republicans, the speech was an inspiration, a tribute to American ideals infused with religious fervor and devotion.

Democrats, however, heard a different speech.[1] When the president proclaimed, to Republican approval, "We are led, by events and
common sense, to one conclusion: the survival of liberty in our land
increasingly depends on the success of liberty in other lands," Democrats wondered where his concern was for liberty in Saudi Arabia or
Pakistan. As he asserted that "Today, America speaks anew to the
peoples of the world," Democrats scoffed: "And who is listening?
You've alienated them all." The President: "All who live in tyranny
and hopelessness can know: The United States will not ignore your
oppression or excuse your oppressors." The Democratic echo: "So why

won't you call what's going on in Darfur genocide? Because they're not sitting on oil?"

Today, Democrats and Republicans seem like two species, living in parallel universes, unable to speak the same language. We hear the same evidence and come to diametrically opposed conclusions, even in simple matters of fact.

The tendency to see what we want to see reflects an accidental by-product of the evolution of our brains. We approach and avoid *ideas* because of the feelings they elicit, just as we approach and avoid things in the world depending on their emotional associations. Precisely the same mechanisms that provide a compass to guide our behavior in adaptive directions also act as magnets for self-deception, rationalization, and the kind of partisan "reasoning" that prevents any kind of rational discourse about political affairs for roughly 80 percent of the population, including the most politically informed voters.

How does this happen?

Through some deceptively simple properties of associative networks. Activation spreads along networks from link to link, gradually weakening as the links get further from the original "source," just as a ripple from a stone thrown in a pond is most intense at the point of entry and then gradually dissipates until it is imperceptible. The words *weapons of mass destruction* spread activation to *nuclear weapons* and *biological weapons,* putting the brain on alert for these concepts. If the next sentence were to begin with "*Nuclear. . . ,*" the brain would readily anticipate *weapon* or some closely related word, but it would not anticipate *family*, even though the latter is a frequent complement to *nuclear*, because activation had spread to a competing network.

Weapons of mass destruction actually activates many more specific associations, which ripple far and wide. Activation spreads from the broad category to a subordinate category, *biological weapons,* and from there to the still more subordinate concepts *anthrax* and *nerve gas*. These more specific examples are a step removed from where the stone hit the water and thus receive less activation, unless something else— like the anthrax scare of 2001—gives them an extra "jolt."

Cognitive psychologists discovered this property of "spreading activation" in research on categories such as animals and birds. After see-

TAE CAT

A simple reading task turns out to be not so simple. Adapted from Rumel-hart et al., 1986.

ing or hearing the word *bird*, people more quickly recognize the word *robin* than *penguin*, even though both are birds. The reason is that a robin is a *prototypical* bird—a good example of a bird, which has all the features of a bird (e.g., it flies, it migrates, it lives in trees) and is highly familiar to most readers. Penguins, in contrast, are highly atypical and unfamiliar birds, with which most people are familiar only through books and occasional trips to the zoo.

Although spreading activation is essential to the functioning of networks, a complementary process is what might be called *spreading inhibition*. Most readers will effortlessly read the handwritten words in the above figure as *THE CAT*.[2] This takes only a fraction of a second, even though the processes by which it occurs are extraordinarily complex—and unconscious.

The letters are somewhat ambiguous, both because of their slant and the way they are drawn (much like ordinary handwriting), yet we readily recognize them. In the figure, the second letter in each word is physically identical, but I doubt many readers saw *TAE CAT* or *THE CHT*.

So how does the brain decipher such hieroglyphics, where physically identical lines are decoded as different letters in two adjacent words?

It does so through a balance of activation and inhibition. When your brain first confronted the middle letter of each word, it activated two out of twenty-six networks of neurons whose job is the recognition of letters in the alphabet. One network represented the letter *A*, whereas the other represented the letter *H*. At the same time, different circuits in the brain were processing each word. The first word could have been either *THE* or *TAE*, but the former received much greater activation because of its substantially higher frequency in the English language. For the second word in the figure, networks representing *A* and *H* were also activated, but inhibition spread rapidly to the *H* network, essentially shutting it off, because *CHT* is not a word.

By this point, your brain was already leaning toward *THE CAT*, spreading activation and inhibition to different interpretations of precisely the same configuration of lines in the middle of each word. The icing on the cerebral cake came as your brain processed the phrase as a whole, further spreading activation and inhibition to the correct and incorrect interpretations of the middle letter of each word because no other English phrase other than *THE CAT* is possible. All you were likely aware of, while your brain was performing these remarkable calculations, was seeing the simple phrase, *THE CAT*.

This act of juggling different possibilities outside awareness until settling on the most sensible solution in light of the data is characteristic of most of human thought, and has enormous political implications. Cognitive scientists refer to this process as *constraint satisfaction* because what the brain is essentially trying to do is to make a judgment that satisfies as many of the constraints imposed by the data as possible. In essence, constraint satisfaction is like a Darwinian process of natural selection in our minds, in which alternative perceptions, memories, ideas, or explanations compete with one another, where survival of one interpretation usually leads to the extinction—or at least the suppression—of the others.

In a slightly more complex scenario, suppose I mention to a friend that "I was really unhappy with the party last night." At this point, two networks are likely placed at a latent state of activation in my friend's brain, each representing a competing "candidate" for what I might be talking about. One network represents the idea of an unpleasant social gathering. The other represents the idea that my political party had done something I thought was a mistake. From my sentence, there is no way to anticipate which way I am heading. As a result, the brain activates *both* networks, rendering it ready to anticipate whatever might follow.

This process is not magical. It is simply born of experience. In the past, when my friend has heard statements about *parties*, these statements have generally been associated either with social gatherings or political organizations, leading to strong associative links to both. Thus, the word *party* initially spreads activation to everything associatively connected to it (i.e., multiple networks with many different meanings) unless the context has already made clear the intended meaning. If I continue, "Almost everybody I invited was out of town," activation continues to spread to the first network, and inhibition spreads to the second. My friend effortlessly follows my train of thought—and is never aware that her brain had even considered the alternative "hypothesis" that the party I was referring to was a political one.

As we will see in later chapters, this process of activation of alternative possibilities outside of awareness, which is basic to human cognition, creates tremendous opportunities for stealth attacks in politics, in which a campaign uses the "cover" of a dominant interpretation of the data to provide plausible deniability for another network intentionally activated under the cover of neural darkness. This is why the Willie Horton ad was so insidious. The network most active by virtue of the verbal content of the ad, and the one of which most viewers were consciously aware, was the "soft on crime" network. But a second, more emotionally powerful network—about scary black men—was also activated. People can choose to accept or reject messages designed to bring ideas to consciousness (e.g., "Dukakis is soft on crime"). They can't as easily protect themselves from the insidious effects of "secondarily" activated networks—what we aptly refer to colloquially as racial "overtones"—whose influence is opaque to them because it is unconscious, particularly when followed by a second ad (in this case, "Revolving Doors") designed to mask it. Republicans exploited precisely the same neural mechanisms to defeat Tennessee senatorial candidate Harold Ford, Jr. in 2006.

The use of processes of activation and inhibition in politics is not inherently bad or insidious. All cognition—and hence all political discourse—works this way. But such processes can be readily misused, particularly if one side understands them and the other doesn't.

Winning Delegates at the Neural Convention

Cognitive scientists Keith Holyoak and Paul Thagard[3] have shown how processes of activation and inhibition explain the way people think with analogies and metaphors in politics and everyday life. Through analogies, people understand a novel situation in terms of a something familiar or better known to them.

As the linguist George Lakoff has made clear, the metaphors used in political discourse set the way voters "frame" issues and play a powerful role in shaping their feelings. When Ronald Reagan framed Nicaraguan death squads as "freedom fighters," he evoked metaphors of those who have died for the cause of freedom in the face of tyrants or invading forces. This set the terms of discourse in the United States, including the discourse of journalists, who could no longer "see" that these "freedom fighters" were attacking innocent civilians in a country that had just, for the first time, freely elected a government that Reagan simply didn't like.

During the Gulf War, President George H. Bush compared Saddam Hussein to Hitler. If we accept the premise—that Saddam is like Hitler—then Iraq's invasion of Kuwait was like Germany's invasion of its neighbors at the start of World War II. This would imply that Saddam must be stopped immediately before becoming a danger to the world.[4] The analogy was compelling to the world community, leading to a powerful coalition of nations willing to send their forces to the Middle East.

Why did Bush's brain equilibrate to this particular analogy? According to Holyoak and Thagard,[5] when our minds are settling on an analogy, the current situation must be similar enough to the analog from the past to activate its networks, and the elements of the two situations (the novel one and the more familiar one) must be readily mapped onto one another. This creates a sense of "fit" between the two.

Hitler was a paranoid, remorseless dictator with a penchant for cruelty and no qualms about mass murder. So was Hussein. Hitler attacked his neighbors and threatened the stability of an entire region. So did Hussein. Both men even sported distinctive mustaches. From the point of view of analogical mapping, Hitler was a good analogy for Hussein.

But Bush could easily have chosen another analogy: the quagmire of Vietnam. In fact, he held back from an assault on Baghdad for precisely the reason his son ignored—that the United States might find itself bogged down for years in a civil war fighting a shadowy insurgency that knew the land better than American soldiers ever could. That Bush the elder initially chose the analog of Hitler and World War II instead of Vietnam likely reflected his own experience in World War II, which was far more direct and emotionally salient to him than the Vietnam analogy that was on the minds of younger politicians. Research suggests that late adolescence and early adulthood are a particularly important period for political "imprinting"— that is, for forming lifelong political attitudes[6]—and fighting in a bloody war, as George H. W. Bush had done in the Pacific as a pilot, likely amplified that imprint.

One other factor, however, probably influenced Bush's choice of analogies: motivation. Neither Bush nor Reagan chose to invoke the Hitler analogy during their twelve years in the White House in response to unprovoked aggression by *African* leaders against their neighbors. Nor, for that matter, did they invoke the metaphor of Hitler gassing his enemies when Hussein used chemical weapon attacks on Iran.

The analogies and metaphors people find compelling depend not only on the extent to which the elements of the current situation map onto elements of the analogy but also on their goals (and on the emotions that provide the "fuel" for our goals). Had George H. Bush not worried about the availability of Middle Eastern oil after the Iraqi takeover of Kuwait, he might well have found the Vietnam analogy more compelling, given that this analog had blocked U.S. intervention in many similar international confrontations for two decades.

By suggesting that oil was in the mix underlying Bush's analogical reasoning, I do not mean to impugn his integrity. As Holyoak and Thagard note, no single constraint is typically definitive in the judgments we make or the analogies we draw. Rather, multiple constraints function "like the various pressures that guide an architect engaged in creative design, with some forces in convergence, others in opposition, and their constant interplay pressing toward some satisfying compromise that is internally coherent."[7]

For Bush, the solution that was both *cognitively coherent* and *emotionally satisfying* in light of his goal of securing U.S. energy sources (and his own personal ties to the leaders of many Middle Eastern countries and oil companies) was the Hitler analogy. Ultimately, however, his politically unpopular decision not to "finish the job" likely reflected not only the concerns of the Pentagon and many in his administration (including both Colin Powell and Dick Cheney) but also the lurking (and, in hindsight, accurate) secondary analogy of Baghdad to Saigon.

The analogies politicians find compelling, and the analogies they try to "sell" to the public, often bear the heavy imprint of partisan goals. When House Republicans wanted to impeach President Clinton, they found remarkable similarities between his actions and those of Richard Nixon. Democrats, in contrast, saw a major problem with the comparison: the original "crime" in Nixon's case was a political crime, whereas Clinton's original sin was a personal matter—and the kind of personal matter that had never been the subject of investigation for any prior president. A few years later, when confronted with an administration that appeared to have broken multiple laws and covered them up—for example, laws on wiretapping, torture, or revealing the identity of covert intelligence officers for political gain—activation never seemed to spread in Republican lawmakers' brains to the Nixon network.

What these examples suggest is that the analogies to which our brains "naturally" gravitate reflect something other than just the similarity between the current situation and potential analogs in memory. They also reflect their congeniality to our *emotional agendas*. The same can be said for the evidence we find compelling or uncompelling, the data we readily believe or dispute, the sources we find credible or incredible, the newspapers and magazines we choose to read, and the television networks we choose to watch.

During the confirmation hearings for Supreme Court Justice Clarence Thomas, Republican commentators maintained that the evidence supporting Anita Hill's claim of sexual harassment was not credible, nothing more than a tawdry he-said/she-said situation. Senator Arlen Specter, whose brutal cross-examination of Anita Hill almost cost him his Senate seat in 1992, publicly accused her of perjury during the confirmation hearing. Many Democrats, in contrast, found her allegations so compelling that they could not vote for Thomas's confirmation.

Yet in a role reversal a few years later, when Republicans learned of Paula Jones's allegation that President Clinton had propositioned her in an Arkansas hotel room, their inferences shifted. They made precisely the same arguments Democrats had offered years earlier— which they had themselves vehemently rejected—about the probative value of evidence such as testimony from the accuser's friends that she had discussed the alleged harassment at the time it occurred. They became convinced of the widespread and pernicious nature of sexual harassment, and some right-wing commentators, such at Pat Buchanan, even began referring to the Jones suit as a "civil rights case" or "women's issue."[8] Democratic pundits were mirror images of their conservative counterparts. They marshaled the arguments to support the view that Jones was not the likely victim of sexual harassment, had not naively walked into the president's hotel room, and had suffered no material harm from the event even if it took place.

These incidents raise fundamental questions about political decision making, both by the general public and political and judicial decision makers. Can members of Congress or Supreme Court justices really decide impartially on questions pertaining to impeachment, removal, or election of the president, or are their judgments little more than rationalizations for their emotional preferences and prejudices? Is it an accident that when Republicans in the House of Representatives "examined the data" and "voted their conscience" in deciding whether to impeach President Clinton, they virtually all reached the conclusion that his actions were impeachable, whereas their Democratic colleagues, who read the same documents and heard the same testimony, reached the opposite conclusion?

The first of the four articles of impeachment (the article charging perjury) passed the House of Representatives by a vote of 228 to 206. Only 5 of over 200 Republicans voted no, and only five of over 200 Democrats voted yes. A quick statistical analysis of these numbers places the chances that rational consideration of the data played any significant role in the deliberations at less than one in a trillion.*

Similarly, can Supreme Court justices, including those appointed by the father of one of the litigants, adjudicate questions that will decide the presidency without influence of their wishes, fears, and values? In speaking to a group of high school students shortly after the Supreme Court's decision in *Bush v. Gore* that decided the presidential election in December 2000, Justice Clarence Thomas expressed disbelief at the notion that partisan feelings could have had any influence on the ruling. "I plead with you," he implored the students (and the nation), "that, whatever you do, don't try to apply the rules of the political world to this institution; they do not apply," contending that "The last political act we [justices] engage in is confirmation."[9] Thus, according to Thomas, when Supreme Court justices put on their robes, they check their political undergarments at the door.

Thomas's words, though seemingly heartfelt, seem very naive in light of the most obvious disconfirming data: the fact that the ruling had split along party lines. Perhaps most damning, the conservative majority, known for its consistently negative attitudes toward federal intervention in state matters, judicial activism, and the equal protection clause of the Constitution, nonetheless stepped in to overrule the Florida Supreme Court and used the equal protection clause to justify its decision. As we shall see, the most charitable explanation of the decision by the conservative majority in *Bush v. Gore* was that the justices lacked any self-awareness of the capacity for self-deception and rationalization they share with the general public. The less char-

---

*The exact likelihood that anything other than partisanship determined the vote is actually $1.75/10^{90}$, which is more zeros than I can even picture. My appreciation to statistician and psychologist Bob Rosenthal who helped me get the right number of decimals.

itable explanation, voiced by Alan Dershowitz after careful analysis of the ruling in light of the justices' prior decisions, is that the conservatives on the court didn't care about the merits of the case and simply concocted whatever arguments were necessary to put their boy in office:

> The decision may be ranked as the single most corrupt decision in Supreme Court history, because it is the only one that I know of where the majority justices decided as they did because of the personal identity and political affiliation of the litigants. . . . No honest person can any longer trust them to do justice, as distinguished from politics.[10]

One Man, One Motive?

In describing how people make inferences about complex political and legal events, rational choice models of decision making make the same assumptions that members of Congress and the Supreme Court expressed when they claimed that they put partisan judgments aside, weighed the evidence, and made impartial judgments. However, in both the impeachment of Bill Clinton and the Supreme Court's judgment in *Bush v. Gore*, the political and legal decision makers precisely mirrored the general electorate, whose judgments could be predicted with over 80 percent accuracy from their prior emotional prejudices and predispositions, irrespective of the facts.

Contrary to rational decision models, the decisions we make and the analogies we find compelling are constrained not only by the available data but by how these decisions or analogies make us *feel*. In politics, as in everyday life, two sets of often competing constraints shape our judgments: *cognitive constraints,* imposed by the information we have available, and *emotional constraints,* imposed by the feelings associated with one conclusion or another. Most of the time, this battle for control of our minds occurs outside of awareness, leaving us as blind spectators to our own psychodramas, prisoners of the images cast on the wall of our skulls.

The brain gravitates toward solutions designed to match not only data but desire, by spreading activation to networks that lead to conclusions associated with positive emotions and inhibiting networks that would lead to negative emotions. Positive and negative feelings influence which arguments reach consciousness, the amount of time we spend thinking about different arguments, the extent to which we either accept or search for "holes" in arguments or evidence that is emotionally threatening, the news outlets we follow, and the company we keep. In short, as suggested by the neuroimaging study with which this book began, our brains have a remarkable capacity to find their way toward convenient truths—even if they're not all that true.

The notion that people can unconsciously protect themselves against threatening information has a venerable history. As the quotation from Sir Francis Bacon that opened this chapter suggests, philosophers (not to mention playwrights and poets) have known about this quality of the human mind for centuries. It was central to Freud's thinking over a century ago. In more recent years, researchers have documented self-serving "reasoning" in a range of domains, including politics.[11] Several experiments have found that people evaluate evidence that disconfirms their cherished beliefs much more critically than evidence that supports their values, attitudes, religious beliefs, or scientific theories,[12] and that the capacity for rationalization and selective scrutiny of evidence starts early, by the elementary school years.[13]

Perhaps nowhere are emotion-driven cognitive distortions more obvious—and more potentially dangerous—than in political affairs.[14] For years, political scientists tended (or perhaps wanted) to believe that emotion-driven thinking is more characteristic of less sophisticated or less knowledgeable voters.[15] However, the more sophisticated people are politically (e.g., the more they know about an issue), the more able they are to develop *complex* rationalizations for dismissing data they don't want to believe.[16] Politically knowledgeable citizens also tend to be partisans, which gives them the strongest reasons for distorted reasoning.

In a seminal study, researchers presented subjects with two alleged studies, one supportive of the efficacy of capital punishment and the other not.[17] Subjects who came in with positive attitudes toward capital punishment had few complaints with the "pro" study, but they discounted the arguments and rejected the conclusions of the "con" study. Subjects with negative attitudes toward the death penalty showed the opposite pattern. Both proponents and opponents of the death penalty walked away from the experiment with *stronger* convictions than when they had come in. Being confronted with mixed data only increased their dogged commitment to their point of view.

Studies during several elections have found that people's judgments of who won presidential debates are strongly biased toward their predebate emotional preferences.[18] A team of investigators assessed subjects' attitudes toward the two presidential candidates just before watching the first Clinton–Dole debate in 1996.[19] Afterwards, they rated who they thought had won, the quality of the candidates' arguments, and how they felt as each candidate was speaking. As in previous studies, subjects' prior feelings toward the candidates strongly predicted not only who they thought had won the debate but their judgments of the quality of each candidate's arguments.

The studies described thus far all made a simplifying assumption: one man, one motive. In these studies, people's biases tugged them in one direction (e.g., toward their party's candidate). But in politics, as in everyday life, we are seldom pulled in only one direction. When parents get a hint that their child is having a problem in some domain (e.g., making friends at school), they are often torn between two motives: the desire to understand the problem so they can help fix it, and the desire not to understand the problem because it would be painful to view their child as hurting or having trouble. So they often find a compromise between the two, such as recognizing the problem but minimizing its severity or significance.

Conflicting motives that require compromise solutions are the norm in electoral politics. They are certainly the norm among political officeholders, who routinely face conflicts, whether consciously acknowledged or not, among the best interests of their constituents, the country, party, and their campaign coffers. But conflict and compromise are also the norm among average citizens, who often have competing emotional loyalties or "special interests" in their minds.

For example, most American Jews have social attitudes that lead them to identify with the Democratic Party. Jews were among the most strident supporters of civil rights for African Americans in the 1960s, and they tend toward tolerance on social issues, such as homosexuality. However, those who are more identified with Israel have a countervailing emotional pull toward the Republican Party, given the tendency of the left wing of the Democratic Party to identify with the Palestinians as an oppressed people. I know a number of Jews, particularly orthodox Jews, who reluctantly pulled the lever twice for George W. Bush, on the presumption that he would back Israel in the event of attacks by groups such as Hamas and Hezbollah (which he generally did), while simultaneously voting for Democrats in House and Senate races.

A relatively new conflict among emotional constraints in another minority group is between the traditional loyalty of African Americans to the Democratic Party and a countervailing emergent loyalty born of participation in an all-volunteer military, which tends to foster right-leaning ideologies. Similar conflicting emotional constraints emerged in the first few years of the new millennium among Hispanic voters, who traditionally found their interests and values in closer alignment with the Democratic Party (except for Cuban-American immigrants, who have always seen the anti-Castro Republicans as their natural ally). Many Hispanics shifted rightward as they attained greater representation in the military, became more prosperous, or simply appreciated the fact that the Bush brothers literally "speak their language."

Four years later, however, many newly conservative Hispanic voters were taken off guard by the xenophobia conservatives revealed in their "debate" about immigration reform. How these conflicting emotional constraints will translate into votes will likely be crucial in deciding many state and national races in upcoming decades, as the number—and power—of Hispanic voters increases in multiple states, and as Florida continues to sway left and right and

potentially to hold presidential elections in the balance for some time
to come.

Empirical research has begun to document compromises of this
sort experimentally.[20] A revealing study attempted to predict which
black women would believe O. J. Simpson was guilty of killing his
wife.[21] African-American women were in an emotionally complicated
position. As women, they were likely to identify with his wife and,
hence, to be emotionally inclined to take seriously evidence such as
DNA samples. On the other hand, as African Americans, they were
likely to identify with Simpson, and African Americans overwhelmingly believed that O. J. was framed.

So how did they resolve this conflict? The answer lies in the relative strength of their identifications—and, by extension, their feelings.
The extent to which African-American women believed Simpson was
guilty depended on the extent to which they identified with being
black or being female. If being female was more central to their identity, they were more likely to believe the evidence against Simpson. If
their African-American identity was stronger, they were more likely to
find the evidence uncompelling.

Beginning in 1998, my colleagues and I began studying these kinds
of compromise solutions in a series of studies involving three crises in
U.S. politics: the impeachment of Bill Clinton, the disputed presidential election of 2000, and the discovery of torture at Abu Ghraib prison
in Iraq.[22] At the risk of giving the punch line before the joke, the joke
turns out to be on all of us: When people make judgments about emotionally significant political events, cognitive constraints matter, but
their effects are trivial. When the stakes are high, people prefer what
Stephen Colbert has called "truthiness" over truth:

> I'm no fan of dictionaries or reference books. They're elitist, con-
> stantly telling us what is or isn't true, or what did or didn't hap-
> pen. . . . Doesn't taking Saddam out *feel* like the right thing?
> Right here, here in the gut? Because that's where the truth comes
> from, ladies and gentlemen: the gut. Do you know you have more
> nerve endings in your stomach than in your head? Look it up.

Now, somebody's gonna say, "I did look that up, and it's wrong . . ." Well, Mister, that's 'cause you looked it up in a *book*. Next time, try looking it up in your gut. I did, and my gut tells me that's how our nervous system works.

The truthiness is, anyone can *read* the news to you. I promise to *feel* the news *at* you.—Stephen Colbert, *The Colbert Report*[23]

Across three major political crises over a six-year period—the impeachment of Bill Clinton, the disputed presidential election of 2000, and the discovery of torture at the Abu Ghraib prison—we were able to predict people's judgments between 80 and 85 percent of the time from emotional constraints alone. Indeed, we could predict the judgments of eight of the nine justices on the Supreme Court in *Bush v. Gore*—the case that decided who would be president—from a single emotional constraint: feelings toward the two parties. And we could do this even if all eight justices had taken a bus trip together, gotten into a terrible accident, sustained traumatic head injuries that left them comatose for several months, and reawakened just as they had to make their ruling, without benefit of hearing the facts of the case.*

In March 1998, in an interview on *60 Minutes,* Kathleen Willey alleged that she had been sexually harassed by President Clinton in the Oval Office. We conducted a study about ten days later. Our aim was to predict the electorate's inferences about what had occurred between the President and Willey, which at this point was (and remained) ambiguous.

We solicited subjects from the voting-age population by administering a brief (five-minute) questionnaire in public places in Boston and New York. To measure people's judgments about what they believed had occurred between the president and Willey, we asked subjects to rate the extent to which they agreed or disagreed with six statements, such as "I think Kathleen Willey went on *60 Minutes* to describe what President Clinton did to her in the Oval Office because she was genuinely troubled by it and wanted to expose the truth," and "I

---

*As numerous commentators have noted, the majority opinion in *Bush v. Gore* actually reads like such a document.

think Kathleen Willey accused the president of sexual harassment and went on *60 Minutes* to try to get a book deal."

In terms of the cognitive constraints on what people could believe, we expected people's judgments to be influenced both by what they knew about Clinton's history and by what they knew about the scandal itself (e.g., whether they had seen her interview and information later released by the White House regarding her prior and subsequent letters to the president). So we created two sets of questions to test cognitive constraints on their judgments.

The *Clinton Knowledge* questions included items about the president's life. Participants who knew the answers to such questions would need to have followed politics over several years. For example, we asked subjects, "What political race did Bill Clinton lose in Arkansas?" (The answer was governor of Arkansas, where Clinton was unseated after his first term before being re-elected.)

The *Scandal Knowledge* questions included items regarding the scandal, from relatively well-known facts to more obscure details that only someone following the situation closely would know. For example, we asked subjects, "How did Kathleen Willey's husband die?" The answer was suicide, something even politically informed readers may by now have forgotten but would have known at the time.[24] Participants in the study received two scores, one for Clinton Knowledge and one for Scandal Knowledge.

The next challenge was to consider the range of potential emotional constraints on people's judgments—that is, emotional reactions that might have little or no *rational* bearing on their judgments about what the president likely did or didn't do in the Oval Office but might sway their judgments emotionally. Four such constraints seemed like prime suspects. The first were feelings toward the two political parties. *Logically*, partisan feelings should have no impact on who voters believe in a he-said/she-said situation, although we suspected they would have an enormous influence. The second were feelings toward Clinton personally. We included these as well as partisan feelings because many Democrats had negative feelings toward Clinton (e.g., those on the left who found him too moderate), and many Republicans (and Reagan Democrats, who leaned to the right) had positive feelings toward him (particularly if they read their financial statements on a regular basis during his term in the White House). The third were feelings toward infidelity, which again bore no *logical* relation to beliefs about Willey's credibility but could, we hypothesized, sway voters. Fourth were feelings toward feminism. We reasoned that subjects with strong negative attitudes toward feminism would be more likely to identify with the man in this situation.

We expected that some of these emotional constraints would likely pull people in the same direction, whereas others would be conflicting. Take a Republican businessman, "Joe," who voted for the first President Bush in 1992 but voted for Clinton in 1996 because he liked the way Clinton was handling the economy and generally found him personable. Joe once had an affair of his own with a female employee, and he was still bitter about the way it ended, when she charged him with sexual harassment. In terms of cognitive constraints, Joe didn't know much about Clinton's past, other than that Clinton had been accused of philandering. But he thought Clinton seemed like a "decent guy" who might slip an attractive supporter the tongue under the right circumstances but was hardly a sexual predator. Thus, his knowledge of Clinton triggered a network representing the president fondling Willey but inhibited the network representing an *unwanted* advance.

In terms of emotional constraints, Joe's positive feelings toward the Republican Party tended to spread activation to networks leading to the conclusion that the Democrat had behaved badly in office. However, his feelings toward Clinton personally spread activation in the opposite direction and inhibited precisely the same networks. Having had an affair once himself, he was less troubled by the idea that Clinton might have behaved unfaithfully, so this emotional constraint had little influence on his judgment. However, his own experience with a harassment charge had colored not only his attitudes toward such charges but strengthened his traditional conservative attitudes about feminism. So strong inhibition spread to the "unwanted advance" network, and strong activation spread to networks that might provide an alternative explanation, such as the possibility of a book deal that would put Willey in a more solvent financial situation.

Joe was thus both cognitively and emotionally predisposed toward the solution that perhaps Clinton made an advance but it was not unwanted, and that Willey had an ulterior motive for her accusation. This example illustrates both the complexity of the processes underlying people's judgments and the simplicity of the underlying principles.

What did we find when we analyzed the data across over a hundred "average Joes"?

Cognitive constraints had minimal influence on people's judgments. But people's feelings toward the parties and toward Clinton each strongly predicted their beliefs about the president's Willey. Independent of any cognitive constraints, simply knowing the strength of voters' feelings toward the parties and the president allowed us to predict with over 80 percent accuracy whether they would find Willey's accusations convincing.[25]

The unfolding scandal gave us an opportunity to replicate and extend these findings three months later, when Monica Lewinsky testified before the grand jury. At that time, Kenneth Starr was pursuing the possibility of obstruction of justice: that the president might have asked Lewinsky to lie, or that his friend Vernon Jordan might have tried to buy Lewinsky's silence by getting her a job.

Once again, what determined people's judgments was not their knowledge of either Clinton or the scandal, but their *feelings* toward the parties and toward Clinton.

The major limitation of these studies is that we were assessing people's political judgments at the same time as we were assessing their feelings, preventing us from concluding definitively that their feelings *caused*, or at least preceded, their judgments about his behavior. Events conspired a few months later to allow us to test this hypothesis more rigorously, when the Republican-controlled House voted to hold an impeachment hearing in December 1998. In the days immediately prior to the hearing, we recontacted as many subjects as we could locate from the first two studies. We used their prior cognitive and emotional constraints, assessed six to nine months earlier, to predict their answers to questions about whether the president's actions constituted impeachable offenses, such as "Do you think what the president has been accused of doing meets the standard set forth in the Constitution for an impeachable offense?"

This time, all four emotional constraints—feelings toward the parties, Clinton, infidelity, and feminism—independently predicted people's judgments about whether the president's actions constituted "high crimes and misdemeanors." In other words, the combination of how they felt about Democrats and Republicans, Clinton, infidelity, and feminism all contributed (roughly equally) to what both rational decision models and most members of Congress considered a quintessentially "rational" judgment, namely how to interpret the impeachment clause of the Constitution. In this third study, knowledge about the scandal was also a significant predictor of judgments about impeachment but a weak one.

Our simple predictive model—based on a five-minute questionnaire administered six to nine months earlier—turned out to be extremely powerful. We were able to predict which way people would go on the question of impeachment 88 percent of the time—a percentage seldom seen in social science research, where so many factors generally affect people's judgments that we're usually delighted when we can predict 60 to 65 percent.

But another way of framing the findings is more sobering, if not chilling. When we left the cognitive constraints out of the model entirely, using only emotional constraints as predictors, we were able to predict people's judgments about impeachment with *85 percent accuracy*. Cognitive constraints essentially bought us only a 3 percent increment in prediction.

These findings were mirrored in the House, where accuracy of prediction based on partisan feelings alone exceeded 90 percent for the votes cast on all four articles of impeachment. In this sense, people's elected representatives were indeed representative of their constituents—they let their emotions overrule their rational judgments—but they did not represent them well.

Overall, irrespective of high-minded claims about following the rule of law, voting on the basis of conscience, weighing the evidence objectively, and the like, the data show that this is not how most people made judgments at any point during the year that culminated in the impeachment trial. When emotion roared, reason buckled at the knees. And the same processes appeared to occur in our everyday voters as in their elected representatives.

The disputed presidential election of 2000 presented another opportunity to compare passionate and dispassionate visions of the political mind. The Bush team was arguing that a manual vote count would allow too much room for political mischief, while the Gore team was arguing that machine ballot counts had failed to read many valid votes cast. In the heat of the moment, no one seemed to recognize their arguments were simply rationalizations. A day before the election, if you had randomly polled 1,000 voters as to whether manual or machine counts are more accurate, you wouldn't have found any relation to party identification. But a day after the election, both sides seemed thoroughly convinced of the truthiness of their point of view.

We used a similar method as in the three studies during the Clinton crisis, administering questionnaires to voting-age citizens in three locations six weeks into the disputed election (December 17–18, 2000), just prior to the Supreme Court's ruling that ended the controversy. We measured cognitive constraints as in the first three studies, by asking questions of fact that would indicate the extent to which subjects had closely followed the events of the election (e.g., "Which Florida county used the butterfly ballot?"). But this time we also varied cognitive constraints experimentally, by presenting subjects with purportedly unbiased new information from a nonpartisan organization that either supported or did not support their desired outcome. We measured four sets of emotional constraints: feelings toward the Democrats and the Republicans and feelings toward the two candidates, although we collapsed them into two dimensions (feelings toward the Democrats and Gore, and feelings toward the Republicans and Bush) because by this point in the election, Democrats and Republicans had polarized around their nominee.

The results were consistent with our three Clinton studies. What people knew about the disputed election had no impact on their judgments. Presenting them with results from a purportedly nonpartisan group had a small effect. But the lion's share of voters's judgments about the relative validity of manual versus machine counts reflected nothing but their feelings toward the parties and candidates.

Using both cognitive and emotional constraints as predictors, we were able to predict voters' judgments about the relative validity of manual versus machine ballot counts 83.5 percent of the time. When we eliminated cognitive constraints completely, however, prediction remained at *83 percent.* In other words, six weeks of intense news and commentary and some new information "hot off the press" from an allegedly independent group had virtually no impact on what people chose to believe.

Four years later, we ran one more study of this kind, following the release of photographs taken at Abu Ghraib graphically depicting acts of sadism, humiliation, and torture of Iraqi prisoners at the hands of their American military captors. Because our prior studies had shown such a surprisingly small effect of cognitive constraints, this time we designed an experiment in which we could make the evidence as compelling in one direction or the other as we wanted, to see if we could override people's emotional biases. We presented voting-age citizens at shopping centers in Atlanta with the following "breaking news" story:

> A case that is likely to receive substantial media attention in the upcoming weeks is the case of Lt. Samuel Miller, who is facing charges of having broken the eardrum of a naked Iraqi prisoner at Abu Ghraib prison by repeatedly inserting a pencil in his ear while threatening, over the course of an hour, to "stick this pencil where it will hurt a lot more."
>
> Lt. Miller has argued that he cannot receive a fair trial unless his lawyers are permitted to question Defense Secretary Donald Rumsfeld and, if necessary, President Bush. Lt. Miller's defense hinges on his assertion that he was not a sadist who took pleasure in inflicting pain or humiliation on Iraqi prisoners, and that he only participated in such practices because he was led to believe by superiors that the rules governing the treatment of prisoners had changed.
>
> A military judge has to make a difficult decision. On the one hand, he must guarantee a fair trial for Lt. Miller. If Lt. Miller was ordered to commit the acts, and if the orders reflected legal interpretations at the highest level of government, this could affect the

verdict or sentence. On the other hand, the judge must be careful not to open up administration officials in the future to constant subpoenas. The standard used in military law in the rare cases of this sort over the last 150 years is that the defendant must show "substantial cause" to believe that he was acting "under directives of the President of the United States or his legitimate representatives."

Voting-age subjects received one of five versions of the questionnaire, which varied in how much evidence Lt. Miller had to back up his case, from virtually none (just his own testimony) to overwhelming evidence (including corroborating testimony and memoranda from senior civilian officials). Once subjects read the evidence, they rated the extent to which they believed Miller's case crossed the rigorous but ambiguous threshold allegedly used for more than 150 years in military courts. In this study we assessed three emotional constraints: feelings toward the political parties and the administration, feelings toward protection of human rights (e.g., how they felt about "international human rights groups, such as Amnesty International and the International Committee of the Red Cross"), and feelings toward the U.S. military (e.g., "I would be very proud if my son or daughter chose to become a soldier").

The results were, once again, sobering. The weight of the evidence had a small effect. But this effect was less than one-sixth the magnitude of the effect of feelings toward the parties. "The evidence" was dwarfed, as well, by feelings toward both human rights and the military, none of which, logically, bears any relation to the judgment people were asked to make. Including both cognitive and emotional constraints, we could predict people's judgments about whether Lt. Miller should be allowed to subpoena civilian officials a whopping 84.5 percent of the time. But emotional constraints alone could predict which way they would decide 84 percent of the time. Thus, even when we handcuffed people to the data with titanium cognitive cuffs, they managed, Houdini-like, to free themselves from any constraints of reality through the power of emotion.

The truth about truthiness is that the intuitive theories of judgment and decision making held by most congressmen, senators, and

Supreme Court justices who commented publicly on their decision making during the most important political crises of the last decade are intuitively appealing but dead wrong. And so are the decision theories that underlie most research in cognitive science, neuroscience, economics, business, and political science.

The dispassionate mind of the eighteenth-century philosophers allows us to predict somewhere between .5 and 3 percent of the most important political decisions people will make over the course of their lives. This may well be an *over*estimate for people who are most politically engaged, and particularly those who are actively involved in politics, who tend to be highly partisan and, hence, more vulnerable to emotional biases in their thinking.

Whereas rational delegates appear to play only a minor role in the selection of candidates for belief, the same cannot be said about emotional delegates at the neural convention. Upwards of 80 percent of the time, the judgments people reach in political affairs reflect compromise solutions arranged in the smoke-filled room between their ears, crafted by competing and collaborating emotional constituencies, largely without benefit of the transparency of consciousness.

Impressionist Politics

The picture I have painted in this chapter is not a pretty one. It suggests that our political beliefs are more like abstract art than anything vaguely representational, covering the political canvas with broad, truthy strokes that represent an expression of our feelings but little else.

But that conclusion may be slightly too severe. It may be that the better analogy is impressionism. Although our findings on the political mind and brain are consistent with other research on partisan bias, several caveats are worth noting.

First, the series of studies we conducted involved high-stakes political situations, in which emotions were running strong. The results are unequivocal that when the outcomes of a political decision have strong emotional implications and the data leave even the slightest room for artistic license, reason plays virtually no role in the decision making of the average citizen. As the vote to impeach the president in 1998 shows, the chances are less than one in a trillion that legislators are any different in this respect from their constituents. And as the Supreme Court's tortured, partisan decision in *Bush v. Gore* suggests, if you're looking for justice and the case under consideration is one about which members of the Court are likely to have strong feelings, you can expect as fair a hearing in the Supreme Court as in Guantanamo Bay.

The only study we have conducted thus far that found a more substantial effect of reality on belief is one in which the stakes were somewhat lower. In this study, we predicted people's judgments about the state of the national economy from objective economic indicators (e.g., gross domestic product, unemployment), their personal finances, and their feelings toward the political parties.[26] We used data from the National Election Studies, a large-scale survey conducted over several decades that allowed us to test hypotheses with a sample of several thousand voters across many electoral years. In this study, cognitive constraints (objective economic indicators) and emotional constraints (partisan feelings) jointly predicted people's judgments about how well the economy was doing. Cognitive constraints had a larger impact than in the political crises we had previously examined, although once again emotional constraints had a stronger impact on voters's judgments than even "hard" economic indicators.

Okay, so that first caveat wasn't so hopeful, but maybe the second is a little more heartening. Although data don't seem to make much of a difference in the short-term, they do, over time, place *some* constraints on judgments, and sometimes those constraints are considerable.

In the spring of 2003, following the invasion of Iraq, the question on the Sunday talk shows was whether and when we would find a smoking nuclear gun in Iraq because we "knew" we would find at least chemical and biological weapons. Within a few months, the question was not whether we would find evidence of a *nuclear* weapons program but whether we would find evidence of *any* substantial stockpiles of nonconventional weapons. And a year later, the question of weapons of mass destruction was no longer even on the table (except to viewers of Fox News, who, according to opinion polls, continue to this day to believe that the question was settled—in the affirmative). Thus, over time, as the constraints imposed by data became more definitive, people's beliefs did change.

The problem, however, is that once beliefs changed, the terms of the argument simply changed to avoid the inconvenient facts. If you stuck with the original terms of the argument—that the war in Iraq was waged to keep terror off our shores—then it was a colossal failure. But for partisan Republicans, when cognitive constraints made the original rationale for the war untenable, the emotionally compelling solution was to find another rationale. So now the war was about spreading freedom. But ultimately, when that rationale failed, *adaptive* emotional processes did kick in for the majority of Americans, just as they did in Vietnam when simply too many body bags were coming home.

Although democracy often fails in the short-term, as the great democratic theorists of the eighteenth century and the framers of the Constitution knew well, it is the least flawed system humans have ever devised to govern themselves. At least in the established democracies in the West, democracy has tended to prove self-righting more often than not, as long as you don't mind choosing your time frame in retrospect.

Sometimes that time frame is quite brief. In 1972, the Watergate scandal had already broken, and McGovern bumper stickers exhorted the public to remember Watergate. But Watergate had no impact. Nixon won every state but Massachusetts.

Yet just one year later, as the hearings unfolded and the facts became undeniable, Nixon was forced to resign. This was very different from the Clinton impeachment, which built up a head of steam as a band of philandering brothers galvanized a Republican-dominated House to impeach the president for a souped-up philandering charge. By the time Clinton was acquitted, a CNN/*USA Today*/Gallup poll showed that 64 percent of Americans approved of the acquittal, 68 percent approved of the job Clinton was doing as president, and only 40 percent approved of the Republican Congress.[27]

Perhaps the best example of a glass that is half empty or half full depending on your time frame is the glass from which white Americans sip their attitudes toward African Americans. As Lyndon Johnson described in his address to the nation a century after Abraham Lincoln had freed the last of the people defined by the founders as three-fifths of a man, many blacks were still not free. They couldn't vote in a substantial percentage of states. They couldn't drink from white water fountains, swim in white swimming pools, or stay in hotels in many states. I remember in the late 1960s when a sincere elementary school classmate warned me, as her mother had warned her, not to get into a swimming pool with black kids, for fear that their blackness might rub off.

Survey results on race in America before and after the height of the civil rights movement show extraordinary social and psychological change. In 1944, only 45 percent of whites agreed with the statement that "blacks should have as good a chance as white people to get any kind of job." In 1972, that percentage had risen to 97 percent.[28] Of course, the same year Nixon was busy dismantling what remained of Johnson's war on poverty, and covert racist sentiments could still be heard around the water cooler. But the fact that most people would not even tell a pollster or researcher that they believed in discrimination against qualified African Americans in 1972 speaks volumes about changes in attitudes regarding the most divisive issue in American history.

One final caveat is perhaps most hopeful. It is true that 80 percent of the time we can predict voters' judgments about complex issues from passions that bear no logical relation to truth. And it is true that a big chunk of that 80 percent—typically over half of it, and sometimes virtually all of it—is partisan sentiment.

But that leaves 20 percent of the electorate who are influenced by something other than their feelings toward the parties. And 15 to 20 percent is an enormous number in electoral politics, when candidates frequently win elections by two or three percentage points, and 55 percent of the vote is considered a landslide.

These are the voters with changeable minds. Precisely what changes their minds is the question to which we now turn.

chapter six

TRICKLE-UP POLITICS

★   ★   ★

The critical roles that . . . emotional processes play suggest what a fully rational, cerebral electorate would look like. First, absent enthusiasm, it would be largely passive and inactive. . . . It would be an electorate disinclined to do much of anything, let alone display the active engagement that philosophers, activists, candidates, and interests, public and special, alike all require. . . . Second, absent anxiety, it would be similarly unmoved by crisis or challenge, moral or material. Though many grievances might warrant public attention and engagement, even the most strenuous efforts to engage the public would find citizens largely unresponsive, too confident that all was well, that all cries for redress were overdone, alarmist, and merited at best a wait-and-see attitude.

— GEORGE MARCUS, *The Sentimental Citizen.*[1]

I f emotions provide the fuel for virtually everything we do, they should predict what happens on election day. Fifty years of research in political science suggests that they do, and that they are far more powerful determinants of how people cast their ballots than "the issues" that have been the preoccupation of most Democratic campaigns since the 1970s.

The primary data available for studying the relative influence of passionate and dispassionate concerns on voting behavior come from the National Election Studies, an enormous database designed from its inception to provide a representative snapshot of American electorate. Begun in 1952 at the University of Michigan, these extensive surveys have extensively probed voters during every midterm and presidential election ever since.

Using these data, researchers produced a landmark study nearly fifty years ago, at the dawn of the television era, showing that voters' choices could be predicted by their feelings toward the two political parties and the two candidates themselves.[2] In analyzing the presidential elections of 1952 and 1956 (both times a contest between Dwight Eisenhower and Adlai Stevenson), a simple equation including feelings toward the parties and the candidates predicted the way people ultimately voted even better than voters' *own* preelection predictions of who they would vote for.[3] Although the personalities of candidates have exerted an increasing influence on voting behavior since the rise of television, the power of partisan feelings has not changed appreciably since the 1950s. Between 1980 and 1996, for example, only 20 percent of the time did the voters "defect" from their party's candidate for the presidency.[4]

A major step forward in understanding the role of emotions in voting behavior came about twenty years later from a study conducted by Robert Abelson and his colleagues at Yale[5], whose results were so powerful that they influenced the questions included in all subsequent National Election Studies. Abelson and colleagues asked voters questions of the following form (using here Jimmy Carter as an example):

> Now I want to ask you about Jimmy Carter. Think about your feelings when I mention Jimmy Carter. Now, has President Carter—because of the kind of person he is or because of something he has done—ever made you feel. . . .

The investigators supplied a list of twelve emotions (e.g., angry, happy, hopeful) and asked the question for each one. They also assessed the *traits* voters ascribed to each candidate, using a list of sixteen emotion-laden characteristics (e.g., honest, smart, inspiring, immoral, weak).

This study produced a number of findings, nearly all of which have held up in the ensuing twenty-five years. Two are of particular significance.

First, just as positive and negative emotion emerge as distinct dimensions from studies of people's emotional experience, the same two dimensions emerged from people's feelings toward presidential candidates, and they were not simply opposites. The same person who could feel warm toward Carter could also feel angry toward him—a finding whose implications for running an emotionally compelling campaign cannot be overstated, as will become clear.

Second, people's positive and negative associations to a candidate were better predictors of their voting preferences than even their judgments about his personality and competence. Voters may disagree with things a candidate stands for or may dislike aspects of his personality, but when feelings about the candidate and more considered assessments of his strengths and weaknesses differ, feelings tend to trump beliefs.

Analyses of data from one election after another since that time have consistently shown that when voters' feelings toward a candidate clash with their beliefs about his *policies*, their feelings also tend to be decisive.[6] George Marcus, a political scientist at Williams College, has been at the forefront of a movement in political science to bring emotions into the equation. Marcus[7] used National Election Studies data from the 1984 presidential election between Ronald Reagan and Walter Mondale to compare the impact of feelings toward the candidates, emotional judgments about their personal characteristics, and their perceived views on the issues.

The take-home message was anything but dispassionate. Two-thirds of voters' decisions to support one candidate or another could be accounted for by two simple variables: their partisan feelings and their feelings toward the candidates.[8] Candidates' positions on the issues had only a modest effect on their electoral preferences. Marcus and his colleagues later obtained similar results when they examined the data from every presidential election from 1980 to 1996.[9]

Although devotees of "reason" might find these results discouraging, the data actually do provide some hope for the rationally inclined. Policies *are* related to voting, but not directly. Policies matter *to the extent that they influence voters' emotions*. Candidates' stands on the issues matter most when voters are anxious or unhappy because of a flagging economy or an upopular vote. Anxious voters are far more likely to "defect" to the opposite-party candidate, particularly when they perceive that candidate as closer to them on the issues. For voters low on anxiety, however, issues have virtually no effect, even when they perceive the other party's candidate as closer to their own attitudes on the major issues of the day.

Other researchers have gone straight for the gut, pitting voters' gut-level feelings ("I like this guy"/"I don't like this guy") against the *reasons* they offer for liking or disliking a candidate.[10] Although both have an impact, gut feelings are about three times as powerful as more "rationally" derived preferences in predicting electoral choices. And when voters' reasoning circuits pull them in different directions from their emotion circuits (as occurred in voters who had a visceral preference for Reagan but could generate more reasons to prefer Carter), about 80 percent of the time, they vote with their gut.[11]

Reason is not irrelevant to people's decisions; nor is a candidate's stance on the issues. But the "issues" that dominate elections tend to boil down to voters' *interests* ("is this good for me and family?") and their *values* ("is this something I think is right?"). Successful election campaigns activate the emotions latent in both.

The political psychologist David Sears has shown, across decades of polling, that people's material self-interests often show surprisingly little connection to their voting patterns.[12] When people's material interests *do* affect their attitudes toward specific policies, it is usually when their interests coincide with their broader values or social attitudes.[13] White voters' attitudes toward affirmative action in college admission, are largely unrelated to whether they have children approaching college age who may be adversely affected by it—*unless* they also hold negative attitudes toward African Americans.

The fact that policies affect voters through the emotions they engender is, I suspect, one of the major reasons values tend to trump self-interest at the polls. Issues of value require little translation to become *emotional* issues. When Al Gore and John Kerry used phrases like "I'll fight for the working people of America," they were trying to appeal to people's materials interests. But these are weak emotional appeals. They don't make people *picture* anything (e.g., wealthy people on yachts, uncorking the champagne with one hand while clutching their bloated tax refund checks with the other), and they don't activate the most important *value* associated with fighting for working people: *fairness*. Appeals, such as "I'll fight for the working people of America," may have generated emotions during the Great Depression, but that was seventy-five years ago. Today, such phrases are among the tired, poor, and huddled phrases of the liberal lexicon that need to be replaced with words that appeal to the average American's values and emotions.

In extraordinary times, people will vote their interests even without particularly compelling appeals because the circumstances of their lives make their material interests, values, or sense of shared community so salient that they don't require great oratory to awaken their emotions. During the Great Depression, when people couldn't put food on the table for their children, it didn't take much to turn interests into feelings, although even then, Franklin Roosevelt used his fireside chats to speak to people's hearts and minds. During the Vietnam War, when people's sons and husbands were dying by the thousands for what increasingly seemed like no good reason, it didn't take much to turn their interests into feelings.

But most times are not extraordinary.

This is what Democrats have often found voters's behavior so perplexing. How gay people express their commitment to one another doesn't affect the marriages of 95 percent of Americans, who aren't likely to start dashing off with their fishing buddies in droves if given the opportunity to tie the gay knot. Whether a few dozen murderers a year get a life sentence or the chair doesn't make much difference to the day-to-day experience of most of us. What *does* affect most Americans' lives is who gets tax breaks and who doesn't; whether they can leave one job and begin another without fear of losing their health insurance because of a pre-existing condition; whether they can take a maternity leave without getting fired; or whether their children are safe in school from the risk of being fired at with automatic weapons.

So, to echo Thomas Frank's haunting title, *What's the Matter with Kansas?* [14]

Frank has arguably penned the most richly detailed depiction ever of what Karl Marx called "false consciousness," in which ideological systems blind people to the realities of an economic system that is taking advantage of them. But the problem is not just that voters need to be made aware of their material interests. They need to *feel* that someone is looking out both for their interests and for the *values* that give their lives meaning. [15]

Marx was no friend of the liberal philosophers, who were the intellectual architects not only of modern democracy but of free-market capitalism before government started to constrain the sticky fingers of its invisible hand with laws regulating child labor, vacations, overtime, minimum wages, occupational safety, and the like. But Marx was himself a product of that emergent capitalist culture, and he unwittingly shared the implicit psychological assumption that guided philosophers from Thomas Hobbes to Adam Smith: that people are ultimately driven by their rational self-interest. [16]

As decades of survey research demonstrate, people are driven in the voting booth by their feelings, and these feelings reflect the extent to which they believe a party or candidate is attending to their interests and values. And as in research on emotion in psychology, the one feeling that doesn't fit neatly into the positive/negative dichotomy in voter surveys is anger, particularly when it is alloyed with fear. The combination of fear and loathing often leads to *enthusiasm* for a candidate— not typically viewed as a negative emotion. It may be more sensible to consider fear and loathing, and the constellation of disgust, contempt, and hatred, as a third dimension of emotional experience, apart from positive and negative emotion, that has its own properties (and requires different ways of addressing when exploited by the opposition).

In the *Federalist Papers* James Madison and the other founders recognized the dangers of fear and loathing. Madison in particular was concerned—and the history of democracies throughout the world bears out his fears—that democracies may not be able to address the most extreme, emotionally intense conflicts among their members, particularly conflicts among competing religious sects. [17] However, Madison, Jefferson, and the other founders hoped they could keep such conflicts at bay through a combination of attachment to the nation, protection of private property, creation of the conditions for prosperity that would strongly motivate people to restrict their battles to the ballot box, and creating a separation of church and state that would discourage sectarian battles waged using the instruments of government. [18]

The political studies reviewed thus far have relied primarily or exclusively on surveys. These studies have the advantage of including large representative cross-sections of the American voting population over several decades. But only experiments, in which scientists can randomly assign subjects to one condition or another and then see how they respond, allow definitive judgments about cause and effect. Few researchers have tested the effects of emotion on electoral decisions experimentally, reflecting, in large measure, the rational choice models that have dominated academic political science. However, the small number of experiments that *have* been conducted paint a similar picture to the one outlined in broad strokes here thus far.

In the 1930s, a socialist candidate for local office conducted a "field study" as part of his campaign in Allentown, Pennsylvania. [19] A week before the election, in one ward, volunteers distributed a leaflet that made an emotional appeal. In a second ward, volunteers distributed a leaflet that instead appealed to a rational electorate. In the third ward (a control condition), no leaflets were distributed.

The results were striking. In the "emotional" ward, votes for the Socialist Party increased by 50 percent over the previous election. In the "rational" ward, votes increased by about a third. In the control ward (no leaflets), votes increased by about a quarter.

University of Michigan political scientist Ted Brader is on the cutting edge of experimental research testing the role of emotions, and especially of images and sounds designed to elicit emotions, on the efficacy of campaign advertisements. Brader conducted two ingenious studies during the 1998 Democratic primary election campaign for governor of

Massachusetts that pitted Attorney General Scott Harshbarger against State Senator Patricia McGovern. One tested the impact of emotionally compelling visual and musical cues in a positive ad designed to elicit enthusiasm. The other study tested the impact of these kinds of sensory cues on a negative ad designed to elicit anxiety or fear. The text of the positive ad offered an uplifting message of hope and progress. The negative ad described a dissolving social fabric that the rival candidate was incapable of addressing.

In each study, subjects viewed one of two versions of the ad. In one version, the narration was accompanied by emotionally evocative images and music that matched the "tenor" of the ad. In the other version, the images and music were more muted, selected for their relative lack of emotional appeal. For example, in the negative ad, the narrator begins, "It's happening right now in your neighborhood. A generation of young people is in danger." In the emotionally evocative version, the narration is accompanied by a dark image of the back of a police officer scanning cars in an urban neighborhood and tense, menacing music. In the less evocative version, the same narration is accompanied by an aerial photo of a suburban neighborhood. The narrator continues, "Violence and drugs threaten to destroy their future." Brader used a similar design for the positive ad, with the narrator beginning, "There's good news in your neighborhood. The future looks bright for a generation of young children."

Brader looked at a range of outcomes, from voters' feelings after watching the ads to their likelihood of voting and even volunteering for the campaign. The results were unequivocal. The reason for voting were the same in each version of each ad because the argument (the text of the narration) was identical. But the addition of emotionally powerful images and music not only influenced the extent to which the ads generated anxiety or enthusiasm. It also affected the likelihood that subjects would both vote and sign up to become involved in the campaign.

These seemingly incidental but emotionally salient "background" features have nothing to do with the logical structure of the argument. But they have everything to do with its emotional structure—and ultimately its impact.

Dueling without a Sword

The data from political science are crystal clear: people vote for the candidate who elicits the right feelings, not the candidate who presents the best arguments.

Imagine what might have happened if Al Gore had known this when he entered into the following exchange with George W. Bush in their first presidential debate in 2000:

MODERATOR (Jim Lehrer): Are there issues of character that distinguish you from Vice President Gore?

BUSH: The man loves his wife and I appreciate that a lot. And I love mine. The man loves his family a lot, and I appreciate that, because I love my family. . . . I felt like there needed to be a better sense of responsibility of what was going on in the White House. I believe that—I believe they've moved that sign, "The buck stops here" from the Oval Office desk to "The buck stops here" on the Lincoln bedroom. . . . It's time for a fresh start after a season of cynicism. And so I don't know the man well, but I've been disappointed about how he and his administration have conducted the fundraising affairs. You know, going to a Buddhist temple and then claiming it wasn't a fundraiser isn't my view of responsibility.

MODERATOR: Vice President Gore?

GORE: I think we ought to attack our country's problems, not attack each other. I want to spend my time making this country even better than it is, not trying to make you out to be a bad person. You may want to focus on scandal. I want to focus on results. As I said a couple of months ago, I stand here as my own man and I want you to see me for who I really am. Tipper and I have been married for thirty years. We became grandparents a year and a half ago. We've got four children. I have devoted twenty-four years of my life to public service and I've said this before and I'll say it again, if you entrust me with the presidency, I may not be the most exciting politician, but I will work hard for you every day. I will fight for middle-class families and working men and women and I will never let you down.

MODERATOR: So, Governor, what are you saying when you mention the fundraising scandals or the fundraising charges that involve Vice President Gore? What are you saying, that the voters should take from that that's relevant to this election?. . .

BUSH: I think people need to be held responsible for the actions they take in life. . . .

MODERATOR: Are you saying all this is irrelevant, Vice President Gore?

GORE: No. I think the American people should take into account who we are as individuals, what our experience is, what our positions are on the issues and proposals are. I'm asking you to see me for who I really am. I'm offering you my own vision, my own experience, my own proposals. And incidentally, one of them is this. This current campaign financing system has not reflected credit on anybody in either party. And that's one of the reasons I've said before, and I'll pledge here tonight, if I'm president, the very first bill that Joe Lieberman and I will send to the United States Congress is the McCain-Feingold campaign finance reform bill. . . . And I wish Governor Bush would join me this evening in endorsing the McCain-Feingold Campaign Finance Reform Bill.

BUSH: You know, this man has no credibility on the issue. As a matter of fact, I read in the *New York Times* where he said he co-sponsored the McCain-Feingold Campaign Fundraising Bill. But he wasn't in the Senate with Senator Feingold. . . .

GORE: Look, Governor Bush, you have attacked my character and credibility and I am not going to respond in kind.[20]

In Gore's response, we see the heavy footprint of the dispassionate vision of the mind. His initial response reveals the networks that were active in his mind as another man told him to his face, in front of tens of millions of his countrymen, that he had no integrity: "I think we ought to attack our country's problems, not attack each other. . . . You may want to focus on scandal. I want to focus on results."

Gore's character had just come into question, and instead he wanted to turn to issues, to *results*, to the expected utility of a Gore versus a Bush presidency. As Bush sharpened his attack—and his fangs— as the interchange proceeded, Gore returned to the language of expected utility, suggesting an instrumental response to the problem of special interest money on government (the McCain-Feingold Bill).

But Bush wasn't talking about the influence of special interest money on government. He was talking about the influence of special interest money on *Al Gore*.

Gore also made the same sequencing error he made in his interchange with Bush on Medicare, leading with the dispassionate, utilitarian response (he was going to provide outcomes) and then *following* it with the more effective emotional appeal, establishing himself as a family man and a devoted public servant. Nor did he respond to Bush's well-crafted effort to associate him with Bill Clinton's personal improprieties, which had nothing to do with Gore, particularly the reference to the Lincoln bedroom, which activated associations not only to fundraising scandals but to sexual indiscretions.

Bush, ever the male primate (and armed with a much better intuitive understanding of the feelings of the millions of other primates tuned in at home), was emboldened by his opponent's failure to respond when attacked in the moral jugular, so he intensified his attack. Whereas his language was initially careful and measured, once he smelled weakness, his language, posture, and movement became ever more aggressive. In his final blow, he stated baldly, "You know, this man has no credibility on the issue" and went on to call Gore a liar.

From the standpoint of primate politics, this interchange reflected a classic display of aggression aimed at establishing dominance, and Bush clearly won. Each time he attacked, Gore backed away, hissed a little, but refused to fight.

At another level, what millions of viewers witnessed was an old-fashioned challenge to another man's honor. Bush was standing in front of Gore, face-to-face, eye-to-eye, attacking his integrity. Two centuries earlier, such an attack would have invariably provoked a duel. To avoid the duel would have been to suffer a disgrace worse than death. But Gore refused to duel even verbally, despite the fact that he was the far better swordsman.

As a southerner, Al Gore surely knew what it meant when a man calls you a liar to your face, and he should have known how every southern voter would respond if he did not defend his honor. Much of the South is characterized by what anthropologists call a culture of honor, in which an attack on a man's honor, or his family's honor, is a fighting matter. [21] To show cowardice, to back off, or to respond with anything other than a display of aggression in the face of an attack on one's honor is to lose face and status, to be deeply shamed.

In a remarkable experiment at the University of Michigan, researchers documented just how important these cultural dynamics can be. [22] Subjects were male college students from either Northern or Southern states. A confederate of the experimenter "accidentally" bumped into them and then walked off into another room. In half the cases, the confederate called them an obscene name after bumping into them.

The researchers then rated how amused or angry the students appeared after the bump. They also asked them to complete a hypothetical scenario in which a woman complained to her boyfriend that a mutual male friend kept making passes at her. Finally, to see just how deep subjects' reactions ran, they analyzed cortisol levels in the men's saliva (because cortisol is a hormone secreted during stressful events) as well as testosterone levels before and after the incident (because testosterone provides, among other things, a physiological index of readiness to fight).

Northern and Southern males responded very differently, both psychologically and physiologically. Whereas the majority of Northern students responded to the insult with more amusement than anger, 85 percent of Southern men showed the opposite pattern. Roughly half of the Northern males completed the scenario about the woman complaining to her boyfriend about the unwanted pass with a violent ending, regardless of whether they had been insulted. Among the Southern men, the ending of the story depended on whether they had first felt dishonored: For Southerners who hadn't been insulted, only 20 percent completed the hypothetical scenario with a violent ending. For those who had been insulted, the number rose to 75 percent. They showed Southern gentility when not insulted, but they demonstrated a readiness for aggression when primed with an insult.

The same differences showed up in their biology. Northerners showed virtually no physiological reaction to the insult. In contrast, both cortisol and testosterone levels jumped dramatically in Southern men following an insult.

The implications couldn't be clearer for candidates who want to win national elections: Make sure you understand the way different emotional constituencies (e.g., males and females, Southerners and Northerners, rural and urban voters) are likely to respond to different campaign strategies. And if you don't have the expertise on your team, get it. To New Yorkers, if someone bumps into you on the street and hurls an obscenity, you're likely to roll your eyes and say, "Screw you, buddy." And that's the end of the matter. To Southern males, them's fightin' words.

By attacking Gore's honor, Bush had actually handed Gore a golden opportunity to appeal to the southern, rural, and working-class voters—particularly male voters—who had voted for Bill Clinton for eight years but weren't so sure about Gore, by giving the Texas governor a good ole southern *ass-kickin'*. Bush had also given Gore a chance to bring into the campaign what the governor had so successfully placed off limits—*his entire life history*—having erased all his sins with his religious conversion just a few short years earlier. Both the media and the Gore campaign had accepted Bush's framing of his life as having just begun a few years earlier. This was a chance for Gore to show the continuities between the Bush who was lost and the Bush who was found, with a response like this:

> Governor, you see those two young women sitting there in the front row? Those are my daughters. And that woman sitting next

to them? That's my wife. And the woman next to her—that's my mother.

You have attacked my honor and integrity in front of my family, the people of my home state of Tennessee, and millions of my fellow Americans. So I think it's time to teach *you* a few old-fashioned lessons about character.

When I enlisted to fight in the Vietnam War, you were talkin' real tough about Vietnam. But when you got the call, you called your daddy and begged him to pull some strings so you wouldn't have to go to war. So instead of defending your country with honor, you put some poor Texas mill worker's kid on the front line in your place to get shot at.

Where I come from, we call that a coward.

When I was working hard, raising my family, you were busy drinking yourself and your family into the ground. And not just in your own home, setting a terrible example for your kids. Why don't you tell us how many times you got behind the wheel of a car with a few drinks under your belt, endangering your *neighbors'* kids?

Where I come from, we call that a drunk.

When I was serving in the United States Senate, your *own father's government* had to investigate you on the charge that you'd swindled a bunch of old people out of their life savings by using insider knowledge to sell off stocks you knew were about to drop. And you know who bought those stocks? The people right out there in America who are listening right now, looking you right in the eye.

Where I come from back home, we call that crooked.

When you were in a tight primary battle with John McCain in South Carolina this year, people started getting these phone calls telling them he'd sired a black baby. Yes, Governor, that baby did have dark skin—because Senator McCain and his wife had adopted that child from Bangladesh. And funny, something similar happened the last time you were in a tight race, running for governor of Texas against governor Ann Richards, when suddenly rumors started flying that she was a lesbian.

Where I come from, we call someone who does those kinds of things a disgrace to his family, his state, and his country.

So, Governor, don't you *ever* lecture me about character. And don't you *ever* talk about me that way again in front of my family or my fellow citizens.

Whether Gore could have mustered an effective response to Bush's challenge on character had he not received the same advice that ran Democratic candidates into the ground all over the country in the next two elections is anybody's guess. Poll results, his strategists informed him with authority, had shown that people didn't like bickering and finger-pointing, and that they wanted to focus on the future, not the past.[23] Virtually every word that came out of his mouth had been market-tested using focus groups and hand-dials indicating when listeners liked and didn't like what he was saying in practice debates.[24] Unfortunately, the more his words seemed market-tested, the less genuine they seemed. And the less genuine he seemed, the less likable.

In December 2004, when Gore was still contemplating a rematch with Bush four years later, he told his friends that if he ran again, this time he would use his gut and not have his hands tied by his handlers. Gore never had the strongest political instincts, which rendered him vulnerable to bad advice even if he hadn't surrounded himself with some of the most powerful purveyors of it in the business. Nevertheless, his courageous, blistering critique of the Bush administration's plans to go to war with Iraq, delivered at the Commonwealth Club in San Francisco in September 2002[25] when few were openly opposing the war and the media were actively attacking anyone who did so, provides a glimpse of what "Gore unplugged" might have looked like on that stage two years earlier, when he went from a nearly double-digit lead over Bush before the debates to defeat pulled from the jaws of a slim electoral victory.

In his speech to the Commonwealth Club, Gore began with the kind of humor that was too rare in his campaign:

Thanks for your kind words on my service as vice president. I felt it was a tremendous honor. I enjoyed the job. I have to tell you that I did some research about the vice presidency and found that quite a number of my predecessors did not really fully appreciate the job. Some of them resigned. . . . John C. Calhoun actually resigned the vice presidency in 1825 to become a senator from South Carolina. And as many of you know, he subsequently lost that seat to Strom Thurmond, who's still there.

When he got into the central message of his speech, he spoke in plain language, integrating intellect and passion, and introducing the kind of emotion-laden colloquialisms that were missing from his 2000 campaign:

> I believe we should focus our efforts first and foremost against those who attacked us on September 11 and who have thus far gotten away with it. The vast majority of those who sponsored, planned, and implemented the cold-blooded murder of more than 3,000 Americans are still at large, still neither located nor apprehended, much less punished and neutralized. I do not believe that we should allow ourselves to be distracted from this urgent task simply because it is proving to be more difficult and lengthy than was predicted. Great nations persevere and then prevail. They do not jump from one unfinished task to another. We should remain focused on the war against terrorism.

In this passage, Gore contrasted the Bush policy with what "great nations do," and made clear that Iraq had nothing to do with the war against al Qaeda. This is the kind of wedding of reason and emotion that both stirs and intellectually engages the political brain. Then Gore continued:

> I believe that we are perfectly capable of staying the course in our war against Osama Bin Laden and his terrorist network, while simultaneously taking those steps necessary to build an international coalition to join us in taking on Saddam Hussein in a timely fashion. If you're going after Jesse James, you ought to or-

ganize the posse first. Especially if you're in the middle of a gun-fight with somebody who's out after you.

This was an old-fashioned, rabble-rousing speech to America's gutland. Gore was talking straight, he was talking tough, and he was using the kinds of metaphors he virtually never used in 2000 and never, to my knowledge, used in the 2000 debates. He was beating George Bush at his own game.

This was the Al Gore who should have run for president.

Why Johnny Can't Run

Given the overwhelming evidence of the impact of emotion on electoral success, why are Democrats so consistently unable to run emotionally compelling campaigns?

Several forces, I believe, are at work.

The first is, well, cerebral. Democrats, and particularly Democratic strategists, tend to be intellectual. They like to read and think. They thrive on policy debates, arguments, statistics, and getting the facts right.

All that is well and good, but it can be self-destructive politically when alloyed with a belief in the *moral superiority* of the cerebral at heart, because moral condescension registers with voters. And, truth be told, the empirical record linking moral action and intellectual rigor isn't very strong. While the philosopher Martin Heidegger was sympathizing with the Nazis, many Germans of far lesser intellectual means were not. Indeed, the most dangerous kind of psychopath is a smart one.

A second reason is a mistaken belief that reason can provide both means and ends, when it can only provide the former. Despite philosophers' best efforts to derive morality from reason, no one has been able to do so successfully, and for good reason: the fuel that drives our actions, including moral actions, is emotional, not cognitive. Nothing is more irrational than spending our lives trying to fend off mortality when no one has ever escaped that fate. There is nothing rational about wanting the best for our children, who themselves are mortal and hence have no particularly good reason for eating the flesh of cows or burning fossil fuels.

Unless the wiring of our brain gets tangled over the course of development, we are endowed by God, Darwin, or natural selection with motives to care about our children and families. To what degree we extend our concern to ever more inclusive groups—community, state, nation, Western people who look enough like us to elicit feelings of sympathy, all humans, all sentient creatures—depends on how high a price we are willing to pay to make them our moral priorities. And that, in turn, depends on a host of factors—all of them emotion-laden—from our capacity for empathy, to our moral and religious beliefs, to how much we enjoy a good burger.

A third source of resistance to the effective use of emotions in Democratic campaigns is the belief that doing so is inherently manipulative. But there is no necessary relation between reason and morality or between emotion and immorality. You can tell the truth or lie with arguments and statistics, just as you can lead or mislead with emotionally compelling words, images, and analogies.

But I suspect the greatest source of resistance among Democrats is the one that represents the biggest impediment to more effective campaigns, because it is both institutional and psychological. It comes in many forms, and it is usually couched in terms that sound lofty or high-minded, which makes it all the more difficult to address.

It is a *discomfort with emotion* characteristic of many cerebral Democrats, including many who make important strategic campaign decisions. I would not be so presumptuous as to diagnose individuals I don't know from a distance. But an anecdote should make the general "syndrome" clear.

I was attending a meeting led by a man with a great deal of power, who had proven himself a great mover and shaker. At this particular meeting, two women representing a relatively powerless contingent of the group presented a proposal. They were clearly anxious, uncertain about his response, and cowed by his intimidating presence. Although I do not believe his response was consciously intended to be hostile, it was abrupt and mildly accusatory, and it immediately closed off discussion. The mood in the room was awkward. He didn't seem to notice and moved on to other items on the agenda.

Later that evening, I turned to a colleague, perplexed, and wondered how someone with such a track record at making things happen, shaking hands and kissing babies, could be so unaware of the emotion in the room. She responded, without blinking an eye, "He understands power. He doesn't understand emotion."

She was absolutely right. He knew who was above him, who was below him, who was a peer, and how to craft coalitions. But he had little idea about what went on in anyone's mind, particularly if the person was feeling something other than dominance or subordination. He could arrange any kind of meeting other than a meeting of the minds.

Psychologists have described and studied people who show a discomfort with or disinterest in emotion in a number of ways and with a number of labels. Of particular interest is a syndrome known as an obsessional personality style, characterized by tone deafness to emotion, usually combined with a preference for viewing emotion as something irrelevant or bothersome, a hard-driving if not overly conscientious attitude toward work, and a tendency to focus on details that often leads the person to lose the forest for the trees.[26] If obsessive individuals express emotion, it is usually righteous indignation.

This is a personality style, not a disorder. People with this style are often highly successful. Their spouses may complain about some emotional distance but usually accommodate to it. In our own research, colleagues and I have found that obsessive people tend to be perfectionistic; to see themselves as logical and rational, uninfluenced by emotion, preferring to operate as if emotions were irrelevant or inconsequential; to have difficulty acknowledging or expressing anger; to be controlling; and to be competitive with others.[27] My colleague Jonathan Shedler has studied a similar phenomenon he calls "illusory mental health," which describes a kind of person who *reports* little or no anxiety or distress but often oozes it from his pores.[28]

Other researchers have studied a style of forming intimate relationships called an "avoidant" or "dismissing" attachment style. By twelve to eighteen months of age, infants with this attachment style have already learned to avoid emotional dependence, usually because of the emotional aloofness or discomfort with closeness and "soft" emotions of their primary caregiver. Avoidant adults shut off or "deactivate" attachment-related feelings, rather than turn them on, as people with a more secure attachment style do, when coping with distress. In one study, conducted during the first Gulf War, researchers examined the way Israeli citizens coped with Scud missile attacks from Saddam Hussein.[29] Whereas securely attached individuals tended to draw together for comfort, individuals with an avoidant style reported feeling more comfortable alone.

In yet another, related line of research, colleagues and I have identified a trait we call "emotional avoidance,"[30] a style of regulating emotion that can be seen in highly functional people but that minimizes their access to emotion. Individuals high on this personality dimension have a tendency to perceive themselves as logical and rational; to prefer to operate as if emotions were irrelevant or inconsequential; to deny or disavow their own needs for nurturance, caring, or comfort, often regarding such needs as signs of weakness; and to be invested in seeing and portraying themselves as emotionally strong, untroubled, and in control, despite clear evidence of underlying insecurity, anxiety, or distress.

What is shared by these various personality styles is a discomfort with emotion that can be deadly to a political campaign. Such individuals are often competitive and driven and may enjoy the fray of politics. They frequently hold values many of us would consider noble. They are particularly comfortable with policy, facts, figures, and poll results. They are often exquisitely sensitive to power dynamics, and may be helpful in coalition building or in recognizing when someone is gaining or losing prominence or power. However, they may also require control in ways that others find overbearing.

Most importantly, their obsessive attention to facts and figures, their caution and risk aversion, their indifference or disdain toward emotion, and their conflicts around anger and aggression (which may lead them to generate rationalizations against attacking or responding to attacks), leave them misattuned to some of the most important emotional signals in electoral politics, such as whether a candidate has charisma, what nonverbal signals he or she is sending, what emotions the candidate is or is not activating in the electorate, and when it is time to capture the moment with a positive or a negative appeal. Such individuals may seem highly competent because of their capacity to read power dynamics, and at times this may lead them to make good calls. But they are fundamentally handicapped by an emotional style that runs contrary to what is required, particularly in the era of television, of someone charged with managing the emotions of the electorate.

From Science to Practice

The passionate vision of mind and brain laid out in this part of the book, and the data described in this chapter, have many implications for how candidates should run their campaigns. Perhaps most importantly, they suggest a hierarchy of goals that should guide every campaign, reflecting the hierarchy of influences on electoral success.

The first goal transcends any given candidate: to define the party and its principles in a way that is emotionally compelling and tells a coherent story of what its members believe in, and to define the other party and its values in ways that undermine its capacity to resonate emotionally with voters. This is the first goal of any campaign because the way voters experience the party is the first influence on the way they will experience the candidate.

The second goal of an effective campaign is to maximize positive and minimize negative feelings toward its candidate, and to encourage the opposite set of feelings toward the opponent. The most important feelings are gut-level feelings, from global emotional reactions (e.g., "I like this person") to more specific feelings (e.g., "She makes me proud to be an American"). Ronald Reagan successfully associated Jimmy Carter with humiliation for his inability to get the Iranian hostages home, just as Bill Clinton associated George H. Bush with anxiety about the economy as well as a range of other negative feelings toward Bush's apparent inability to "get" what the average American was experiencing. Both men, as challengers, associated themselves with hope.

It may seem obvious that these are the feelings a candidate wants to elicit and avoid. But my point is much more specific: *managing positive and negative feelings should be the primary goals of a political campaign*. It is important to engage on issues and offer some specific positions. There is plenty of time for that in a campaign. But candidates should use policy positions to *illustrate* their principles, not the other way around.

When Bill Clinton was running for re-election in 1996, he didn't hide values in the fine print of his policies. His policies and actions illustrated his values, as can be seen in the opening paragraphs of his party's platform that year:

> Today's Democratic Party is determined to renew America's most basic bargain: Opportunity to every American, and responsibility from every American. And today's Democratic Party is determined to reawaken the great sense of American community.
>
> Opportunity. Responsibility. Community. These are the values that made America strong. These are the values of the Democratic Party. These are the values that must guide us into the future.
>
> Today, America is moving forward with the strong presidential leadership it deserves. The economy is stronger, the deficit is lower, and government is smaller. Education is better, our environment is cleaner, families are healthier, and our streets are safer. There is more opportunity in America, more responsibility in our homes, and more peace in the world.[31]

The first paragraph promises to address Americans' interests (opportunity) and their values, including values more often associated with the right (responsibility). The second paragraph draws its emotional power from its literary style. Presenting the words *opportunity*, *responsibility*, and *community* as sentences in their own right literally forces the reader to "speak" these words as they would be delivered in oratory—punctuating each one with significance. The next paragraph describes the basis for the claim that the Democrats can deliver on these promises. As was so characteristic of Clinton's appeals, the sequence of the paragraphs is not incidental. It begins with an appeal to emotion, wedding voters' interests with quintessentially American values, and then follows with an authoritative presentation of what he had accomplished.

This document was just the opening act of a campaign that would stay on message from start to finish, with the same principles and sequencing, to the very end. Consider Clinton's opening statement from his second and final debate with Republican Senator Bob Dole in late October 1996, which used statistics to illustrate his values, to show concretely what he cared about:

> I have a simple philosophy that I tried to follow for the last four years: Do what creates opportunity for all, what reinforces responsibility from all of us, and what will help us build a community where everybody's got a role to play and a place at the table. Compared to four years ago, we're clearly better off. We've got ten and a half million more jobs, the deficit's been reduced. . . . Incomes are rising for the first time in a decade, the crime rates, the welfare rolls are falling. We're putting 100,000 more police on the street. Sixty thousand felons, fugitives, and stalkers have been denied handguns.[32]

The third goal of a campaign is to manage feelings toward the candidates' *personal characteristics*. This goal is related to the previous one, although emotional associations tend to hold more sway with voters than judgments about a candidate's particular traits (as Clinton's global approval ratings even after his impeachment demonstrate). In general, the goal is to convince voters that your candidate is trustworthy, competent, empathic, and capable of strong leadership, and to raise doubts about the opposition along one or more of these dimensions.

The fourth goal of a campaign is to manage positive and negative feelings toward the candidates' policies and positions. This goal is not only fourth but a *distant* fourth. And it is higher still than the more "rational" goal of presenting voters with cogent arguments for a set of policy prescriptions. These arguments tend to influence behavior at the polling booth, if at all, to the extent that they engender positive or negative feelings toward the candidates.

This hierarchy may seem obvious, but it has been remarkably opaque to many Democratic strategists for the better part of three decades. Democrats have instead insisted on starting at the bottom of the hierarchy, practicing what might be called *trickle-up politics*. Trickle-up politics is the theory of electoral success associated with the dispassionate vision of the mind. It assumes that voting decisions trickle up from voters' rational assessments of specific policies, and that these specific assessments additively create an overall judgment of the expected utility of electing one candidate or the other.

Trickle-up politics is as valid as trickle-down economics.

The assumption of trickle-up theorists is that voters not only *do* but *should* make their electoral decisions this way. But in a republic such as our own, where we vote for candidates from president on down to county commissioner or sheriff, ordinary citizens—including even well-informed citizens—can't possibly keep up with all the data required to know which aspects of which bills are likely to yield results conducive to their values and interests and which candidates hold which positions in more than a handful of races. Although the media tend to be disinclined to play much of an educative role in elections (other than to inform voters of who's winning or losing at any particular point in time), even an information-seeking, educated voter might know the details on three or four issues in a high-profile race, but knowing much more than that would be a full-time job. That's the job of a legislator, not a citizen.

What a voter needs to know most in deciding whether to vote for one candidate or the other are four things, roughly in this order: First, do they share the values that matter most to me, and do they care about people like me? Second, can I trust them to represent me faithfully? Third, do they have the personal qualities that lead me to believe they'll do right by my values and interests, such as integrity, leadership, and competence? And fourth, if there's an issue that really matters to me (e.g., the Iraq War), what's their stand on it, and can I trust them to think about it and make decisions which I would probably make if I had all the information they'll have as my elected representative?

And those turn out to be just the questions voters *do* ask when casting their ballots, and in just that order.

Part Two

A BLUEPRINT
FOR EMOTIONALLY
COMPELLING CAMPAIGNS

chapter seven

WRITING AN EMOTIONAL CONSTITUTION

★ ★ ★

Success [in politics] has less to do with brains than guts. . . .
Democrats have failed at the basics: defining their message, attacking their opponents, defending their leaders, inspiring
their voters. . . . Americans don't like what Republicans stand
for, but they don't know what Democrats stand for.
— JAMES CARVILLE AND PAUL BEGALA[1]

I n a classic experiment, cognitive psychologists asked their subjects
to try to remember the following paragraph:

The procedure is actually quite simple. First you arrange things
into different groups. Of course, one pile may be sufficient depending on how much there is to do. If you have to go somewhere
else due to lack of facilities, that is the next step, otherwise you are
pretty well set. It is important not to overdo things. That is, it is
better to do too few things at once than too many. . . . After the
procedure is completed, one arranges the materials into different
groups again. Then they can be put into their appropriate places.
Eventually they will be used once more and the whole cycle will
then have to be repeated.[2]

The task isn't easy. But it's a lot easier if you're first given the title: "Washing Clothes." Suddenly the "gestalt" or gist is clear, the description is comprehensible, and you would likely remember the essence of it a week later. Without the title, each sentence stands alone for its meaning, more like a list than a story. By first activating a network about "washing clothes," however, the incomprehensible becomes comprehensible, the sentences assume the structure of a narrative, and the story can be readily remembered and retold.

The first and most central task of any campaign is to capitalize on the partisan feelings of those who tend to identify with the candidate's party. That percentage ebbs and flows over time and differs by state and region. But as the history of independent candidates for both the Congress and the presidency shows, it's a big help to start with 30 to 40 percent of the electorate kindly predisposed.[3]

That kind of disposition is only possible, however, when a party has a coherent, emotionally compelling "story"—a narrative of what it means to be a Democrat or a Republican—sometimes described inelegantly in the language of advertising as a "brand." You know a "brand" or "master narrative" exists when it is amenable to titles such as liberal or conservative that carry with them deep connotations (i.e., that activate extensive, emotionally powerful networks), and when it can be placed in the form of an emotionally compelling, coherent story that tells the tale of what the party stands for.

Research suggests that our minds naturally search for stories with a particular kind of structure, readily recognizable to elementary school children, and similar across cultures.[4] A coherent story has an initial state or setting ("Once upon a time. . . "), protagonists, a problem that sets up what will be the central plot or story line, obstacles that stand in the way, often a clash between the protagonists trying to solve the problem and those who stand in their way or fail to help, and a denouement, in which the problem is ultimately resolved ("And they lived happily ever after"). Most stories—and all that try to teach a lesson, as political stories do—have a moral. Many stories are complex with subplots and submorals. But in general, they follow a similar and recognizable structure that gives them their rhetorical power.

Any compelling political narrative must have the following elements:

☆ It should have the structure our brains expect of a narrative so that it can be readily understood, told, and retold.

☆ It should have protagonists *and* antagonists, defining both what the party or candidate stands for and what the party or candidate *cannot* stand, most centrally, what the antagonists represent.

☆ It should be coherent, requiring few leaps of inference or imagination to make its plot line move forward or the intentions of its central actors clear.

☆ It should have a clear moral (and generally subordinate morals, which refer to the party's values).

☆ It should be vivid and memorable.

☆ It should be moving.

☆ It should have central elements that are readily visualized or pictured, to maximize its memorability and emotional impact.

☆ It should be rich in metaphor, both so that it is emotionally evocative and so that it creates and reinforces its intended analogies.

☆ It should take elements of the opposition's story, including its metaphors, and recast them as its own.

☆ Finally, if the story is the party's master narrative, it should be a story its framers would want to tell their children—that could be illustrated in a children's book—because it should be so clear, compelling, and central to its members' understanding of right and wrong that they would want their children to internalize the values it embodies.

Most of us have read to our children the quintessentially American story, *The Little Engine That Could*. Although we may have thought we were just participating in a bedtime ritual, we were transmitting values, whose faithful transmission depended not just on the words on each page but on its narrative structure. This simple children's story is

rich with moral meanings—meanings so implicit I wasn't even aware
of most of them even though it was my favorite story as a young child,
and one I have read to my own children many times.

The story begins with a good little train, whose mission was to
bring toys and treats to girls and boys on the other side of the mountain. It wasn't going to bring the toys to just *any* old boy or girl. It was
going to bring them to the *good* boys and girls, transmitting, under the
radar screen of our children's imaginations, messages not only about
good behavior but about *justice*, that goodness is rewarded.

But then something happens: through apparently no fault of its
own, the train stops with a jerk, unable to move (the obstacle that sets
up the plot). At first, the toys on the train panic, but then they realize
they have nothing to fear because many trains would pass by that could
give them a helping hand—inculcating the value of community and
the expectation of trust in the goodness of others.

But that's not what happens. One locomotive after another—a
shiny engine with fine carriages and elegant dining cars that carries
people, not lowly toys, apples, and lollypops; a powerful engine capable of much heavier lifting—ignores the pleas for help because each
felt it was *too good* for the little train and its cargo (the antagonists).
The implicit message is that no train, no matter how rich or powerful, should put itself above others and refuse to help out a poor neighbor in need.

Eventually, just as the clowns and dolls on the stalled train are
about to lose hope, a little blue engine approaches. The clowns and
dolls explain their dilemma. The little blue engine isn't very strong and
has never been over the mountain. But those poor little boys and girls
on the other side must get their treats. Although she has no material
interest in helping the train and its cargo, she takes their plight as her
plight and decides to do everything in her power to help them. Again,
the moral lesson is clear but implicit: to help those in need—even when
you don't know them, even at a cost to yourself, even if you're not sure
you can do it—is the right thing to do.

So then the little engine begins pushing them up the mountain. It
isn't easy, and it takes all her strength. But as she climbs up the mountain, she expresses the central theme of the story: "I think I can, I think

I can, I think I can." Because she has confidence, the motivation to succeed, and a worthy goal, she does succeed (the denouement). And as
she begins to roll down the mountain, she smiles to herself and chugs,
"I thought I could, I thought I could, I thought I could."

What a magnificent set of messages this little story teaches our children. It teaches them to have good hearts, and that the good should be
rewarded. It teaches them the dangers of pride, class, and division, and
the importance of helping those in need. It teaches them that those
who are truly rich are those who are rich in spirit, not in the trappings
of success. And perhaps the central theme of the story is that if you try
hard enough, you can overcome adversity to achieve whatever you
want.

It is difficult to imagine a more *American* story of the relation between personal achievement and the welfare of the community.

For years, Democrats have been running campaigns that lack the
story structure to which our minds are so receptive, competing not
only against an ideological "brand" that has a highly compelling, well-
honed story but also against the natural disposition of our brains.
Against a coherent narrative, the Kerry campaign ran a rational-utility
laundry list. As James Carville and Paul Begala, two of the best political storytellers in the business (and the only ones to engineer the re-
election of a Democratic president since Franklin Roosevelt) put it,
instead of telling a story, the Kerry team focused on issues: "They
talked about the economy. They talked about health care. They talked
about the environment. They talked about Iraq. They talked prescription drugs and Social Security."[5]

They practiced trickle-up politics, listing all the ways a Kerry presidency could offer high expected utility. But without a storyline, without a plot, without protagonists, and having *deliberately* chosen to leave
out the antagonists (the Bush administration and its extraordinary failures) because of a misguided belief that voters dislike "negativity," they
provided voters with a list, a description of the steps they would take to
wash our collective clothes. But they forgot to mention that the clothes
were dirty, that they needed washing, and that the other party had
muddied them up.

And as a result, they got taken to the cleaners.

Just as we share our values with our children through stories, candidates and parties need to share their values with voters through stories. And the first and most important story—the story that picks up the first 40 percent of votes, and may well carry the election on its own if it is coherent, well crafted, resonates with the electorate, and is read with enough of the right vocal intonation by a reasonably good storyteller— is the story of what the party stands for, which should be an extension of the story of the nation and its principles.

So the next time a political strategist tells a Democratic candidate to run an "issue-oriented" campaign, to offer a laundry list of policies instead of a genuine story of who the candidate is and what he or she stands for, I suggest that candidate stop memorizing all those facts and figures and simply read voters *The Little Engine That Could*. That little book contains all the "issues" that really matter to most Americans and all the values that define the American dream and the Democratic Party: Try to be a good person, don't put yourself above others no matter how rich or strong you are, understand that you are a part of a community, show your appreciation for what you have by sharing your blessings with others who are less fortunate, achieve so that you may become the best person you can be, and in so doing you will not only become strong and virtuous, but you will contribute to the strength and virtue of your community.

★ ★ ★

The Big Blue Engine That Couldn't

Political ideologies are conveyed from generation to generation, and from leaders to citizens, through stories. They include beliefs about what *is* as well as what *should be*, and they shape the way people respond to new information, issues, dilemmas, and candidates.

Ideologies are hierarchically organized, with principles at the highest level and attitudes toward policies at the lowest. At the top of the hierarchy are broad principles and emotional commitments— views of right and wrong, of how society should be organized, and of what it means to be a good person and a good citizen—for which we use labels such as *liberal* or *conservative*. The principles at the top of the hierarchy tend to revolve around feelings toward change (tradition vs. progress), hierarchy (relative equality vs. inequality), and authority (obedience vs. autonomy).[6]

One level below these broad ideologies are values,[7] enduring emotional dispositions toward domains infused with moral feelings, such as fairness, responsibility, gender roles, religious faith, or the use of military force. And one level further down we see more specific attitudes about potential solutions to problems defined by our values. Should we try to eliminate inequalities of opportunity through affirmative action? Should we impose quotas to insure that the pace of change is fast enough? To what extent can we change the problems that beset our inner cities through governmental initiatives?

To be compelling and durable, the master narrative of a party—the "big picture" story that defines its principles—must be clear, coherent, and emotionally alive, allowing flux and change at the level of specific attitudes and gradual change at the level of values. This master narrative is the *emotional constitution* of a party, a living document that resides in the minds of its adherents and defines the overarching message of its framers, its leaders, and those who identify with it. As a "constitution," it must allow for changes in the "laws" (attitudes) associated with it, and, over time, even amendments to its core values as times change.

Democrats can't hope to achieve anything but default victories—victories that occur when the Republicans are so incompetent, corrupt, or morally bankrupt that voters have no direction to turn but left—if they do not develop a master narrative, an ideology that stands *for* something and that stands *against* something. Democrats have been unable to do the former—to develop a narrative that stands *for* something, other than disparate liberal causes—and have been afraid to do the latter—to tell a story that stands against anyone or anything, for fear of offending someone or being branded as immoral, unpatriotic, or antireligious. As a result, for most of three decades, the two parties in America have been playing on vastly uneven fields, with the

Republicans offering a clear and compelling master narrative that is the only master narrative in the public domain, and hence the one that is most often adopted by the media, by independents, and even by left-leaning centrists.

Who Hid the Flyswatter?

For fifty years, from the early 1930s to the early 1980s, Congress was dominated by the New Deal ideology and coalition forged by Franklin Roosevelt. People who lived through the Great Depression and those who heard about it from their parents remembered well the ugly under-belly of unregulated capitalism. Even conservative presidents, such as Eisenhower and Nixon, accepted the basic premise of Democratic ideology, that capitalism is a good thing but government must serve as a watchdog. Nixon created the Environmental Protection Agency and the Occupational Safety and Health Administration, hardly the acts of a president and a party ideologically opposed to government intervention.

But by accepting the premises of the New Deal, Republicans found themselves in the unenviable position, now assumed by the Democrats, of a party without a story. The New Deal was the Democrats' morality tale, and the best Republicans could be was Democrat-lite. By the mid-1970s, the position of the Republican Party had gone from unenviable to untenable, compounded by Watergate, as less than 20 percent of voters identified themselves as Republicans.

Fortunately for the Grand Old Party, a confluence of forces led to the birth of a new master narrative. The Democrats' endorsement of civil rights had alienated many white southerners, turning them from Democrats to Dixiecrats, ripe for the picking by Republicans. The Vietnam War and the eventual revolt from the left led many Americans to resent what they perceived as an anti-American insurgency within their own country, symbolized by flag burning. And perhaps most importantly from a psychological standpoint, the cultural revolution of the 1960s, brought on in no small measure by the combination of affluence and the birth control pill, was deeply disquieting to many Americans, as it upended traditional values that extended directly into the lives of their families.

The impact of this cultural revolution continues to reverberate to this day. In the mid-1970s, as today, this revolution was not only a source of consternation to those threatened by change but also a source of unacknowledged conflict for many who embraced it. Many people continue to struggle between conscious attitudes favorable to the expanding roles and freedoms of women and deeply held but largely unconscious mental models, forged in childhood, of their stay-at-home moms. Such conflicts can be seen in most of the "liberal" marriages I know, including my own. The issue is even more salient in families where the wife might well have been happier to stay at home and the husband may feel diminished for not earning a large enough paycheck to allow her that option. Similar conflicts run through public discourse about sexual morality, with politicians on the right preaching abstinence without having practiced it themselves in their youth or seriously thought through the implications of a later-marrying population, and politicians on the left tongue-tied for fear of appearing to support sexual hedonism instead of speaking openly and truthfully about the conflicts they share with their fellow citizens.

By August 24, 1984, when Ronald Reagan accepted his party's nomination for a second term at the Republican Convention in Dallas, he had solidified a set of organizing principles that would galvanize the conservative movement for a generation. His agenda, his story, his master narrative, was the wistful hope of the conservatives who had "lost the war" to Roosevelt's New Deal fifty years earlier. It was the dream of the Goldwater Republicans in 1964. It was a narrative whose story line was crafted over many years by well-financed conservative think tanks that first emerged in the 1970s, whose goal was to hone its message, its language, its plot, its protagonists, its candidates, and its talking points. It is now a narrative that will constrain any efforts at change for at least thirty years after its resonance with the public has passed, as its judicial proponents will retell their story in the language of constitutional law.

Reagan described the choice confronting the voters in August of 1984:

America is presented with the clearest political choice of half a century. . . . The choices this year are not just between two different personalities or between two political parties. They're between two different visions of the future, two fundamentally different ways of governing. . . .

He went on to offer a devastating critique of the villains of his story, the tax-and-spend Democrats and their standard bearer, Walter Mondale (who, in Reagan's gentlemanly manner, he never mentioned by name). The phoenix of conservatism then began to rise from the ashes of fallen New Deal liberalism:

> It's up to us to see that all our fellow citizens understand that confiscatory taxes, costly social experiments, and economic tinkering were not just the policies of a single administration. For the twenty-six years prior to January of 1981, the opposition party controlled both houses of Congress. Every spending bill and every tax for more than a quarter of a century has been of their doing.

In Reagan's hands, taxation became "confiscation," attempts to solve social problems became "costly social experiments," regulation of market failures became "economic tinkering." Reagan was reshaping the language of public discourse about the nature and role of government as profoundly as had Roosevelt fifty years earlier. But Reagan was just beginning to sharpen his teeth—and his story line:

> By nearly every measure, the position of poor Americans worsened under the leadership of our opponents. Teenage drug use, out-of-wedlock births, and crime increased dramatically. Urban neighborhoods and schools deteriorated. Those whom government intended to help discovered a cycle of dependency that could not be broken. Government became a drug, providing temporary relief, but addiction as well. . . .
> The people told the liberal leadership in Washington, "Try shrinking the size of government before you shrink the size of our paychecks."

Our government was also in serious trouble abroad. We had aircraft that couldn't fly and ships that couldn't leave port. Many of our military were on food stamps because of meager earnings, and re-enlistments were down. Ammunition was low, and spare parts were in short supply.

By this point, Reagan had offered a clear characterization of those with the black hats. They were pessimistic, irresponsible, self-satisfied liberals who never saw a tax they didn't want to levy, a social program they didn't want fund, or a flag they didn't want to burn. Now it was time to develop the character of the conservative cavalry and to describe their dramatic rescue of American democracy:

> Together, we began the task of controlling the size and activities of the government by reducing the growth of its spending while passing a tax program to provide incentives to increase productivity for both workers and industry. . . .
>
> Today, of all the major industrial nations of the world, America has the strongest economic growth; one of the lowest inflation rates; the fastest rate of job creation . . . and the largest increase in real, after-tax personal income since World War II. We're enjoying the highest level of business investment in history, and America has renewed its leadership in developing the vast new opportunities in science and high technology. America is on the move again and expanding toward new eras of opportunity for everyone.

Not only was the economy strong, but our powder kegs were full and dry:

> Today our troops have newer and better equipment; their morale is higher. The better armed they are, the less likely it is they will have to use that equipment. But if, heaven forbid, they're ever called upon to defend this nation, nothing would be more immoral than asking them to do so with weapons inferior to those of any possible opponent. . . .

None of the four wars in my lifetime came about because we were too strong.

The years of big government and deficit spending were coming to a close, but the villains had not yet been run out of town:

> For three years straight, they have prevented us from adopting a balanced budget amendment to the Constitution. We will continue to fight for that amendment, mandating that government spend no more than government takes in. . . .
> They call their policy the new realism, but their new realism is just the old liberalism. They will place higher and higher taxes on small businesses, on family farms, and on other working families so that government may once again grow at the people's expense. You know, we could say they spend money like drunken sailors, but that would be unfair to drunken sailors.

Reagan then brought the crowd to its feet, as he described the choice between the freedom he promised and the totalitarianism that would be the natural endpoint of the path to which liberals had been taking the nation:

> We believe in the uniqueness of each individual. We believe in the sacredness of human life. For some time now we've all fallen into a pattern of describing our choice as left or right. . . . But is that really an accurate description of the choice before us?
> Isn't our choice really not one of left or right, but of up or down? Down through the welfare state to statism, to more and more government largesse accompanied always by more government authority, less individual liberty and, ultimately, totalitarianism, always advanced as for our own good. The alternative is the dream conceived by our Founding Fathers, up to the ultimate in individual freedom consistent with an orderly society.
> We don't celebrate dependence day on the Fourth of July. We celebrate Independence Day.
> *Audience*: U.S.A.! U.S.A.! U.S.A.![8]

Reagan did not create the agenda of the radical right on his own, but he created, packaged, marketed, and embodied in his own persona a "brand" so simple and emotionally compelling that it was able to sustain itself through eight years of moderate Democratic leadership far closer to the values of the average American. What distinguished the conservative ideology of Reagan was its crystal-clear narrative coherence and its emotional resonance.

The right-wing conservatism that began with Reagan and is now the official ideology of the Republican Party tells a coherent story, which goes something like this:

> Once upon a time, America was a shining beacon. Then liberals came along and erected an enormous federal bureaucracy that handcuffed the invisible hand of the free market. They subverted our traditional American values and opposed God and faith at every step of the way.
>
> Instead of trusting people to choose how to govern themselves in their own states based on their own local mores and values, they trusted so-called experts and liberal elites in Washington and Massachusetts to tell the rest of us how to think. Instead of trusting businessmen to make decisions that would produce prosperity, they imposed regulations that stifled it. Instead of letting people send their children to their local schools, they bused children to neighborhoods far from home. Instead of letting people spend their own hard-earned money, they thought they could spend it better.
>
> Instead of requiring that people work for a living, they siphoned money from hard-working Americans and gave it to Cadillac-driving drug addicts and welfare queens. Instead of punishing criminals, they tried to "understand" them. Instead of worrying about the victims of crime, they worried about the rights of criminals.
>
> Instead of adhering to traditional American values of family, fidelity, and personal responsibility, they preached promiscuity, premarital sex, and the gay lifestyle. Instead of promoting the family, they turned a blind eye to escalating rates of teenage

motherhood and paternal irresponsibility, and they encouraged a feminist agenda that undermined traditional family roles. Instead of demanding personal responsibility and self-restraint, they preached unbridled pursuit of pleasure.

Instead of promoting faith, they tried to keep the Almighty out of schools, town squares, and courthouses. Instead of letting people use their tax dollars to send their children to the schools of their choice, they discriminated against schools that preached religious faith. They fought every effort to instill Christian values in our children, and they persecuted the faithful.

Instead of projecting strength to those who would do evil around the world, they cut military budgets, disrespected our soldiers in uniform, burned our flag, and chose negotiation and multilateralism instead of asserting our military strength and sovereignty.

Then Americans decided to take their country back from those who sought to undermine it.

Like all good narratives—and this one is very coherent indeed—it is easy to tell and retell. It was easy to write. Everyone knows exactly what someone who calls himself or herself a conservative purportedly values: military strength, tax cuts, minimal government, fiscal restraint, traditional values, patriotism, and religious faith. This clear message starts conservative candidates with 35 to 60 percent of the vote before opening their mouths, depending on the state or district.

It isn't easy to write a similar story of what it means to be a Democrat—something very ominous for the Democratic Party. We don't even know what to *call* people on the left. *Liberal* has accreted the same kinds of connotations as *Negro* did in the 1960s, and *progressive* is probably the best alternative, but it sounds, well, retro.

Like any good political story, however, the conservative narrative is defined as much by what it neglects to mention as by what it mentions. In fact, it has four major elements of narrative incoherence.

The first and most fundamental (because most of the others derive from it) is the failure to explain the *intent* of the villain, who seems to be little more than a Manichean, Ann-Coulteresque liberal who does evil for the sheer pleasure of liberal evildoing. On the face of it, it seems rather unlikely that half of Americans wish ill on their own country.

Second, the story leaves out the reason liberals began to "tinker" with the free market: because during the Great Depression, unfettered capitalism failed. Government regulation was the answer to a problem, not a spontaneously generated evil plot from a James Bond movie. And as for those failed social experiments, they, too, reflected the market failures of capitalism, the fact that capitalism had not only recruited and maintained slavery for two centuries in America but had left almost 20 percent of the population in poverty as of 1960. Census data show that after less than a decade of those "failed social experiments," that percent had dropped by half.[9]

A third element of narrative incoherence is the suggestion of a liberal assault on God. Why, in a nation that is roughly 85 percent Christian, would half the country want to wage war against the Almighty, who presumably will have the last word? The assault was not in fact on religion but on the theocratic imposition of *particular* creeds—precisely the kind of religious encroachment that had led many of those who founded this country to flee religious persecution and come to the New World.

Then, there's the matter of race, which creates a fourth element of narrative incoherence. Why would anyone who lives in a local area with its own mores (which is all of us) want the federal government to step in to tell us what to do? The reason is that just as unregulated capitalism can produce market failures, unregulated democracy can produce "democracy failures," in which a majority can discriminate against a minority with relative impunity. In such cases, a larger majority (in this case, an entire nation) may need to step in to regulate these failures.

These are four pretty big flies in the Republican ointment. The remarkable thing about them is not that they somehow found their way into the conservatives' master narrative. One of the *aims* of any such narrative is to emphasize what its authors want to emphasize and to define what's "unimportant" or "off message" by ignoring it.

What is remarkable is that someone seems to have hidden the fly swatter. Democrats have periodically rolled up a copy of the *New York Times* to take a shot at one fly or another, but they have never *systematically* retold the conservative narrative, putting back in what has been so carefully omitted.

The failure of Democrats to challenge the conservative narrative at its core reflects, I believe, less a failure of imagination than a failure of nerve, a fear of aggression that remains one of the genuine Achilles' heels of the left. Democrats tend to be conflicted about the appropriate use of aggression, and, hence, to hide their fear of confrontation behind the compassion, empathy, and tolerance that are central features of the morality of the left.

Over twenty-five years ago, Democrats had an early chance to challenge the conservative narrative before it became so dominant. But as has been the case so many times since, they didn't take that chance.

After a successful convention at the end of July 1980, at the urging of Senator Trent Lott, Reagan opened his general election campaign in Philadelphia, Mississippi. This was the town in which, just sixteen years earlier, three civil rights workers had been slain (and subsequently immortalized in the film, *Mississippi Burning*). Reagan's message: "I believe in states' rights."

In case those in attendance weren't listening, Reagan, who knew he needed to make inroads on Jimmy Carter's home turf to win the election, made the intent of his proclamation crystal clear to his cheering audience. He added that, if elected, he would "restore to states and local governments the power that properly belongs to them"—language very close to that of his 1984 convention address. And for any dyslexic readers who read 1984 as 1948, yes, it was the same language used by Strom Thurmond in his bid for the presidency on a blatantly racist platform in 1948 that picked off four southern states. This language is central to the conservative master narrative, which allegedly emphasizes states' rights because they are part of the broader goal of getting "government off our backs."

But once again we see an extraordinary element of narrative incoherence. "Getting government off our backs" and "states' rights" bear no logical relation to one another. What difference does it make whether the government on our backs or in our bedrooms is the federal government or the state government? A Leviathan with a drawl is still a Leviathan. The incoherence in Reagan's narrative betrayed the intrusion of a *covert political agenda*—a racist appeal designed to dislodge the south from its native son.

Clinically, this is precisely the kind of causal lapse, patch of illogic, or narrative inconsistency that signals the intrusion of an emotional conflict worth examining explicitly—that is, bringing to the patient's conscious attention. And it is no different in politics.

In political discourse, narrative incoherence indicates to the opposition party precisely what it needs to make explicit.

Reagan's southern strategy succeeded. He won all but one state in the backyard of a man whose family had farmed southern land for 200 years.

In 1980, as today, Americans were deeply conflicted about race. Many whites had easily triggered negative feelings toward black people, but they no longer believed in overt discrimination. Reagan was playing with fire using language associated with an era most Americans wanted to put behind them. A skillfully worded, direct assault on Reagan's character, aimed at unveiling one of the seamy underbellies of his antifederalist agenda, may well, I believe, have dealt a lethal blow to his candidacy, in large measure because it would have challenged his greatest asset: his likeability.

Unfortunately, Jimmy Carter could not seem to decide whether to jump on Reagan's bigotry, to reference it obliquely, or to run from the issue altogether.

He ended up doing all three.

The issue did not come to the fore until several weeks later, when Reagan brought race back into the campaign at another event. But Carter, likely responding to the public perception of Reagan as affable and grandfatherly, couldn't decide whether to challenge Reagan's public persona—a chronic mistake of Democratic presidential candidates, who routinely allow their opponents' self-styled life story to go unchallenged. In a press conference held shortly after Reagan's second allusion to race, Carter responded to a reporter, "I believe it is better to leave these words—code words to many people in our country who have suffered from discrimination in the past—out of the election this year."

This comment exquisitely betrayed Carter's ambivalence, and exemplifies the kind of compromises described in Chapter 5, in which competing emotional constraints—in this case, motives to attack and to avoid—produce a compromise solution. Reagan's words were not code words to the *victims* of discrimination. They were code words to its *perpetrators*, telling them that he was one of them. And Reagan had been on record as one of them the very same year those three civil rights leaders had been slain, opposing the civil rights legislation of both 1964 and 1965.

In a speech at Ebenezer Baptist Church—Martin Luther King's church—Carter was more direct: "You've seen in this campaign the stirrings of hate and the rebirth of code words like 'states' rights' in a speech in Mississippi. . . . That is a message that creates a cloud on the political horizon. Hatred has no place in this country. Racism has no place in this country." Yet when pressed by reporters as to whether he was accusing Reagan of racism, he backed down, saying he didn't believe Reagan was "a racist in any degree" and adding in response to further pressure from a right-wing reporter, "I am not blaming Governor Reagan. That's exactly the point. The press seems to be obsessed with this issue. I am not blaming Governor Reagan."[10]

In fact, he *should* have been blaming Governor Reagan, and he should have gone for the jugular with direct, fiery prose the day Reagan delivered that speech in Philadelphia, Mississippi:*

> Governor Reagan, what you have done today makes my stomach turn. It's un-American, it's un-Christian, and it shows a callousness that not even your well-honed acting skills can cover. You know exactly what it means to talk about "states' rights" in Philadelphia, Mississippi, a town still torn up over the brutal slaying of three civil rights workers just sixteen short years ago.
>
> And in case anyone is too young to remember, let me spell it out for you. "States' rights" was the smokescreen used to stop black people from voting for a hundred years. We've worked hard in the South to overcome the painful wounds of bigotry and hatred, and today, Mr. Reagan, you've deliberately reopened those wounds today with a nod and a wink and an "aw shucks," for no other reason than your personal ambition.

What you have done today is to desecrate the memory of three young men who gave their lives for our nation's freedom, just as surely as those who have served our nation in battle over 200 years have done. Well, let me tell you something, Governor. You can take your brand of hatred back to where you came from. We don't need your kind in the land where my father and his forefathers have farmed for 200 years. We don't need outside agitators like you, fanning the flames of racial hatred.

You ride in like a cowboy with a white hat, but it isn't a white hat you're wearing. It's a white hood.

Your hood is off, Governor, and I have to tell you, what's underneath is ugly.

A response like that would have aired on all three networks that evening and for several days afterwards and would have been the only political topic discussed on the Sunday talk shows for the next two weeks. It would have put Reagan on the defensive just as he was beginning his campaign, forcing him not only to explain the meaning of his comments but also making him explain his opposition to the Voting Rights Acts fifteen years earlier—something Democrats have never forced any incumbent Republican to do. It would also have said to southerners that Reagan *isn't one of us.* It would have turned the tables pitting "us"—good Southerners—against "them"—outside agitators.

A swift and decisive response would also have suggested that Carter could boldly confront aggression, something he desperately needed to demonstrate in light of the ongoing events in Iran and of the blistering attacks from Reagan on what many Americans perceived as his weakness in the face of aggression. And it would have allowed Carter to use Reagan's eloquent delivery against him every time he delivered a moving line, by reminding people that he is an actor and can say anything with conviction, just as Bush eliminated Gore's ability to challenge his policies by declaring any challenge by Gore as relying on "fuzzy math."

Calling Reagan on his appeal to prejudice would not only have been the morally right thing to do but the pragmatic one as well, because it would have signaled to Republicans in the future that Democrats know how to make the strategy backfire. One of Reagan's first acts as president was to try to defy federal law by securing tax exempt status for Bob Jones University despite the fact that it practiced racial discrimination (forbidding interracial dating). This reflected a deliberate, conscious decision, not the kind of implicit racism that can be more readily forgiven because it is under less conscious control. And the Supreme Court was not forgiving, ultimately rebuking Reagan in an 8–1 decision. Yet the Republicans have used this same "southern strategy" in every presidential election they have won since 1968, and Democrats have never once made them pay for it.

As Kathleen Hall Jamieson and her colleagues have shown, the media creates frames through which voters view a candidate. Like a picture frame or camera angle, these frames determine what journalists include and exclude from their reporting. The media had decided that Reagan was affable (as many saw him on a personal level), which ruled out the seemingly incompatible frame that he was racist. The Carter team made the mistake of not going after the dominant frame. As long as Democrats continue to acquiesce in the stories Republicans tell about themselves and the ways they define such crucial terms as *fairness* and *character* (e.g., isn't prejudice a character issue?), the longer the media will accept and transmit those stories and definitions. And once the media accept them, the party's over.

The Master Narrative of—Waddyacallit?

By the time of Reagan's election in 1980, Democrats were in disarray, not dissimilar to the Republican disarray of the mid-1970s. And since the 1980s, the Democratic Party has seemed more like a loose confederation of single-interest groups,[11] each with its own issue to place on the party's laundry list, than a party with any unity of purpose, principles, or master narrative.

The Democratic Party has been washing clothes without a title.

When I wrote the story of conservatism, it was easy. It flowed. There was no question what elements to include, how to frame the arguments, what words to use, who the good guys and the bad guys were, what obstacles the protagonists had to face to defeat the evildoers, and what the desired and ultimate outcome would be.

That's branding at its finest. When even people who don't like your product are humming your jingle, you know you've got them where it counts: in their networks.

But when I tried to write the same kind of story from the left, I drew a blank. I couldn't even figure out whose story it would be.

The story of liberals? That would be a tragic tale. The term has been so contaminated by the branding of the right that no Democratic presidential candidate has called himself one for over twenty years—and no one who dared to do so has occupied the Oval Office in over forty.

Suppose we set aside the issues and policy fixes that have defined Democratic campaigns for years, the slogans from the sixties and seventies that once had emotional resonance but no longer do, and the single-cause agendas that may once have filled a big tent but now keep pulling out its stakes for the sake of single stakeholders. Suppose we start instead with principles rather than interests or coalitions. Is it possible to construct a master narrative on the left with comparable emotional power to the well-constructed narrative of the right?

How much we can improve on *The Little Engine That Could* I can't say, but there is little doubt that a set of principles underlies most of the causes, issues, and interests that matter to those who pitch their tents left of center. The task, as I hope to show in the remaining chapters, is to make conscious the "rules" that unconsciously guide most of us on the left as we make moral and political judgments in everyday life, and to weave them into a story that resonates with the average American.

That story should feel to the majority of Americans like *their* story. The story of the party and its principles should sound like a natural extension of the story of the nation and its principles. If the master narrative of the Democratic Party doesn't make 60 percent of the electorate feel at home (roughly the percent of self-identified Democrats and Independents), it isn't a good narrative. The party's narrative needs to have enough elasticity that candidates in different parts of the country can draw out its implications in ways that fit their values and those of their neighbors. And it needs to draw on shared sentiments that have become associated with the other party, allowing moderates to cross over without feeling like strangers in a strange land. Democrats believe every bit as much in hard work and personal responsibility as Republicans. The problem is that they rarely say so.

Conversely, if the master narrative *doesn't* alienate about 30 percent of the electorate, it isn't a good narrative, either. About a third of the electorate won't turn left under any circumstances, and if the Democrats' story doesn't make them angry, there's something wrong with it. A substantial minority of Americans hold authoritarian, intolerant ideologies driven by fear, hate, and prejudice that are fundamentally incompatible with Democratic (and democratic) principles. They are the antagonists of the Democratic story, and if they aren't antagonized by it the same way liberals are antagonized by listening to George W. Bush's storytelling, the Democratic story isn't getting its message across.

The flipside of a compelling story about what it means to be a Democrat and why one would want to be one is a compelling story about the other party and its values.[12] Conservatives have had no trouble telling *their* version of the story of liberalism, as Reagan so deftly demonstrated. So to see what the shoe feels like on the other foot, let's revisit *The Little Engine That Could,* conservative style:

> Once upon a time, a little train carrying toys and treats got stuck on its track. Then the rich and mighty trains came by. When they heard its pleas, they responded with derision and contempt, "If you'd kept your engine in better shape, you would never have had this problem. Now get out of my way," and they chugged on.
>
> Over time, the rich and mighty trains became more contemptuous of the little train and its cargo. Each time they passed it, they would complain about the smell of the rotting fruit, the rust that was gradually accumulating on its idle engine, and the laziness of the nasty little dolls and clowns inside who just sat there

doing nothing, expecting something for nothing and getting in the way of trains that were pulling their own weight.

And then on Sundays they chugged to church and praised the Lord. But somewhere along the way they forgot that those who are truly fortunate wear their gold in their hearts, not on their sleeves.

Many years ago, satirist Art Buchwald wrote a wonderful essay that asked, "So you want to be an anti-Semite?" Buchwald then proceeded to rattle off an impressive list of things a person who wants nothing to do with Jews should avoid, starting with taking the polio vaccine, invented by a Jew, Jonas Salk.

The Democrats should take a leaf from Buchwald's book, challenging conservatives repeatedly with a set of inconvenient truths so that the conservative "brand" begins to take on different emotional connotations. With my apologies to Buchwald, who could have done it better, here are some examples of what such a "master counternarrative"—a rebranding—might include:

So you want to be a conservative? Let me tell you something about your heritage.

When conservatives have had a choice between tax cuts for the upper 1 percent of Americans and the middle class, they have chosen the super rich.

When conservatives have had a choice between tax cuts for the super-rich and funding for the National Institutes of Health, which supports the development of cures for cancer, heart disease, and other serious illness, they have cut funding for the National Institutes of Health.

When conservatives had the choice between tax cuts for the rich and body armor for American troops dying in Iraq, they chose tax cuts.

Every time working people have asked for a rise in the minimum wage, conservatives have opposed it, saying that wealthy businesses can't afford it—even as they gave huge bonuses to their CEOs.

When scientists discovered that research on fetal tissue transplants and stem cells might help people with Alzheimer's disease or quadriplegia overcome their illnesses, conservatives blocked it, saying that God was against it.

When Congress proposed a national holiday honoring Dr. Martin Luther King, conservatives opposed it, calling him a communist on the floor of the United States Senate.

When people in wheelchairs, including World War II veterans who lost their limbs defending our nation, asked for accessible sidewalks and buildings, conservatives opposed it, saying it was too expensive.

When Franklin Roosevelt tried to create a safety net for senior citizens, conservatives opposed it, saying we couldn't afford it, and they have been trying to dismantle Social Security, Medicare, and Medicaid ever since.

When Bill Clinton proposed a law that would allow any new mother to take three months of unpaid leave from her job without fear of getting fired for having a baby, conservatives opposed it, saying it would be too costly for businesses.

When half the people who were going bankrupt every year were doing so after a catastrophic illness that wiped out their life savings, conservatives changed the law to make it impossible for them to file for bankruptcy, so that credit card companies could expand their profits.

When oil profits soared beyond all previous heights, and the price of gas at the tank doubled from $1.50 a gallon to $3.00 a gallon, conservatives pushed through the Congress a taxpayer-financed, multibillion-dollar "incentives package" for oil companies to keep up the good work.

So you want to be a conservative? That's your heritage. Stand tall.

Democrats should be reminding voters of these flies in the conservative ointment in every election in every part of the country. With enough repetition over enough years, Republicans would be dodging and weaving like liberals when asked, "Are you a conservative?"

And this list is just the tip of the iceberg.

What is disconcerting about this list, is not what's on it. It's the fact that most Americans would be shocked by almost everything on it. They would have no idea that conservatism has stood on the wrong side of virtually every effort to expand freedom in the last century.

But the fact that most Americans would be shocked by this list is not the fault of conservatives. It is the fault of the left.

Ask anyone in America to write a similar essay called "So you want to be a liberal?" and they could create a long list off the top of their heads: liberals tax and spend, they cut and run, they believe in big government, they're fiscally irresponsible, they take money from hard-working people's paychecks and give it to able-bodied welfare loafers, they're weak on defense, they're soft on crime, they support the gay lifestyle, they preach promiscuity to our children, they lack family values, they persecute people of faith, they want special rights for gays and minorities, they cater to special interests, they appoint activist judges who overrule legislators and propositions with broad popular support.

That's branding. And the success of that branding can be measured in just how many phrases come to mind in a matter of seconds, even among those who don't accept them: "tax-and-spend liberals," "big government," "able-bodied welfare loafers," "weak on defense," "soft on crime," "the gay lifestyle," "family values," "special rights," "activist judges."[13]

What are the comparable phrases and caricatures on the left?

I can't think of a single one. Why?

Because the left has no brand, no counterbrand, no master narrative, no counternarrative. It has no shared terms or "talking points" for its leaders to repeat until they are part of our political lexicon. Instead, every Democrat who runs for office, every Democrat who offers commentaries on television or radio, every Democrat who even talks with friends at the water cooler, has to reinvent what it means to be a Democrat, using his or her own words and concepts, as if the party had no history.

If this is how Coke marketed itself, we would all be drinking Pepsi.

chapter eight

ABORTING AMBIVALENCE

★　★　★

As long as I can remember, the tone of the liberal message on abortion has been defiant, sometimes even celebratory. . . . Still, for those of us who came after *Roe v. Wade*, there is a significantly different reality. The context has changed. Back alleys and coat hangers are not part of our visceral memory. To this generation, the "choice" of a legal abortion is no longer something to celebrate. It is a decision made in crisis, and it is never one made happily. Have you ever talked to a woman who has had an abortion?. . . I promise you, such a woman does not talk about exercising the "right to choose." You may accuse her—and me—of taking such rights for granted, and maybe you'd be right. But mainly she will tell you how sad she is, how she wished she hadn't had to make that "choice," how unpleasant the procedure was. She is more likely depressed than defiant.

—Sarah Blustain, *American Prospect, 2004*[1]

When pollsters first entered into the mix of political consultants in the 1960s and 1970s, politicians used polls to tell them where they stood with the electorate. Polls informed them about what they needed to worry about and where the electorate was with them.[2] Today, however, pollsters frequently *determine* the themes of a campaign, telling a candidate what's hot and what's not.

171

Polls, from the vista of modern campaign strategy, are not just *de*-scriptive but *pre*scriptive, pointing the way toward issues and policies *on* which and *from* which to run. In both 2002 and 2004, most Democratic candidates ran on precisely the same issues, often using versions of the same speeches, as pollster-strategists in Washington determined the issues most important to voters. From a dispassionate standpoint, these were the issues on which any reasonable candidate would run because they were scientifically shown to have the "highest numbers." Candidates who had their own agendas were by definition displaying an irrationality that did not bode well for electoral success—or party funding.[3]

Pollsters, in this view, are like oracles who can see the signs of success and failure in particular issues or positions, much as Tiresias, the blind soothsayer of ancient Greece (immortalized in *Antigone*), could see tragedies unfold before his eyes. Unfortunately, many of our modern-day soothsayers have created more of the tragedies than they have foreseen.

A different vision of mind leads to a very different way of thinking about polling. On virtually every contentious political issue—abortion, guns, welfare, gay marriage, tax cuts—polls show a seemingly mixed pattern of results. Ask the question one way and you get one answer, ask it another way, and you get a different answer. In part, this simply reflects technical issues of little interest to anyone but experts in survey construction. A difference as subtle as asking a question in the affirmative or the negative ("Are you in favor of tax cuts?" versus "Do you oppose tax cuts?") can substantially affect the way people respond.[4]

But another sense in which polls show "mixed" results is of tremendous significance. Take almost any contentious issue, and you'll find that the electorate will endorse what seem like contradictory positions on it. The vast majority of Americans supports gun control. But the vast majority also supports the right to bear arms. So are Americans pro-gun or anti-gun?

That's the wrong question.

The question seems natural to a dispassionate mind that considers the mutual implications of its various values, attitudes, and beliefs, and comes to a unitary, conscious position that resolves potential inconsistencies. But it's a question that doesn't even come to mind if you think in terms of competing and conflicting networks that represent "special interests" in the mind with disparate concerns, which may forge momentary "alliances" to come to a consensus when answering the questions of a pollster.

The advice dispensed by many leading Democratic pollsters reflects a one-dimensional reading of three-dimensional data. When consultants inform a candidate they don't know well who is winning a primary in a distant state that one of the candidate's signature issues is "a winner" or "a loser," or when they tell a candidate to avoid an issue because it "isn't safe" or could be turned to advantage by the opposition, they are engaging in one-dimensional thinking. This view of polls as divining rods for determining which issues or policy positions are "up" or "down" in the polls—and, by extension, which ones candidates should emphasize or downplay—literally represents public opinion in one dimension: a straight line that goes from up to down, high to low.

One-dimensional thinking is especially problematic when the average person is of *two minds* about an issue—that is, when the same issue activates at least two networks that lead to different feelings (e.g., concern about guns in the hands of criminals and support for the rights of law-abiding citizen to protect their families). Democratic pollsters, unlike their Republican counterparts, frequently advise candidates to downplay, avoid, or "stay away from" these kinds of issues because the numbers are ambiguous or mixed. Unfortunately, these happen to be the issues that arouse the most passion and, hence, have the biggest impact on both voting and get-out-the-vote efforts.

Contentious issues are the issues that arouse emotions. If you cede the contentious issues, you cede passion to the other side. And given that people vote their passions, that's always a losing strategy.

Republicans go straight for these issues, and they now have the confidence that they can do so even when support for their position is in the range of 30 percent, as is the case with their absolutist stance on abortion: that abortion is murder and should be illegal under all circumstances. They can do so with impunity because they know that Democrats usually won't contest them for fear of offending some constituency or being branded with a slippery-slope argument (e.g.,

"My opponent believes in abortion on demand," "My opponent views abortion as just another form of birth control"). The result is that Republicans assert an extreme principle, the public never hears a compelling counternarrative, and gradually public opinion shifts to the right.

Polls don't reveal whether voters support or do not support abortion, gun control, or gay rights. Nor should they be used to tell candidates what policies to support or not to support. That's what the candidate's values are for. And polls should *never* be used to tell candidates what issues to avoid. Candidates should never avoid anything, particularly when the other side is running on it, because doing so gives the opposition exclusive rights to the networks that create and constitute public opinion.

Looked at from a different angle, polls provide a *three-dimensional map of the emotional landscape*. What they can tell a candidate is this, and nothing more: *in light of your values and the things that matter to you*, which hill is high enough that you can preach from it, which valley is so low that no one will hear your voice even if you're right, and which path might be worth clearing because people might just follow you there. A three-dimensional map takes seemingly conflicting poll results on an issue like gun control (that people support it, and that they also support the Second Amendment) and creates a "thick description" of the conflicting and competing networks that account for those results, so that candidates can find better ways to talk about the things that matter to them and their constituents.

The view of pollsters as master agenda setters who pick and choose issues for candidates is a natural extension of the dispassionate vision of mind. If the way to win elections is to take the right stance on the right issues, maximizing candidates' utility to voters, then rational candidates will let the experts who have done the statistics tell them what the right stance and the right issues are.

But from the perspective of the passionate mind, candidates shouldn't be running on issues in the first place. Candidates should be running on *principles*, bolstered by a compelling personality, a compelling life story, a shared sense of values with their constituents, the emotional intelligence to identify and communicate these shared values, and some good ideas about how to actualize them.

The last thing a campaign should sever is the link between the candidate and what he or she believes in. In an article in the *New Republic* in 2003, Noam Scheiber reported how Democratic candidates opposed to the Iraq War in 2002, whose constituents were often equally divided, were told by Washington pollster-strategists (who not only advised them but also advised those who controlled the party's campaign war chest) to run pro-war television ads. In a stinging article in the *Washington Monthly* two years later, called "Fire the Consultants," Amy Sullivan described many similar tales from the next election, in which risk-averse party strategists who had lost one close congressional race after another in the previous election cycle were rehired to serve up the same warmed-over populist themes to the next generation of candidates—and with the same predictable results.[5]

If we abandon the trickle-up assumptions embedded in the dispassionate vision of the mind, there is a simple way for Democratic leaders charged with helping elect their party's candidates to retain accountability, spend their limited resources wisely, and play to the strengths of candidates and their indigenous staffs: they should use exactly the same principles to select and put resources into candidates that voters use. That is, they should put their support behind candidates who can arouse the passion of the electorate with their own variations on the themes of the party's master narrative (the most important influence on voting), who are likable and charismatic (the second most important influence), and who have personal attributes that render them likely to be successful both as candidates and as leaders (the third most important).

The specific issues candidates choose to make central to their campaign and the positions they take on those issues should vary by candidate and region. Where pollsters can be valuable for candidates at every level of government is in helping them decide which of the issues that matter to them might serve them well as "signature issues" to illustrate their values and principles, as well as in helping them hone the way they talk about those principles, values, and issues. But pollsters can only be helpful if they start with the candidate's principles.

A Memorial for a Choice

For more than forty years, abortion has stirred deeply felt passions. The majority of Americans believe abortion should be legal. A recent study by the Pew Research Center found that two-thirds of Americans endorse the view that we should find a "middle ground" on abortion.[6] Less than one-third believe that "there's no room for compromise when it comes to abortion laws." Remarkably, the majority of Democrats (70 percent), independents (66 percent), and even Republicans (62 percent) support some kind of compromise. Over *60 percent of white evangelicals* and Catholics support some kind of "middle ground."

Even as a one-dimensional map, these numbers should have been guiding Democratic campaigns toward this issue, not away from it, in every election over the last thirty years. Democrats should be talking about abortion virtually everywhere, including Republican districts and Christian radio stations that reach evangelicals, by emphasizing the extremist position that has dominated the Congress, the White House, the judiciary, and state governments all over the country since the turn of the twenty-first century, which is far outside the mainstream of public opinion.

But a number of conflicts, both within and across people, regions, and "demographics," suggest a more complex three-dimensional image.[7] The vast majority of Americans (85 percent) believe abortion should be permitted when the mother's life is in danger, and three-fourths believe a woman has the right to terminate a pregnancy if she is the victim of rape or incest. But nearly 90 percent support some restrictions on abortions, particularly in the last trimester, and over two-thirds believe that girls under age eighteen should have to obtain parental consent.

The most frequent interpretation of these seemingly conflicting results is that Americans are "divided" on abortion, a position that makes Democrats anxious, particularly in red or purple states, and typically leads either to silence or to a defensive, "I'm kind of pro-choice, but not really" response. A prototypical example is Missouri Senator Claire McCaskill's response in a debate with then–Senator Jim Talent on *Meet the Press* in 2006:

MR. RUSSERT: Do you support a ban on partial-birth abortion?

MS. McCASKILL: I do, within the constitutional framework that we currently have, with the exception for the life of the mother. I also support parental notification. On the whole issue of abortion, what we need to do—I, I, I certainly believe that abortion should remain safe, legal and rare in the early term, but why don't we concentrate on prevention? Why don't we all—none of us want abortion, none of us support abortion [turns to her opponent, as if seeking support]. Let's come together and work on preventing abortions in this country, making adoption easier and, and, and do the right thing to, to drop the number of abortions instead of making health care more unavailable to poor women, which in fact drives up the number of abortions in this country.

McCaskill was one of the sharpest, most emotionally intelligent candidates the Democrats fielded in any race in 2006 and was able to defeat an incumbent in a state that usually sees red in national elections. Yet her response was defensive, indexed by the initial retreat to legalism ("within the constitutional framework. . . "), followed by a gratuitous reference to her position on parental notification (which Russert hadn't asked about), followed by an uncharacteristic stumbling for words and a barrage of half-measures designed to change the subject from what she apparently believed was an unpopular stance in her home state.

What is remarkable about this response is not that such a gifted Democratic candidate would be at a loss for words on such a major issue, but that, *thirty years* after *Roe v. Wade,* the Democratic Party has been unable to generate a principled stand that could spare its candidates from having to invent their own response from scratch in every election and could spare voters from having to play the all-too-familiar game of Pin the Principle on the Donkey.

The poll numbers suggest that the story of abortion in America runs far deeper than "pro-choice versus pro-life." Most Americans do *not*, as McCaskill clearly understood, support unrestricted abortions. They do not support so-called "partial-birth abortions" (a term that was actually invented by the right to create the desired emotional reaction, which Democrats repeat without realizing they are reinforcing their opponent's "brand"). Most Americans don't like the idea of teenage girls getting abortions without consulting their parents, although Democrats have largely been too timid to use emotionally evocative examples of circumstances in which most voters would find parental notification laws morally unacceptable, as in cases of incest (permission from *whom?*), in which parents are abusive, or in which parents and their seventeen-year-old daughter who recently started college would be at odds on what she should do.

That 66 percent of Americans support abortion rights in some form but 85 percent support imposing restrictions on it makes clear that we are not only looking at conflicts *between* Americans but conflicts *within* Americans. Americans are *ambivalent* about abortion, and this has powerful implications for how Democrats should talk about it.

Implicit in the poll numbers are two things most people couldn't tell a pollster because they reflect unconscious processes that structure both their beliefs and their moral intuitions. Whether they know it or not, most people have a graded view of when a fetus becomes a person and a graded view of when a person becomes an adult (and hence a girl becomes a woman capable of choice). These views reflect the way our minds naturally classify phenomena that are fuzzy around the edges (e.g., when adulthood *really* begins). And they are actually more sensible than the arbitrary cut-offs people impose when they proclaim that "life begins at conception" or "at age eighteen, you're an adult" (as any parent can attest).

The Republican response to Americans' conflicts on abortion, and to our unconscious sense that reality is fuzzier than our abstractions, has been unequivocal: describe abortion as murder, define an uncompromising stance as the only *moral* stance one could take, get the 30 percent of Americans with the least tolerance for ambiguity on moral questions to the polls, and let the Democrats offer dozens of different positions as they follow the polls one way on confirmation of Justice Alito, another on confirmation of Justice Roberts, and another on "partial-birth abortion." In so doing, Republicans can portray themselves as principled and Democrats as unprincipled with respect to abortion.

And the Republicans are absolutely right.

A registered Democrat for thirty years, I have no idea where the Democratic Party *really* stands on abortion. My own suspicion, which I assume is shared by most voters, is that most Democrats *really* believe that abortion should be a woman's choice but are afraid to admit it outside the Northeast and California coasts. Where the electoral market will bear it, Democrats repeat a shibboleth such as "a woman has a right to choose." But such shibboleths, while more consistent with what most moderate and progressive voters believe, actually don't reflect what most of us feel in our guts.

Given that most people vote with their guts, we would do well to know what's in ours as well as theirs.

As Sarah Blustain observed in a thoughtful article in *American Prospect*, the notion of a "right to choose" emerged in the 1960s as part of the broader struggle for women's rights. In that context, and in the context of the coat-hanger abortions that led to *Roe,* the language of choice presented a simple, coherent, *moral* message—that a woman unequivocally has the right to choose what to do with her body.

But like any good narrative, that one leaves certain things out of the story. If we think about polls as describing the emotional landscape, the poll results tell us precisely what it leaves out, and precisely why Democrats have been unable or afraid to offer an emotionally compelling counternarrative to the morally repugnant—but largely morally uncontested—narrative of the extreme right. There is a *principled moral position* embedded in the poll numbers, one that, I have come to believe, is more morally sophisticated than the one-dimensional (pro-choice) position I have held all my life.

What Americans are expressing as they offer seemingly disparate answers depending on what questions they are asked is that abortion represents a genuine moral conflict between the rights of a person—a pregnant woman—and the rights of a potential person—a fetus that becomes progressively more person-like over the course of pregnancy. In the early stages of pregnancy, when the fetus lacks most of the properties that implicitly define our concept of personhood (the ability to think, feel, and move purposively), most people find the rights of the mother far more emotionally compelling. That's also why most people find the potential benefits of stem cell research to living, hurting human beings far more compelling than abstract concerns about discarded embryos, particularly when they see the devastation with their own eyes (as when Michael J. Fox courageously appeared in ads all over the country in 2006) or in their own loved ones (as was the case with Nancy Reagan).

But the longer the pregnancy continues, the more we are confronted with a conflict between the rights of a person and the rights of an emerging person. That's why the vast majority of Americans oppose late-term abortions even though they favor a woman's right to choose. Those two positions are *entirely consistent* if you implicitly *feel* that a fetus isn't a person at conception but that it also doesn't suddenly attain personhood when it utters its first cry. The closer to term, the more uncomfortable most people feel about terminating a pregnancy without good reason, because a nine-month-old fetus is far more like a person than not.

Let me give a personal example that should make the point in a way that is far more emotionally compelling than any description of poll results.

My wife and I experienced a late miscarriage, at around twenty weeks. We are, were, and remain firmly committed to the moral belief that a woman, and not the government, is the one who should make decisions about her body. But as most people who have had a miscarriage (or abortion) will understand, a miscarriage five months into the pregnancy was a deeply painful experience, particularly for my wife, as she had carried what she experienced as *her baby* everywhere for five months, both physically and emotionally.

So why did she experience a late miscarriage as so painful? Because no matter what she or we might believe about a woman's right to choose, she experienced a *person* growing inside her. Was it a person the way our first child, then a toddler, was a person, and did we grieve for it the way we would have grieved if something had happened instead to our daughter? No—and this example should give pause to anyone who has experienced anything similar but asserts that "life begins at conception," because it says something important about what most people *really*, in their guts, feel about whether a fetus is a life the same way a child is a life. But the fact that the experience was painful—that emotionally it felt far closer to losing a baby than removing a benign growth—betrays our own conflicting networks regarding the human status of a fetus at five months.

We were taken aback at the "frame" hospital personnel kept trying to impose on us, which we suspect would have been very different if we had still lived in Boston, where we had our first child, rather than in Atlanta, where we had our second. The culture was different, and the language of personhood—rather than the language of medicine—was dominant. Time after time, a nurse or doctor would say, "Would you like to see your baby?" or "Do you want to hold your baby when she's delivered?" even though our "baby" was a fetus, not a baby, and would be delivered dead. And I remember being tremendously relieved when finally, the next morning, a nurse spoke to us in the terms that were consistent with the frame with which we had entered the hospital, when she asked, "What would you like to do with the fetal remains?"

Our response to that question, and to those that followed, betrayed something about our own implicit attitudes toward when life begins in ways of which I had been previously unaware. We were relieved that someone finally referred to the fetus as a fetus. And we chose neither a burial nor a funeral, as did some "parents." (Even the term I use here betrays my own ambivalence. Truth be told, I entered the quotation marks *after* typing the word.)

But we *did* attend a collective memorial a month later with about a hundred other couples who had undergone the same experience, and we gave the "baby" a name when asked for a name to be listed on the program and to be called as her turn came to be memorialized. (We named her Baby Ashley, the name our toddler, Mackenzie, had insisted was going to be the name of her little sister.)

Our choice of a collective memorial rather than a burial was an unconscious compromise, reflecting the activation of two networks, one representing "losing a fetus" and the other representing "losing a baby." Had we conceptualized the miscarriage as losing a baby, we would have had to have a funeral. So why did we attend a memorial?

I've never attended a memorial for a choice or a right.*

I use this example because it calls into stark relief the reason Democrats are so tongue-tied about abortion and demonstrates precisely the kinds of stories candidates should be telling when they talk about issues filled with conflict and emotion. Even a one-dimensional reading of the polls makes clear that two-thirds of Americans are ready to hear an alternative to the conservative morality tale. But it takes a three-dimensional reading to know what that story is.

A Principled Stand on Abortion

You know you have a three-dimensional understanding of poll results when you can tell a good story about them—one that that makes sense of the available data (i.e., that confers intelligibility on otherwise incoherent poll results), that is emotionally compelling (i.e., that leads most emotionally reasonable people to nod their heads), and that has narrative coherence (i.e., that has no clearly missing links).

The Republican story is a Manichean one, a tale of good and evil, in which the good guys stand for life and the bad guys prefer death. The incoherence, as is so often the case with conservative narratives, lies in the ascription of intent. Two-thirds of Americans cannot possibly be pro-death.[8] Democrats should be retelling the conservative story to Americans over and over, and calling conservatives on this deeply offensive caricature of the values of the majority of their fellow citizens.

The Republican story is incoherent in a second respect, which Democrats frequently note parenthetically but rarely use systematically to attack their opponent's position on abortion: it is in direct conflict with the master narrative of the conservative movement, namely that government should be small and nonintrusive. It's hard to argue that government should stop interfering with the rights of corporations to emit mercury that is now poisoning the bloodstream of 20 percent of

---

*If Democrats don't start speaking honestly about abortion, however, and about a range of other emotionally charged issues, I suspect we'll all start attending such memorials on a regular basis (until we lose the right of assembly). Today, a woman can obtain an abortion in less than 15 percent of the counties in the United States, despite the right bestowed by *Roe*.

pregnant women while simultaneously arguing that government has a compelling interest in forcing them to carry an unwanted child.

The current Democratic story on abortion, however, is also incoherent. It leaves out the conflict, the reason there are protagonists on both sides. Most importantly, it leaves out the explanation of why Democrats are *generally* pro-choice but then, for some unexplained reason, periodically vote for some Republican initiative (e.g., a ban on particular forms of late-term abortions). Democratic narratives present the same pattern of incoherence on virtually every social issue: we're for gay rights, but not completely; we're for gun control, but only sort of; we're for banning flag burning, but we'd rather have a law than an amendment.

In each of these cases, you could take a principled stand from either the center or the left.[9] But *you have to take a principled stand*, in the form of a compelling narrative, or no one will know—or trust—what you believe. The positions of Democrats on these issues virtually always seem like post-hoc rationalizations or compromises between their *real* values and what opinion polls indicate is politically safe. As a result, Democratic politicians look opportunistic and "weak on morals," when, in fact, they are trying to uphold certain moral positions but just can't find the high ground.

If you tell the truth about what you believe, people are more likely to hear your message. And they're even more likely to be receptive if what you feel happens to converge with what they feel.

So here is a simple, compelling, three-dimensional distillation of what the average American feels about abortion, which can account for the seemingly mixed poll numbers on abortion. As with the principled stands, I will offer throughout the remaining chapters, it is not the only such stand one could devise. My goal in this book is to offer a way of thinking about how to communicate with voters, not to advance a particular political agenda, whether toward the center or the left. But the principled stand I offer here, like those to follow, has several features that any alternative must share. It represents a compelling *moral* vision that Democrats can contrast everywhere with the moral vision of the right. It reflects core progressive values while cognizant of where the public stands. And it is deceptively simple, and in this case readily summarized in three sentences:

Abortion is a difficult and often painful decision for a woman to make. It's a decision only she can make, based on the dictates of her own conscience and faith, not on the dictates of someone else's. But except under exceptional circumstances, such as rape, incest, or danger to her health, she should make that decision as early as she can, so she is not aborting a fetus that is increasingly becoming more like a person.

This simple principled stand would allow candidates in different parts of the country to endorse the same narrative but with variations on the theme that resonate with their constituents (e.g., what constitutes "early enough"). It is up to candidates to decide whether this stand is congruent with their own moral compass, and if so, precisely how to give voice to an emotionally compelling version of it.

But compare this counternarrative to the Republican stand on abortion: Abortion is murder under all circumstances. Anyone who aborts a fetus or performs an abortion is a murderer. If a woman is raped, she should be forced to have the baby. If a teenage girl is molested by her father or grandfather, she should be forced to have the baby. If a pregnant woman has a condition that will lead her to die in childbirth, that's a tough break.

If Democrats started making clear that *these are the two competing moral visions on abortion*, and began enunciating the same kinds of choices on a range of social issues, we could start telling the truth again about what we, and most Americans, believe.

And that truth always comes in three dimensions.

Rebranding the Culture of Life

Mapping the emotional landscape on abortion or any other issue that arouses passion requires distinguishing two sources of seemingly "conflicting" poll results: conflict *within* voters and conflict *between* them. In describing abortion, I have emphasized conflict within voters, because it is the most overlooked aspect of the abortion issue in public discourse, which is usually summarized with headlines such as, "The

American Public Is Split on Abortion." Although that is true, we are also a house divided within ourselves.

We owe to Freud the recognition that more often than we know or would like to acknowledge, we are of more than one mind about the most important things and people in our lives. When I teach Freud to undergraduates, I often begin by asking them who they love the most in the world. The answer is usually one or both of their parents. Then I ask them who can make them the angriest of anyone in the world. And you can guess the answer. For older audiences, the answer to the first question is usually their spouse, partner, or lover. And when I ask who they have been *nastiest* or *most hateful* toward in the last two weeks—it is, you guessed it, the same person.

Why is that the case?

From a developmental perspective, conflict is virtually built into human existence. The people children first learn to love—their parents—are the same people who first frustrate them in ways that make them both distressed and enraged. The first time a child utters the phrase, "I hate you," the word that completes that proposition is invariably "Mommy!" or "Daddy!"

Conflict and ambivalence are built into our earliest social expectations, feelings, wishes, and fears, simply by virtue of the fact that memory is built on principles of association. We associate the same person with different feelings because the same person arouses different feelings in us at different times. This is particularly true for someone to whom we are deeply attached, both as children and as adults. Thus, how we answer a question like, "How do you feel about your mother?" depends on which networks are most active at the moment.

Ambivalence is the norm in political life as well. Take a simple example, which turns out not to be so simple: party affiliation. I was born into a Democratic household. My parents understood the meaning of Roosevelt's New Deal "up close and personal," as his leadership put food in their mouths in the early 1930s when they first experienced the pangs of hunger. My brother took an interest in politics at an early age, and as his greatest fan and admirer, I leafleted my first shopping center with "big" brother (then age ten) for Hubert Humphrey in 1968. I was eight years old, and I remember our mother taking us to party head-quarters to pick up bumper stickers and buttons.

As a voter, I came of age shortly after Watergate but a few months too late to vote for my state's governor, Jimmy Carter, in his first bid for the presidency. (Although a devout partisan, I actually cast my first vote for John Anderson in 1980 because of my concern about Carter's failure to set a firm example in response to what I believed was going to be one of the first, but not the last, instances of Islamic extremism holding the United States hostage.) Since that time, I may have cast an occasional ballot for a Republican in a local election but have voted with my party in every presidential, house, and senatorial contest I can remember. I was thrilled when Bill Clinton was elected, as I shared many of his values, and, like most Democrats, I valued competence, and he was supremely competent. I attended his second inauguration and some of the parties that night, and felt humbled and proud to be there. I've always donated what I could to the party (which as an academic was never much) and to Democratic candidates and causes whenever the phone or doorbell rang.

So I'm about as "pro-Democratic" as they come, highly identified with the Democratic Party, even when I disagree with it on specific policy issues. It's my party, and it sends my frontal pole (the part of the brain most associated with the self and identification) aflutter.

So if a pollster were to call and ask me, "What do you think of the Democratic Party?" you'd think my answer would be unambivalent.

But it would actually depend on the moment you caught me. Over the last several years, I have become highly ambivalent about a party that embodies most of the values I hold dear but has run one strikingly incompetent campaign after another. Like most Democrats today, if I were asked the standard National Election Studies questions about what emotions the Democratic Party elicits from me, the four most salient would probably be pride, happiness, anger, and disgust. And by early 2006, whether I gave money to the party when the phone or door-bell rang came to depend, in a way it had not before, on which of those emotions was active at the moment.

If people can be deeply ambivalent about their mother, and politically passionate people can be deeply ambivalent about their party, imagine what they might feel on the range of emotional issues that capture the public's attention in any given election?

In politics, you win or lose depending on which networks you activate, which dots you connect, and which dots you leave unconnected. The conservative master narrative, and the subsidiary "values narratives" that support and reflect it, has worked so well over the last twenty-five years because Republicans have been able to count on Democrats to avoid issues on which they felt vulnerable and, hence, *not* to connect the dots in ways that would create inconvenient associations.

The conservative story on abortion has a number of elements of narrative incoherence that would show how far it is from what most Americans would consider morality if only Democrats would connect the dots. Consider the abortion plank in the Republican Party Platform of 2004, in a section called "Promoting a Culture of Life":

> As a country, we must keep our pledge to the first guarantee of the Declaration of Independence. That is why we say the unborn child has a fundamental individual right to life which cannot be infringed. We support a human life amendment to the Constitution and we endorse legislation to make it clear that the Fourteenth Amendment's protections apply to unborn children. Our purpose is to have legislative and judicial protection of that right against those who perform abortions. We oppose using public revenues for abortion and will not fund organizations which advocate it. We support the appointment of judges who respect traditional family values and the sanctity of innocent human life.[10]

Several implications of that moral stance would create some very discordant associations for conservatives if Democrats, armed with a coherent narrative of their own, would simply talk about them. Here is one example:

> My opponent puts the rights of rapists above the rights of their
> victims, guaranteeing every rapist the right to choose the mother
> of his child. What he's proposing is a rapists' bill of rights.

This is the logical entailment of the Republicans' "culture of life."
Perhaps the most fundamental right of a woman is to choose whose
children she will bear. Yet in the Republican morality tale, if a woman
is raped, she must have her rapist's baby. She can give up the child—
who is her own flesh and blood, mingled with the DNA of her
rapist—or she can wake up every morning and see the eyes of her
rapist in her child. Those are her two choices. Tell that to the father of
a teenage girl in rural Virginia and see how he responds. It is a deeply
repugnant, and deeply immoral, position. But its repugnance is only
apparent when you make the associative links.

Here is another example:

> My opponent believes that if a sixteen-year-old girl is molested by
> her father, she should be forced by the government to have his
> child, and if she doesn't want to, she should be forced by the gov-
> ernment to go to the man who raped her and ask for his consent.

This is another dot conservatives don't want Americans to connect.
If the rights of the unborn are so unequivocal that they override the
rights of the mother, then a teenage girl molested by her father must
give birth to her father's child. She must give him a grandchild.

Nothing could arouse more gut-level moral disgust than granting
a man who molests his daughter the right to see her bear his grandchild—and to be the arbiter of whether or not she is permitted to terminate the pregnancy. Yet that is implicit in the platform of the
Republican Party and explicit in many parental notification laws.

Those are the unconnected dots, the associative links Democrats
need to create to flesh out the moral position of the Republican Party on
abortion. And no Democrat should ever run against an abortion-is-mur-
der extremist—or *any* Republican, now that this is the official position of
the Republican Party and of virtually every federal judge appointed by

the president and confirmed by the Republican Senate since George W. Bush assumed the presidency—without making those links.

It's difficult to offer a coherent narrative—or to call attention to the missing links in the other side's narratives—if you feel compelled to squeeze your own three-dimensional values into one dimension. For decades, Democrats have been afraid to acknowledge our ambivalence on a host of issues, and we have paid dearly at the polls, for one simple reason: *ambivalence leaks*. It leaks through defensive responses, and it leaks through silence.

The Sounds of Silence

The question of when to avoid certain issues because "the poll numbers look bad" has an unambiguous answer: *never*. If a strategist tells a candidate "avoid that issue," the candidate should avoid that strategist, because he or she doesn't understand how the mind and brain work. As I argue in the chapters that follow, the answer is the same to the question of when to cede regions and put your resources instead into "winnable" states, when it is best to leave a subtle racist appeal alone, and when it is best to avoid "dignifying" an attack made by your opponent. In all four cases—ceding or avoiding issues, regions, racist appeals, or attacks—the basic principle is the same: silence is the surest way to let the other side shape and activate their associations of choice, and if you let them do it long enough, you've lost several generations.

Yet on virtually every issue that arouses passion in American politics, the Democratic Party has taken a self-imposed vow of silence, which has allowed Republicans to reshape our political lexicon.[11] There is a reason no one remembers the Democratic stand on abortion, guns, affirmative action, or gay marriage. We don't have one. And there is a reason most voters don't associate Democratic positions on poverty, the environment, education, or the concerns of middle-class families with the same kind of passion they associate with the death penalty, illegal immigration, or gay marriage: we don't define them as "values" issues.

If Republicans repeatedly link the words *values* and *morality* with right-wing positions on sexuality, abortion, war, and guns, those associations will eventually be transferred from their minds to ours, building a conservative infrastructure into the structure of our own brains. The networks of those who developed and refined the conservative lexicon have metastasized their way into the neural tissue of the left, as progressives have ceded the meaning of words like values, morality, and character to the right. If we fail to offer competing narratives about what is right and what is wrong—if we remain tongue-tied on questions of value—we cannot counter ideologies we consider malignant.

Using both historical data and survey research over many years, political scientist John Zaller[12] has shown how the discourse of "political elites" enters into public discourse and shapes public opinion. As we have seen, when political elites offer a single message—as is often the case in matters of war, at least early on, when politicians of both parties put aside their differences to support the war effort and the commander-in-chief—the vast majority of the public tends to adopt this shared understanding. Political scientist (and sometimes-consultant) Samuel Popkin[13] has argued that this tendency to play "follow the leader" is a sensible strategy for most voters, who have their own lives to lead and don't have the time or interest to study all the affairs of state. Accepting uncontested elite opinions represents a form of what Popkin calls "low-information rationality." If no one on either side of the aisle is contesting an issue at the top of the information chain, why would most voters, who have far less direct knowledge, contest it at the bottom?

But as Zaller has documented, when political elites begin to offer competing stands on the same issue, as when the consensus on the Vietnam War fell apart by the late 1960s, and when the consensus on the Iraq War began to dissolve, people rely on the opinion leaders they trust—most importantly, the leaders of their party—for cues as to what to feel. Again, from Popkin's standpoint, this represents low-information rationality, given that the people whose opinions voters are most likely to accept are those they trust, whose values most resemble their own, and who have more information available to them.

What has distinguished the Democratic Party since the departure of Bill Clinton from the White House is something Zaller could not have foreseen when he wrote his groundbreaking book on the nature and origins of public opinion in 1992: its inability to offer a compelling counternarrative on virtually any issue that matters to the American public. Even in the watershed election of 2006, when voters overwhelming cast their ballots for Democrats, they reported that they had little idea what the Democrats stand for.[14] This abdication of one of the most central roles of political leaders has produced the appearance of elite unanimity to the average voter, allowing conservatives to define what voters should consider important and how they should think and feel about the issues of the day.

The midterm election of 2002 provides a case study of the dangers of the politics of avoidance. Democratic pollster Mark Mellman, who crafted the message for the entire slate of Democratic Senate candidates, counseled candidates to stay away from the issues that mattered most to voters, most centrally national security.[15] In the wake of September 11 and the initial military success in Afghanistan, polls showed Bush running strong on national security. But the polls also suggested that Americans were not enthusiastic about his tax cuts. Joined by other prominent Democratic pollsters and strategists, Mellman decided that the best thing to do was simply not to talk about either issue, and if a candidate had to answer a question about one or both, simply to agree with Bush and "move on." That way, Democrats could focus on issues, such as health care and prescription drugs, that were their traditional strengths. As one aide to the Democratic leadership put it, "The strategy all along has been that, if you can take the war and taxes off the table, we can have a debate on the issues where we are strongest."[16]

On the face of it, it's hard to see how even a one-dimensional reading of the polls could have led to that strategy. Bush was riding high on national security, but voters had never expressed enthusiasm for his tax cuts, and 60 percent opposed them in 2002. So why did the same pollsters who were pushing traditional Democratic issues advise Democrats to *support* a tax giveaway to the super-rich? Because they were afraid Republicans would brand them as "tax-raisers."

The job of a political strategist is not to turn an asset into a liability for fear of a counterattack. It is to prevent or counter that attack, and to be a good enough chess player to have thought a few moves ahead.

The advice to avoid the major issues of the day and "move on" to traditional Democratic workhorses not only undercut everything the Democratic Party stands for (whatever that is), but it flew in the face of history, including recent history. In 1992, Bill Clinton ran *squarely* on the tax issue, by making a simple differentiation that Americans could understand: between the middle class, whose taxes he would cut, and the rich, who needed to pay their "fair share." For Clinton, the tax code was an extension of the country's moral code,[17] a phrase that should be repeated by Democrats everywhere until it is part of the political vernacular.

Whereas the party strategists of 2002 advised Democrats to run from contentious issues on which they were on the *right* side of public opinion, Clinton understood how to turn even a large deficit in the polls into an asset. Carville and Begala tell the story of how Clinton met with them early in the 1992 campaign, noted that Democrats were running thirty points behind on welfare, and went straight for the issue like a moth to a flame: "Boys, they're killing us on welfare. We'd better talk about welfare."[18]

The first ad they ran was about welfare reform, and the rest is history.

At the root of the problem with the strategy of 2002 was that it had all the hallmarks of the dispassionate vision of the mind. When people are worried about their security, you don't cede security and talk about the price of pills. When you hear the drumbeat of war, you don't get out the laundry list and search for the Cheer. When your opponent is running on fear, if you're going to counter with prescription drugs, they'd better be valium.

And most importantly, you don't instruct your candidates to run against their own and their party's most fundamental principles. Because the first two questions voters ask in every election are, "Does this person embody my values and the values of my party?" and "Is this person genuine, trustworthy, and enough like me I can feel comfortable with him or her as my representative?" If the answer to either of those questions is no, nothing else you say will make any difference.

chapter nine

GUNNING FOR COMMON GROUND

★   ★   ★

> Democrats need to know that *40 percent* of our population
> hunt, fish, or watch wildlife, and *50 percent* of all homes have at
> least one gun. This is not some fringe element of our society. It
> is every other household. It is half the parents of kids who play
> on your son's baseball and your daughter's softball teams. It is
> half the people you work with; indeed, it is half the people you
> sit next to in church.
>
> — STEVE JARDING AND MUDCAT SAUNDERS,
> *Foxes in the Henhouse*[1]

I n politics, we often speak of "demographics," such as women or
Hispanics. These distinctions are obviously important. Women, for
example, tend to vote Democratic more than men do, and to be less
receptive to saber rattling then men, although in 2004, soccer moms became "security moms" whose fears for the safety of their families led
many to vote for George W. Bush. As Louann Brizendine has pointed
out in *The Female Brain*,[2] women differ from men by their first months
of life. As infants, they are more attuned to the emotional signals of
those around them. By adulthood, the only emotion more commonly
reported by men is anger.

Although demographics such as gender and ethnicity are useful
for parsing the electorate, they provide a crude shorthand for what

might be called *emotional constituencies*, people who share highly similar networks. As members of the same country, we all share certain networks. Without them, we couldn't understand each other. But the same words can activate very different associations—and, by extension, emotional reactions—in different people. The networks of a wealthy Cuban immigrant are very different from those of a poor Dominican immigrant, even though both may fall under the rubric of "Hispanic."

The last chapter focused on conflicts within voters. This one focuses primarily on conflicts between voters.

Winning elections requires crafting messages attentive to the disparate emotional meanings of words, phrases, images, and symbols to different emotional constituencies. Unionized and nonunionized workers may respond very differently to the same appeal because union members have been exposed to rhetoric and experiences that foster their solidarity. The difference between a successful and an unsuccessful campaign often lies in understanding how to appeal to voters in the middle of the political spectrum, whose networks are likely to overlap to some extent with partisans on both sides of the aisle, and in identifying voters who normally vote for the other side but have particular networks that render them emotionally available, such as Republicans, who believe abortion should be legal under certain circumstances or evangelical Christians who could be moved by a candidate running a values-based campaign against poverty.

A prime example, which contributed to electoral success in 1992 and 1996 and defeat in 2000 and 2004, is the way Democrats talk and think about what it means to be "middle class." Democratic rhetoric about the concerns of working and middle-class families has recently led many to believe the Democratic Party is no longer in touch with either their interests or values.[3] This is particularly the case for those in the most rapidly growing districts in the country, the "exurban" districts (the areas sprawling outward from the suburbs of large cities), 97 percent of which voted for George W. Bush in 2004. Exurban voters typically own large, new homes on large plots of land a commute away from the city. Rhetoric about fighting for workers has only fostered the impression of the Democratic Party as the party of the disenfranchised.

The importance for the Democratic Party of broadening not only its language but its view of the meaning of *middle class* can be seen in the exit polls from the 2004 presidential election.[4] The richest and the poorest Americans were mirror images in their support for Kerry and Bush. Among those with incomes below $15,000 a year, 63 percent voted for Kerry—the exact same percent of those making over $200,000 a year who voted for Bush. But if we look carefully at those with incomes between $50,000 (including two-income, working-class families) and $200,000, economics didn't make the slightest difference in their voting behavior: 56 to 58 percent voted for Bush regardless of where they fell within that very large spectrum.

Neither Al Gore nor John Kerry carried the majority of families earning $50,000 or more, and the majority of American families are now in that bracket. One in five American families has an annual income above $100,000, and more families now earn between $100,000 and $150,000 than those who earn less than $15,000.[5] These economic data, along with poll results asking people to place themselves on the socioeconomic spectrum, suggest something very important about the way Democrats should frame their messages to the majority of Americans: *most Americans consider themselves middle class.*

If we think in traditional terms about class boundaries—about whether people wear a white collar or a blue one to work, or whether they push a broom or a pencil—the old rhetoric captures something important. But if we think in terms of *middle-class values* and *traditional middle-class concerns*, it is no wonder that people with a family income between $50,000 and $200,000 consider themselves middle class. After taxes, childcare expenses, health care expenses, retirement savings, and mortgage payments, an income of $100,000 does not translate into a huge cache of disposable income. Add college tuition, and a family in this salary range may be living month to month despite what sounds, in 1960s money, like a large income.

Families in this income bracket also tend to have *traditional middle-class aspirations.* They want to feel secure in their retirement and to have a few thousand dollars in cash reserves for emergencies. They want to give their children a better life than they had—to be able to send them to the best college they can get into; to help them buy a first home, which will likely be out of their reach for years; and to leave them enough of a legacy that they can have fewer financial worries than their parents did. In a word, most people in this income bracket—which is most Americans—want their children to live more freely and comfortably than they did themselves.

This is why Bill Clinton positioned the Democratic Party well when he spoke of the "forgotten middle class." And this is why the party should target programs to middle-class voters—such as 100 percent tax amnesty for child care and education expenses, not a few thousand dollars that barely covers the gas to and from day care—and make up the shortfall from revenues from corporations that don't treat their middle-class workers well and from the super rich.

My point here is not just that we should *use* words better. It is that we should *mean* words better. And the only way to do that is to know who we are speaking with, to understand the language of their emotions, and to be sure we don't inadvertently use words, images, and metaphors that would have appealed to their grandparents but have a different meaning to them.

Hunting for Principles

An issue Democrats have unnecessarily ceded to an extremist narrative on the right is guns. The vast majority of Americans support gun control, but the vast majority also supports the right to bear arms. Carville and Begala offer a telling tale. When their pollsters asked people if they supported a ban on assault weapons, an overwhelming majority said yes. But when they added a second question—"When I hear a politician talk about gun control, it makes me think he doesn't share my values"—the *same people* said yes.[6]

If we look at the numbers, we get another one of those mixed pictures that so often leads Democratic strategists to run for the hills (or, more accurately, to fail to look for them). In a 2004 Harris poll (the latest available as of this writing), slightly over half of Americans reported favoring stricter gun control laws, but far fewer—only one in five—wanted to relax the current laws. When Harris framed the question more specifically in terms of *handguns*, the percentages became even more lopsided, closer to 3:1 in favor of stricter regulations. But from a one-dimensional perspective, it's probably safer to stick with Social Security and prescription drugs. Only a bare majority supports tougher gun regulations, and many who do are clustered in large ur-ban areas and on the coasts. So guided by their pollsters, Democrats generally either avoid or concede the issue, and when forced to talk about it, they often offer incoherent stories.

Al Gore epitomized Democrats' discomfort with guns in an ex-change with George W. Bush in their second presidential debate in 2000:

> MODERATOR: So on guns, somebody wants to cast a vote based on your differences, where are the differences?

> GORE: . . . I am for licensing by states of *new* handgun purchases . . . because too many criminals are getting guns. There was a re-cent investigation of the number in Texas who got—who were given concealed weapons permits in spite of the fact that they had records. And the *Los Angeles Times* spent a lot of ink going into that. But I am not for doing anything that would affect hunters or sportsmen, rifles, shotguns, existing handguns. I do think that sensible gun safety measures are warranted now. Look, this is the year—this is in the aftermath of Columbine, and Paducah, and all the places in our country where the nation has been shocked by these weapons in the hands of the wrong people. The woman who bought the guns for the two boys who did that killing at Columbine said that if she had had to give her name and fill out a form there, she would not have bought those guns. That conceiv-ably could have prevented that tragedy.

Aside from the usual dispassionate mistakes—the gratuitous refer-ence to the *Los Angeles Times*, the reference to Columbine without of-fering an evocative image—what is most striking about this response is the lack of any coherent *principle* that might explain why he would place restrictions on new handguns but not on old ones. Nor does he justify why he is excluding hunting rifles, although the viewer can in-fer that it's because he wants to get elected. Like Senator McCaskill's response on abortion, Gore's response on guns, which is prototypical of Democratic candidates' hedges on so many social issues, seems ad hoc and defensive at best and opportunistic at worst.

Gore's response ended well, however, with the story about the woman who purchased the guns for the Columbine shooters. Bush couldn't respond to this appeal, which was not only emotionally compelling but revealed an enormous gap in the conservative narrative about the right to bear arms: the fact that it gives criminals, terrorists, and disturbed teenagers the right to bear arms (a dot Democrats should routinely connect). So Bush simply got out the remote and switched networks:

> BUSH: Well, I'm not for photo licensing. Let me say something about Columbine. Listen, we've got gun laws. He says we ought to have gun-free schools. Everybody believes that. I'm sure every state in the union has got them. You can't carry a gun into a school. And there ought to be a consequence when you do carry a gun into a school. But Columbine spoke to a larger issue. It's really a matter of culture. It's a culture that somewhere along the line we've begun to disrespect life. Where a child can walk in and have their heart turned dark as a result of being on the Internet and walk in and decide to take somebody else's life? So gun laws are important, no question about it, but so is loving children, and character education classes, and faith-based programs being a part of after-school programs. Some desperate child needs to have somebody put their arm around them and say, we love you.[7]

To a Democrat, or to anyone listening to Bush's response with even a slightly dispassionate mind (which, as we have seen, is almost no one), Bush's response was cognitively incoherent. Gore was offering a very modest proposal on gun control—simply requiring a photo ID for any new handgun purchases—and Bush was taking a position difficult to defend in light of the comments of the woman who had handed the guns to teenagers who had massacred their classmates and teachers at Columbine.

But to many voters, Bush "won" the exchange, shifting voters' attention—and hence their emotional activation—from one network (keeping guns out of the hands of disturbed teenagers) to several "values" networks—fostering a culture of life (an implicit allusion to abortion), loving our children (family values), and faith-based after-school programs (bringing prayer back into the public schools)—and to the goodness of his heart (something he did often in his debates with Gore).

Gore ceded the emotional agenda to Bush, switching to Bush's "culture of love" message, which Bush had actually lifted from a phenomenally moving eulogy *Gore* had delivered at Columbine just a year and a half earlier. Remarkably, Gore never mentioned that he had *been* at Columbine. With all his debate preparation, it never occurred to his campaign strategists that his best weapon on guns was the magnificent eulogy he had delivered at Columbine:

> Nothing that I say to you can bring comfort. Nothing that anyone else can say can bring comfort. But there is a voice that speaks without words, and addresses us in the depths of our being. And that voice says to our troubled souls: peace, be still. The Scripture promises that there is a peace that passes understanding.
>
> I would be misleading you if I said I understand this. I don't. Why human beings do evil, I do not understand. Why bad things happen to good people, I do not understand. Like every one of you, at such a time as this I go on my knees and ask, "Why, Oh Lord, Why?"
>
> I do know this: at such a time we need each other. To the families of all those who died here, I say:
>
> You are not alone: the heart of America aches with yours. We hold your agony in the center of our prayers. The entire nation is a community of shock, of love, and of grief. May you feel the embrace of the hundreds of millions who weep with you.
>
> "Blessed are they that mourn, for they shall be comforted.". . .

Gore then called those assembled to arms:

If our spiritual courage can but match the eternal moment, we can make manifest in our lives the truth of the prophesy: "that the sufferings of this present time are not worthy to be compared with the glory that shall be revealed in us." All of us must change our lives to honor these children.

More than ever I realize that every one of us is responsible for the children of our culture. There are children who are hungering for their parents to become more involved in their schools, and to fill the spiritual void in their lives.

If you are a parent, your children need your attention. If you are a grandparent, they need your time. If you do not have children, there are kids who need your example and your presence. Somewhere—somewhere in reach of every adult in this country—is a child to hold and teach—a child to save. . . .

Parents, we can stop the violence and the hate. In a culture rife with violence—where too many young people place too little value on a human life—we can rise up and say no more. We have seen enough violence in our schools. We must replace a culture of violence and mayhem with one of values and meaning. It is too easy for a young child to get a gun—and everywhere we look, there are too many lessons in how to use one. We can do something about that.[8]

Had Gore's strategists not been so bewitched by the dispassionate vision of the mind, they might not have put a silencer on their most potent weapon: Al Gore speaking from his heart. Bush presented Gore with a golden opportunity to *personalize* the issue, to put the face of a child on it. With a response like the following, he would have placed in bold relief the callous indifference implicit in Bush's response and the extremism of the conservative narrative Bush was embracing:

Governor, I walked with those shocked and grieving parents, teachers, and children at Columbine, I shed tears with them, and I delivered a eulogy that Sunday by their graveside. I remembered with them the heroism of their beloved coach and teacher, Dave Sanders, who bravely led so many to safety but never made it out of the building himself. I remembered with them a young girl named Cassie Bernall, whose final words were: "Yes, I do believe in God." *

I *just told you* how the woman who bought the guns that took the lives of Dave Sanders and Cassie Bernall wouldn't have done it if she'd just had to fill out a form and show a photo ID. And you *still* can't feel for Coach Saunders' wife and children, who'll never wrap their loving arms around him again? You *still* can't weep for Cassie's parents? You *still* think it's sensible to require someone to show a photo ID to *cash a check* but that it's too much to ask that they show an ID to *buy a handgun?*

Americans have a clear choice in this election. And it *is* about a culture of life. They can do something to honor the lives of those who died that day at Columbine. Or they can vote for a man who, as governor of Texas, signed a law allowing people to bring guns into *church*.

Our Constitution proclaims that every law-abiding American has the right to own a rifle to hunt and to protect his family. I believe in our Constitution, and I believe in the right to bear arms. I spent a lot of time hunting as a kid with my Dad, as many of us did and do. But the right to bear arms *doesn't* extend to felons and children, and it *doesn't* extend to weapons with no other purpose than to take human lives.

Gore's failure—and the failure of the Democratic Party ever since—to understand and respond to Americans' conflicting feelings about guns with a *principled position* has led to a self-fulfilling prophesy. In 2000, Gore actually didn't need to dance the Pollster Polka with the Two-Steppin' Texan. In May of that year, four months before the debate, the same Harris poll that looked so "mixed" just four years later showed unequivocal support for tougher regulation of handguns, with three-quarters of the electorate favoring stricter control.[9]

---

*I took the words about Dave Sanders and Cassie Bernall from Gore's eulogy at Columbine, to illustrate how he could have used his own language in response to Bush.

Why? Because under Bill Clinton and Al Gore's leadership, Democrats had *led* on guns. Between the time Clinton signed the Brady Bill into law in 1993 and the time George W. Bush and the Republicans let it sunset, it had prevented roughly 100,000 felons from getting guns. But by cowering in silence for the next four years and letting the only narrative on guns be the conservative narrative, Democrats ceded voters' neural networks to the National Rifle Association (NRA). And the results were just as John Zaller might have expected: within four years, support for handgun control had dropped by 15 points.

When political elites are silent, the public assumes consensus. And when Democrats lose their nerve, they lose their voice.

Different Networks, Different Targets

America is alone in its "division" on guns. No other industrialized nation has laws resembling ours or a gun-related murder rate (or, for that matter, a handgun-related suicide rate) even approaching ours, at 30,000 a year. The only countries that top our murder rates are those in the midst of civil wars or genocide, and many of those deaths are by machete.

The peculiarly American conflict about firearms reflects our history. The framers of our Constitution were suspicious of a government with a monopoly on force because they had seen what such governments could do. They didn't have the benefit of our 200-year history of democracy and peaceful transitions to power. American attitudes toward guns are also a legacy of our history as a frontier nation. The idea that a family would travel in a wagon westward unarmed would simply have been unthinkable in nineteenth-century America. And the attachment Southerners have to their guns may also reflect networks passed from generations of which they are unaware, reflecting what the historian C. Vann Woodward called "the burden of Southern history"—the fact that only Southerners in the United States have had the experience of war on their own soil and "foreign" occupation during the Civil War.[10]

As in the case of abortion, a substantial part of the conflict reflected in the polls reflects voters' ambivalence (e.g., wanting a gun to protect their homes but not wanting criminals to have ready access to guns).

However, a substantial part reflects a conflict between rather than within voters—and a failure of imagination on the left to find the high ground from which to challenge an extremist, but coherent, principle on the right.

To understand the conflict over gun control, and the silence of the lambs on the left, consider the different associations the word *gun* evokes in urban and rural America. Prime voters who have grown up in big cities with the word *gun* are likely to activate a network that includes handguns, murder, mugging, robbery, killing, crime, inner-city violence, machine guns, and criminals. If someone in New York City is packing a piece, he probably isn't hunting quail.

If you've spent much of your life in any big city, not only have you been exposed to stories of gun violence on a daily basis on the local news, but you may have had some firsthand experience of your own. When I first moved back to Atlanta as an adult after twenty-five years in the Northeast and Midwest, I was minding my own business in a local coffee shop in a suburban, middle-class area when a man told me to put my hands behind my head. Engrossed in my work, I didn't even hear his instruction the first time. But he caught my attention the second time by adding visual and tactile stimulation, putting a long, shiny, silver revolver to my temple.

That time I heard him.

So if your associations to guns are to images of crime scenes, body bags, and scary-looking drug dealers on television being hauled off in handcuffs, perhaps enhanced by a firsthand experience of your own, when a politician says, "I'm for gun control," you can't imagine how any reasonable person could disagree.

But to frame a coherent principle on guns, Democrats need to consider some other statistics.[11] Seventy-five percent of the land in the United States is rural, and roughly sixty million Americans grew up and live on that land. Nearly half of all American households have at least one gun owner, with a heavy concentration in Southern and rural areas. More than sixty million Americans own guns, and they spend more than $21 billion a year on hunting.

In light of these numbers, suppose we replicate our priming experiment in rural rather than urban America, and let's say we use men as our subjects, since rural males tend to have strong feelings on the issue. We prime them with precisely the same word, *gun,* that activated fear networks in our urban sample. But this time, the words that come to mind include *hunt, my Daddy, my son, gun shows, gun collection, rifle, shotgun, protecting my family, deer, buddies, beer, my rights,* and a host of memories that connect them to their fathers and grandfathers. If you live in a rural area—whether one of those ubiquitous 60-acre homestead parcels or a smaller plot of land—if an armed intruder enters your house, it could take a long time before the county sheriff arrives. The idea of being defenseless in the face of a threat to your family is not one that sits well with Southern and rural males, whose identity as *men* is strongly associated with the ability to protect their families.

If Democratic strategists don't recognize the different emotional constituencies comprising urban and rural voters on guns, they won't understand what's being heard on 75 percent of American soil when a Northeastern or urban Democrat at the top of the ticket says he or she is for "gun control." As with "pro-choice," Democrats should avoid labels like "pro-gun control," which do an injustice to the complexity of the emotional landscape by reducing it to one dimension—and unnecessarily alienate half the population. The word *control* itself has problematic associations for gun owners, suggesting curtailment of their freedom.

Democrats should use a simple rule of thumb to determine whether to woo an emotional constituency (i.e., to build their concerns into the stories they tell and the principled stands they articulate) or to write them off: Are their networks closer to ours or to those who represent extremist positions on the other side? For guns, that means asking, "Are they more like us or Charlton Heston?" If the answer is Heston, the only place they belong in a Democratic narrative is as the antagonist. But if it's even close, the job of a strategist is to understand their concerns and map their networks because that map may point to some uncharted electoral terrain.

In *Foxes in the Henhouse,* Steve Jarding and Mudcat Saunders have written what should be the Democrats' Bible on how to understand and win back rural America. They helped turn Democratic Governor Mark Warner into a folk hero in Republican Virginia—including rural Virginia—in part by teaching him the lay of the farmland, and they advised both his successor, Tim Kaine, and now-Senator Jim Webb. They describe in extraordinary detail just what the Republican Congress and the Bush administration have done to rural America, especially to the hunters, anglers, and wildlife enthusiasts whose way of life depends on the presence of unpolluted, undrilled, undeveloped land, rivers, and streams. And they meticulously document the way the Democratic Party has unnecessarily ceded tens of millions of voters who hunt, fish, and watch wildlife by sending unintended signals that say "I'm not like you" or "I'm not interested in understanding your values or culture."

As is the case with so many "values" issues, the left has failed to offer a counternarrative to the increasingly radical right-wing narrative of the NRA, whose position is now the official position of the Republican Party. The NRA refused to cancel its annual convention in Denver just days after the Columbine massacre—with no consequences (i.e., no ads) from the Democrats. Its spokesman, Wayne LaPierre, suggested that agents of the federal government's Bureau of Alcohol, Tobacco, and Firearms are the moral equivalents of Nazi storm troopers—a position that led President George H. W. Bush to resign publicly from the organization but did not dampen his son's enthusiasm for it (or for the dollars that have helped elect literally hundreds of Republican candidates to the U.S. Congress). Had Democrats not taken the bullets out of their own rhetorical revolvers, they might have asked George W. Bush why he disrespected his father's denunciation of the NRA and took their position as his own.

The NRA's stance on guns is the moral equivalent of "abortion is murder under all circumstances." It would not resonate with many voters if Democrats simply presented them with its logical implications and with a counternarrative that seemed principled rather than opportunistic. Once again, however, silence by the Democrats has allowed the far right to tell, without any interference from the left, both its own story and the story of the "liberal" position on firearms, with its evocative title, "They want to take away your guns."

Jarding and Saunders provide some sobering examples of just how much difference it makes when you fail to engage in a conversation with an emotional constituency that may share many of your networks but not know it because you haven't told them in words or actions.

John Kerry lost gun owners to George W. Bush by a whopping two to one margin in 2004. Kerry lost Ohio, and with it the presidency, by 135,000 out of roughly 5.5 million votes cast. Had he attempted to court gun and wildlife enthusiasts, he might have picked up the meager *68,000* votes he needed out of the 3.7 million hunters, fishers, and wildlife enthusiasts of that state to become president. The same was true in Iowa, where he lost by 12,000 votes in a state with 1.3 million hunting, fishing, and wildlife enthusiasts—just 6,000 of whom he needed to sway to capture the state's electoral votes.

Democrats have consistently shot themselves in the foot by failing to link traditionally "conservative" networks—hunting and fishing—to a network generally thought of as "liberal"—environmental protection.[12] The conservative movement's destruction of the air, water, forests, and national parks is by far the greatest threat to outdoor enthusiasts, including hunters, since the Republicans began handing their regulation over to their malefactors in 2001. Democrats do themselves a tremendous disservice by failing to fill in this associative link at every opportunity.

Those on the left also do themselves—and the earth—a disservice by continuing to trot out words such as *environment* and *environmentalism* in public discourse. Not only are these tired workhouses emotionally bland, but they are also precisely the words Republicans have successfully branded as the domain of effete, tree-hugging, spotted owl-saving liberals. Instead, we should be using more evocative, less abstract, more emotionally compelling, and hence less readily co-opted phrases. We should be talking about protecting the land of our forefathers, the air we breathe, the water our children drink, the streams we fish, the game we hunt, the trails we climb with our children, the gracious majesty of our landscape, and God's earth. These are evocative images, some for most Americans, and others for distinct emotional constituencies. They say exactly the same thing as "the environment," but they speak the language of Georgia and the Upper Peninsula of Michigan rather than the language of Northeastern environmentalists.

Al Gore has spent his life studying the earth and how to protect it. That has been his deepest, most sustained political passion since entering public life. But he never mentioned it in the presidential campaign of 2000. Why not?

Because his handlers told him it wouldn't win him any additional states.[13]

That's one-dimensional thinking.

It wouldn't be difficult to figure out how to craft an ad for, say, the Michigan voters about whom Gore's strategists were preoccupied. Try depicting the days when you used to be able to fish in the Great Lakes (96 percent of whose shoreline is now so polluted that you can't go near it), with a black-and-white newsreel clip of a child excitedly reeling in a fish with his dad in the 1930s, followed by grim footage—also in black-and-white, but this time conveying bleakness, not the "good old days"—of chemicals pouring into the Great Lakes. Add the sound of pollutants rushing into rivers and tributaries. Then conclude with a message, accompanied by video in bright sunshine and full color, about cleaning up the Great Lakes, with images of children splashing in the water, followed by a camping scene in the early evening, with a family cooking its fresh catch over an open fire. You couldn't craft a much more emotionally compelling ad for the people of Michigan—let alone for senior citizens old enough to remember when they could eat those fish, or outdoorsmen who'd never thought of Gore as someone who shared their values.

Although Gore shared Americans' positions on gun control in the May 2000 Harris poll, the same poll showed that they thought George W. Bush was stronger on gun control. Although Kerry had hunted all his life, Bush was the choice of American sportsmen, even though he'd purchased his Crawford ranch as a prop only two years before running for president—something Democrats never thought to mention in two presidential campaigns. Nor did they mention that he had stocked its manmade lakes because the river running through it was too polluted to fish.[14]

These are *just the kinds of facts and images that win elections.* And they are just the kinds of facts and images that *should* win elections because they tell where a candidate *really* stands, not just where he stands for photo ops.

This is precisely the kind of information that *informs the emotions of the electorate.*

So how did Kerry, the avid hunter, end up losing two-thirds of the hunting vote to the Andover-Yale-Harvard MBA from Connecticut? (And why, for that matter, didn't Democrats tag George Walker Bush, son of George Herbert Walker Bush, grandson of Connecticut Senator Prescott Sheldon Bush, with that pedigree every chance they got, to undercut the story he was telling about himself as the "average Joe?")

Kerry actually did one "photo op" in which he shot geese, but his handlers wouldn't let the media take a picture of him carrying away a dead goose like a real hunter for fear of offending the wheat germ and tofu crowd who might find the scene distasteful.[15] This represents yet another profound misunderstanding of the emotional landscape of both the electorate and the Democratic Party, given that an angry vegan was hardly going to cast a protest vote for Bush. In contrast, an unambiguous, unapologetic image of *Kerry the hunter* would have sent two very important messages to fellow sportsmen: that he *meant* it when he said he wasn't going to take away their guns, and that *this guy's like me.*

Outgunning the Right

I have described rural and Southern voters as if they are unambivalent in their feelings toward guns, but that is an oversimplification. The position of the NRA—a chicken in every pot, and an M–16 under every pillow—is not the position of most Americans, urban or rural, and it is so powerful today only because no one has offered a sensible counternarrative. Rural voters have little fondness for what happened at Columbine, and they have little true affection for handguns or automatic weapons. If the NRA scares them with its "slippery slope" argument about "taking away your guns," the fault lies as much with the Democratic Party, which has put such a powerful safety lock on its own rhetoric that no one knows where the party really stands.

When a party finds itself caught in a bind between emotional constituencies with seemingly incompatible views, the first task of its strategists should be to look for two things: *areas of ambivalence* in one or both constituencies that may mask shared networks, and *ways of bridging seemingly unconnected networks* to create common ground.

Many voters have both positive and negative associations to guns. Some city dwellers, and particularly suburban homeowners, want the freedom to own a gun to protect their homes and families, and others take trips to the country to hunt, but they don't want criminals to have them. Most rural voters don't want guns in the hands of criminals, terrorists, or troubled adolescents. These two caches of ambivalence, one in the city and the other in the countryside, provide hints about an alternative to the conservative narrative that may be more emotionally compelling to both constituencies than "Everyone has the right to buy whatever kind of gun he wants, no questions asked."

A skillful strategist should also be able to find common ground even between voters who share few associations toward guns by linking guns to other networks they *do* share. One such "bridging network" is protection of the land, rivers, and streams that sustain wildlife. It's not much fun to fish or hunt when your prey have already been hunted by toxic chemicals, and it's a lot easier to fish when you don't have to drive six hours to get to an unpolluted stream. An ad such as the following would put the emotion back into the environment for sportsmen:

[Image: A rugged looking man with a fishing pole, walking along a stream, with his young son tagging along behind him, face turned downward in disappointment. The two continue to walk along the bank, kicking at stones, as the father speaks to the camera, sometimes directly, and sometimes with a faraway look in his eyes] I used to fish here with my dad and grandpa. Always thought I'd take my son here and teach him how to catch bass. [The man is now obviously holding a rancid fish in one hand] But we can't fish here anymore. They're dumping some kind of chemicals up there [pointing] in the Potomac, and now most of the male bass, like this one, have ovaries and eggs. It's just unnatural. [Look of disgust, as the man throws the fish back on the bank, and turns to walk away, with his arm around his son]

> Announcer: Six years ago, you could fish in this stream. But now the polluters are in charge of regulating pollution. Protect our rivers and streams. Vote for common sense and traditional American values. Vote Democratic.

An ad like this bridges the concerns of traditional voters with the concerns of environmentalists, while co-opting the message of the right. It activates feelings associated with the bonds across generations and traditional masculine genders roles. By calling attention to the ovaries and eggs now found in male bass in West Virginia, it implicitly threatens traditional viewers' ideas of masculinity, associates the threat with the polluters, regulators, and Republicans who've put them in charge, and calls attention to the fact that what's happening is *unnatural*—a feeling long used by the right to discredit progressive policies. You don't have to care about the spotted owl to experience the images in this ad as disturbing.

A second bridge that extends the gun network into common ground is terrorism. Linking terrorism to unregulated firearms creates a far more powerful network for Democrats than either network by itself because it establishes Republicans as both weak on terrorism and extreme on gun control. The Democrats could take a page from the Republican playbook, using a "revolving door" ad like the one used by George H. Bush on crime against Michael Dukakis:

> [Image of a gun shop in a rural area. A few "locals" are chatting with the owner and his wife, a couple in their early sixties. In come a steady stream of Middle Eastern men, pulling automatic weapons off the shelves, putting their cash on the table, and leaving with three or four apiece. As the door swings behind each one, the next one enters. The woman casts a worried look at her husband, who shrugs with a facial expression that implies, "What am I supposed to do?" In the background can be heard the faint sounds of automatic weapon fire]
>
> Candidate: [Video of candidate walking through the woods in hunting gear, with a rifle tucked over his shoulder] My opponent

thinks you shouldn't have to show a photo ID or get a background check to buy a handgun. He thinks anyone who wants an AK–47 should be able to buy one, no questions asked. What's the point of fighting terrorists abroad if we're going to arm them over here? Last time I looked, you didn't need a semiautomatic to hunt deer.

An ad like this establishes, through visual images alone, the absurdity of the conservative story on gun control, even before the candidate has said a word. It makes clear, at first visually and implicitly and then explicitly (to reinforce the message), that the Republican's stance on gun control has nothing to do with the right to hunt since the ad is being narrated by his Democratic opponent, a hunter. Not only does the first scene (the revolving door) link fear to the conservative narrative (unregulated guns in the hands of terrorists), but the second scene (the candidate hunting) inhibits the association conservatives have repeated for years between gun regulation and the right to hunt. The ad fosters identification between rural voters and the Democratic candidate, showing him as strong, masculine, and certainly no foe of hunting, while maintaining a principled position toward unregulated sales of guns that have no purpose but to kill people. Most importantly, the ad associatively links terror and terrorists to the Republican Party and its uncompromising stand on guns, showing the obvious inconsistency between two of its central values issues, opposition to gun control and protection against terrorists.

A third bridging network could be readily activated because it is already associated with guns in the minds of both urban and rural voters: *law and order*. One of the appeals of conservative ideology is that it emphasizes the protection of *law-abiding citizens*. Those in the cities who want gun control for the protection of their families and those in the countryside who decry the lawlessness of the cities share the same concern: the freedom and safety of law-abiding citizens and the freedom from the threats posed by criminals.

This convergence of networks suggests a principled Democratic narrative on guns. This narrative can be summarized in four sentences, the first of which defines the core principle that underlies it:

Our moral vision on guns reflects one simple principle: that gun laws should guarantee the freedom of *all* law-abiding Americans. We stand with the majority of Americans who believe in the right of law-abiding citizens to own guns to hunt and protect their families. And we stand with that same majority of Americans who believe that felons, terrorists, and troubled teenagers don't have the right to bear arms that threaten the safety of our children. We therefore support the right to bear arms, but not to bear arms designed for no other purpose than to take another person's life.[16]

Now compare this principled stand to the narrative of the NRA, taken from its Web site:

The Founding Fathers trusted an armed citizenry as the best safeguard against the possibility of a tyrannical government. . . . Some claim that banning only certain firearms does not constitute an infringement of Second Amendment rights. That measured ploy is not new. . . . Our founders risked their lives to create a free nation, and they guaranteed freedom as the birthright of American citizens through the Bill of Rights. The Second Amendment remains the first right among equals, because it is the one we turn to when all else fails.[17]

Which narrative would you rather have to defend to the American people? The NRA has helped elect virtually every Republican congressman to whom it has funneled money in the last fifteen years, which includes most Republican members of the House and Senate, and this paragraph should be used against every one of them. Not only does it take a radical, nonmainstream stand on gun regulation (i.e., there should be none), but it offers a rationale for that stand that every American should understand is the reason behind the Republican Party's endorsement of it: to prevent the men and women who wear the uniform of the United States from tyrannizing their fellow citizens. Most Americans, including those with ties to the military, would consider that viewpoint repugnant, reflecting the views of extremists armed with both weapons and a paranoid worldview, the combination that led to the Oklahoma City bombing of 1995.

Listen clearly to what they are saying: *They want to carry guns so they can shoot the police, American soldiers, and National Guardsmen "if all else fails."* Tell that to the parents of American soldiers and to members of the National Guard and their families.

Most Americans don't know this is the position of the NRA and the Republican Party because Democrats won't tell them. They won't tell them because they won't talk about guns. They won't talk about guns because they have no counternarrative. And they won't offer a counternarrative because they don't distinguish reasonable Americans who want to own a rifle to hunt or protect their families from extremist bullies who know how to push Democrats down slippery slopes.

You only have to worry about slippery slopes if you aren't standing on the high ground. And the way you get to the high ground is with a coherent narrative.

There are certainly alternative stories the Democratic Party could advance on guns. But whatever story Democrats decide to tell must be principled, with a rationale that is coherent, readily recognized, and embedded in the narrative. It must be framed in the context of fundamental American values. It must appeal to a broad range of emotional constituencies. And finally, like the principled stand on abortion presented in the last chapter, it must give latitude to candidates in different parts of the country to define for themselves the specifics, such as which kinds of guns would be licensed or regulated.

Seeding, Not Ceding

Just as avoiding difficult issues is always a bad idea, so is avoiding parts of the country. Aside from strategic "geopolitical" reasons (you don't want to have to count on a quadruple bank shot off Pennsylvania, Ohio, Michigan, and Florida, and you don't want to cede local elections to Republicans who will then gerrymander districts to reduce the number of winnable Democratic seats in Congress), the fact is that if you can't get your crops to grow south of the Mason-Dixon line or west of the Mississippi, you have a tough row to hoe if you want to win a national election. In the immediate future, Democrats need to look for patches of fertile ground all over the country, even where the clay may seem red. Over the long run, they need to plant some hardier seed that can grow in different climates. And there's no time like the present to start seeding.

In the short run, aside from focusing on the party faithful, Democrats need to focus on voters who share many of the networks that define the party's principles but often don't vote. These are the voters who don't come out when they think what's being heaped on them is the same old fertilizer. In the 2004 election, these voters made the difference for the GOP, who brought ten million new voters to the polls, in large measure through what is known as "micro-targeting"—or, more colloquially, "slicing and dicing"—breaking the electorate down into ever more refined segments, and using targeted messages to elicit the right emotions. Corporate marketers use this practice all the time: they collect reams of data on what kinds of cars, drinks, and CDs a person buys; what cable channels or television shows the person watches; and demographic information such as age and sex. They then use "data mining" procedures to identify likely buyers of their products.

Equally important for short-term electoral success are swing voters, both those who tend to vote and those who don't. By definition, swing voters share enough of our networks that we can speak their language if we take the time to learn it. In his reelection bid in 1996, Bill Clinton, with the help of some talented pollsters, targeted Republican-leaning swing voters (e.g., through ads on Christian radio stations in the South) by emphasizing issues and values that spoke to them emotionally, such as reforming welfare and putting 100,000 police officers on the street.[18] In 2004, Karl Rove took the same tack of targeting winnable Democratic voters in Democratic precincts throughout the entire country.[19] Because swing voters are not just found in swing states—and can make the difference between winning and losing a state's electoral votes—they have to be cultivated everywhere, not just in specific states or regions.

For example, the rural farm and cattle country of South Dakota and Wyoming would rarely be considered fertile soil for Democrats. But something has recently changed so dramatically that a well-crafted appeal could likely turn these areas blue as fast as you can say "catastrophic climate change." As of this writing, the Plains states (including North and South Dakota, Wyoming, Nebraska, and Montana) are facing a disaster of seismic proportions that appears to be one of the first post-Hurricane Katrina canaries in the coal mine of climate change. In South Dakota, up to 90 percent of the traditional watering holes for cattle have dried up, ranchers can't find food for their cattle in blistering, unprecedented heat, and farms are being destroyed by the heat and drought. This economic and ecological disaster has actually been in the making for several years, with startlingly little snow in the winter and record heat in the summer several years running, leading to dry, scorched earth.[20] Recent research suggests that because of global warming, American's "breadbasket"—it's huge swath of land that supports the harvesting of wheat—is moving north into Canada, as American land becomes decreasingly hospitable to the growth of wheat.

Anyone who has seen Al Gore's *An Inconvenient Truth* will recognize immediately that this is precisely the kind of catastrophe scientists predicted, which Gore illustrated graphically in his PowerPoint presentation, and the Bush administration and its Republican allies in Congress repeatedly called "just a theory" while they abandoned the Kyoto Treaty. A barrage of ads juxtaposing images of cattle dying, land drying up, and dead cornfields with footage from Gore's movie predicting exactly what has happened and Republican leaders declaring it a hoax could readily convert hundreds of thousands of Great Plains voters to Democratic voters.

This is the kind of event, like the Great Depression and September 11, that turns voters' material concerns for their safety and livelihood directly into votes, especially if the issue is tied to a moral one (destroying the earth so that greedy corporations and politicians can line their pockets). Great Plains voters should be among the *first* targets of a new "environmental" campaign that avoids the old language of spotted owls and endangered species and focuses on *our* endangered species.*

Micro-targeting should be a staple of Democratic campaigns. Democrats should be targeting coal miners with e-mail, direct mail, and commercials on programs they watch with images of recent deaths among miners working for companies with long records of violations. And they should target everyone who has hit the Web site of every nonprofit organization or nursing home that deals with diseases such as Alzheimer's, head injuries, spinal injuries, schizophrenia, and Parkinson's disease, and send some pointed, graphic messages about which party supports stem cell research that could save lives and which party is condemning their loved ones to death by dogma.

The capacity for micro-targeting is expanding by the minute, as search engines like Google provide advertisers with information that allows them to place targeted ads on the Web pages of users depending on the words they have searched and the sites they have visited. For example, in 2006, Yahoo! began using complex models to analyze what their 500-plus million users look for when they search, the pages they read, and the ads they click. Yahoo! users then receive custom-designed advertisements that directly address their interests.[21]

Over the long run, the most important reason for seeding rather than ceding large swaths of electoral terrain is that partisan minds are generally closed for business, and they close early. Voters' positions on issues of values, and their feelings toward the parties and their candidates, largely reflect ideological commitments formed by early adulthood.[22] The greatest influences on these emotional commitments are their parents' values and party identities, but salient events in adolescence and early adulthood (e.g., the Great Depression, the Vietnam War, the Iraq War) can lead to realignments in both partisan commitments and specific values and attitudes (e.g., regarding the appropriate use of military

---

*South Dakota Governor Michael Rounds' declaration of a week of prayer for rain in late August of 2006 seems touching only if voters aren't confronted with the fact that he and his party had shown a willful indifference to twenty years of scientific evidence that had *predicted* the dire situation in which the citizens of his state had found themselves. Many people pray when their child is diagnosed with leukemia, but that doesn't stop them from listening to the doctor.

intervention).[23] Every year new voters come of age, and an emotionally compelling message can have the durability to last a lifetime.

Branding is a long-term investment, but now is a particularly important time to present the public with a new master narrative—and to do so quickly. Roosevelt's message sustained a Democratic majority in Congress for half a century, but neither the message nor the coalition that coalesced around it can continue to be the foundation of the Democratic story.

We are coming toward the end of one of the most destructive administrations in American history, which has taken the nation into a disastrous war, allowed a major city to drown and remain in disrepair, plundered our national treasury, trampled on our Constitution, destroyed our prestige abroad, and increased the number and plight of the poor. The Democratic Party is approaching its last chance to win back those Reagan Democrats who swung to Reagan, returned to Clinton, and swung back again to Bush, in large measure because of the Democrats' failure to provide a compelling counternarrative. Campaign decisions made in 2008 will have ramifications for Democratic prospects in 2080.

Politics—like the market, and like the brain—is dynamic, ever responsive to changing times. Normally, when a party has been in power too long or has shifted, as the contemporary Republican Party has, too far to one side, new ideas and new candidates naturally emerge from the other side to fill the ideological vacuum, usually from just to the right or just to the left of center. They win, the middle shifts, and the center of political gravity changes.

Within the constraints imposed by incumbency and gerrymandering, over time, there should be few genuinely unwinnable seats or states. The nature of equilibrium renders that impossible. As national Democratic leaders recognized, in their choice of candidates to support in the 2006 midterm elections, if Republicans can elect pro-choice Republican governors repeatedly in the three most liberal states in the country (Mitt Romney in Massachusetts, George Pataki in New York, and Arnold Schwarzenegger in California), Democrats can afford to let the marketplace of emotions in a given region determine the stances Democratic candidates take. And if the national Democratic Party were to begin crafting principled stands on issues, such as abortion and guns, that resonated with voters all around the country, Democratic candidates might not have to adopt Republican language or positions in places like North Carolina to stand a chance.

Progress has no starting point. A party of progress—the literal meaning of *progressive*—must meet people where they are, expanding freedom and opportunity from where they are *now*, wherever that happens to be.

When we cede large sections of the electoral map—notably the South, which John Kerry effectively conceded at the beginning of the 2004 race, requiring George W. Bush to earn only about 100 electoral votes on his own—the fault lies not in our stars but in ourselves. The marketplace of emotions has plenty of room for competition.

Nature abhors an ideological vacuum. If Democrats are conceding entire regions, it means that the party and its pollsters are forcing candidates into procrustean beds with "issues" that don't resonate with voters; that the party has no master narrative, allowing the other side to brand its candidates before they can define themselves; that the narratives it does offer are one-dimensional, forcing candidates in red states or districts to make Hobson's choices (e.g., between "pro-life" and "pro-choice") that do an injustice to the emotional complexity of their own and their constituents' values; or—as we now explore—that the party is failing to address emotional undercurrents, such as racial prejudice, that are catching candidates in the undertow.

chapter ten

RACIAL CONSCIOUSNESS
AND UNCONSCIOUSNESS

★　★　★

On August 15, 2006, at a campaign stop, Senator George Allen of Virginia showed a side of himself that would lose him his job three months later. Having spotted a young man of Indian descent named S. R. Sidarth in the crowd, who he knew worked for his Democratic challenger, Jim Webb, he tried to poke some fun at him. But what came out of his mouth betrayed sentiments that were ultimately his undoing:

> This fellow here, over here with the yellow shirt, Macaca, or whatever his name is. He's with my opponent. . . . Let's give a welcome to Macaca, here. Welcome to America and the *real* world of Virginia.[1]

The scene was replayed many times on television and hundreds of thousands of times on the Internet. Webb didn't immediately respond himself, but his communications director did, noting that "The kid has a name," and that he was a Virginia native. Allen was forced to apologize, claiming he'd meant nothing derogatory by the interchange: "I would never want to demean him as an individual. I do apologize if he's offended by that." But the damage was done. Allen had smeared himself with his own Macaca.

Allen never recovered from the incident. His twelve-point lead dissolved within a week,[2] and Webb pulled slightly ahead in the polls by mid-September 2006 in a race the Democratic Party hadn't even put in the "potentially winnable" column.[3]

But Allen went on to lose by a razor-thin margin. By the end of the race, he had regained substantial ground, as Webb never turned the incident into a voting issue. New to the Democratic Party, Webb nevertheless responded like Democrats traditionally have to racist appeals, remaining "above the fray" by sending out a surrogate or hoping the media will do the job for them.

So why do Democrats routinely allow Republicans to get away with overt racial slurs, or, more typically, coded racial appeals? Because they know most people harbor prejudice at some level.

But the operative phrase is *at some level.*

Welcome to America

Confronted with Americans' mixed feelings on race, Democrats tend to speak evasively about issues such as affirmative action, welfare, or crime in our inner cities.* Republicans are well aware of Democrats' conflicts on these issues. When Nixon spoke of "law and order," Reagan made liberal use of phrases such as "welfare queens" and "states' rights," and George H. W. Bush declared Dukakis "soft on crime," they knew Democrats would be afraid to call them on what they were really saying for fear that the electorate shared their prejudices. And so, on yet another set of issues on which passions run strong, Democrats silently cede to the opposition exclusive rights to shape the networks of the electorate.

What both Democrats and Republicans know is that if you dig deep enough, you'll find wellsprings of prejudice in the associative sediments of many voters. But the *last* thing Democrats should try to do is

---

*This was not true of Webb, who spoke his mind about other issues related to race.

to keep issues related to race out of the public consciousness because on matters of race, *people's conscious values are their better angels.*

When Allen ridiculed an *American citizen* about his color, he tipped his hand too low, showing cards most Americans, including rural and southern Americans, don't want to see anymore because, whatever their unconscious sentiments, overt racist displays offend their *conscious* sensibilities. The same was true when Trent Lott effused "without thinking" at Strom Thurmond's 100th birthday party: "I want to say this about my state. When Strom Thurmond ran for president, we voted for him. We're proud of it. And if the rest of the country had followed our lead, we wouldn't have had all these problems over all these years, either."

Thurmond was a notorious racist who ran on a white supremacist agenda in 1948. Lott's remarks revealed so much about what he *really* believed—in 2002, not 1948—that he was forced to step down from his leadership post in the Senate. Democrats should have called for his resignation from the Senate, and had they simply googled their way to quotes like the following from Thurmond's 1948 convention address, I suspect they would have succeeded:

> Ladies and gentlemen . . . there's not enough troops in the Army to force the Southern people to break down segregation and admit the nigger race into our theaters, into our swimming pools, into our homes and into our churches.[4]

Particularly in light of the Senate Republicans' vote to restore Lott to a position of leadership in 2006, Democrats should run ads all over the country using the newsreel of Thurmond's words in 1948, followed by Lott's unambiguous comment supporting it, followed by photos associating Lott and Thurmond with every incumbent Republican Senator who either voted for him or said nothing publicly afterward—which is every Republican Senator. The message should be clear: "Your Senator thinks Trent Lott and Strom Thurmond are moral leaders. Your Senator put these men in positions of power and leadership." Then replay that last line about letting "the nigger race" into our churches—a particularly jarring juxtaposition for twenty-first-century church-goers, who no longer resonate with such clearly abhorrent sentiments—and watch the effects of shining the light of twenty-first-century conscious values on mid-twentieth-century bigotry.

Americans implicitly understand what it means when something "slips through the cracks" of consciousness. When movie star Mel Gibson began ranting about Jews in an unscripted moment with a police officer, they understood that the target of his drunken tirade was not accidental. Questions about Gibson's anti-Semitism had already been raised by what many Americans perceived as an anti-Semitic slant in *The Passion of the Christ* and by the subsequent media attention to the fact that Gibson's father is a virulent anti-Semite and Holocaust denier. There are many things a drunk could scream at a police officer who pulled him over, but the evildoings of Jews are not typically toward the top of the list. It was precisely the idiosyncrasy of the rant that laid bare Gibson's soul.

The media made plenty of George Allen's "misstep," but by showing the video over and over, they also unintentionally primed the networks Allen had intended to activate. It is never advisable to let voters connect their own dots, or to rely on the media to do so, because a message of this sort activates two networks simultaneously: a conscious one about the ugliness of racism, and an unconscious one associated with negative feelings toward people of color and foreigners. The available research suggests that the second network—the unconscious one—is likely, over time, to exert the more powerful impact on behavior—in this case voting behavior—*unless* candidates make sure people view the issue through the prisms of their conscious rather than their unconscious values and attitudes.

In cases like this, an immediate response, particularly one that weaves together a coherent story that includes not only the current incident but past behavior consistent with it, is essential to focus people's attention on their conscious values, as Webb could have done with a response like the following:

> I share with all Virginians a deep disgust for what we witnessed in our state today. Whatever your feelings about race, I don't think there's a decent, God-fearing Virginian who believes that

publicly ridiculing a young man for the color of his skin is anything short of morally repugnant. As the Bible tells us, "You too must love foreigners, for you yourselves were foreigners, in the land of Egypt" (Deuteronomy 10:20).

In ridiculing Mr. Sidarth today, and "welcoming him to America," Mr. Allen wasn't just attacking a fellow child of God, or a fellow American. He was attacking a *fellow Virginian*. In this country, and in this state, we don't care where your ancestors came from. If you're born in Fairfax, Virginia, where this young man was born, you're just as much of an American as Senator Allen, and you don't need him to welcome you here.

Mr. Allen will try to tell us that it's all a misunderstanding, that he didn't mean anything by it. But it's consistent with everything he's done from the time he was a lawyer, when he hung a noose on a tree limb on the wall of his office, to the time as a state legislator he opposed a holiday honoring the Reverend Martin Luther King.[5]

Senator Allen has disgraced himself and he has disgraced our state. What we heard today are not the sentiments befitting of a U.S. Senator. And they certainly do not represent the sentiments of the good and decent people of the Commonwealth of Virginia.

Welcome to America, Senator.

Three principles guide this kind of response. First, when people have conflicting conscious and unconscious values and emotions, you want to appeal to the level of consciousness that activates the right emotions—in this case, moral outrage. Otherwise, you allow reverberations in the networks you want to inhibit. Second, if you live in a state in which most people go to church, remind them of their better angels. Quote scripture. Frame the issue as it should be framed: as a moral issue, and for people of faith, as a spiritual one. And third, when dealing with issues of race, you have to *control the "we"*—to define who "we" are in a way that fosters identification with the person who has been wronged. The issue is not about being respectful to people who are *different*. It is about being respectful to *one of us*, a member of our community.

Out of Sight, but Not out of Mind

In 1911, a Swiss physician named Claparede shook hands with a patient suffering from Korsakoff's disorder, a disabling condition that can produce complete amnesia for recent events. Claparede had concealed a pin between his fingers, which pricked the patient as their hands clasped. At their next meeting, the patient had no memory of having met Claparede. But for reasons she couldn't describe, she didn't want to shake his hand.[6] What the patient knew in her gut—that the good doctor was not so good—and what she consciously knew—that she was meeting a doctor, whom she had no need to fear—were two very different things.

You don't have to be brain-damaged to be unaware of why you do most of the things you do—or, for that matter, how you do them. Try explaining how you know to say *knew* instead of *knowed*, how close to stand to another person in conversation, or when and how often to avert your gaze in conversation. What becomes clear is just how little we actually know about the workings of our own mind, and how difficult it is to put things into words that we normally do automatically without the benefit of consciousness.

In virtually every domain of psychological functioning, neuroscientists have come to recognize the importance of the distinction between processes that are conscious (also called *explicit*) and unconscious (or *implicit*). One way researchers activate people's unconscious networks is by outfitting them with earphones that play different messages in each ear. People can learn rapidly to attend to one channel and ignore the other, at first by repeating everything they hear in one channel, so that when given a list of words a few minutes later and asked which ones were presented in the unattended channel, they have no idea. (Readers who are married are probably thinking, "You needed *experiments* to prove that people can learn to tune each other out?")

But these studies show something quite counterintuitive: that even when people don't know what they heard in the unattended channel, the message may have gotten through anyway. Suppose an experimenter presents the words *taxi* and *cab* in the unattended channel and later asks subjects to spell some words. Subjects whose networks about taxis and cabs have been activated outside of awareness are more likely to say "fare" than "fair" when asked verbally how to spell the word, despite the fact that *fair* is the much more common spelling (because it is more widely used in the English language and, thus, is generally at a higher state of activation).[7]

About fifteen years ago, Harvard psychologist David McClelland, along with his colleagues Richard Koestner and Joel Weinberger, wrote a tremendously important article on conscious and unconscious motivational processes, which was so far ahead of its time that no one really knew what to do with it. It remains largely unknown to both political scientists and political strategists. It should be required reading for both.[8]

McClelland and his colleagues were attempting to explain a paradox from decades of research on motivation. When psychologists measure the strength of people's psychological motives, they usually use one of two methods. The first is simply to ask them how much they care about achievement, power, intimacy, and so forth. The second is to present them with a set of pictures, each depicting an ambiguous social scene, and ask them to make up a story about each one. Researchers then code the stories for motivational themes. The assumption behind this method is that people may not know what motives lurk in their networks, but what matters to them will be more likely to show up in their stories than what doesn't because it's generally at a higher state of activation.

Motives coded from stories are highly predictive of people's behavior over time. For example, the number of intimacy themes expressed in stories at age thirty predicts the quality of marital adjustment almost twenty years later.[9] Researchers have applied the same method to political speeches of presidents, and the motivational profiles they obtain are remarkably predictive of historians' ratings of presidential success.[10]

The conundrum described by McClelland and his colleagues[11] is that these two ways of measuring people's motives—one relying on their self-reports, and the other on the stories they tell—both provide useful information about what people want, and both predict behavior in the real world. But the two methods don't predict *each other*.

Whether your stories show a lot of power motives doesn't predict whether you believe power is important to you. So if both measures predict people's behavior, how can they not predict each other?

The answer to the apparent paradox lies in distinguishing between unconscious motives, assessed by the story task, and conscious motives, assessed by self-report. People express their unconscious motives in their everyday behavior. If they crave power, it will show up in the way they treat their employees, their spouse, or their children. If they are competitive at heart, it will show up in the way they play sports, the way they jockey for position at the office, or the way they look a potential "competitor" up and down at a social engagement.

In contrast, people act on their conscious motives when they are focusing their conscious attention on them. Conscious motives can override unconscious ones, as when we remind ourselves to be tolerant, compassionate, or fair-minded when we have just met someone who has triggered a stereotype. But conscious motives only direct behavior as long as they are conscious—or as long as they produce a clear decision that will be remembered the next time the situation comes up.

Why is this research so important? Because it suggests what might happen in politics if we had a better sense of what's going on both above the surface of consciousness and in the wellsprings of emotion and motivation below.

Coded racial appeals present one message consciously and another unconsciously. They provide "plausible deniability" while simultaneously activating unconscious networks that usually work in tandem with the conscious message to ratchet up its emotional power. If you simultaneously activate an unconscious network about scary black men while focusing people's conscious attention on a furlough program for dangerous criminals, you'll get a very different effect than if you run the furlough appeal without the unconscious prime. And although people may have thought they were responding emotionally to Dukakis's record on crime, the Bush campaign was actually manipulating the strength of their feelings—both fear and outrage—outside of awareness.

McClelland and his colleagues provided the most compelling evidence of the importance of distinguishing motives and values at different levels of consciousness. Other research, however, points in the same direction.[12] For example, someone who has just attended a lecture on alcohol-related driving fatalities isn't likely to stop at the bar on the way home. When we speak of "consciousness-raising," that is exactly what we mean: creating or reinforcing a particular set of associations and "raising" them to consciousness. However, the same person may overindulge a few days later at a happy hour when his or her unconscious attitudes toward alcohol are again active, particularly if these attitudes reflect years of positive associations between drinking and pleasure. And unconscious attitudes toward alcohol and drugs (measured by a simple word association test, in which the person is asked to say what comes to mind in response to words such as *liquor* or *beer*) turn out to predict people's drug and alcohol use over time better than their conscious attitudes.[13]

Playing the Race Card

The politics of race infiltrate discussions of a number of "hot button" issues such as crime, violence, affirmative action, immigration, "family values," and welfare. Race has left Democrats particularly tongue-tied, as it is a matter about which our nation has a three-century-old conflict, and it dovetails with another issue Americans tend to find uncomfortable (and Republicans have successfully managed to sweep under the rug), namely class.[14]

Avoiding being at a loss for words on race requires a willingness to speak honestly with the American people. Perhaps most importantly, it requires being honest with ourselves, because if we can't do that, we can't be honest with our fellow citizens.

Americans' ambivalence about race permeates virtually every aspect of our culture, from religion to sports to music. Americans, including those most vulnerable to racist appeals, do not have *one* attitude toward African Americans. Whether their vote follows their hate, fear, or admiration depends on which networks are most active in the polling booth. And which networks are most active depends on whether only one side is talking to them, and in what dialect.

The music of the Southern rock band Lynyrd Skynyrd exemplifies the complex feelings of many Americans, particularly those in the

South, about race. Lynyrd Skynyrd's best known song, "Sweet Home Alabama," was written in the early 1970s and reflects the attitudes of the time. The song is not primarily about politics, but it carries a strong political message. Neil Young had chastised Southerners for their history of bigotry in his song, "Southern Man". Its refrain, written in the heat of the civil rights movement in the late 1960s, was a powerful indictment of the hypocrisy of those who both worshipped and burned the cross. In "Sweet Home Alabama," Lynyrd Skynyrd issued their "response" to the eastern, liberal, Woodstock attitudes expressed in "Southern Man" (lattes hadn't yet been invented but no doubt would have been featured in the song if they had).[15] In a verse aimed squarely at Young, they told him to butt out and admonished him that "Southern man don't need him around anyhow."

One could easily take this verse to mean that the authors of "Sweet Home Alabama" were bigots, who were unmoved by "bullwhips cracking" of the southern past and the contrast of "tall white mansions and little shacks" that Young so poignantly described in "Southern Man". But on the same album as "Sweet Home Alabama" was a lesser-known but just as deeply felt ballad with a very different message, "The Ballad of Curtis Loew". The song tells the story of a dobro (steel guitar) player who so inspired the narrator as a child (guitarist Ronnie Van Zant) that he would tolerate "whoopins" from his mama—who, like everyone else in town, considered the old alcoholic black man a low-life—just to sit at the feet of the master to listen to him play. With the same scorn heaped on Neil Young, the refrain describes how the townspeople thought Loew was useless "but them people all were fools, 'cause Curtis Loew was the finest picker to ever play the blues."

The song's central theme is that Loew never got the recognition he deserved. He died unsung, with no one at his funeral but the young narrator, a preacher perfunctorily performing his duties while holding his nose, and the grave diggers who "chunked him in the clay." Although the song never states explicitly that Loew's race had anything to do with his fate, in the final verse, the narrator makes clear that Loew was not just a great blues player but a blues player of a particular kind: a man who had spent his lifetime "playin' the black man's blues." And anyone who heard the band's music—including the prominent steel guitar on "The Ballad of Curtis Loew"—understood that Loew's legacy was live on stage with this white Southern band.

So how do we reconcile the Lynyrd Skynyrd of "Sweet Home Alabama" with the Lynyrd Skynyrd of "The Ballad of Curtis Loew"? How could the same band that opened "Sweet Home Alabama" to cheering crowds as a large confederate flag unfurled behind them— not dissimilar to the crowd that cheered for Ronald Reagan a few years later in Philadelphia, Mississippi, as he boomed, "I believe in states' rights"—feel so strongly about an alcoholic old black man who couldn't drink from their water fountains but took the "black man's blues" to such heights that, decades later, they would give him a proper memorial in verse?[16]

The answer lies in the broader networks in which different attitudes toward African Americans are embedded and the different "primes" that activate those networks. In "Sweet Home Alabama," the prime was an attack on the honor of the South, an attack that cut deeply into an intense regional pride that lingers to this day. The inextricable—but to many Southerners, uncomfortable, and hence unacknowledged—links between southern pride and bigotry would be woven together and exploited thirty years later by Sonny Purdue, who became the first Republican governor of Georgia since Reconstruction by playing on white Georgians' feelings about a proposal to expunge the confederate flag from the state flag. In the context of a perceived attack on southern honor and dignity—an attack intertwined associatively with strong feelings about both race and humiliation—the feelings activated toward blacks and carpetbaggers like Neil Young were the feelings of the Old South.

But with a different prime—"the black man's blues," one of the strongest musical influences on southern rock, and on all rock music since Elvis Presley cut his teeth on a blend of the blues and Gospel— came a very different set of associations—and feelings—toward blacks. These feelings included not only admiration for Curtis Loew but a sense of *injustice* for his treatment at the hands of the tone-deaf white folk who couldn't hear the music.

This seeming contradiction between bigotry, admiration, and identification with black heroes is manifest in public opinion polls today. It is, and was, characteristic not only of Southern culture but of American culture more broadly, where Willie Horton could sway precisely the same people who swayed with Louis Armstrong, Tina Turner, or Stevie Wonder. Conflicts in public opinion toward race can be seen only obliquely in polling questions that ask directly about feelings toward African Americans (because people may not know or want to admit what has seeped into the well water of their associative networks) but with slightly greater clarity in issues linked to race, such as affirmative action, welfare, poverty, and violence.

Three-quarters of Americans believe that "The position of blacks in American society has improved in recent years."[17] The numbers are relatively similar for whites and blacks, suggesting that they are seeing many of the same realities—namely that the position of African Americans has substantially improved since the days of separate bathrooms and drinking fountains. At the same time, however, two-thirds of whites endorsed the view in 2004 that "blacks who can't get ahead are responsible for their own condition," whereas only 43 percent of blacks agreed. The results were similar to a Harris Poll from four years earlier, in which nearly half the respondents blamed people for their own poverty, compared with one-third who believed instead that people "are poor through no fault of their own," with substantial differences in responses by whites and blacks.[18]

At the same time, an equally low percentage of whites and blacks— about one-third—endorse the view that "discrimination against blacks is rare." Thus, many whites may blame blacks for their poverty, but they don't believe the playing field is level.[19] And the same percentage of Americans who believe that people stay on welfare by choice (three-fourths) also believe that "this is a rich country, which could afford to do more to help the poor." Fully two-thirds believe that "most people on welfare could suffer very seriously if they did not get their welfare payments." A 2004 poll taken just after the re-election of George W. Bush and a large slate of Republicans who didn't include poverty among their "values issues" found that the percent of Americans favoring increasing aid to the needy actually increased over the last decade.

Whites and blacks report similar attitudes toward work, and although they differ on the value of welfare programs, they do not differ substantially on what they perceive to be their long-term effects. Nearly two-thirds of African Americans believe that "Most people can get ahead if they're willing to work," and three-quarters believe that "Everyone has it in their own power to succeed."[20] These numbers suggest shared networks regarding the virtues of hard work, even where impediments to success are substantial. Roughly the same percentage of blacks as whites (about two-thirds) expressed concern that people are too dependent on government aid.[21] Three-fourths of black respondents also endorsed the item, "I have old-fashioned values about family and marriage."

The poll numbers on affirmative action may be surprising to readers who watched the presidential debates in 2000 and 2004, given the ease with which Bush stated his position and the obvious discomfort of his Democratic opponents. According to a 2003 Pew survey, two-thirds of Americans continue to favor affirmative action to overcome past discrimination for minorities and women.[22] Although support for affirmative action is weakest among white males, a substantial majority of Americans, white and black, support affirmative action in college admissions programs. I suspect this reflects the reality many people can see in their own workplace, that such programs have been effective in helping create an educated black middle class, and that the color of the workplace looked very different twenty-five years ago. But as importantly, it reflects a *confluence* of networks too infrequently paired in public discourse: affirmative action paired with hard work, responsibility, and achievement.

With such a maze of conflicting poll numbers, it's easy to see why Democrats have been talking around these issues for most of four decades, rather than telling the kind of coherent stories our brains naturally crave. Democratic strategists have been looking for order in apparent disorder and have been unable to find it on a one-dimensional map.

Republicans, in contrast, have been happy to tell a coherent, if, yet again, Manichean story, which resonates with their rank and file: black people ought to put down their ghetto blasters and pull themselves up by their bootstraps. They should stop whining about what they don't have, stop demanding special privileges, stop taking hard-earned money out of the paychecks of hard-working taxpayers, start working for a living, stop dealing drugs, get off crack, stop making those nasty rap CDs, and stop shooting people.

In fact, if you had to interpret this maze of numbers in one-dimensional terms, you'd likely conclude, particularly in light of the effectiveness of coded racist appeals for four decades, that white people just don't care for black people, blame them for their own poverty, and see them as constantly picking their pockets, whether at gunpoint or at the Treasury Department. And recent research suggests that this is truer in the South than elsewhere in the country, no matter how you slice it.[23]

But there's a three-dimensional image hidden in this statistical jumble, which not only tells a coherent story (one with far richer character development than the Republican narrative) but does so in a way far more congenial both to Democratic principles and to most Americans' values.

We can only see that image if we distinguish what these numbers are telling us about race from what they're telling us about class and the social ills that accompany poverty—and if we see what they're telling us about some networks about work, responsibility, and respect for those who help themselves that are shared by white and black Americans alike. We can see this image most clearly if we take a look at one more set of poll numbers that weren't designed to tell a story about race at all. These numbers tell us exactly where Americans would follow if we chose to lead with the courage of our convictions and a little more faith in our fellow citizens.

In 2004, Harris issued a release with the following title: "For Third Year in a Row Oprah Retains Her Position as America's Favorite TV Personality."[24] Actually, this was the fifth time in recent years that Oprah had found herself in the top spot.

The following year, Harris released a poll on Americans' top choices for the Oscars.[25] A plurality of Americans chose *Ray*, the story of Ray Charles's life. This is particularly striking because some of the most poignant scenes addressed race and racism, as when Charles cancelled a whites-only concert in Georgia, was condemned by the Georgia legislature, and years later was immortalized by the same legislature when it formally apologized and made "Georgia" the state song.

Charles was not the only black man that year to capture the imagination of the movie-going public. In the same poll, actor Jamie Foxx was the runaway favorite for best actor for his brilliant portrayal of Charles.

The next year Harris released a poll with the title, "Tiger Woods Becomes Nation's Favorite Sports Star as Michael Jordan Drops to Number Two for First Time in Thirteen Years."[26] Following Woods and Jordan on the male side were athletes who provided an eclectic mix of athletic and racial backgrounds: Green Bay Packers' quarterback Brett Favre, New York Yankees' shortstop Derek Jeter, NASCAR driver Dale Earnhardt Jr., and Miami Heat center Shaquille O'Neal. And on the female side, tennis star Venus Williams was first, with sister Serena following close behind at number two.

So what do the polls tell us about the emotional landscape of race in America?

White Americans are of several minds about black people. On the one hand, Americans value hard work and fairness, and they believe that anyone who works hard and plays by the rules deserves whatever his or her talents will bring—a theme Bill Clinton trumpeted from the mountaintop. In the last forty years, as a nation we have extended those values to people of color, which is no small accomplishment, considering where we came from. The poll numbers on Oprah, Ray Charles, Tiger Woods, and the Williams sisters don't lie. The same people who were energized by Sonny Perdue's racist appeals in the 2002 Georgia governor's race also wear shirts to Braves' games with the name and number of their favorite players, including third baseman Willy Aybar and shortstop Edgar Renteria, who you'd think would start with two strikes against them, being both black and Hispanic.

The veneration for Tiger Woods and the Williams sisters reflects not only their extraordinary talents but precisely the fact that they broke into "white" sports and proved that they could overcome the odds and become legends—by playing by the rules and excelling. Rather than whites resenting their success in the last bastions of white athletic supremacy, Woods and the Williams sisters are, by the best poll results, our most revered athletes.

Americans understand that we have made great strides on race, but that we aren't done yet. They have told us as much in the polls: that the condition of blacks has improved dramatically, that there is still discrimination, and that we can't entirely abandon affirmative action without abandoning the gains we have made in bringing African Americans into the mainstream of American life. Americans understand that outside the ball field, the playing field isn't level for African Americans. And they are right: black men earn about $0.70 for every $1.00 earned by comparably educated white men.

If we activate most Americans' networks about fairness, equality, and playing by the rules—and lead them to evaluate racially charged issues *consciously* in the context of *those* values—they will support measures that level the playing field, even if it costs them a little. Few Americans begrudged Colin Powell for the help he got from affirmative action because he earend their respect and served his country with distinction. And most Americans would be very disturbed by recent data—if Democrats would just tell them about it—showing that where ballot initiatives have eliminated affirmative action in college admission, we are seeing a precipitous return to segregation in public universities.[27]

Americans won't, however, support anything they perceive as land-grabs by "special interests" because such efforts violate precisely the same values of fairness and justice that motivate their acceptance of the need for affirmative action. That's why Republicans constantly use terms such as "special interests" to describe minorities. And most Americans won't support efforts increasing equality of opportunity if they perceive them as making it impossible for others to achieve *their* dreams despite hard work and talent. Looked at this way, *the same values that lead most Americans to support affirmative action lead them to reject quotas.*

More indirectly, we can also see in the polls that Americans are vulnerable to what social psychologists call the assumption of a "just world," the comforting belief that people get what they deserve and deserve what they get.[28] Particularly when alloyed with negative racial sentiments, this assumption allows people to blame those who are poor for their misfortune, particularly when many are having children out of wedlock, using and selling drugs, failing to take on parental (especially paternal) responsibilities, and unwittingly starring on local television news shows after fatal shootings.

So what do the poll data say in three dimensions? Americans really don't like people who don't work hard, care responsibly for their children, and obey the law. That's more about poverty than about race, but it's easy for Republicans to activate one network with the other because the two are so strongly correlated in America. If most Americans were *consciously* hostile to black people, they would resent Oprah and Venus Williams, not venerate them. Americans don't like the idea of tithing a part of their paycheck to people who are having children without first thinking about how they'll support them, particularly when they're struggling to pay their own bills. And they don't like having parts of their own town they're afraid to drive through. Link those concerns to networks reflecting prejudices that have largely gone underground, of which many people are not even aware, and you have fertile ground for appeals that elide bread-and-butter issues, values issues, and racism, using code words such as "law and order," "welfare queens," "special rights," and the need for "color blind" college admissions.[29]

When black people work hard, play by the rules, and excel, Americans have no trouble seeing "them" as "us." They consider African Americans like Venus Williams or Tiger Woods not only *like us* but *inspirations* to us, and they have no trouble identifying with black and Latino baseball players. This identification is reflected in our language, when we say things like, "Hey, we beat the Dodgers last night," when "we" includes a lot of people of color. This fact cannot be emphasized enough because it means that barriers to identification with people of color are now highly permeable. Americans are willing to help hardworking people who have been victims of discrimination, but most aren't willing to do that for people who they see as violating middle-class values, and they aren't willing to do it if they see it as "throwing good money after bad" through social programs they are convinced have failed.

Polling data provide a rough approximation of the emotional landscape on race, but understanding conflicts between conscious and unconscious networks on race requires technologies that can drill deeper than self-reports to assess networks that have gone underground. Research on these unconscious networks finds that, irrespective of what we may feel and believe consciously, most white Americans—including many who hold consciously progressive values and attitudes—harbor negative associations toward people of color.[30] White jurors tend to impose stiffer penalties for black criminals. The more "African" a defendant's facial features appear (e.g., the darker his skin, the broader his lips), the more time he is likely to find himself in prison, even though jurors are typically screened for their *conscious* prejudices. White jurors are more likely to impose the death penalty on killers whose victims are white. When examining identical resumes, employers tend to have a "better feeling" about those with "white" names (e.g., Mary, Tom) than "black" names (e.g., Tiara, Tyrone), and they are more likely to call them for an interview. These are all examples of unconscious prejudice, which occurs through the activation of thoughts, feelings, motives, and stereotypes outside of awareness.

A growing body of research has demonstrated how different people's conscious and unconscious feelings toward African Americans can be.[31] In one study, the investigators presented participants with a series of black and white faces, followed immediately by a positive or negative adjective.[32] The task was simply to press a key to indicate whether the adjective was positive or negative. What subjects didn't know was that the length of time it took them to recognize a word as negative following a black "prime"—measured in milliseconds—provided a good index of the extent to which they harbored unconscious associations between African Americans and negative emotions. The stronger the link, the more quickly a person primed with a black face recognized a negative word, because the black face had already activated negative feelings outside awareness.

As in the McClelland studies of conscious and unconscious motives, this measure of unconscious racial attitudes was unrelated to people's conscious attitudes (e.g., their responses to questions about the Rodney King beating and the riots that followed the acquittal of the police officers who beat him). But their unconscious attitudes *did* predict something very important that their conscious attitudes did not:

how comfortably they interacted with a black research assistant who "debriefed" them at the end of the study. Among those with a more rapid response to negative words after seeing a black face, regardless of their conscious attitudes, their ambivalence leaked. It leaked the same way it often leaks when candidates who lack genuine comfort with African Americans try to talk with black leaders or constituents. It's hard to control largely nonverbal signals you're sending when you don't know you're sending them—especially when you believe (or want to believe) you're not prejudiced.

Voters range considerably in their emotional unconscious associations to African Americans, and the same is true of politicians. When Bill Clinton sat with African Americans in the pews of their churches, he didn't have to pretend not to be prejudiced. He didn't shuffle uncomfortably, use stilted language, or struggle to figure out whether to call his hosts black or African American (or Ross Perot's gaffe, "you people"). African Americans know when someone is liberal on the outside but uncomfortable on the inside. It shows, either through nonverbal behaviors or through overcompensation.

Neuroimaging data suggest that prejudiced waters run deep. Recall that the amygdala plays an important role in generating unpleasant emotions, particularly fear, in animals ranging from rats to humans. The higher people score on measures of unconscious racism, the more their brains show activation of the amygdala when they look at pictures of black faces. This is even true when the faces are presented *subliminally*, so that they never even registered consciously.[33]

Findings similar to those uncovered by psychologists are beginning to emerge in research by political scientists. Simply inserting the phrase "inner city" before "violent criminals" into a question about whether to increase spending on prisons or antipoverty programs leads to dramatic differences in the way people respond—but only if they hold negative attitudes toward African Americans.[34] And black Republican candidates are discovering that prejudice permeates the Republican rank and file—not in what they say, but in what they do. Across the country, white Republicans are 25 percent more likely to vote for the Democrat when the Republican senatorial candidate is black.[35]

The Truth Will Set You Free

The worst thing you can do when the other side is sending racist appeals under the cover of darkness is to leave the light off. Doing so lets these appeals resonate with the darkest of people's unconscious networks. Because these networks are generally opaque to voters' consciousness, what they become aware of, instead, are their emotionally acceptable derivatives in consciousness: the issues to which such networks can attach themselves and provide emotional energy, such as outrage at welfare recipients with six kids, people getting "special privileges," or immigrants being given "amnesty" for "breaking the law."

How, then, can Democrats tell coherent narratives about issues such as affirmative action and poverty that might resonate with a public divided within itself? What messages will resonate with voters' conscious values while inhibiting deeply held sentiments most people wish weren't on their own psychic soil?

There are two truths embedded in our unconscious networks that Democrats need to tell the American people. If they want to tell an emotionally resonant story, they will need to tell them both together.

The first truth is that despite our conscious values, most of us are prejudiced in ways we can only see through a glass darkly. If we tell this truth in a highly personal, emotionally evocative way, most people will hear it, particularly if we make clear this is about *us,* not about *them.* If we frame the problem as a conflict between what most of us consciously value and what we unwittingly find under our skin, most people would be willing to acknowledge that they've had a few thoughts they'd rather not show on their faces—or that they may have shown without knowing it. This wouldn't be such a bitter pill for most Americans to swallow if Democratic leaders *take it with them*, if they don't stand in judgment. It's not that most people *want* to be racist anymore. It's that three hundred years of history just aren't erased in a few generations.

That's not a complicated message to convey.

But there's a second truth that needs to be told, or many people will immediately discount the first. And that second truth is about some of those conscious beliefs and unconscious associations that aren't just right-wing propaganda or prejudice. They are associations born of experience. We fail as a party and as a nation when we deny those truths rather than turning moral problems into moral imperatives. Paradoxically, if Democrats were just to acknowledge the legitimate concerns of conservatives—concerns about violence, drugs, absent fathers, and teenage mothers—they could turn conservatives' descriptions of these problems into a prescription for change and their callous indifference into a moral problem. Acknowledging what is wrong in our inner cites—and in many parts of rural America, where poverty and its attendant social problems are just as devastating to children, whether white or black—and making it our national calling to do something about it, would appeal to the values of many in the political center. It would also appeal to many evangelical Christians, whose faith tells them that there is no greater sin than having two coats when your neighbor is cold and has none.

Over the last four decades, the Democratic Party has lost many voters because of its principled stand against racism. Sometimes, courage has its costs. That's what makes it courage.

But Democrats have also lost many voters—including moderate suburban, rural, and working-class voters—by failing to acknowledge a number of realities that they could see with their own eyes.[36] By the mid- to late 1970s, not only was welfare becoming a way of life that was a dead end for its recipients and a drain on the taxes of working people, but violence was turning our inner cities into war zones. The breakdown of the family and the skyrocketing rate of illegitimacy was not just a concern of right-wing, sex-obsessed ideologues, although it was that, too. It was a prime cause of a host of social ills that not only could have been predicted but *were* predicted by Daniel Patrick Moynihan in the early 1960s when he was an academic, and for which many branded him a racist.

In the intervening thirty years, Democrats have done little to convince the average American that they "get it." Instead, when faced with unpleasant facts about poverty—for example, that child abuse and neglect are rampant in our inner cities—those on the left often respond with denial, including denials that are patently absurd to anyone who has ever worked as a teacher or case worker in the inner cities.

This kind of defensiveness about inconvenient truths not only prevents us from seeing the truth clearly enough to try to figure out what to do about it, but it provides ammunition to those who see liberals as "coddling" people who behave badly or as responding to moral questions with social-scientific explanations.

Democrats also spoke too euphemistically about the fact that affirmative action was, and remains, a necessary evil. It is necessary because we are not yet color-blind. It is an evil because one person's affirmation is another's negation, based on a quality, skin color or ethnicity, that most Americans wish we didn't have to factor in when making decisions about people's lives and livelihoods.

Democrats spoke in the language of euphemism when they denied that, no matter how you slice it, affirmative action *did* reduce the portions of the American pie to those who were not its recipients. That group included many who had traditionally feasted on it and who, by all rights, could afford to give up more than a few bites to those who had gone hungry for decades. But it also included others who were just trying to get their own small slice, including many working-class males who were incensed at being called "privileged" by virtue of being white and male as they worked at deadening assembly line jobs.

The problem with the language of euphemism is that it's probably the one language everyone understands.

Nor, as a nation, did we ever have an honest discussion of how and why to extend affirmative action to people other than those who had been forcibly torn from their homelands—African Americans and Native Americans—and suffered not only discrimination (which virtually every immigrant group entering the United States has experienced, except some white people of English descent) but destruction of their cultures. To most Americans, reparation to these groups still seems just and fair. Advocates for expansion of affirmative action *could* have made a principled case for shifting its meaning to diversity for diversity's sake, or for recognizing more subtle forms of discrimination faced by Hispanic immigrants. They could have taken that case to the electorate. But they didn't. As a result, Democrats have often appeared to voters to be pandering to "special interests," a truly ironic designation for people who had been disenfranchised, but one that has "stuck" because of our failure to speak the truth.

So let me suggest a principled stand that tells the story I believe Democrats have been struggling to tell about affirmative action. It reflects a combination of progressive values and an effort to meet voters on both a conscious and unconscious level:

> Our commitment is to *all* Americans who are willing to work hard to make a better life for themselves and their children, to have a chance at the American dream. We believe in the words of our founding fathers, that we are all created equal, and that no matter what the color of our skin or where our ancestors came from, we're all Americans, and we're all children of God. We have witnessed with our own eyes the extraordinary strides toward racial equality of the last forty years, but we also know that our task is not yet complete. We know that because if we're honest with ourselves, most of us can remember those moments when we've encountered someone whose skin color was different from ours, whose accent was different, or whose face bore the scars of poverty, who we judged in ways we would not want to be judged ourselves. But we are a compassionate nation, and we believe in going the extra mile for people who have not yet shared in the American dream but are willing to work hard for it. And for the same reason, we reject quotas, because they deny other Americans their chance at that dream.

This narrative clearly endorses continued efforts to redress racial inequalities through affirmative action (a term that has accreted so much emotional baggage that it doesn't fit easily in most people's overhead compartments), but it places boundaries on those efforts on *principled*, not pragmatic, grounds. It acknowledges the progress we have made toward racial equality, something the average American wants to hear in considering extending affirmative action into the future, but it avoids the use of rhetoric that carries negative connotations for much of the electorate. It draws on shared language and shared symbols to elicit people's compassion rather than their prejudice, and encourages them to look inward for all the evidence they need that the task is not yet complete. And like the narratives on abortion and guns in the prior two chapters, it circumvents slippery-slope arguments and incorporates many of the values of those in the political center, including those just right of center.

Now consider a similar narrative on welfare and poverty. Once again, the narrative takes the principles shared by Democrats and extends them in ways shared by the vast majority of Americans:

> We stand with all Americans, white and black, in our belief that it's time to end the welfare culture, that welfare should be a safety net and not a way of life, and that the way to end welfare dependency is to put an end to the poverty that breeds it. If we can fight wars in distant lands, we can dedicate ourselves as a nation to the eradication of poverty on our soil, which is the only way to defeat the crime, violence, drug abuse, and hopelessness that afflict our inner cities and parts of rural America. The way to win this war is through hard work and personal responsibility on the part of those who want a better life for themselves and their children, and through a partnership of government, business, and religious institutions. That means providing tax incentives to businesses that provide jobs and affordable health care to those who want to help themselves, and creating the conditions for people of faith to *demonstrate* their faith, by partnering wealthy churches, synagogues, and mosques with places of worship in the inner cities, to help build homes, hope, and connections across our communities. And it means building colleges instead of prisons so that poor teenagers who want to work hard and lift themselves out of poverty can see a light at the end of the tunnel other than the dim red light of crime and drugs.

What is perhaps most central to this narrative is that it bridges networks that are usually seen as competing: ending welfare, ending poverty, and doing so through personal responsibility, corporate responsibility, and religious institutions. It offers a principled stand that not only co-opts much of the rhetoric of the right but steals its thunder (what infuriated conservatives so much about Bill Clinton, who repeatedly took conservative issues, acknowledged what was sensible in them, and then offered a more compassionate solution). It suggests something far more popular than big government tackling social problems alone: creating a genuine partnership of government, business, and religious institutions.

Once again, this is not the only principled stand one could offer. The suggestion that government could help bring together religious institutions for the common good, for example, might engender many legitimate concerns, and would have to be handled with care to avoid the slippery slope of state-sponsored religion that the framers of our Constitution inveighed against.[37] At the same time, anyone with any acquaintance with inner-city African-American culture knows that religious faith is one of the most powerful forces for good in our inner cities. The inclusion of religious institutions in this narrative also challenges people of faith *outside* the inner cities to partner with inner-city religious institutions, to put their money where their mouth is, and to build bridges across different parts of town. If members of white suburban churches were simply to break bread with members of black inner-city churches and participate in a common effort, they would readily discover their shared humanity. Social psychologists discovered over fifty years ago that the best way to overcome antagonism between groups is to have them work together toward shared goals.

This principled stand would, however, be very difficult to assail from the right. It is not proposing to maintain a welfare culture. It is about putting able-bodied people to work, dealing with the problems of drug abuse and violence, restoring traditional family structures, and bringing together people of faith to do what the Good Book says they should be doing: helping the poor. This is a progressive narrative, but it draws on the language and resources of the right and center as well as the left.

Getting Corkered

If Democrats were to start to speak the truth about race, they would be free to retell the Republican story on race.

Since the mid-1960s, the party of Lincoln has desecrated his memory. Republicans have opposed every effort to extend equal rights to anyone who isn't white. They have played the race card in every presidential election they have won since 1968. As long as Democrats don't turn racism into a *character issue*, Republicans will continue to use it as an instrument of political persuasion.

Perhaps the most egregious example of a successful racist appeal occurred during the midterm election of 2006.[38] Democrats outflanked Republicans in every closely contested Senate race except one: Tennessee. At first blush, the loss in Tennessee was surprising, given that Harold Ford, like so many of the other Democrats who defeated Republican incumbents (e.g., Bob Casey, Sherrod Brown, Claire McCaskill), was an emotionally compelling candidate. Ford, however, was taken down by an extraordinarily sophisticated stealth campaign orchestrated by now Senator Bob Corker and the Republican National Committee. The centerpiece of that campaign was an infamous ad created by a protégé of Karl Rove.

The stealth attack, designed to fly far enough below the radar to allow plausible deniability, played unconscious racial networks like a fiddle at Opryland. As Corker began to run into trouble in public opinion polls, he began describing himself as the "real Tennessean," using as a cover story that Ford was a city slicker from Washington. The Republican National Committee then ran an ad the Corker campaign predictably disavowed, allowing Corker to claim distance while taking advantage of its effects. Corker then followed it up with another ad of his own that made clear that the ads were coordinated.

The ad that drew media attention featured a scantily clad white woman declaring excitedly, "I met Harold at the *Playboy* party!" She returned at the very end of the ad, appearing as if an afterthought, with a seductive wink, saying "Harold, call me." The obvious goal was to activate a network about black men having sex with white women, something about which many white men still feel queasy (particularly if they imagine their daughter with a black man). Martin Luther King understood the power of this image for white men and disarmed it, declaring, "I want the white man to be my brother, not my brother-in-law."

The "call me" line came just after the ad had ostensibly ended with the following words on the screen, while the narrator was distracting viewers with a different message, effectively rendering the words implicit: "Harold Ford. He's Just Not Right."

When I first saw the ad, something about the syntax of that last sentence struck me as peculiar. What did they mean by "He's just not right?" That's a phrase often used to describe someone with a psychiatric problem, and no one was suggesting that Ford was disturbed.

Then I realized what was wrong. If you were going to use that syntax, you'd say "He's just not right *for Tennessee*." What viewers of the ad were not aware of (unless they were Tweetie Bird, or couldn't pronounce their *r*s) was that another network was being activated unconsciously. This second network was primed both by the racial overtones of the ad and by the broader campaign emphasizing that Ford isn't "one of us": He's just not *white*. In fact, had the narrator spoken the words, the intent would likely have been too obvious, especially when followed by the "call me" line.

As Corker began gaining in the polls following the "Call Me" ad, he followed it with a radio ad, whose cover story was again to compare and contrast the two candidates on the extent to which they were "real" Tennesseans. In the radio ad, music plays continuously in the background, but every time the narrator talks about Ford, the listener is exposed to the barely audible sound of what, with close listening, is the sound of an African tom-tom.

The ads run against Ford suggest that Rove and crew are well aware of recent research on subliminal priming. It is difficult otherwise to explain the tom-toms, and I have not heard an alternative explanation for them.

Unfortunately, Democrats responded to twenty-first-century science with twentieth-century intuition. They lacked the knowledge to respond with the only known antidote to racial appeals made below the radar of consciousness: *make them conscious*. George Allen was heading for an easy victory in his bid for re-election to the Senate and a serious run at the presidency in 2008, but he took a nosedive when he flew his prejudice at the wrong altitude. Bob Corker succeeded with a stealth appeal that largely stayed below the radar.

Harold Ford couldn't have been his own messenger in this case, as he well knew, and as evidenced by his muted response. Doing so would have activated another network that would have blown up in his face: *black person crying racism*. What he needed was a Southern white elder statesman to do it for him.

The person who could have done it was Bill Clinton, who won Tennessee twice and stumped for Ford in the final days of the campaign. A fiery response like the following would likely have shifted the dynamics of the race from Ford's color to Corker's character and put Corker on the defensive:

> Mr. Corker, the people of this state know what a skunk smells like, and they know when they've been sprayed. You knew exactly what you were doing when you ran that ad with the white woman saying with a wink, "Call me, Harold." The first time I saw that ad, a phrase came to my mind that I hadn't heard in fifty years: "All they want is our white women." And if it came to my mind, it came to a lot of people's minds. And that was just the point.
>
> The fact is, you couldn't beat Harold Ford Jr. in a fair fight so you decided to beat him however you could. You started talking on the stump about how he wasn't *really* from Tennessee, how he wasn't *really* one of us. Who, exactly, did you mean by "us," Bob?
>
> That young man was *baptized* in a church in *Memphis*. If that doesn't make him a "real Tennessean," perhaps you can tell us just how you tell a real Tennessean when you see one.
>
> You want to know what it means to be a *real* Tennessean? It means to understand the words of our founding fathers: that *all* men are created equal.
>
> Mr. Corker, the difference between you and Harold Ford Jr. isn't in the darkness of your skin. It's in the darkness of your heart.

As of this writing, many Democrats are expressing tremendous enthusiasm about Barack Obama in his running for the 2008 Democratic presidential nomination. And rightly so: he has enormous charisma, all the nonverbal behaviors that portend political success, and a first-rate intellect combined with an ability to talk to people where they live. But Obama, like every African-American candidate for Senate or president in the near future, needs to study the tapes of the Ford–Corker race, and study them well. The orchestrated campaign against Ford was as psychologically sophisticated as it was racist, and it took no time for Republicans to call attention to Obama's middle name: Hussein.

The only way to put an end to ever more sophisticated versions of race baiting is to understand it, to use the best available science to counteract it, and most importantly, to put Republicans on notice that they will pay for it.

Democrats failed to make Corker pay for it in 2006. But there's no time like the present to turn *Corker* into a verb, as in "We're not going to get Corkered again." Democrats should use the phrase so frequently that it enters into popular political language.

No one wants *that* as his legacy. And no one deserves it more.

But the Corker campaign is just the latest subplot in the Republican story on race, a story Democrats should be telling and retelling in elections all over the country. The constant efforts to keep black voters from the polls, the refusal of invitations to speak at the annual conventions of the NAACP, the indifference to the suffering of the urban poor, the fact that the poverty rate among minority children rises every time Republicans get control of the instruments of state (something Democrats should shout from the high ground because children inherently elicit positive feelings, and you can't blame them for being born into poor neighborhoods), the fact that George W. Bush had never *heard of* the Civil Rights Act of 1965 when first asked whether he would allow the law to sunset—none of this has elicited a clear and cohesive *moral* rebuke from the Democratic Party.

Fearful of talking about race, Democrats have failed repeatedly to weave these facts into the only coherent story they actually tell: that the leaders of the Republican Party think it's morally acceptable to play on people's prejudices to win elections, and that if you vote Republican, you are voting against every principle for which our nation stands.

Virtually every Republican incumbent over age sixty is on record as having opposed the Voting Rights Acts of 1964 and 1965. Ronald Reagan was. George H. Bush was. Yet no one made an issue of it.

Every Republican in the Senate who voted to make Trent Lott their leader—twice—knew his beliefs about Strom Thurmond and the racism that fed those beliefs. Yet no one made an issue of it.

George W. Bush vociferously attacked affirmative action on moral grounds, even though he was its poster child, a man of little talent who found his way into Yale and Harvard Business School *despite* his record. This is a story Democrats should have told in both 2000 and 2004 because it would have emphasized his privilege, his hypocrisy, and his opposition to affirmative action when it lends a helping hand to poor black people but not to rich white "legacies."

By definition, every Republican local, state, and national official who has been devising methods of disenfranchising black voters— whether through keeping the number of voting machines in black districts disproportionately low, devising new versions of the poll tax dressed up as efforts at preventing black voter fraud, or setting up arbitrary procedures that hinder the actions of voter registration workers—is a racist, and Democrats should use that word to describe them. Democrats should pull the white hood off of every Republican incumbent who has not spoken out vociferously against such practices, challenging them with a single question: *just what is it about "all men are created equal" that you don't understand?* Or in parts of the country that speak a different political dialect: *just what is it about "we are all God's children" that you don't understand?*

Keeping people from voting because of the color of their skin isn't "fair game" in politics. It's crossing a moral line. It's un-American. And it is part of a consistent, organized pattern of Republican activity since the 1960s.

That is the high ground on which Democrats should stand on race.

chapter eleven

DEATH AND TAXES

★　　★　　★

. . . [T]he victory that we seek in November will not be easy. . . .
We recognize the power of the forces that will be aligned
against us. We know they will invoke the name of Abraham Lincoln on behalf of their candidate—despite the fact that the political career of their candidate has often served to show charity
toward none and malice toward all.

We know that it will not be easy to campaign against a man
who has spoken or voted on every known side of every known
issue. Mr. Nixon may feel it is his turn now, after the New Deal
and the Fair Deal—but before he deals, someone had better cut
the cards. . . .

But we are not merely running against Mr. Nixon. Our task
is not merely one of itemizing Republican failures. Nor is that
wholly necessary. For the families forced from the farm will
know how to vote without our telling them. The unemployed
miners and textile workers will know how to vote. The old people without medical care—the families without a decent
home—the parents of children without adequate food or
schools—they all know that it's time for a change. . . .

The Republican nominee-to-be, of course, is also a young
man. But his approach is as old as McKinley. His party is the
party of the past. His speeches are generalities from *Poor*

> *Richard's Almanac.* Their platform, made up of left-over Demo-
> cratic planks, has the courage of our old convictions.
>
> —SENATOR JOHN F. KENNEDY,
> *Acceptance Speech at the Democratic Convention, 1960*[1]

John F. Kennedy is certainly not remembered as a "negative" candidate or president. But in his nomination speech at the 1960 convention, he clearly took off the gloves, and although he ran a
generally positive campaign, he was unsparing in his criticism of his
Republican opponent.

Kennedy did not hold back from attacking either Nixon the partisan or Nixon the person. He zeroed in on the central Republican
dilemma of the day: moderate Republicans had accepted the premises
of Roosevelt's New Deal, and could only argue around the edges of it.
But he wasn't content to scorch the earth *around* Richard Nixon. He
went straight for his character. In retrospect, Kennedy's comments
about the man who later would occupy the Oval Office appear uncanny, almost as if they had been written *after* listening to Nixon's
White House tapes.

Investing in an Emotionally Balanced Portfolio

Successful campaigns present both positive and negative messages.
The reason is less political than neurological: it is inherent in the structure of the human brain.

Positive and negative emotions are not the opposites of each other.
They are psychologically distinct, mediated by different neural circuits, and affect voting in different ways.[2] Focusing primarily on the
positive and leaving the negative to chance is simply ceding half the
brain to the opposition.

You can't win an election with half a brain.

Although some of the circuits that create various positive and negative feelings are shared, different neural regions are associated with
positive and negative emotions. Experiments using EEG to measure
electrical activity in the frontal lobes have found that positive feelings

associated with "approach" are associated with greater activation in the left cerebral hemisphere. Avoidance-oriented negative emotions (e.g., anxiety or fear, which lead humans and other animals to back off or stay away) are associated with greater activation on the right.[3]

The distinction between positive and negative emotions has emerged in multiple research domains in psychology and neuroscience. Research on marital satisfaction finds that people who experience little excitement in their marriage but have minimal enmity toward one another other may report the same level of marital satisfaction as a couple with lots of sparks on both sides of the conjugal equation. The same is true in children's relationships, where the stormiest friendships are sometimes the closest.[4]

The same distinction emerges when political scientists analyze voters' ratings of candidates in large election surveys. From a strategic point of view, this means that candidates have to attend to both. They can't afford high negatives, but they won't usually win with low positives, either.

Whether you're on the road to the White House or the grocery store, you can't go far in neutral.[5] A telling example occurred in early 2006, when, after three electoral debacles, the Democrats tried to fashion a slogan that would convey who they were and how they differed from the Republicans. They couldn't find one everyone agreed upon, so they came up with a compromise that was a variation on a 2004 campaign theme: "Together, we can do better."

The problem with that slogan, aside from the fact that warmed-over pabulum tastes worse the second time around, was that it was such a good compromise between an intended positive appeal and a muted attack (for fear of seeming negative) that it activated neither strong positive feelings toward the Democrats nor strong negative feelings toward the Republicans. As a positive appeal, like the similar slogan foisted on Virginia Governor Tim Kaine in his response to the president's State of the Union address around the same time ("There *is* a better way"), it essentially conveyed the message, "We're slightly less bad than the GOP." That's not exactly heartwarming. As a negative appeal, it suggested that things were going along well, but perhaps we could increase the gross domestic product by a quarter of a percent.

You can't grow political capital by investing in low-interest bonds.

Like Reagan's "Morning in America" ad, many of the best appeals—whether commercials, stump speeches, television appearances, or—activate positive *and* negative emotions. A prototypical example is this passage from Bill Clinton's convention address in 1992, which does an extraordinary job of indicting his opponent while associating himself with dignity, compassion, and reverence:

> Of all the things that George Bush has ever said that I disagree with, perhaps the thing that bothers me most is how he derides and degrades the American tradition of seeing and seeking a better future. He mocks it as the "vision thing."
>
> But just remember what the Scripture says: "Where there is no vision, the people perish."
>
> I hope nobody in this great hall tonight, or in our beloved country has to go through tomorrow without a vision. I hope no one ever tries to raise a child without a vision. I hope nobody ever starts a business or plants a crop in the ground without a vision. For where there is no vision, the people perish.
>
> One of the reasons we have so many children in so much trouble in so many places in this nation is because they have seen so little opportunity, so little responsibility, so little loving, caring community, that they literally cannot imagine the life we are calling them to lead.
>
> And so I say again: Where there is no vision, America will perish. . . .[6]

Courage Under Fire

Political strategists and media advisors often make use of the "message grid," which consists of four simple questions every campaign should ask at the beginning: What will I tell voters about me? What will I say about my opponent? What will my opponent tell voters about himself or herself? What will my opponent say about me?[7]

From a psychological point of view, this grid emphasizes two essential points. First, campaigns are about managing positive and nega-

tive feelings toward *both* candidates. Successful candidates create enthusiasm toward themselves *and* negative feelings toward their opponents (whether about their principles, character, competence, or close
association to other people who have earned the public's disrespect),
and they effectively anticipate and counter their opponents' positive
and negative messages.

Second, emotionally compelling campaigns tell good stories. Associations don't "stick" in voters' minds unless they're embedded in coherent narratives. And they stick all too well if the other side tells
stories that go unanswered.

Campaign strategists who start with a dispassionate vision of the
mind, like the ones who advised both Al Gore and John Kerry, tend to
lose in all four quadrants of the grid because they don't realize the importance of either emotions or storytelling. As someone who closely
watched both campaigns, I can readily recite the stories told by the
Bush campaign about all three men—Gore, Kerry, and Bush—but if
Gore and Kerry offered a coherent story about either themselves or
Bush, I can't recall it.

Kerry had a very compelling story he *could* have told about himself, which would have undercut the stories Bush was telling about
both himself and his Democratic challenger. The story of who John
Kerry was and why he should be president might have had the title,
"Courage Under Fire," and would have gone something like this:

> These are times when we need a strong leader, who knows what
> war is like, not in the abstract but up close and personal. We need
> a leader who knows what to do when someone is firing at you.
> But we also need a leader who has held a dying comrade in his
> arms, who truly understands what it means when he signs an or-
> der to send your children into harm's way.
>
> My father was a diplomat, and I was a soldier, and I learned
> from both of those experiences that strength lies not just in boots
> on the ground but in knowing when to talk and when the time
> for talk is over. When I was a young boy, I remember standing in
> awe at the Berlin Wall. I learned then what despotism looks like,
> and why the world needs America to be strong and resolute, to

stand up to those who threaten our freedom and who have to put up a wall to fence their own people in.

When I was a young man, I enlisted in the Vietnam War, and I put my life on the line for my men. I was awarded the Purple Heart for courage under fire. But to be honest, it took greater courage to do what I did when I came home.

In Vietnam, I saw what happens when you face an enemy that doesn't wear a uniform. I saw what happens when you never know whether the child walking toward you is desperate for food or carrying his older brother's grenade. I saw what happens when the other side doesn't follow the rules of war, doesn't believe in the Geneva Conventions, and tortures what it considers enemy combatants. And I saw what happens when our government doesn't have a clear plan and a clear exit strategy.

So when I came back home, I stood before the most powerful body in the world, the United States Senate, and with the moral authority of someone who had not evaded his duty to his country but had served honorably, I testified about what I had seen—about how our policies were destroying not only the Vietnamese people, including millions of innocent children—but also the hearts, limbs, minds, and lives of our own men, who were trapped in a war waged without a clear plan for either victory or exit.

In Vietnam, I did whatever I could to save the lives of the men under my command. But now it was time to try to spare the lives of the tens of thousands more who had not yet been sent and who wouldn't be coming home.

That's what a leader does. He shows courage under fire, whether it's on the battlefield or in the United States Senate.

We need a leader who isn't afraid to fight with bombs and bullets, but who knows that courage doesn't mean talking tough, it means being tough. In a world in which our enemies know no borders, we need a commander in chief who knows that our strength lies not just in our might but in our right.

We need a commander in chief who can command not just our own troops but the respect of our allies, and of nations all around the world, who know what America stands for, and what we won't stand for.

From the standpoint of the message grid, this simple narrative would have told a powerful story about Kerry's strength and courage, the most important qualities he needed to convey in the first presidential election after September 11. Without mentioning George W. Bush by name, it repeatedly undercut the message Bush was telling about himself, that he was strong and resolute, that he was a hero. It undercut his go-it-alone foreign policy, by redefining strength as both military strength and the ability to lead other nations.

In the first three quadrants of the message grid—the story Kerry wanted to tell about himself, the story his opponent wanted to tell about himself, and the story Kerry wanted to tell about his opponent—it offered two emotionally powerful narratives: one about Kerry's strength and the other about Bush's weakness. Without ever mentioning the president, simply by juxtaposing their life histories, it recast Bush as Oz, a tiny little man projecting an image of the all-powerful wizard of terror.

Most importantly, it told the truth.

This simple story about "John Kerry: Courage under Fire" would have also accomplished something very important in that crucial fourth quadrant of the message grid: it would have undercut the story George W. Bush wanted to tell about John Kerry. By the time Kerry emerged as the likely Democratic nominee, the Bush campaign was already telling the story that he was weak, that he sold out our veterans by testifying before the Senate and describing the atrocities they committed, and that he was not resolute in his convictions. Kerry needed to define what the Bush team wanted to cast as his first and most fatal "flip-flop"—his service in Vietnam followed by his testimony before the Senate—as reflecting a single underlying quality: courage under fire.

Kerry could have taken that message to veterans' groups all over America, a "demographic" he managed to lose handily to a man who had evaded the draft. Displaying courage under fire yet again, he could have told those veterans:

You may not agree with me on Vietnam. Many of us fought there, and we have different opinions about the path our government should have taken. All of us wanted to win that war, but after years of fighting without a clear strategy for victory, we disagreed on what to do next. If those differences forty years later make you want to vote for a man who chose not to fight when called, you have to follow your own moral compass, and I respect your decision. But I would never doubt in you what you should never doubt in me: that what we share as veterans is our love of country, our willingness to serve and die for our nation, and the memories of those who fought bravely by our side but never returned to freedom's shores.

By taking this message to veterans groups, Kerry would have redefined the "we," not as those on one side or the other of the Vietnam conflict, but as veterans who, unlike the president, had risked their lives for their country. And by taking this message to a group he knew included many who had negative preconceptions of him because of his Senate testimony, he would have let them know that he was a man of conviction, even if his conviction was not theirs, and he would have emanated strength.

What is deeply disturbing is how easy it was to write "John Kerry: Courage Under Fire." It took fifteen minutes. And it is equally disheartening to realize how easy it would have been to write it in 2004 by simply sticking the message grid in front of Kerry's emotionally tone-deaf campaign team and firing anyone who couldn't figure out which way was up.

Principles of Managing an Emotional Portfolio

From a psychological standpoint, the primary goal of every campaign appeal should be to elicit emotions that *move the electorate*. And that means activating, reinforcing, and creating networks that associate your candidate or party with positive emotions and the opposition with negative emotions.

In the first part of this book, I laid out a vision of mind and brain that places networks and narratives at the heart of electoral success, and the chapters that followed have laid out the implications of this view for running winning elections. Successful campaigns build on a strong party brand defined by core values, address conflicts within and between voters, offer principled stands on issues that matter to voters, attend to both conscious and unconscious values and attitudes, activate and inhibit networks associated with positive and negative emotions, and, perhaps most importantly, speak the truth to voters in a way that is emotionally compelling.

The remainder of this chapter describes four principles for managing emotional associations designed to guide the construction of persuasive political appeals, from the master narratives candidates use to frame their campaigns to the specific messages contained in direct mail, television, or Internet appeals. These principles are based on the best available science as well as an analysis of successful political ads and rhetoric from the right, left, and center.* They are not the only such principles, but they are among the most important.[8] Whether implicitly or explicitly, Republicans understand and use most of these principles, whereas Democrats too seldom use any of them.

Principle 1: If You Don't Feel It, Don't Use It

The point of every ad, stump speech, position statement, or page on a candidate's Web site should be to elicit a specific emotion or set of emotions. This is the first and most important principle of political persuasion. As the great unsung political strategist Ella Fitzgerald put it, "It don't mean a thing if it ain't got that swing."

Every time campaign strategists craft an appeal, they should be thinking about what they want voters *to feel* after hearing or seeing it. Campaign messages should inform voters, but they should inform their hearts as well as their minds.

---

*Most of these principles apply to positive and negative appeals, and most of them apply to virtually every form of persuasion, from marketing to effective leadership.

It isn't easy to give up beloved phrases. But progressives have to stop using the kind of language that has left the left so right but so wrong, such as "Poverty is a serious social problem," "We have to do more to protect the environment," and "Income disparities in the country have increased at an alarming rate." If you didn't feel anything as you read those phrases, you're not alone.

This doesn't mean those on the left have to give up their values and principles to win elections. It means they have to describe them with *emotional clarity*.

The Contract with America in 1994 was a superbly constructed document for establishing the Republican Party's message, taking as its starting point the values and concerns of Republicans running for office, and then honing the language they used to appeal to the American public with a combination of good intuition and good science.[9] Newt Gingrich asked Frank Luntz, then a rising Republican pollster and consultant with an extraordinary intuitive understanding of how to use words to activate emotions, to poll all Republicans running for the House on what they considered the top agenda items for the party. Using the "top ten" list with the most support, Luntz then market-tested different versions of each item until he found the right wording that would "sell" to the American public.

For example, he discovered that cutting the "estate tax" didn't turn people's dials (he was one of the prime proponents of the "dial group" now seen on television, in which people turn a dial indicating their feelings as they hear certain "pitches"), but the "death tax" sure did.[10] Luntz then provided Republican candidates with a pamphlet providing them the vocabulary with which to speak to voters, based on both his dial-a-message device and his gut-level ability to hear the emotional music behind even seemingly monotonic, emotionless issues, such as budget balancing.

And he and others have been doing this for the GOP ever since, generating what he has called *Words That Work*.[11]

The Contract with America was exemplary in its emotional clarity. It was literally written as a contract, in a language that resembled the Declaration of Independence and capitalized on the association. Each plank had a name, and each name was written in a way that no sensible person could oppose the sentiment. As a result, every title evoked an intended set of associations and "set the mood" before the reader even read what followed.

Consider three planks from the Contract, each of which was linked (for those who wanted to go further) to a more thorough description or an actual bill:

> **The Fiscal Responsibility Act:** A balanced budget/tax limitation amendment and a legislative line-item veto to restore fiscal responsibility to an out-of-control Congress, requiring them to live under the same budget constraints as families and businesses.

> **The Job Creation and Wage Enhancement Act:** Small business incentives, capital gains cut and indexation, neutral cost recovery, risk assessment/cost-benefit analysis, strengthening the Regulatory Flexibility Act and unfunded mandate reform to create jobs and raise worker wages.

> **The Common Sense Legal Reform Act:** "Loser pays" laws, reasonable limits on punitive damages and reform of product liability laws to stem the endless tide of litigation.[12]

What is striking about the Contract is how well it evokes values and goals with which most Americans would agree at face value—unless they read the fine print.[13] Who could be against "Job Creation and Wage Enhancement"? And who could be against small business incentives and raising worker wages? Of course, the devil is in the details. You wouldn't know that this plank of the Contract came along with Republican opposition to any increase in the minimum wage.

Although in retrospect the Contract was too heavily loaded with "inside politics" terms (e.g., "neutral cost recovery"), not only its common-sense tone but its use of metaphors is central to its emotional appeal. Consider the "Common Sense Legal Reform Act," a title that creates an immediate context for understanding—and feeling about—what follows. Changing product liability laws will "stem the endless tide of litigation," a metaphor that leads the reader to imagine a billowing ocean, taking us all under with a sea of lawsuits. It doesn't mention that the poor beachgoers who are drowning in that sea are mostly wealthy corporations.

Democrats don't need to emulate the Orwellian Newspeak characteristic of some of the planks embedded in the Contract. As the linguist George Lakoff has suggested, when Democrats hear what sounds like Newspeak (euphemistically describing something as its opposite) from conservatives, they should use that as a clue that Republicans are hiding a vulnerability.[14] But Democrats should study the Contract closely for the way it turns emotionally neutral language into emotionally evocative language through simple turns of phrase and metaphors that have rich emotional overtones (i.e., that activate emotion-laden networks).

That starts with the titles. Republicans don't propose legislation without a name, and they make sure that the name, chosen to suit their purposes, is how a bill or act will be referred to. In so doing, they not only get free advertising, but they frame the terms of the debate. If you go to the Department of Education's Web site looking for the "No Child Left Behind Act," you get what is essentially a paid advertisement for the Republican Party—paid for by the American taxpayer. At the top of the page describing the act you see an American flag with the face of a child, accompanied by the following words: "Signed by President George W. Bush on January 8, 2002, the No Child Left Behind Act gives our schools historic educational reform based on:

☆ Stronger Accountability for Results

☆ More Freedom for States and Communities

☆ Encouraging Proven Education Methods

☆ More Choices for Parents"[15]

Each bulleted point is hyperlinked to a Web page that allows interested readers to dig slightly deeper. Although I presume it must be there somewhere, I couldn't find the statute number anywhere on any of the links, or any other name for the legislation. So ever since its passage, Republicans, Democrats, and the media have all referred to the act with a name specifically crafted by the Bush campaign and the Republican Party to market its product—not just education reform, but this particular president and this particular party and their effort to capture a traditionally Democratic "issue." If you read the bulleted links carefully, you recognize that they all relate exquisitely to the conservative master narrative.

Now *that* is branding—requiring Pepsi executives to refer to Coke as "The Real Thing"—and using their own advertising budget to do it.

Whenever Democrats refer to No Child Left Behind, even to attack it, they are reinforcing its feel-good message and contributing to the fortunes of the Republican Party because they are reinforcing the networks it was designed to draw upon and create. The same is true of the notoriously Orwellian "Clear Skies Act" of 2003, designed by America's leading polluters.

When Democrats introduce an issue or bill, they need to give it a name that is evocative, suggests why it should be passed, makes opposition to it difficult because of the values it expresses (after all, who would want a child left behind or dirty skies?), and relates it to the party's master narrative. Democrats should avoid using inside-the-beltway phrases such as "McCain-Feingold" either to name a bill or to refer to it in public. Such terms evoke nothing (other than, in this case, perhaps a joke about a Jew and an Irishman) and create distance between them, as "Washington insiders," and their constituents.

To see how Democrats could give Republicans a taste of their own medicine, consider the Flag Burning Amendment Republicans have run up the flagpole every year at election time for decades. This amendment is by far the most vapid of the symbolic "Democrat-baiting" legislative initiatives introduced between 1994 and 2006 when Republicans gained control of the House. It was designed for no purpose other than to put Democrats on record as opposing something for which they can be attacked (in this case, something of no real significance, since virtually no one has burned a flag in the United States since the Vietnam War, and that was forty years ago).

Democrats have repeatedly been, or felt, compelled to take stands on such "issues," which usually put them on the defensive. For example, Senator Hillary Clinton took the position that she would support a *law* banning flag burning but didn't believe the issue rose to the level of a constitutional amendment. Although one can certainly make an argument for such a position, to the average voter it seems like hairsplitting. If you *really* want to stop flag burning and avoid the inevitable legal challenges to it, why not go for the real thing? Positions such as this cede morality and patriotism to the right and leave Democrats looking like Republican-lite.

So suppose, instead, when Republicans introduced this amendment during the Iraq War in 2004 and 2006, Democrats had offered their own amendment to the Constitution, designed to address an issue that was *not* trivial:

> **The Flag-Hiding Amendment**: The Bush administration has taken the unprecedented action of refusing to allow the flag-draped coffins of the thousands of soldiers returning from Iraq to be seen publicly, instead whisking their coffins into the United States under cover of darkness. Mothers and wives of soldiers killed in action have had to lodge lawsuits—all of them unsuccessful, as conservative activist judges have turned them down—for the simple right to meet the bodies of their dead sons and husbands as they return to U.S. air force bases.[16] At the same time, with an average of two flags burned in the United States per year, the Republicans in Congress have voted repeatedly for a flag-burning amendment to the Constitution. We propose instead a *Flag-Hiding Amendment to the Constitution*, which would prevent government officials from hiding the flag-draped coffins of brave American soldiers as they return to their native soil in defense of our freedom. We are deeply proud of our fallen heroes, and we should not be playing public relations games with their honor.

Whether or not such a proposal rises to the level of a constitutional amendment, it underscores the cynicism of a flag-burning amendment while the memories of men and women who served their country are being desecrated as part of a public relations campaign. And perhaps most importantly, it insures that the public *sees* and *feels*, in a daily and visceral way, what the costs of war are so they can weigh those costs against its benefits (including the costs and benefits of Bush's post–election "surge" in U.S. troops). What ended the Vietnam War—and what *should* have ended it—were the feelings engendered by daily images of body bags on the evening news. Such images spoke far more loudly to the voting public than statistics about war dead. Democrats could present such a proposal in 2008 against Republican incumbents who championed or voted for the flag-burning amendment while remaining silent about what was happening to *their own constituents' children*— which includes most Republican incumbents.

Principle 2: Frame Messages for Emotional Impact

George Lakoff has written masterfully about the importance of "framing" issues so that they elicit the right connotations and of the dangers of inadvertently accepting the other party's framing of an issue.[17] As Lakoff[18] notes, framing people's attributes as *choices* renders their actions capable of moral condemnation and makes it easier to abridge their liberty. That's why right-wing religious groups are so intent on denying the clear scientific evidence for the genetics of homosexuality. If homosexuality is strongly influenced by genes, you can't hate people for their sexual orientation, and you have to struggle with the question of why God gave some people gay genes.

Conservatives have gone a step further in framing homosexuality as a *lifestyle*. This is a particularly insidious frame, similar to an unconscious appeal to racial prejudice, because it not only suggests choice but activates implicit associations to promiscuity among single gay males (and images of gay men having anonymous sex with each other at peep shows). The problem with the frame becomes clear if you try to think of heterosexuality as a lifestyle. What is the heterosexual lifestyle? The lifestyle depicted in *Sex and the City* or *Desperate Housewives*? Or the lifestyle of the couple with young children at home, who plop down in front of the tube at the end of the day to watch reruns of *Sex and the City* or make sure they record *Desperate Housewives* because they can't stay up that late when they know the children will be up at five o'clock in the morning?

Frames influence not only what people think and feel about an issue but what they *don't* think about.* As media analyst Kathleen Hall Jamieson and her colleagues use the term, with an analogy to *picture frames,* a frame literally determines what is and is not in view. Thus, by framing the Iraq War as a war of liberation and part of the broader war on terror, all the carnage and destruction in Iraq became so invisible that U.S. journalists rarely even ventured a guess about how many Iraqis had died in the initial "liberation" and subsequent occupation of Iraq (something not called an occupation, or a civil war, until long after both labels were the obviously more appropriate frames).[19]

Compare this with the frames used to describe the war in Lebanon that began when Hezbollah guerillas crossed the border into Israel and killed and kidnapped several Israeli soldiers in 2006. One could certainly have framed the war that ensued as analogous to the attack by al Qaeda on September 11, in which a terrorist organization, unprovoked, attacked the citizens of a democratic country on their native soil. Yet news coverage focused extensively on the civilian casualties of the war on the Lebanese side, showing their bloodied bodies, interviewing them, focusing on children killed, and most importantly, *giving them names.* They were in the frame. Several reports even used the term, "The Israeli-Hezbollah conflict." Yet never has an American journalist referred to the "war on terror" as "the United States-al Qaeda conflict"—a frame that would suggest two equal sides, with equal legitimacy, and an equal claim to be heard.

Americans are of many minds about the legitimacy of Israeli counterattacks in Lebanon and elsewhere, but my point is simply that the

---

*Readers familiar with popular writing on framing may wonder why I have introduced the language of networks in this book rather than sticking with the now more familiar concept of frames. Although I suspect one could get to many of the same places with the frame concept, the language of networks has a number of advantages, including its more direct links to the way the brain works and its ability to address conflicts among and within networks, conflicts and compromises among conscious and unconscious networks, nonlinguistic networks involving sounds and images, and, most importantly, emotions associated through learning and experience with ideas and images encoded on networks. None of this is to diminish the concept of frames, which has proven useful in multiple domains, including politics.

media have wide latitude in the frames they employ, that these frames, in turn, determine the frames used by the electorate, and that a party cannot compete in elections if it leaves media frames to chance. In contemporary American politics, "leaving it to chance" invariably means leaving it to conservatives, who have spent years creating frames that have been absorbed by both the media and the popular culture so even those on the left, to use the phrase of the linguist Geoff Nunberg, are *Talking Right.*[20]

The most prominent contemporary examples of framing, beginning with the Contract with America, have been the handiwork of Frank Luntz, who has recently disclosed some memos written to provide Republicans with "translations" for common phrases that didn't serve them well. For *foreign trade,* he substituted *international trade*; for *tort reform, lawsuit abuse reform.*[21] In each of these cases, and dozens of others, Luntz recommended using words that evoked the right networks, rather than those that elicited little emotion or unintended negative associations to Republican policies (e.g., the word *foreign*).

A perennial problem for Democrats has been the failure to recognize Trojan horses that smuggle in frames from the other side. This has allowed conservative think tanks and strategists like Luntz to generate language that seeps, uncontested, into the frames used by the media, and ultimately into the language of public opinion. It also constrains the imagination of Democrats themselves.

A prominent example is the Republican framing of taxation. The translation of the *estate tax* into the *death tax* was clearly a stroke of genius. Whereas the *estate tax* sounds like something to be handled by estate attorneys, the notion of a *tax on death* is emotionally compelling. How fair can it possibly be that someone who has worked hard all his or her life, and presumably paid income taxes already on the earnings, be taxed just for *dying*? Shouldn't people be able to pass along their hard-earned savings to their children? Similarly, we'd all love "tax cuts," but as Lakoff has emphasized, its substitution with tax *relief* implies a narrative with a hero (President Bush) who relieves helpless sufferers of a burden or affliction imposed by something or someone powerful and dangerous (big government and the liberals that love it). These are frames that come straight from the conservatives' master narrative.

These frames have become so powerful because Democrats have not only failed to contest them but have used them themselves, initially offering a competing "tax relief" package to the one eventually passed by President Bush and the Republicans after September 11, once again putting political capital into the bank of the GOP.[22] Acceptance of these frames has also immobilized Democrats for fear that any attempt to roll back the Republicans' billionaire bonus (an alternative frame, which would ring much truer to most Americans if Democrats simply paraphrased Ronald Reagan and asked, "Are *your* taxes lower than they were four years ago?") would leave them vulnerable to being branded as tax-raising liberals. Even after taking back both houses of Congress in January 2007, Democrats couldn't see their way to revisiting the enormous tax giveaways to the wealthy that Republicans had just re-passed the prior summer.[23] It would have been much easier if they had initially turned back the Trojan horse and used their own language to refer to the president's billionaire bonus or caviar cuts.

When you find yourself afraid to move for fear of being branded, you know you've bought into the other side's frame, and you'd better sell your shares. When Bush was running against the "death tax" in 2000, his language was evocative, but his tax plan actually never polled well among American voters. The massive tax break he subsequently enacted into law had nothing in it for the *98 percent of Americans* whose estates were *already* below the existing exemption on inheritance taxes.[24] With their tongues tied by the fear of being branded, Democrats didn't drive home that the estate tax was established by the first republican president, Abraham Lincoln, to pay for the Civil War, and that another great Republican president, Teddy Roosevelt, argued for the estate tax on grounds of fairness, suggesting that a tax on earned income from the fruit of one's labors is far less fair than a tax on the results of "gambling in stocks."[25]

With a pound of creativity and an ounce of nerve, Democrats could readily reframe the Republican billionaire bonus, the Iraq adventure that was supposed to pay for itself, and the spending spree for special interests that turned the first budget surplus in thirty years into the largest deficit in American history, into a *feeling*: moral outrage. The reality is that by racking up such massive deficits, President Bush and his party have instituted the largest new tax ever levied in American history: *a tax on the unborn*. They eliminated the tax on death and replaced it with a tax on *birth*. Who do they think is paying for that $70-plus billion a year going to the super rich at a time of massive deficits? Who is "sacrificing" for the Iraq War when its costs aren't even built into the budget?

The people who have just been hit with an unprecedented *birth tax* are our children, grandchildren, and their unborn children, who'll be paying for the sins of their parents and grandparents for decades— with interest. As the father of two young children, it makes my blood boil that my young daughters are being saddled with debt so that George Walker Bush's friends in Kennebunkport can cheer about their untaxed capital gains and inherit the large fortunes neither they nor most of their parents sweat a drop for, while my children pay off the debt for their newly refurbished yachts. And I'll bet a lot of middle-class parents would feel just like I do if someone told them what was being done to their children so that *2 percent* of the country could clink their glasses of Grand Marnier with a toast to their good fortune.[26]

Perhaps the most fundamental maxim Democrats should follow when responding to Republican initiatives or rhetoric is always to *assume* that they have carefully selected their frames, words, analogies, and imagery, and that they understand branding.

This has two implications. First, Democrats should study the words carefully, particularly the names and slogans, to see what emotions and networks the Republicans are trying to activate and where they are laying traps. Second, they should never repeat Republican slogans, except to attack them. If Republicans propose a Contract with America that keeps low-paid workers' wages stagnant and blocks those who have suffered readily foreseen injuries from suing large corporations, Democrats should talk about how the Republicans have "taken out a Contract on America" for the benefit of rich corporations. If Republicans pass a bill designed to take the "burden" off polluters and call it the "Clear Skies Initiative" (or simply "Clear Skies"), Democrats should refer to it as "The Dark Lungs Initiative," or "Clear Lies." If Republicans try to reframe a failed strategy in Iraq as "Flex and

Adapt," Democrats should call it "Hem and Haw," "Dodge and Weave," or "Bend and Stretch."

It is easy to get outflanked if you don't think about the networks being activated by the opposition. Unless something profoundly changes by November 2008 (e.g., another major terrorist attack on American soil), Republicans will do their best to frame the 2008 election as a "fresh start," with two years having passed between the era of unfettered Republican control over the entire federal government, and with neither Bush nor Cheney on the Republican ticket. If Democrats accept that frame, they will be making a tremendous mistake, and they should begin offering an alternative frame now, always using in one breath, "Bush and the Republican Congress" whenever they criticize the policies of his administration.[27]

Although most discussions of framing have focused on verbal frames, a final issue worth mentioning brings the concept closer to the metaphor of a picture frame. Framing can be done with images just as it can be done with words. The kind of visual framing involved in "setting the stage" for a speech can be just as important in shaping the way a message is heard and felt as the words.

From the time of Ronald Reagan, Republican strategists have been acutely aware of the importance of *staging* as a way of shaping the context for the president's speeches—down to the angles from which media cameras would be filming. Reagan never traveled without a royal blue background for his speeches,[28] aimed at transmitting the message conveyed repeatedly in his campaign ads: that he was *presidential*. The Bush team has similarly left nothing visual to chance, always placing behind him a screen with the theme of his talk written all over it. Not only is the screen likely to activate networks outside of awareness, but it also increases the likelihood that people who aren't listening closely will catch the message as they walk by the television and associate the message with the president. The Bush team hired television news and entertainment producers to craft the setting and lighting of every speech so that it would appeal both to those listening *and* to those glancing while making dinner or channel-surfing.[29]

Democrats, in contrast, are often tone-deaf to staging. A prime example was the choice of convention sites for 2004. By January 2002, when Karl Rove publicly telegraphed that national security after September 11 was going to be the major campaign theme for the Republicans during the Bush presidency, Democrats should have booked New York as the site of their convention, both to associate themselves with the city that had shown such resoluteness in the face of a devastating attack and to preempt the Republicans from using it as the ideal backdrop to showcase their war on terror and the "hero" of September 11.

New York made a bid for the Democratic Convention, but the Democrats declined, selecting instead Boston, the capital of "liberal Massachusetts." Even putting aside the obvious symbolic importance of holding the first post-September 11 convention in the city of the Twin Towers, it is hard to imagine how anyone could have imagined that the most liberal state in the union would be the best "backdrop" (i.e., visual frame) for Democrats to anoint their nominee, when Democrats had lost every state in the South in the last presidential election and the country had taken a decided rightward tilt in the interim.[30]

Principle 3: Pitch Your Message at the Right Level

A woman walking down the street in a dark blue overcoat belongs to the categories *mammal, vertebrate*, and *human* just as clearly as she belongs to the category *woman*. Yet we are more likely to say "Look at that woman in the blue coat" than "Look at that vertebrate in brightly colored apparel."

About thirty years ago, Berkeley psychologist Eleanor Rosch discovered that people around the world naturally tend to categorize objects at what she referred to as the "basic level." The basic level is the level to which our minds tend to gravitate because objects at that level share many features in common, and these features help distinguish them from other objects.[31] *Woman* is a basic-level category, as are *dinner, car*, and *bird*.

The existence of basic-level categories reflects one of the properties of neural networks, that they can link concepts hierarchically. At the top of the hierarchy are broad, superordinate concepts (e.g., "political parties in America"). Basic-level concepts tend to be in the middle ("Democrats" and "Republicans"), with subordinate categories or

instances below (e.g., "Southern Democrats"). Although the brain naturally gravitates toward the basic level, people often categorize at a
higher or lower level depending on their goals and level of expertise, as
when they distinguish moderate Christians from evangelical Christians
(or at even more subordinate levels, evangelical versus fundamentalist
Christians, and all the way down to specific instances, e.g., Billy Graham versus Jerry Falwell).

One way to control public opinion is to obscure these levels, as
when leaders of the religious right appropriated the term *Christian* to
apply only to a narrow subset of American Christians and created organizations with names such as the "Christian Coalition" that imply
that they speak for all Christians. Whether out of ignorance or fear,
Democrats have repeatedly failed to recognize and call attention to
these efforts to co-opt the meaning of fundamental concepts for partisan ends. As a result, they have frequently acquiesced to the framing of
extreme or bigoted positions as "the Christian" position on issues such
as race (in a prior era, when "mixing of the races" was seen as unnatural) or homosexuality. In so doing, they have not only ceded large blocs
of voters to the right but failed to offer principled progressive coun-
ternarratives for those in the political center (e.g., moderate Christians).

Although no one to my knowledge has ever studied the concept of
basic-level categorization in political persuasion, the level that appears
to have the most emotional impact in politics is what I have referred to
in prior chapters as a *principled stand*. A principled stand is neither an
abstraction (too superordinate) nor a detailed policy proposal (too subordinate). Unfortunately, these seem to be the two levels toward which
Democratic minds naturally gravitate. A principled stand has clear implications for policy, but it does not lay out the specifics of programs.
Rather, it is an emotionally compelling *application of a value* or ideological principle to a particular issue or problem.

You know you have a principled stand when it generates an immediate emotional response, whether an intuitive, gut-level sense of
recognition ("Yes, that's what I feel!") or a moral emotion, such as
compassion or anger. You know you've pitched your tent at the wrong
emotional altitude—either too high or too low—when you don't see
heads bobbing enthusiastically, eyes tearing, jaws dropping, or other

indicators such as smiles of recognition that indicate that your listeners feel you "get it." Most importantly, you know you don't have a principled stand when you don't feel anything yourself.

An example of what I'm getting at can be seen in an interaction between a Republican and a Democratic member of Congress in a segment on MSNBC during the 2006 campaign on "whether the Democrats *really* plan to raise your taxes, or whether this is just a Republican scare tactic."[32] Both participants in the debate were affable and socially skilled (which is always a relief for those of us on the left, since conservatives actually *invest* in candidate training, whereas the left has neither the talent scouts nor the extensive "farm teams" of the right).

Although my partisan brain was positively disposed toward the Democrat, I had no idea what he was talking about. It was some mix of inside baseball and policy statements—something about this or that provision for the middle class, and tuition tax breaks that either were or weren't going to be extended. And I was actually listening, something you can't count on from most voters. His emotion was right—he was reassuring—but I had no idea what principles he or any other Democrat would use to make decisions about what percent of my salary I'd be bringing home next year.

Enter the Republican Congresswoman. She first took a couple of quotes from Democrats out of context and then rapidly got to what she really wanted to offer: some well-honed, pithy, affably delivered phrases like, "They like to call it revenue stream. We call it your paycheck."

It wasn't a fair fight. One side was talking at the right level of emotional abstraction, using well-crafted phrases designed to elicit anxiety about Democrats and convince the average voter that Democrats, as the president had recently said, have it in their DNA to raise taxes. The other side was speaking at the wrong level, with the hapless Congressman making up the words as he went along because Democrats *have* no "party line" on taxes—even though it would probably take about one day's work to derive a single Democratic principle on taxation along with some pithy, emotion-laden phrases to make it stick.

All the Democratic Congressman really needed to say when asked, "Do people need to worry that the Democrats will raise their taxes if they win the Congress?" was "Only if their name is Exxon. If you're an oil company that's been ripping off Americans at the pump while reaping record profits, and getting a corporate welfare check to boot from the Republican Congress, you bet you're going to see your taxes go up. We're going to roll back the Republicans' no-tuxedo-left-behind tax plan and give that money back to middle-class Americans who actually work for a living. We're going to make the tax system fair again, by cutting, not raising, taxes on people who work hard and play by the rules because our tax code should be an extension of our moral code, not of the mission statements of big oil and big drug companies." He could have stopped there because nothing his Republican counterpart could have said after that would have made a difference.

That's a principled stand.

Consider another example from the elections of 2004 and 2006, the Democrats' stand on the Iraq War. From the time weapons of mass destruction did not materialize in 2003 through the summer of 2006, Democrats had more positions than candidates. But when they began to speak with one voice in opposition to the war, the question raised by both the media and the Republicans was, "So what's *your* plan?"

Democrats searched for language, but they couldn't find it because they were looking at the wrong level. Some were calling for a phased withdrawal, but most just sounded defensive, backing away from the specter of "losing Iraq" or "not supporting our troops" when pushed.

But if you think in terms of principled stands rather than policy statements, and if you bear in mind our evolutionary heritage (i.e., the things we evolved to care about), it isn't difficult to generate an emotionally compelling stand that Democrats could have used everywhere in both election years:

> This administration has so badly misled the American people about Iraq that it would be irresponsible for me to pretend to have some detailed plan before I've been in the position to ask the hard questions of our generals and get some real answers. But I *can* tell you the *principle* I'll use in any vote I cast on the Iraq war, or in any other situation that might put our troops in harm's way: *If I wouldn't send my child, I won't send yours.*

That's a principled stand. And when you think about it, that's exactly the principle a legislator *should* use when weighing the risks and benefits of foreign policy decisions that could mean life and death for the sons and daughters of the people they represent.

Principle 4: Appeal to the Whole Brain

Our brains represent the world in multiple modes, both linguistic and sensory. The creation of rich networks joining words with images and sounds is essential to political persuasion. The more neural "tracks" a message activates throughout the brain—through words, images, intonation, and music, all of which activate different neural circuits—the more evocative and memorable it is likely to be. And perhaps most importantly, the richer, more sensory-based the neural tracks, the more likely they are to create and activate *emotional* associations.

That's why the Bush administration worked so hard to keep soldiers' caskets out of the public eye. Video showing a dead American soldier being dragged through the streets of Mogadishu in October 1993 was enough to lead President Clinton to bring a halt to a humanitarian intervention in Somalia. In contrast, statements such as, "We have lost 1,834 American soldiers thus far in Iraq" had little impact on public opinion for three years.

Al Gore's documentary, *An Inconvenient Truth,* illustrates the point. Before seeing the film, like most Americans, I had heard about global warming hundreds of times but simply hadn't understood the urgency. The term itself activates weak and counterproductive associations. "Warming" has positive connotations, suggesting, at worst, the need for a little extra sun block. "Greenhouse gases" sound like a problem a florist might worry about as Valentine's Day approaches or something generated by tainted spinach. And for most people, dire warnings about the ocean getting a degree or two warmer led to little more than the thought, "Good, maybe the ocean won't be so cold on Memorial Day weekend."

But two features of Gore's presentation changed all that. The first was his evocative choice of words. He talked about a "climate crisis"— a phrase with very different connotations than "global warming"—

and he ended the film with stirring words about the earth that were anything but abstract: *"This is our only home."* This simple sentence brought the climate crisis into the metaphorical domain of family (hearth and home). Gore then made it still more immediate and personal, as he wondered what our kids would think of us if we were to continue down the path we were on now and bequeathed them a home far less hospitable than the one our parents, grandparents, and their grandparents bequeathed to us.

But perhaps the most powerful aspect of the film was precisely what can't be captured by linguistic analysis of frames and metaphors because it was beyond words: the visual imagery. The most powerful moments of the movie came as viewers literally watched the polar ice cap crumble before their eyes and major pieces of Antarctic ice melt away. These images made all the more palpable his visual depiction of how the map of the world and the United States would change—for example, how much of Manhattan and Florida would be under water—if the sea level worldwide were to rise by twenty feet.

Words can carry us to the doorstep of change, but it is often images that carry us over the threshold. This likely reflects the evolution of the brain itself, and the closer links between the circuits that mediate feelings to sensory states than to words. It was the images from Selma, Alabama, that catalyzed support for the Voting Rights Act of 1965. And just weeks after millions of Americans saw Gore's images of Florida, Manhattan, and the polar ice cap in *An Inconvenient Truth,* several states leapfrogged the federal government to pass their own laws regulating emissions of carbon dioxide.

The political scientist Ted Brader[33] has studied the visual and auditory qualities of political ads intended to evoke hope on the one hand ("feel-good ads") and fear on the other ("attack ads"). He describes the way political consultants elicit emotional responses using these sensory cues in attack ads:

> ... the soundtrack of fear ads features tension-raising instrumentals full of minor chords, ominous rhythms, and discordant tones. Sound effects such as sirens, crying infants, and howling wind punctuate the visual storyline. These ads use grainy, black-and-

white images or dark and muted colors. They show scenes of war, violence and crime, drug use, desolate landscapes, sewage, poverty, and death.[34]

An ad produced by Ned Lamont's campaign team that contributed to his primary victory over Connecticut Senator Joe Lieberman provides a good example of both the power of imagery in political advertising and the importance of watching out for unintended associations. Lamont ran on Lieberman's close alliance with President Bush at a time when Bush's approval ratings were in the low thirties. Lamont made the point in a brilliantly produced ad called "Speaking for Bush." The ad showed issue after issue on which Lieberman had cast his vote—and his lot—with the unpopular Republican president, followed by film clips of Bush speaking, with Lieberman's voice superimposed over it:

NARRATOR: Joe Lieberman on Presidential Power.

LIEBERMAN: [Video of Bush giving a speech to the nation without the sound, replaced with Lieberman's voice] In matters of war, we undermine presidential credibility *at our nation's peril*.

NARRATOR: Joe Lieberman on the Iraq War.

LIEBERMAN: [Clip of Bush speaking, once again with the sound off, flanked by General Tommy Franks and Secretary of Defense Donald Rumsfeld, replaced with Lieberman's voice] We're now at a point where war in Iraq is a war of necessity.

NARRATOR: [Image of a smiling Joe Lieberman] Joe Lieberman may *say* he represents us, but if it *talks* like George W. Bush, and *acts* like George W. Bush [photo of Lieberman slowly morphs into a broadly smiling photo of George Bush], it's certainly not a Connecticut Democrat. Let's get our voice back in Congress.

LAMONT [looking at the camera]: "I'm Ned Lamont, and I approve of this message [spoken enthusiastically].

CHORUS: [Campaign supporters in background holding campaign signs, smiling, as the candidate turns toward them as they shout in unison] So do we!

This ad uses principles of association with tremendous effectiveness. The Lieberman voice-overs are superbly placed on top of well-chosen video clips of a somber-looking Bush speaking with what to most Democratic primary voters appears to be feigned gravitas by a president attempting to spin the realities of an unsuccessful war. The voice-overs, combined with the videos, create precisely the impression intended by the ad's title: Lieberman is speaking for Bush.

Worth noting, however, are two flaws in the visual imagery. The first is the use of *smiling,* flattering photos of both Lieberman and Bush in the morphing at the end of the ad. Smiling faces innately activate parts of the brain (and facial mimicry on the part of the observer) that reinforce happiness, not distaste. Smiles elicit smiles and positive feelings, even if unconsciously. The second is the setting. Both men were flanked by a prominent American flag, a symbol associated not only with positive feelings but patriotism, sending the unintended message that Lieberman and Bush were patriotic. In using such images, the ad worked against itself.

Although these kinds of unintended associations are often elicited by poorly chosen images, they can equally occur through careless use of sound, music, or words. In an attempt to defeat incumbent Marilyn Musgrave for a House seat in Colorado, Angie Paccione ran an attack ad in which she linked her Republican opponent to a series of votes for special interests. The content of the ad was powerful, but it was undercut by uplifting, swelling orchestral music playing in the background that made Paccione's words seem silly in juxtaposition. This kind of mistake is extraordinary in a fiercely contested, multi-million dollar race decided by 7,000 votes. To a dispassionate mind, the music doesn't matter. But to a human mind, watching the ad is like listening to the screeching sounds of Hitchcock's *Psycho* while listening to a sermon on love.

One final example illustrates what can happen when campaign strategists and speech writers don't understand principles of association and thus don't manage their associations wisely. In an extraordinary blunder in his convention speech that had dozens of moving, well written, well-delivered lines, John Kerry called to mind symbols strongly associated with President Bush's strength as the man who brought the nation together after September 11:

> Remember the hours after September 11, when we came together as one to answer the attack against our homeland. We drew strength when our firefighters ran up the stairs and risked their lives, so that others might live. When rescuers rushed into smoke and fire at the Pentagon. . . . It was the worst day we have ever seen, but it brought out the best in all of us.
>
> I am proud that after September 11 all our people rallied to President Bush's call for unity to meet the danger. There were no Democrats. There were no Republicans. There were only Americans. How we wish it had stayed that way.[35]

Somehow Kerry's strategists failed to appreciate that they were using words to evoke *images of firefighters* on the days surrounding the destruction of the World Trade Center that were indelibly associated in voters' minds with their most positive memories and images of *George W. Bush*. To activate these images and then reemphasize how the country had stood behind President Bush was to cede a major portion of the speech to the incumbent president. The line, "How we wish it had stayed that way" was irrelevant by the time Kerry had primed the "Bush as hero" network.

A Gut and a Lab Coat

To invest their emotional assets wisely, political strategists need two characteristics. The first is a good gut, which allows them to know when they've hit what Tony Schwartz, who produced Johnson's "Daisy" ad, called *The Responsive Chord*.[36] The second is a healthy respect for data, and a corresponding humility in the face of data that don't support their intuitions.

Republican strategists tend to have both. Democratic strategists too frequently have neither.

The failure to appreciate the importance of a good gut reflects the spell cast on the Democratic Party by the dispassionate vision of the mind, which views emotions, stories, associations, images, frames, analogies, sounds, and music as distractions in a campaign that have to be "thrown in" to woo irrational voters. But the failure of Democrats to make use of data—let alone cutting-edge technology—is difficult to fathom.

Republicans govern with faith and intuition but campaign with the best available science. Democrats govern with the best available science but campaign with faith and intuition.

In managing campaigns, Republicans use data at every step of the way, starting with the win-loss records of their strategists.[37] They pay close attention to strategists in the hinterlands who rack up a string of victories because they realize that, empirically, they seem to know something. Karl Rove moved to Washington after he had spent years converting Texas from the land of LBJ to the land of W.[38] Democrats, in contrast, hire the same consultants regardless of the outcomes of their ministrations. After James Carville and Paul Begala helped Democrats re-elect their first president in over fifty years, the next two presidential campaigns sidelined them in favor of Bob Shrum, who had lost one presidential contest after another, using the same failed tactics each time.

If *Wittgenstein: The Musical* isn't a blockbuster, perhaps it's best not to start producing the sequel.

Republicans also draw on a mixture of market forces and experimental methods to identify the best language and campaign ads. In 1988, George H. W. Bush's strategist and media consultant, Roger Ailes, began the practice of using market forces—competition among consultants or ad agencies—to make the best use of his gut instincts, by giving multiple agencies the "gist" or theme he wanted for an ad and letting them compete to produce the best script. Karl Rove went a step further, examining "rough cuts" of actual campaign ads before finalizing them. This kind of pre-testing allows a skilled consultant to preselect ads for their emotional resonance, rather than to be stuck with a flat ad that doesn't accomplish its intended aims.

The Republicans have also made ample use of the talents of Frank Luntz, who not only has a good ear for words that might work but a good understanding of *scientific method* and what it can do for you. The most common use of polling is to measure what the public believes about an issue. What Luntz does, however, is to turn polls into mini-experiments, testing alternative phrasings of the same idea to see which ones resonate best with the public.

Democrats shouldn't be floating slogans like "Together, we can do better" or "There *is* a better way" without first testing them against alternatives designed by their most emotionally savvy wordsmiths.

Oddly, Democrats have been behind Republicans on technology in every election since Eisenhower's campaign saw the value of television ads over fifty years ago. Making use of two technological advances would go a long way toward changing that.

The first is simply to market-test ads and other political appeals using basic principles of experimental method, by combining the sampling techniques perfected by pollsters and micro-targeting firms with the instant access to potential voters afforded by the Internet. The procedure is simple. Show one group of voters one ad or script, and show a similar group an alternative one. Immediately afterward, ask each group to rate what the candidate makes them feel and how they feel about the candidate on characteristics generally important to electoral success (e.g., leadership, integrity) and on qualities specifically targeted by the ad. If simply handed a list of e-mail addresses selected for the appropriate demographics by a polling firm, a consultant with expertise in Internet technology and experimental method can conduct a test like this from start to finish in less than a week.[39]

Although something as simple as this could have an enormous impact on the effectiveness of campaigns, it shares with polls and focus groups the limitation that it can only assess conscious responses. Much of political persuasion occurs through changes in unconscious networks, which are inaccessible to consciousness. If you ask people conscious questions about unconscious processes, they will be happy to offer you their theories, but most of the time, these theories are wrong.

Recall the experiment in which subjects exposed to the word-pair *ocean-moon* were more likely to respond with *Tide* when asked for the name of a laundry detergent. The reason was that *ocean-mood* spread activation to an unconscious network that included *tide*. I've done this experiment many times in lectures, and people are happy to explain why Tide came to mind: because they use it themselves, because their mother used it when they were a kid, because they can picture that orange box, and a host of other reasons that seem eminently sensible— most of which have little to do with why Tide really came to mind.

They aren't lying. They are simply offering their best intuitive theories of how their minds work. And in this case, as in many others, their theories happen to be wrong.

And that leads to the second technological advance: the use of cutting-edge technology designed to measure unconscious associations, so that consultants can test how well an ad, slogan, or political appeal is working in ways people can't consciously report. A maverick consultant named Bill Hillsman, who helped engineer the successful campaigns of some very unconventional candidates such as Russ Feingold (the most left-leaning member of the Senate) and Jesse Ventura (the straight-talking wrestler who became the governor of Minnesota), understood the importance of the unconscious appeal of a message in the way he ran focus groups. He would turn on the television in the corner of the room and let people do what they normally do while watching television—drink, eat some snacks, and wander around. He wasn't interested in their *opinions* about the ads. He was interested in when they would *stop to listen*.[40] That's an implicit measure, and a highly valid one.

We now have the technologies to accomplish the same goal instantaneously on the Internet. My colleague Joel Weinberger and I ran a preliminary study to test our intuition on the spectacularly unsuccessful "Ask Dr. Z" ad campaign featuring DaimlerChrysler CEO Dieter Zetsche, which was put to bed after a $100 million marketing debacle.[41] The ads were intended to be humorous and light-hearted, narrated by the German chief executive as he placed himself in unlikely positions (e.g., under a car in a driveway, displaying the quality of German engineering in the company's new cars). When I first saw the ads, I thought they were an extraordinary mistake, activating a negative unintended message: that a foreigner was now at the helm of an iconic American company. The ads appeared right in the middle of the Republicans' introduction of "immigration reform" in the 2006 midterm election, which rendered their timing particularly bad, as antiforeign sentiment was running high.

So we conducted a test on the Internet.* We showed subjects one of the Dr. Z ads and then used two tasks to assess its effects on their unconscious networks.

The first task presented subjects with a series of words (e.g., *Chrysler, Ford, Toyota, stylish, power, bland*) and asked them to ignore the word and simply click on the color in which it was printed (red, yellow, blue, or green) as quickly as they could. This is actually a variant of a test developed years ago in which psychologists presented subjects with color words (e.g., the word *blue*) printed in different colors, and asked them to ignore the meaning of the word and just report the color of the ink in which it was printed (e.g., red). It's a very difficult task because our brains automatically process the word but then have to inhibit the meaning of the word to report instead the color of the ink.

Dozens of studies have used this method to assess the level of activation of unconscious networks, whether they've just been primed (e.g., people's associations to Chrysler after just seeing the Dr. Z ad) or are often on this person's mind (e.g., snakes in people with snake phobias, whose brains stay "on the lookout" for anything that could signal the presence of one). Networks at a high state of activation will interfere more with the task of identifying the color of the ink than networks at a lower state of activation. If you're afraid of snakes, it's very difficult to ignore the word *copperhead*. As a result, it will take you a few extra milliseconds to click on the color in which *copperhead* is printed because the word catches your eye. Similarly, if the Dr. Z ad activated a network about Chrysler (as opposed, for example, to a network about Germans, or silly old men), it would take consumers a few extra milliseconds to click the color in which *Chrysler* came up on the screen.

What we found fit not only with our initial intuition but with the enormous failure of the Dr. Z campaign: after exposure to the ad, people were actually more likely to think of *Ford* than Chrysler. Although they were slowed down by the words *power* and *stylish*, suggesting that the ad *did* activate those associations, they were slowed down as much by *bland*,

---

* To see how these methods work, see www.thinkscan.com.

and not by *durable* or *engineer*. The unconscious impact of the ads was that the cars they saw were stylish and powerful but not durable or well-engineered (the point of the ad). Most importantly, the ad would not likely lead consumers to think of Chrysler the next time they went shopping for a car.

We followed this task with a subliminal task. We presented one group of subjects with a subliminal photo of Dr. Z followed by a picture of a smiling, middle-aged businessman. The other group saw the same businessman preceded by his own subliminal image. In other words, the only thing subjects in both groups *consciously* saw was the smiling businessman, but subjects in the first group were first primed with a subliminal photo of Dr. Z. We then asked all subjects to give their impressions of the businessman, rating him on a series of words (e.g., *sleazy, smart, lecturing, boring, would buy from*).

Dr. Z generally left a weak impression on people, only minimally influencing their ratings of the businessman. But Dr. Z had different effects depending on consumers' gender and age. Men tended to dislike him and to see him as lecturing, and people under thirty-five tended to see him as sleazy. Women had a more favorable impression, as did people over thirty-five, probably because they identified more with him since they were closer in age.

I wouldn't bet the store on this single study. It would take a larger sample to reach more definitive conclusions. But the implications are clear for campaigning (and other forms of marketing) in the twenty-first century. Media consultants should routinely assess both the conscious and unconscious effects of ads, slogans, scripts, or other messages on the electorate and on specific groups, who might have very different responses to the same message (as occurred in our test of the Dr. Z ad).

In the twenty-first century, the exclusive reliance on polling and focus groups is no longer tenable. These methods can't dig deep enough to assess networks that people either don't know about or don't want to admit, whether to a pollster, a group of strangers in a focus group, or themselves.

chapter twelve

HOPE, INSPIRATION, AND POLITICAL INTELLIGENCE

★   ★   ★

I was about to add that ahead there lies sacrifice for all of us. But it is not correct to use that word. . . . It is not a sacrifice for any man, old or young, to be in the Army or the Navy of the United States. Rather it is a privilege.

It is not a sacrifice for the industrialist or the wage earner, the farmer or the shopkeeper, the trainman or the doctor, to pay more taxes, to buy more bonds, to forego extra profits, to work longer or harder at the task for which he is best fitted. Rather it is a privilege.

. . . And I am sure that the people in every part of the nation are prepared in their individual living to win this war. . . . I am sure they will cheerfully give up those material things that they are asked to give up. And I am sure that they will retain all those great spiritual things without which we cannot win through.

. . . We are now in the midst of a war, not for conquest, not for vengeance, but for a world in which this nation, and all that this nation represents, will be safe for our children. So we are going to win the war and we are going to win the peace that follows.

. . . And in the difficult hours of this day—through dark days that may be yet to come—we will know that the vast majority of

the members of the human race are on our side. Many of them
are fighting with us. All of them are praying for us.
— FRANKLIN D. ROOSEVELT, *Fireside Chat,*
On the Declaration of War with Japan, December 9, 1941.[1]

I f a person can speak words like those and bring his countrymen
enthusiastically with him, he deserves to be president of the United
States for a decade or two.

You know you have a good candidate when he or she can make
you laugh, move you to tears, enunciate your shared values in a way
that puts a shiver down your spine, deliver a eulogy or address a national tragedy in a way that puts a lump in your throat, criticize the
other side with a sharp joke that is so disarming that you barely realize
it's more than a scratch until you see the bandage, and elicit moral outrage so powerful you want to go to the polls tomorrow.

That's charisma. That's Franklin Roosevelt. That's Ronald Reagan. That's Bill Clinton.

Research in political science suggests that eliciting positive emotions is the best predictor of the success of a candidate.[2] The first and
most important goal of any campaign, then, is to associate the candidate with positive feelings, such as excitement and hope. The goal of
this chapter is to describe how that's done.

Political Intelligence

Throughout most of the nineteenth and early twentieth centuries, the
focus of American politics was more on parties than personalities. Each
party had its own local "machines" and newspapers to do its bidding.
In many respects, Fox News is a throwback to an earlier day in American politics; the only difference is that it would have had a competitor
on the left with an equal and opposite bias.

Although partisan feelings remain the most potent influence on
the way people vote, after World War II the personalities of candidates
became increasingly important,[3] likely reflecting a mix of forces. One
was the charismatic appeal of Franklin Roosevelt, and the corresponding fear and hatred of him on the right, which ultimately led to presi-

dential term limits. Another was the rapid industrialization that occurred during this period, which always brings with it individualism and a greater focus on individual personalities.[4] Still another was the emergence of radio and then television, which gave viewers the kind of multisensory connection with candidates more similar to the early Greek democracies than the newspaper and whistle-stop democracy of nineteenth century America.[5]

There was once a time when a sincere, plain-speaking Midwestern style was an asset, but that was in the days of newspapers. Today, a successful candidate needs to be able to energize voters, to tell moving stories, and to emanate both strength and warmth. Democratic primary voters ignore these characteristics at their peril.

That Americans pay too little attention to competence in electoral decisions is beyond doubt. They put an exterminator (Tom DeLay) in charge of the Congress and a man who spent the better part of his life with his liquor cabinet better stocked than his bookshelf in charge of the world. But the reality is that no job that prepares a person for the presidency of the United States, and many of the qualities that make for a president who can lead a nation and a world are the same qualities that inspire voters on Election Day. Bill Clinton's foreign policy experience as governor of Arkansas didn't extend much beyond negotiating trade deals with Oklahoma, but he was one of the most beloved international leaders in modern American history. He was also able to move legislation through a Republican Congress—a family leave act, gun legislation that saved thousands of lives, welfare reform—that a person without his charismatic cache with the American public could never have accomplished.

If Republican voters should pay more attention to competence (which they should), Democratic voters should pay more attention to political intelligence, particularly when choosing their party's nominee. As long as the two parties are equally adept at selecting and "marketing" politically intelligent candidates, voters will do a reasonable job at selecting their leaders.

But when one party fails, so will voters.

The 1984 presidential election provides a case in point. By all accounts, Walter Mondale is a very decent man, whose values most

Americans admire, and who had an unparalleled record of public service. But when Amherst political scientist Roger Masters and his colleagues studied voters' responses to television clips of Mondale from the 1984 election—including clips designed to capture him at his most positive and expressive (happy or reassuring)—they could barely detect any signs of emotional life in their respondents. And they looked for it every way they could, from people's ratings of how Mondale made them feel, to physiological indicators of excitement, to facial muscle movements measured by electrodes on their cheeks that can pick up even the glimmer of a smile.[6] Mondale just didn't *move* people.

About twenty years ago, Harvard psychologist Howard Gardner reshaped conventional thinking about intelligence by proposing a theory of *multiple intelligences*. A person with high interpersonal intelligence may become a superb salesperson despite having only average mathematical abilities, or a brilliant composer may have poor linguistic skills. Rather than focusing exclusively on the kind of intelligence that intelligence tests measure, Gardner described several types of intelligence (e.g., mathematical, musical, linguistic, interpersonal) identified, among other things, by their distinct neural circuitry. As he pointed out, two forms of intelligence must be distinct if one of them can break down after a brain injury or stroke, such as the ability to use language, while the other remains intact, such as the ability to play the piano.[7]

Without getting too far into the business of inventing new intelligences, if we were to describe what might be called *political intelligence*—the constellation of overlapping qualities useful to winning elections in a republic such as ours—it would no doubt include several dimensions: emotional intelligence, empathy, the ability to emanate and elicit comfort, the ability to form coalitions, the ability to manage dominance hierarchies, and general intelligence.

Although theorists have defined emotional intelligence in different ways, central to the concept is the ability to *use* emotions well: to recognize them in yourself and others, to use them effectively in relationships, and to regulate them so that they don't get the better of you.[8] This dimension is obviously central to the capacity to create enthusiasm, particularly in the era of electronic communication.

Having good emotional intelligence doesn't guarantee that a person is high on political intelligence. Many people who are both self-reflective and able to "read" other people well are better in one-on-one encounters, and may even seem rigid, distant, or uncomfortable in groups. Others who are high on emotional intelligence simply aren't interested in power and, hence, don't develop particularly strong skills in reading power dynamics. And many successful politicians get by with some aspects of emotional intelligence but not others. It isn't hard to think of politicians who know their way around a room a lot better than they know their way around their own minds. Americans are ambivalent about self-reflection, and so are many of our leaders.

A second dimension of political intelligence related to emotional intelligence, and one of the prime personality characteristics voters consider when casting their ballots, is empathy, the ability to understand and *feel* what other people are feeling. Although empathy and the ability to read people usually go together, that isn't always the case. Adolph Hitler was a master at both reading and shaping public sentiment, but he was not only devoid of empathy but was expert at inducing others who might normally have it to shut off the empathic distress for others that is part of our evolutionary heritage.

A third dimension of political intelligence is the candidate's comfort in his or her own skin, comfort with emotion, comfort in responding to questions, and comfort with other people.[9] Voters are exquisitely attuned to signs of discomfort and defensiveness, and people who have trouble projecting comfort have trouble eliciting it.

A study of the first presidential debate between Gerald Ford and Jimmy Carter found that voters who watched the debate responded much more negatively to Carter during the first part of the debate than the second.[10] Voters who simply read the transcript responded positively to Carter in both parts. The difference was that in the initial moments of the debate, Carter leaked anxiety, as expressed in less fluent speech, high rates of blinking, and high rates of gaze shifts. Once he got comfortable, these behaviors disappeared. (I don't mean this as a criticism of Carter; it's remarkable that *anyone* can get up in front of tens of millions of people, knowing that his or her performance could substantially influence the election, and *not* leak anxiety.)

Emotions are contagious.[11] An emerging body of research suggests that when we watch other people do or feel something, neurons became active in the same regions of our brains as if we were doing or feeling those things themselves. Italian scientists first discovered this in monkeys when they were studying cells in the brain that normally became active whenever the monkey was planning or carrying out movements, such as reaching for a banana.[12] What the researchers discovered was that these same neurons fired when the monkey watched *another* monkey grab for the banana. These "mirror neurons" were essentially simulating the experience of reaching for the banana in the monkey's brain as it watched another monkey do it.

Scientists later discovered that humans have well-developed mirror neuron systems in several parts of the brain. These neural systems allow us to experience other people's intentions directly (e.g., to know, unconsciously, whether they are planning to hit someone when they raise their arm by the angle and velocity with which they raise it because our brain is simulating the experience).[13] They also literally allow a politician to "feel your pain," because seeing someone in pain actually activates our own pain circuits.

Seeing another person in pain or distress usually leads to empathy, but people want their leaders to be confident as well as genuine, and they respond negatively to anxiety, vacillation, refusal to admit obvious mistakes, or defensiveness. Defensiveness is particularly damaging, and there is nothing more important for a campaign to address than pockets of defensiveness around particular subjects or issues, which erode public enthusiasm. Sometimes candidates become defensive for personal reasons, as when they've made a bad call and are asked to defend it. At other times, however, their defensiveness reflects the fact that their party lacks a coherent stand on an issue.

Two examples from the 2006 *Meet the Press* debates between senatorial candidates in close races provide good illustrations. The first was an interchange between Tim Russert and now Virginia Senator Jim Webb.[14] Russert brought up an article Webb had written in 1979, with the headline, "Women Can't Fight." Russert read Webb some of his own words, including the following: "No benefit can come to anyone from women serving in combat. . . . Their presence at institutions dedicated to the preparation of men for combat command is poisoning that preparation. . . . I have never met a woman, including the dozens of female midshipmen I encountered during my recent semester as a professor at the Naval Academy, whom I would trust to provide those men with combat leadership."

Russert then showed a video clip from Commander Kathleen Murray, who enrolled at the Naval Academy just a few years later, and had this to say: "There is no question that James Webb's attitudes and philosophy were major factors behind the unnecessary abuse and hazing received by me and my fellow women midshipmen. This article was brandished repeatedly by our male upperclassmen. They quoted it and they used it as an excuse to mistreat us." Then came the following exchange:

> MR. RUSSERT: Now, you issued a statement that said, "To the extent my writing caused hardship," you were sorry. And Ms. Murray has sent me a letter saying, "That's not enough. It's not 'to the extent that my writing caused hardship,' the content of the article was just plain wrong and Mr. Webb should say that." Do you agree?
>
> MR. WEBB: I—this article was written from the perspective of a Marine rifle platoon and company commander, and to that extent, I think it was way too narrowly based. I wrote that article . . .
>
> MR. RUSSERT: But was it wrong? Was it wrong?
>
> MR. WEBB: I don't think it was wrong to participate in the debate at that time. It's, it's been twenty-seven years, it's a magazine article, and it's something, if, if I may say, I am fully comfortable with the roles of women in the military today . . .
>
> MR. RUSSERT: . . . Bottom line, do you now believe that women can, in fact, provide men with combat leadership?
>
> MR. WEBB: Absolutely . . .

MR. RUSSERT: So that's a change.

MR. WEBB: Well, no, no...

The issue almost cost Webb the election. Webb obviously had mixed feelings about the role of women in the military, both in 1979 and 2006, as many military men did and do. But you don't work out your answer to questions like this on national television. There is no more important task of a lead strategist or debate coach for a candidate than to identify areas of ambivalence or defensiveness and to work with the candidate until he or she has an emotionally resonant response to tough questions. (I suspect, however, that Webb was not one for being "handled." Our strengths and weaknesses tend to flow from the same wells, and Webb's "you get what you see" attitude is also one of his greatest strengths as a politician.)

The last phrase politicians should ever use is one that begins with something like, "I'm sorry if my words were interpreted to mean..." Non-apologies dressed up as apologies always seem insincere, as when President Bush declared in his prime-time address in support of his "new" Iraq policy in January 2007, "Where mistakes have been made, the responsibility rests with me."[15] The passive voice reveals that the president wasn't really taking responsibility for anything.

A second example of the kind of defensiveness that erodes voter enthusiasm and leaves a bad taste in voters' mouths occurred in a debate between then-Senator Jim Talent from Missouri and now-Senator Claire McCaskill. In this example, Tim Russert simply asked Talent the kinds of questions Democrats should have been asking their opponents about their stands on abortion for years, challenging them on the natural entailments of their black-and-white position on when life begins:

MR. RUSSERT: When do you believe life begins?

SEN. TALENT: I believe it begins at the beginning, at, at conception.

MR. RUSSERT: So that embryo is a human being?

SEN. TALENT: Yeah. I think whatever it is that makes—if I . . .

MR. RUSSERT: And so, and so to use that for research is taking of a life?

SEN. TALENT: Yeah, it's the, it's the use—instrumental use of a person for some purpose . . .

MR. RUSSERT: Then why do you favor exemptions in abortion law for rape. . . ? If it's a human being, why are you allowing the taking of that life?

SEN. TALENT: OK. Well, I've, I've supported those exemptions over the years. It's a situation where the pregnancy was not voluntary, and I think the law ought to draw a different balance under those circumstances. But as I said before, I mean, I support . . .

MR. RUSSERT: But it is the taking of a life under your . . .

SEN. TALENT: That's, that's right.

Russert continued to probe the edges of Talent's position, during an election in which stem cell research had become a prominent issue and Michael J. Fox was appearing in ads for Democrats all over the country, including Missouri, in support of stem cell research that might help people like him suffering from Parkinson's disease:

MR. RUSSERT: Senator Danforth, who held a Senate seat, said if you had to go into a fire—a house with fire and yet a—save a three-year-old or a Petri dish with cells, you'd save the three-year-old?

SEN. TALENT: That's a, that's a choice that's between two different—that's a choice that's between two different people. That doesn't mean, though, that you would, you know, you would sacrifice, you know, actively sacrifice the one for the other.

MR. RUSSERT: Well, if you have a three-year-old with juvenile diabetes, people believe that research on the embryonic stem cell may in fact bring about a cure.

SEN. TALENT: That's right. The research—I've said I think the research is promising, I think it's speculative. And the good news, Tim, is we're not in a position where we have to make this kind of choice, we have alternatives that science is developing. At MI . . .

MR. RUSSERT: Right now?

SEN. TALENT: Well, yeah. I mean, look, all this is speculative. They haven't, they haven't been able to clone an embryo, they haven't been able to get cures yet out of pluripotent stem cell research . . .

In Talent's response, we see all the signs of defensiveness: stammering, hemming and hawing, making illogical leaps, inserting abstruse language ("pluripotent stem cell research"). And Talent's response set McCaskill up for one of the most brilliant displays of political intelligence of the 2006 midterm elections:

MS. McCASKILL: My faith directs me to heal the sick. God gave us the miracle of human intelligence to find cures. Our country has never turned its back on medical research and we shouldn't in Missouri. . . . I respect people who disagree with me on this issue on principle, I understand there are differences. I come down on the side of hope, hope for cures and supporting science. And I think it's very important that someone be principled, strong and not muddled, but very clear and straightforward about their position on this issue.[16]

Normally Democrats are the ones hedging on "values issues." But in this case, the shoe was on the other foot. Talent's moral principle (life begins at birth, so a discarded embryo has the same moral status as a child with diabetes) made clear that he was putting a moral abstraction above the life of a living child. McCaskill artfully contrasted their *two opposing moral positions*. She appealed to hope and compassion and challenged Talent's religious position with one of her own. In speaking of the miracle of human intelligence, she used a word that signaled to many conservative Christians that she cared about their values and culture, while enunciating a stance with strong appeal to those in the political center. She acknowledged her respect for people with principled stands other than hers but made clear that her stand was a deeply principled one.

McCaskill's political intelligence was apparent from her first moments on the political stage in 2006. One of the reasons Democrats won more elections than expected in 2006 was that party leaders carefully picked candidates high on political intelligence. In some cases, that meant the kind of "alpha male" toughness of Jim Webb or now-Senator Jon Tester from Montana.[17] In other cases, it meant the timeless, raw political and emotional intelligence Chuck Schumer saw in then-Ohio Congressman Sherrod Brown, whom he literally tracked down in the congressional gym to suggest he start training for the Senate.[18]

Many of the aspects of political intelligence described here can be seen in other primates, such as the ability to read and respond to subtle social signals.[19] Darwin wrote an entire book about the expression of emotional expression in animals. Two additional dimensions of political intelligence in humans are best understood in the context of knowledge of primate politics: the ability to enter into coalitions, and the ability to recognize and negotiate dominance hierarchies.[20]

In humans, as in chimpanzees and bonobos (our other nearest neighbors), knowing how to "play well with others"—and which others to play with—can be crucial to political success. Male chimpanzees will often ally themselves with the second-most powerful male, rather than the most powerful, because they understand that they have more "chips" to cash in with an alliance partner who needs them more. In chimpanzees, dominance or status hierarchies tend to be established by males, with female status depending substantially on connection to powerful males. (The analogy to Donald Trump comes to mind.) In bonobos, in contrast, females tend to establish dominance, with males often hanging onto their mothers' coattails (or just tails).[21]

Humans have much more flexibility, although characteristics such as physical size that influence dominance hierarchies among males of other species continue to influence perceptions of dominance unconsciously even in our most advanced democracies. Not accidentally, our language for leadership, greatness, and status includes words such as *stature*. As Malcolm Gladwell describes in *Blink*, tall men are overrepresented not only among American presidents but among corporate CEOs.

A final dimension of political intelligence is what psychologists call *general intelligence*, the sheer capacity to solve problems, think quickly, and juggle a lot of mental balls at the same time. It's not an accident that we use words like *quick* and *slow* to describe people because mental speed is a central aspect of general intelligence that tends to cut across many intellectual domains. One of the most important components of general intelligence, particularly in politics, is verbal or linguistic intelligence, particularly when alloyed with the kind of emotional intelligence that allows a candidate (or his or her strategists) to find words that sing.

Curb Appeal

The political intelligence that leads to voter enthusiasm is complex, but it is often expressed in subtle ways that register with voters, largely unconsciously. One of the main determinants of electoral success is simply a candidate's "curb appeal." Curb appeal is the feeling voters get when they "drive by" a candidate a few times on television and form an emotional impression.

Much of that impression comes from facial expressions, body language, voice quality, intonation, and other subtle characteristics that fall under the rubric of nonverbal communication. Psychologists Nalini Ambady and Bob Rosenthal demonstrated just how important nonverbal communication can be in a series of studies focusing on what they called "thin slices of behavior." [22] In one study, raters watched 30-second video clips of college teachers at the beginning of a term. They rated them using a number of adjectives, such as *accepting, active, competent*, and *confident*. The investigators wanted to know whether these brief ratings from a single lecture would predict student evaluations at the end of the term.

The investigators added one extra difficulty: they turned off the audio on the videotapes so raters could rely only on nonverbal cues.

The findings were extraordinary. Raters were able to predict end-of-term student evaluations with phenomenal accuracy by simply watching 30 seconds of behavior with the sound turned off. Lecturers who initially appeared confident, active, optimistic, likable, and enthusiastic in their nonverbal behavior were rated much better teachers by their students months later. Raters could even predict teacher success from *two-second* film clips, although their accuracy declined when given that little information.

Similar findings have emerged across a range of settings. A study just completed found that untrained raters watching brief videos of interviews with men in a federal prison could distinguish those who were psychopaths from those who may have committed equally egregious offenses but lack the ruthless, remorseless personality characteristics that define a psychopathic personality style.[23] Raters in this study actually did better with *5-second* than *30-second* clips with the sound off. The most likely explanation is that the capacity for "conning" people—one of the defining characteristics of psychopaths—may rapidly override initial split-second impressions, so that by thirty seconds, people are already "taken in" nonverbally.

Research on thin slices turns out to be relevant to politics as well. And the slices that predict voting behavior can be extremely thin.

A recent study by Princeton researchers asked subjects to view photographs of the winners and losers of House and Senate races from 2000, 2002, and 2004 with whom they were unfamiliar.[24] For each pair of candidates, subjects rated which candidate seemed more competent, trustworthy, honest, and so forth. Remarkably, their judgments of a dimension that included competence predicted the winner about 70 percent of the time, even when they had only *1 second* to make their judgment.

Competence was the only dimension that predicted winners and losers; ratings of trustworthiness and likeability didn't predict anything.

Precisely what cues subjects were using, and what they were really detecting (since they obviously couldn't judge competence from a still photograph) is unclear, but the findings are all the more impressive because they predicted electoral success over and above factors such as party affiliation and incumbency, that are powerful predictors of victory or defeat in congressional races.

A recent study similarly predicted winners and losers from 10-second slices of behavior with the sound turned off, using governors' races from 1988 to 2002.[25] Subjects' simple ratings of who they thought would win was roughly three times as good a predictor of outcome as the state's economic condition, which is one of the major variables typically used to predict electoral success, and as good a predictor as incumbency, which is a strong predictor of outcomes in gubernatorial elections. The only variable that was more predictive was the amount of money spent on the campaign.

These studies have three very important implications for political campaigns. The first is that primary voters would do well to weigh a candidate's curb appeal heavily in the primaries because it will play a decisive role in the general election. After party affiliation, the most important predictors of how people vote are their gut feelings toward the candidates. Although the gut is an imperfect instrument, particularly for judging the soundness of a candidate's policies, it has millions of years of evolution behind it, and nonverbal cues are a big part of that evolution. The gut can be fooled, as when psychopaths overcome its momentary resistance, but it also provides a good gauge of what really matters to candidates, when they aren't totally leveling with the public, and whether they will be able to inspire as leaders. If Democratic voters set a higher bar in the primaries for curb appeal, their candidates would fare far better in the general elections.

The importance of nonverbal signals was apparent in the Democratic primaries in 2004.* Dick Gephart and Joe Lieberman both seemed

---

*For readers who suspect I might be writing with the benefit of twenty-twenty hindsight, much of what I describe here is taken from my comments on a Canadian Broadcasting Company radio show on the nonverbal behavior of the Democratic candidates on February 5, 2004, as Democrats were rapidly jumping on the Kerry bandwagon.

like men of integrity, and both seemed like nice people to the average Democratic voter, but both were rapidly eliminated because of their lack of charisma. Neither could elicit enthusiasm, not because their ideas were particularly weak, but because their presence was weak.

John Kerry was in the middle of the pack from a thin-slice perspective, both with and without the sound on. He was an inconsistent campaigner who sometimes seemed impassioned in both his words and intonation, while at other times seemed flat, uninspired, and uninspiring. His face was often impassive, and his voice frequently followed. He had a habit of throwing stiff punches above his head, which seemed stilted and conveyed neither the sense of power nor authority they seemed intended to elicit.

At the other end of the thin-slice spectrum was John Edwards, who had a winning smile, an ability to inspire, an ability to deliver lines with a range of emotions, and a natural ease and grace to his body movements that gave him strong curb appeal. His good looks didn't hurt either. Although some complained that he was "too smooth," they should have learned their lesson from Bill Clinton, who many called "slick Willie," but who was unbeatable on the campaign trail. Americans like a hopeful, confident leader, and most aren't bothered by an overly smooth presentation unless it seems clearly disingenuous, which Edwards didn't.

It's worth noting, however, that even candidates with as natural a grace as Edwards will always have idiosyncrasies that a campaign team should address. For example, when anxious, particularly early in the primary campaign before he got his footing, Edwards had a tendency for the right corner of his mouth to curl up. Humans innately dislike facial asymmetries, and this should have caught the eye of his advisors. Similarly, although subtle, at times he would clench and move his fist toward his chest in a way that seemed unnatural. These are the kinds of things you can see instantly on film clips and are readily addressed. They also *should* be addressed because nonverbal "noise" can get misinterpreted by voters as "signal." Not everyone can be as charismatic as Edwards (or in the current race, Obama as well), but there's no reason candidates should deliver lines they believe in without delivering the emotional punch the message is intended to convey, whether because of weak vocal intonation or mixed or unintended nonverbal signals.

Howard Dean provides a particularly interesting example from 2004. He had a number of strengths as a candidate. When most Democrats were continuing to suffer from ideological laryngitis, Dean stood up at a Democratic National Committee meeting and asked why Democrats were kowtowing to Bush, voting for No Child Left Behind, and supporting the Iraq War, concluding with his most notable line of the entire campaign: "I'm here to represent the Democratic wing of the Democratic Party."[26]

Dean also had the passion to be president, and a good sense of humor. But he gave off signals of too much passion of a particular kind: anger. Americans appreciate leaders who can be moved to anger and aren't afraid to speak with outrage or moral indignation. Perhaps the most notable examples are George W. Bush's "dead or alive" remarks after September 11, which inspired and reassured most Americans, and Ronald Reagan's indignant, "Mr. Gorbachev, tear down that wall!" Reagan, the quintessentially "gentlemanly" candidate, used a castigating, angry tone of voice with regularity against his political opponents, although he always sandwiched it between appeals that emanated strength, warmth, or humor.

The key to making use of anger to inspire enthusiasm is to fire it *at* someone or something, to keep it focused, and not to let it spray like buckshot. Diffuse anger backfires because it becomes associated with the candidate instead of its intended object. If John McCain were to get the Republican nomination in 2008, this (along with his remarkably foolish decision to abandon his trademark honesty by the side of the road along with his Straight Talk Express) would be his major Achilles' heels.

Dean's famous "scream" was not the scream of an unbalanced, raving lunatic, as it was portrayed on television. It was a failed attempt to use a style of political rhetoric (the old-fashioned, pre-microphone style of yelling into a megaphone) with which he wasn't comfortable, to fire up his base on an evening that was a tremendous disappointment to both him and those who participated in his meteoric rise. The interpretation spun by the media was deeply unfair. It was particularly unfair

in light of the fact that Dean had a highly temperate record as governor of Vermont. It wasn't as if there were no data on his temperament
available that might bear on his suitability for the presidency.

But the interpretation of the "Dean scream" wasn't accidental. It
reflected the fact that too often when he spoke, stood on the stage, or
responded to other candidates in primary debates, he looked tight or
prickly—the way McCain often looks when his jaw is taught. What
didn't help was that Dean, at least in public settings, had a relatively
immobile neck so that he either wouldn't fully turn toward someone
or would turn with his entire torso, which made him appear tense or
"inflexible." It may well have been that he simply had a cervical disc
in his neck that was constricting his motion, or that in public speaking situations his muscles tensed up, but his tight jaw and neck and
appearance of prickliness should have been the first thing his advisors
addressed.

The second implication of research on nonverbal behavior is that a
campaign should monitor carefully the nonverbal messages its candidate is transmitting *over the course* of a campaign and be sure the candidate isn't losing his or her nonverbal "edge." Candidates often become
tired, angry, or demoralized during a long campaign, which is under-
standable given the grueling nature of it, but when these feelings become expressed in their demeanor, they can create a self-fulfilling
prophesy. These unintended messages are particularly important to
monitor when confronted with negative press coverage, which often
feels, and is, unfair, or when confronted with the constant "horse race"
questions ("Senator, the latest polls show you trailing Candidate Y")
that reflect the preoccupation of journalists trying to market their
product as a sporting event.

At other times, a change in nonverbals can signal that a candidate
is being over-managed. When General Wesley Clark first entered the
Democratic primaries late in 2004, his campaign generated tremendous enthusiasm. He had a freshness and nonpolitical quality about
him, an easy manner that approached that of Edwards, a good sense of
humor, and the military bona fides to take on George W. Bush. Like
Dean, he had also expressed serious concerns about the Iraq War long
before doing so was popular.

Within a few weeks, however, his nonverbals began to change, as he appeared more measured in his language, more deliberate in his speech, and generally more "managed" in his style. As of this writing, he has not yet entered the Democratic field for 2008, but if he does, he would do well to capitalize on his natural curb appeal and shy away from speaking like a more traditional Democratic candidate (i.e., one who seems more worried about offending than moving people).

The third implication of research on curb appeal in politics is that campaigns should "watch the tapes" carefully and coach candidates to maximize their nonverbal appeal, just as they try to hire the best speechwriters to maximize their verbal appeal. Bill Clinton was a masterful verbal as well as nonverbal campaigner, but even his advisers coached him on his nonverbals. Before his town-hall debate with George H. Bush in 1992, they advised him to move *toward* audience members in response to their questions,[27] knowing this would emphasize the difference between Clinton and the more uncomfortable, more patrician, Bush, who would be a stationary target. Whether or not Clinton's team knew the research on nonverbal behavior, they were right: moving toward the audience happens to be one of the strongest predictors of liking in thin-slice studies because it indicates approach rather than avoidance, and it suggests an interest in creating a closer connection rather than more distance.

In 1993, Roger Masters and Denis Sullivan wrote a brilliant summary of research on "Nonverbal Behavior and Leadership" that should be known to every candidate, campaign manager, and political strategist.[28] For many years, Masters and his colleagues studied the nonverbal behavior, and particularly the facial expressions, of political candidates, with a focus on how well they elicited emotional reactions in voters. They found that when different presidential candidates displayed the same emotions (happiness, fear, and anger), they did so in very different ways. Ronald Reagan could excite positive emotions even in *Democrats*—as long as they watched him with the sound turned off. Although they weren't aware of his impact on them, his emotional effects could be detected in their facial movements and physiology. Male Independents were particularly moved by Reagan's facial expressions, which may have been important in his appeal to those who became known as Reagan Democrats.

Masters and colleagues coded facial displays and other nonverbal behaviors from the neck up and studied the effects of politicians' facial and head movements on the emotional responses of voters. Voters unconsciously register natural movements of the face and body that convey emotional signals, and candidates differ substantially in the signals they send. For example, happy or reassuring emotional displays include not only the obvious grin with upper and sometimes lower teeth showing but side-to-side and up-and-down head movement. Angry or threatening emotional displays include either the lower teeth only or no teeth, with minimal head motion. One of the features of Ronald Reagan's demeanor that emanated comfort was his relaxed head, which moved to the side with ease and fluidity. This may seem like an inconsequential detail to the dispassionate mind, but knowing about it could have made the difference between victory and defeat for Howard Dean—and between life and death for many in Iraq.

These comments on nonverbal behavior apply as much to representatives of the candidates or the party on television as they do to the candidates themselves. When Republicans put spokespeople or campaign operatives on the air, they virtually always choose people who not only have been thoroughly briefed on how to "talk right" but who also have been selected for high political intelligence, good nonverbals, and strong emotional appeal. In contrast, Democrats seem to confuse the roles of party leaders and party spokespeople. Democrats should put their best orators and most interpersonally comfortable party leaders and legislators in the public eye, regardless of their rank or seniority, to convey their most important messages. What happens within the walls of Congress is one thing. What happens on CNN or MSNBC is another.

Master Narratives and Signature Issues

A politically intelligent candidate with curb appeal provides the medium to deliver a message, and an effective message always comes in the form of a narrative. Research on juror decision making has found that juries are most likely to reach a particular verdict if they can tell a story that makes sense of the evidence, and attorneys who present their cases using the story structure our brains search for have an easier time convincing juries than those who present even highly compelling evidence out of sequence or without an obvious story line to tie it all together.

To "make their case" to the public, candidates similarly need to offer a story of who they are, what matters to them, and what hurdles they have helped the country overcome (if they are the incumbent) or what problems they have come to solve (if they are the challenger).[29] A good master narrative answers the question, "Why is this the right person for the times?" In 1980, the country wanted someone to restore majesty to the presidency, to make America feel proud and powerful again, and to offer hope for a stronger economy, and Ronald Reagan presented himself as the right person to do all three. By 1984, when Reagan was seeking reelection, his enthusiasm numbers hovered in the 60 to 70 percent range.[30]

Although a compelling master narrative usually places the candidate's principles in the context of his or her life story, it is sometimes more about the principles and sometimes more about the person. Reagan, for example, was a towering political figure, but his master narrative revolved less around his history than his principles (although he used his record of fiscal conservatism in California to illustrate his principles). I suspect that most people who voted for him never knew much about his history, other than that he had been an actor and a popular governor.[31] Eisenhower, in contrast, campaigned on a narrative that was more about who he was than about any ideological principles, as is often the case with successful generals-turned-president. In 1952, his campaign produced the first truly powerful presidential commercial in television history, which told the story of his life, moving rapidly from his humble birth to his wartime leadership. The goal of the ad was to reinforce his hero status and to recast him from the role of general to the role of president.

Aside from a master narrative, successful candidates offer what might be called "signature issues"—issues they use to illustrate their values and principles, and on which they offer greater specificity about what they will actually do. Every successful presidential candidate in the last 30 years has chosen a small number of signature issues rather than blitzing the public with detailed plans on every issue. Ideally, signature issues should derive from the master narratives of both the party and the candidate, and they should have the same narrative structure.

So to pick up from a theme from the last chapter, consider two possibilities for signature issues for Democrats today that would send the message to working and middle-class Americans that this is *their* party, with their interests and values at its heart:

> **A Parents' Bill of Rights.** When a corporate executive flies his private jet to meet with a client, that's a business expense, and it's a tax deduction. But when working parents take their children to day care, or when they invest in their children—and their country—by paying school or college tuition, that's their problem. That isn't right.
>
> Child care expenses, tuition for children with working parents who are trying to get the best education for their children in the context of their values and religious beliefs, and college expenses are not disposable income, and they should not be taxed. At all. We don't tax business expenses, and putting your children in day care so you can go to work is a business expense.
>
> We should therefore roll back the Bush tax cuts to the upper 2 percent of Americans and replace them with *100 percent amnesty* for middle-class parents who are taking care of and *investing in their children and their country's future.*

The principled stand behind this signature issue should be clear from the initial paragraph: child care is a business expense, and college expenses are not "disposable income" in an era in which college is no longer a luxury. By juxtaposing what rich businesspeople get with what the average parent currently gets, this narrative draws a compelling analogy.

Sticking with child care and college tuition alone would give tens of millions of voters between 10,000 and 50,000 reasons per child per year to think twice about which party to support the next time they enter the polling booth. And it would make crystal clear which party is speaking for them and which one is speaking for the Kennebunkport crowd.

Extending the federal tax exemption to middle-class families who struggle to afford putting their children into private or parochial schools adds an additional dimension that would draw even more voters into the Democratic orbit, although it would be more controversial to those on the left. For parents (I happen to be one of them) who live in a state where public education is poor (Georgia ranks fiftieth out of fifty), public school is not always a viable option. And for parents who prefer a progressive or parochial school for their children, this signature issue gives them a tax break for doing so, without costing the public schools a cent, as long as the tax break does not extend to state taxes. It actually gives *more* money per pupil to the public schools and encourages competition because the tax break comes from federal taxes, not state or property taxes that pay for the public schools, as in the voucher programs proposed for years by Republicans. By supporting choice in education this way, the Democratic Party becomes friendly to people who want their children to get either an education congruent with their values and to moderate Republicans who like the idea of market incentives in education, while supporting traditional progressive concerns for funding public education.

Now consider a second example, which again begins with a principled stand, embodied in a narrative, and then moves into a greater level of specificity:

The Fair Salaries Act. The average income, bonus, and retirement packages of CEOs have skyrocketed in the last decade. CEOs are receiving annual pay increases of 15 percent on top of additional perks, whereas their workers are receiving salary increases averaging about 3 percent a year, which doesn't even keep up with inflation.[32]

Corporations can't simultaneously argue that they don't have the resources to pay workers a higher wage or as much of their health benefits while lavishing huge salaries and bonuses on their executives. The performance of CEOs is directly related to the performance of those who work for them. If their performance is strong, so is the performance of the people under them. It's hard to imagine that someone working hard making a product deserves $20,000 a year while the head of the company, with his eight weeks vacation a year, deserves $10 million. That's unfair, and it's un-American.

So we will reward companies that close the income gap between workers—from the assembly line up to middle managers—and senior management with tax breaks, and will impose strict tax penalties on companies that continue to escalate the size of the packages they give their CEOs.

The relative salaries of CEOs and employees today represent a market failure, where justice and supply and demand don't intersect. There is nothing to stop corporations from offering more and more extravagant packages to senior management while telling their employees that the coffers are empty, especially as the percent of unionized workers plummets each year. The packages offered to senior management are also unfair to shareholders—the rest of us, who depend on the boards of directors of the companies in which we own stock to secure our retirement—for whom every extra million in stock options to a CEO is a million less owned by the shareholders.

The point of these examples is how they draw middle-class voters back into the Democratic fold, by appealing not only to their self-interest but also to their sense of fair play, an important *value*. These signature issues are derived from principled stands, and could be an integral part of the master narratives of candidates all over the country. They offer a level of specificity well beyond a principle or value but short of the kinds of specific details about how they will be implemented that might be provided in pamphlets to the press.

The Truth About the Truth

The central thesis of this book—that successful campaigns compete in the marketplace of emotions and not primarily in the marketplace of ideas—may at first blush be disquieting to many Democrats. But the reality is that the best way to elicit enthusiasm in the marketplace of emotions is to *tell the truth*. There is nothing more compelling in politics than a candidate who is genuine. And the issues that most tempt politicians to spin and parse are precisely the ones on which they should tell the whole truth and nothing but the truth.

A campaign manager once asked for my advice on how to handle an attack that was threatening to stick. At an event, someone asked the candidate why his own kids were in private school. The candidate fumbled for an answer, and his opponent was now starting to advertise his privilege and hypocrisy.

The candidate was actually very committed to public education. When I asked what the real reason was for sending his kids to private school, it happened that his parents helped found the private school to which he was sending his children, and he liked the values it taught children, which are the values he grew up with. So I responded, "There's your answer: The truth." It was about family values—about honoring his parents. You can't get more Ten Commandments than that. The reality was that he was torn between his commitment to public education and his loyalty to his parents, and he couldn't turn his back on his parents.

If you are a candidate for public office, whether the issue is a seemingly small one such as this or a larger issue of your life story, values, or policy positions, in general, the truth will set you free. You just have to tell it in a genuine, emotionally compelling way. If you fought bravely in a war but came to believe the war could not be won and should not be fought, you should say so. If you voted for a war you shouldn't have voted for, the best strategy is not to compound error with error, but simply to say, as John Edwards did in an op-ed piece in the *Washington Post* in 2005, "I Was Wrong."

People forgive honest errors. Over the long run, they're less likely to forgive what looks like rigidity, half-truths, or opportunism.

In *Politics Lost*, Joe Klein laments the way consultants have sapped the genuineness out of candidates. The Gore campaign was a case in point.

Gore's greatest passion was the environment. As a college student, he was moved by a professor who laid out the data he was collecting on global warming, and Gore never forgot what he learned in that class. He became the first vice president to become a movie star with his brilliant and passionate documentary, *An Inconvenient Truth*.

Yet he barely uttered a word about the earth in his 2000 election campaign. Why? His consultants told him that it wouldn't win him any states. But if Gore was passionate about the environment, the role of his advisors was to find a creative way to turn his passion into a message that would get others to share his passion. It wouldn't have been hard, as Gore showed in his movie.

The same strategists who doused Gore's passion with cold water in 2000 did the same to John Kerry in 2004. They advised Kerry, who fought for years to find missing Vietnam veterans who had been killed or tortured, to look the other way on Abu Ghraib. They wanted the man who had cut his political teeth testifying against Nixon's war effort to take the position on Iraq that it's unpatriotic to criticize the president in times of war.[33] Rather than trying to get a feel for the message and master narrative latent in *Kerry's* values, aspirations, and life history, they imposed their own vision of what they believed would "work"—the same "issues" they had been pushing for years, which had never won a presidential election.

If you're going to paint a portrait of a candidate, you need the candidate to sit for it. And if you want to paint anything other than a caricature, you need to sit still long enough yourself that you know every line on his or her face. It's easy to forget—particularly if you start with a dispassionate vision of the mind, where a candidate is just a vessel for carrying the right issues—that if a candidate has become prominent enough to get to the attention of the national party (and, hence, to a prominent strategist or pollster), he or she has presumably gotten there for a reason. That reason should be central to the campaign.

The Kerry campaign ended up a grab-bag of policies and position statements, a potpourri of good intentions that lacked a unifying theme. But it didn't start out that way. Several of the ads Kerry ran in Iowa and New Hampshire had an emotional appeal that was undeniable, using the life stories of everyday people to illustrate what mattered to John Kerry. The most powerful of those began with video footage of a man under his command in Vietnam, Del Sandusky (the same footage that appeared briefly in the most effective moment of Kerry's first ad in the general election, described in the first chapter). Sandusky plainly described Kerry's courage and leadership in a way that resonated with Democratic voters, who were seeking not only a strong leader but someone who could beat the militaristic incumbent: "The decisions that he made saved our lives. He had unfailing instinct—and unchallengeable leadership." Sandusky, who epitomized down-home, middle-American genuineness, concluded the ad with a simple statement exquisitely designed (and exquisitely, plainly, and genuinely delivered) to disrupt the message George W. Bush would ultimately run successfully against Kerry: "This is a *good American*."

Kerry's Iowa ads worried the Bush campaign. Joe Klein reports a conversation he had with Bush strategist Matthew Dodd, who was at first concerned and then perplexed about what the Kerry team was doing: "I watched those early ads in Iowa and I thought, uh-oh, these guys get what this is all about. . . . It wasn't just Del Sandusky. They had a woman with health-care problems . . . who said, 'John Kerry understands what's going on in my life.' But we didn't see those ads, or that clear focus, after the primaries. What happened?"[34]

What happened was that Kerry's early ads reflected the sense and sensibilities of a Democratic consultant and ad-man named Jim Margolis who *did* get it. Margolis' approach was essentially a "clinical" one—and one campaign and media strategists should emulate. He got to know the candidate, and he got to know the people who could speak passionately about him.

At one point, Margolis asked Kerry what had spurred his interest in foreign affairs.[35] Kerry described being the son of a U.S. diplomat, riding his bike in Berlin as a child, and coming to a visceral appreciation of the threat of communism. Margolis advised him, "You should use that in speeches, make your interest in national security into something that's human and part of your personal story." And Kerry did. Margolis also interviewed Kerry's brother and sisters and his war buddies to get a real picture of the man (and some magnificent footage of their testimony, such as the Sandusky clips). Margolis did what a good clinician does when trying to understand a person's wishes, fears, passions, strengths, and weaknesses: he interviewed Kerry about his life.

Over the last fifteen years, my colleagues and I developed a method of interviewing people to get a complex portrait of their personalities, by obtaining a detailed autobiography. The same interviewing techniques can be adapted to assess the qualities that make a good leader, or to identify the most compelling aspects of the life history and values of someone who wants to represent his or her district, state, or country. The interview focuses on people's narratives about who they are, what matters to them, who the important people in their lives are and were, where they came from (i.e., what it was like growing up), and what their work and relationships have meant to them.

Although we ask a number of questions that require people to generalize about what matters to them or what a particular relationship or occupational choice was like, that is always the starting point, not the end-point. If you really want to know a person, the devil is in the details—in the specific examples—not in the generalizations. It's difficult for people to get worked up about abstractions. It's the memories of specific incidents that reveal who a person is—his or her wishes, fears, values, strengths, and weaknesses.

When interviewing a patient struggling with depression, the stories that often tell the most are the ones about what happened before the depression hit—the first time the person became depressed and each subsequent episode. Who was involved? What happened? What did it mean to the patient? How did he or she try to cope with it?

In interviewing a candidate for a leadership position in an organization, the examples that matter most are stories about interactions with peers, subordinates, mentors, and bosses. Those stories provide a window into how the person handles conflict, stress, interpersonal problems at work, and other challenges in the workplace.

And when consulting with a candidate to develop a master narrative, the memories I'm most interested in hearing in detail are moments in the candidate's life that aroused his or her passion—whether tragedies, triumphs, or sometimes interactions with a stranger that triggered strong feelings. In exploring the candidate's values and principles, there is nothing more important than the *memories* associated with them, which tell something about where they came from and why they matter to him or her. The goal is to identify the dominant themes for the campaign, to figure out how to weave those themes together with inspiring aspects of the candidate's autobiography, and to draw out the stories the candidate can use on the campaign trail to make that narrative and those themes come alive.

Conclusion: Running on Empty

Positive emotions rally voters to the polls and convince the uncommitted that they have someone and something to be excited about. The most successful politicians know how to elicit a range of positive feelings—enthusiasm, excitement, hope, inspiration, compassion, satisfaction, pride, and even sanctity.

Failing to capitalize on the positives can be as disastrous as failing to defuse the negatives, as two spectacular missed opportunities illustrate.

The first was one of the few significant political (as opposed to policy) miscalculations made by George W. Bush in the first six years of his presidency: his misuse of the five-year anniversary of the World Trade Center in the run-up to the 2006 midterm election. The Republican Party had orchestrated a day of events to place Bush back at the scene five years later, starting his day with a photo op with New York firefighters to reactivate the image of Bush with his bullhorn.

But instead of using the event to call for national unity, Bush went negative in a speech to the nation on September 11, 2006, claiming, once again, that only he and the Republicans truly understood the dangers posed by terrorism. His speech came toward the end of a series of speeches over the previous weeks aimed at linking Islamic fundamentalism to fascism and at branding all who opposed his faltering Iraq War as Neville Chamberlains who didn't see the severity of the threat of Adolph Hitler. That effort itself was failing, as the media were now beginning to question Bush openly when he used Osama bin Laden and Iraq in the same sentence, and the analogy to Hitler was so strained that it didn't even sell to mainstream media outlets, who had reported on Bush's pronouncements on war and peace so uncritically for years. Iraq was dissolving into a civil war, which Americans could see on television every night with their own eyes, and there was simply no way to spin his way out of it.

The anniversary was an opportunity for Bush to appear to rise above the rancor, the partisanship, and the war in Iraq, to remind voters of the Bush of September 11, 2001. Here was a chance to deliver a eulogy, to bring Americans back to the realm of the hallowed and the sacred, and to associate Bush once again with that realm.

But instead of a eulogy, the president delivered a political speech. He used the wrong literary genre. It was an extraordinary blunder.

This was a prime opportunity for a president whose *positives* were tanking to *go positive* in a way that would reactivate people's pre-Iraq associations to the Bush of September 11. The moment called for reverence and unity, best prefaced by an acknowledgment of the partisanship of the times and an admonition that this was not a moment for partisanship.

Instead, Bush allowed his critics to attack him for giving a political speech on a national day of mourning. Harry Reid stood on the floor of the Senate and castigated Bush for taking the anniversary of the terrorist attacks of September 11 and politicizing it, turning it into an opportunity to defend his war in Iraq. And just as could be predicted, neither the carefully orchestrated day nor the president's speech produced the post-September 11 "bump" Republicans had anticipated. The president's popularity plummeted further.

The second example of a failure to generate positive emotions was Al Gore's decision to run from Bill Clinton—and, hence, from his own record—in the 2000 election.

In 2000, Gore faced what he and his advisors perceived to be a dilemma. The country had just gone through a year of scandals leading up to the impeachment trial of an otherwise very popular president. By all accounts, Gore himself was enraged, not only feeling betrayed by Clinton, but believing that the Clinton scandal had seriously damaged his own chances in the upcoming presidential election. What he didn't realize was the extent to which he would create a self-fulfilling prophesy.

The question Gore and his advisors asked and answered to their own satisfaction reflected the kind of one-dimensional thinking we have seen repeatedly in Democratic campaigns. Is Clinton an asset or a liability to the Gore campaign? Is he a positive or a negative?

Even if they were going to ask a one-dimensional question about a president about whom voters had multiple feelings, they should have at least asked it in a more nuanced way: for *which* voters is Clinton a net asset, and for which voters is he a net liability? Gore's poll number shot up in the last week of the election when he finally threw a Hail Mary pass and let Clinton stump for him, leading him ultimately to win the popular vote. Had he done so a few months earlier, the race wouldn't likely have been close.

The problem, though, was not the answer at which Gore and his advisors arrived but the question itself. Had they understood emotional associations, they would have asked a very different question: *given* that Clinton and Gore are inextricably linked in people's minds, how do we activate the positive associations people have formed to Bill Clinton over eight years and reinforce those links to Gore, and how do we inhibit the associations between Clinton's personal scandals and Gore's personal attributes? Had they asked this question, they wouldn't have conceded all claims to the accomplishments of the Clinton–Gore years (enjoying none of the positive associations) while simultaneously tying their hands against all attacks for fear of invoking Clinton's name (accruing every negative association George W. Bush and Karl Rove threw at them).

Asked this way, as a question about how to manage voters' ambivalence toward Bill Clinton the president and Bill Clinton the womanizer, the answer is obvious. And the answer would have set Gore free the first time Bush telegraphed that he intended to make the election a referendum on "character."

The character charge made heavy use of guilt by association, essentially saying, "We need to restore integrity to the Oval Office"—the room associated in people's minds with the Lewinsky scandal. Although Bush mentioned fund-raising "scandals" (such as the use of White House phone lines for campaign phone calls), those were just the conscious story line, which had little emotional power on its own. The real message was that Clinton's sexual escapades had tarnished the dignity of the presidency, and what Bush–Rove hoped to do was to cast a wide associative net with "character" and "integrity" that would blur the lines between Clinton's personal indiscretion and Gore's integrity.

Unfortunately, blinded by his anger and feelings of betrayal, and surrounded by advisers either deaf to the rising character crescendo or unable to imagine a way to bring the dissonant concerto to a close, Gore let the charge fester. To answer it, he would have had to utter Clinton's name. He and his advisers seemed to think that if they just didn't talk about Clinton, the association would go away.

But as has been the case every time Democrats have turned to avoidance as a campaign strategy, the strategy backfired, for two very important reasons. First, whether Gore liked it or not, he was *inextricably linked* associatively to Clinton. He was Clinton's *vice president* for eight years, and their names appeared in two election cycles on bumper stickers as *Clinton–Gore*. You can't get much more associated than that. Second, the Bush campaign was *talking about* Clinton, referring constantly to Clinton–Gore, and doing everything they could to create a network around "character" and "integrity" that made Clinton and Gore partners in crime.

Gore simply ceded the networks, allowing Bush to tell whatever stories he wanted about Clinton–Gore's integrity because Gore didn't want to mention that he had been Clinton's vice president. The irony is that although Clinton's poll numbers were low for personal integrity, his numbers were high for overall job performance—remarkably high for a president who had spent eight years dealing with well-financed right-wing efforts to destroy him, supplemented by the Starr inquisition, financed handsomely by fifty million in American tax dollars.

So imagine if Gore had responded the first time Bush first uttered any words vaguely insinuating character issues with something like this:

> George Bush wants to make character an issue in this election. Governor, I wouldn't go there, if I were you because it's not exactly your strong suit.
>
> But let me say something about Bill Clinton, so the American people know exactly where I stand.
>
> No one in America, not you, not me, not Bill Clinton, is proud of what happened between him and Monica Lewinsky. A

314 THE POLITICAL BRAIN

day doesn't go by that he doesn't think about the pain he caused his family, knowing that every time Chelsea turned on the television set for a year all she heard about was her father's affair. We are all well aware of the pain he and an out-of-control Republican Congress, determined to destroy the president no matter who they had to take down with him or how much filth they had to expose our children to on the evening news, caused this nation.

Am I proud of what Bill Clinton did with his personal life? Of course not. But I'll tell you what I *am* proud of.

I'm proud of what Bill Clinton and I have accomplished together over the last eight years for the American people. We began with an economy in disarray, left that way by Mr. Bush's father. We were deep into a recession that was costing Americans their jobs, with a federal government out of control, spending your grandchildren's money by the bushel, running up enormous deficits.

Now look where we are today. We've created millions of jobs, we've cut unemployment to historic lows, we've put a hundred thousand new police on our streets, we've cut the number of people on welfare by more than half, and on top of that, we balanced the budget for the first time in thirty years. We've cut the numbers of abortions for the first time in twenty-five years, and we've given every woman in the United States the right to stay home for three months with her new baby without fear of losing her job. We've taken guns out of the hands of criminals while protecting the rights of hunters, and we've dramatically cut the crime rate.

If that isn't a record to be proud of, I don't know what is.

So Mr. Bush, let me give you a little word of advice. If I were you, I don't think I'd make integrity and values your campaign theme. If someone is going to restore dignity to the Oval Office, it isn't a man who drank his way through three decades of his life and got investigated by his father's own Securities and Exchange Commission for swindling people out of their retirement savings. If you want to be president, you're going to need to convince the American people that they should abandon everything Bill Clinton and I did that has made Americans safe, secure, and prosperous again, and instead vote for a man whose biggest concern seems to be that the yacht tax is too high.

Had Gore begun his campaign that way, he would have made clear that what united him and Clinton was not Clinton's handling of Monica Lewinsky but their administration's handling of the country. As importantly, he would have warned Bush and Rove that if they took off the gloves about character, so would Gore. The way you respond to your opponent's first attacks sends a crucial signal not just to the public but to the other campaign. A weak response does nothing but embolden the opposition. And a swift response to the character issue that included a brief reference to Bush's own moral failings would have prevented Bush, and ultimately the media[36], from framing the campaign as a contest between a man with questionable integrity and a man with questionable experience and intellect. Americans don't care much about experience and intellect, but they do care about integrity.

Nothing can ever be said with certainty, but in this case, the hypothesis that the association with Clinton could have been used to Gore's advantage was scientifically testable. My colleague Joel Weinberger and I got a chance to test it during the recall election of Governor Gray Davis of California using subliminal technology on the Internet.[37]

In 2003, Davis, like Gore, was uncertain whether he should ask Clinton to stump for him, for the same reasons. So we conducted an experiment, comparing two groups of subjects. We showed both groups a photo of Gray Davis and asked them to rate their attitudes toward him on a number of dimensions (e.g., trustworthiness, likeability, competence). The only thing that differed between the groups was what they saw before Davis's face. We presented subjects in one group with a subliminal image of Clinton's face just prior to presenting Davis's. (As in the Dr. Z study, none of them had any idea who or what they had seen subliminally, and most didn't know they'd seen *anything* before the photo of Davis, although we told them in advance, for ethical reasons, that they might be exposed to subliminal stimulation.) The other group got a subliminal image of Davis himself before his consciously visible photo. Our aim was to test whether an association between Davis and Clinton would be an asset or a liability for Davis.

316 @ THE POLITICAL BRAIN

The results were unambiguous: Subliminally flashing Clinton's face before Davis's significantly decreased people's negative ratings of Davis.* For committed Democrats and Republicans, who already tended to have relatively entrenched feelings toward Davis, the effects were minimal. But for Independents—precisely the group who had voted for Clinton twice but switched to Bush in 2004—the effects were very strong. An association with Bill Clinton was a strong plus for a Democratic candidate, even an unpopular one like Davis.

And it should have been for Al Gore.

---

*As in the Dr. Z study, we didn't use subliminal procedures to manipulate people's votes, as in the RATS ad against Gore. Doing so would clearly be unethical. Our goal was to *test* people's unconscious associations, not to alter them. In accord with scientific standards of ethical conduct, we both told them at the beginning of the study that they might be exposed to a subliminal stimulus and we debriefed them afterwards about the actual procedure.

chapter thirteen

POSITIVELY NEGATIVE

The problem with American politics today is that one party has the monopoly on all the anger. . . . Look at John Bolton—if you can. Now, I don't know if this man has human relationships, but . . . his hair's not speaking to his mustache. . . . And to be a Democrat means—I dunno, your guess is as good as mine. It seems like ever since Michael Dukakis was asked how he'd feel if his wife got raped and he said "whatever," the Democrats have been the party that speaks softly and carries Massachusetts.

—BILL MAHER, *New Rules*[1]

For years, politicians, pundits, and political scientists have decried the negativity of political campaigns in the television (and now the Internet) era. They have argued that negative campaigning has been on the rise, that it is destroying the quality of information getting to the public, that it is depressing voter turnout, and a host of other ills.

Several myths have colored discussions about negative campaign appeals. One is that campaigns are getting nastier. Whether this statement is true or false depends on your time frame. In his book *Going Dirty*, David Mark has shown that American political campaigns are actually much more civil today than they were at the start of the republic and throughout the nineteenth century. In the nineteenth century,

317

virtually all newspapers were partisan newspapers whose diatribes against the other side would have made even Bill O'Reilly blush. On the other hand, content analyses of campaign ads in the television era suggest that negative ads are indeed becoming more prevalent,[2] and some of the highly personal ads that ran in the 2006 midterm election represent an unmistakably new low.

A second myth is that negative campaigning depresses voter turnout. This belief, widely held for years by many political scientists, was belied by the 2004 election, when the percent of eligible voters who chose to go to the polls jumped from 54 to nearly 60 percent. The increase in voter turnout largely reflected a concerted—and highly targeted—negative campaign by Republicans aimed less at changing the minds of undecided voters than on bringing conservatives who normally don't vote to the ballot box by making them angry.[3] The high turnout in 2006 for a midterm election also reflected voter anger and concern about the War in Iraq.

Voters are usually moved by positive or negative emotions.

Three other myths are unique to the left and uniquely dangerous, having contributed to the failed campaigns of the last two Democratic presidential candidates: that negative appeals are unethical, ineffective, and when made by the other side, better left alone.

All three fly in the face of everything we know about mind and brain. And there is no better evidence against them than modern American electoral history.

Positively Unethical

The first myth is that negative campaigning is inherently unethical. Anyone who believes this should read the *Declaration of Independence*. A content analysis found that about 70 percent of the statements in that document are negative (toward British rule, despotism, taxation without representation, and so forth).[4] If you're trying to convince people to change course, you generally have to elicit emotions such as anxiety or anger along with enthusiasm for your cause, particularly when your point is that an incumbent has behaved in ways that are incompetent or unethical.

Understanding the use and misuse of negative emotion in campaigns (which is what negative ads try to engender) requires distinguishing between attacks that are unfair, misleading, or unethical and those that are not only accurate but essential for catching voters' attention and informing their emotions.

As we have seen, voters tend to take their cues from party leaders on what to feel. If party leaders or candidates deliberately mute their responses, whether because of fear, misplaced ethical concerns (many of which are "front men" for fear), or a misunderstanding of what polls and focus groups can and can't offer, they misinform the electorate, project fear and weakness, and cede values, patriotism, or whatever other social good the opposition is claiming as its exclusive territory.

Fairness, like beauty, is in the eye of the beholder, but it isn't difficult to distinguish prototypes of ethical and unethical appeals and to use those to guide the ethical use of negative emotions in political campaigns. Democrats err when they confuse negative campaigning with sleazy campaigning. Politicians can and do make unethical negative appeals to voters, but they also make unethical positive appeals, as when President Bush told voters up until November 7, 2006 that the United States was "winning" in Iraq all the while he and his advisors were plotting a new course based on what they knew wasn't true.

Whether an appeal is rational or emotional, or positive or negative, is completely independent of whether it is ethical. The conflation of reason, positivity, and ethics is a profound logic error that has had profound effects on Democratic campaigns for decades.

Consider this exchange from *Meet the Press* between now-Senator Bob Casey of Pennsylvania and then-incumbent Rick Santorum:

MR. RUSSERT: It is interesting, Senator Santorum, hearing you distinguish your voting records in some cases with the president. . . . [I]f you go to *Congressional Quarterly* and review your voting record in support of the president, here it is: In 2005 you were with him 95 percent of the time, 100 percent of the time in '04, 99 in '03, 96 in '02, 97 in '01. . . . You think he's a great president?

SEN. SANTORUM: I think he's been a terrific president, absolutely.

MR. CASEY: . . . Tim, when you have two politicians in Washington that agree 98 percent of the time, one of them's really not necessary.[5]

Casey's amusing line was no doubt "negative" in that it had some fun at Santorum's expense, but it also made an important point: That Santorum was part of a Republican Congress that had moved in lock-step with the president and had failed in its constitutional obligation to exercise independent oversight. Voting 98 percent of the time with the president, particularly during a time of foreign policy disasters and out-of-control spending, was a sign that Santorum was not exercising the independent judgment expected of a senator.

Because Casey's response occurred in a debate, many Democrats would likely have little trouble with it from an ethical standpoint. But consider the following from an attack ad Casey ran against Santorum:

NARRATOR: Rick Santorum's record? [An image of Santorum appears, against the backdrop of the Capitol, with words super-imposed to underscore the narration] Voted three times to give himself a *pay* raise [An image appears of a working-class woman hard at work] while voting 13 times against raising the *minimum* wage. [An image appears of a smiling Santorum sitting next to a grinning George Bush, with words again underscoring the narrative] And he votes 98 percent of the time with George Bush. Even to privatize Social Security.[6]

What made this ad (versions of which ultimately ran against incumbent Republicans all over the country) powerful were two features. The first was its use of *juxtaposition*, one of the most powerful tools in negative political advertising. Juxtaposition essentially connects two networks that were previously unconnected. By creating a link between Santorum's generosity to himself and his lack of generosity to the hard-working men and women he was supposed to represent,

Casey two took facts that alone carried little weight for many voters but put them together in a way that *told a story* about the kind of person who, if you do the math, actually raised his own salary by more money than a Pennsylvanian working forty hours a week at the minimum wage *earned*. That juxtaposition raises serious questions about Santorum's sense of equity and his ability to empathize with constituents who worked just as hard as he did.

And it should.

Second, a feature of ads that often renders them more powerful than speeches is the impact of multimodal networks linking words, images, sounds, and emotions. This creates more room for mischief, but it also creates a greater opportunity to activate emotions. In this case, the ad linked Santorum both visually and verbally to an increasingly unpopular president, and emphasized one of the president's signature issues that most Americans didn't trust (privatizing Social Security). It also superimposed the words "Voted 13 Times Against Raising the Minimum Wage" on a hard-working woman, clearly conveying a lack of compassion by Santorum.

The reality is that Santorum and his Republican colleagues *did* show a lack of compassion for hard-working Americans who just didn't resemble them enough to elicit the empathy they showed for beneficiaries of multi-billion dollar inheritances. Making that point in a way that elicited emotions, was central to Casey's electoral success—and to the lives of millions of American workers and their families.

This ad is a prototype of both an effective and ethical negative appeal. It didn't distort Santorum's record. It didn't mislead by leaving out details that a reasonable person would consider exonerating (e.g., if Santorum had opposed the minimum wage because it was attached to billions of dollars of pork-barrel spending that would have driven up the deficit). It didn't link him to a president he had opposed on numerous important occasions.

It told the truth with emotional clarity.

Now compare this to the barrage of *personal* attack ads run by the National Republican Congressional Committee in House races all over the country in the final weeks of the 2006 midterm election. These ads reflected a year of private investigations of Democratic candidates' personal lives. Republican Congressman Tom Reynolds, who headed up these efforts, responded candidly in an article in the *New York Times* as the ad blitz was about to commence, that "These candidates. . . . have never seen anything like this before," and "We haven't even begun to unload this freight train."[7]

An ad run against Democrat Michael Arcuri in New York, ironically titled "Bad Call," provides a prototype of an unethical attack ad:

FEMALE VOICE: [Speaking in a sexy, licentious tone, with an image of an undulating exotic dancer in silhouette, juxtaposed with a moving image of Arcuri designed, in this context, to appear as if he is leering and then leaning back, as if in ecstasy] Hi, sexy. You've reached the live, one-on-on fantasy line.

MALE ANNOUNCER: The phone number to an adult fantasy hotline appeared on Michael Arcuri's New York City hotel room bill [close up photo of part of an unidentifiable man's face talking on the phone in front of a keyboard, with words similar to the narration superimposed in text, with *adult hotline* in italics] while he was there on official business [images rapidly move from left to right showing the bottom half (i.e., just the pants) of a man wearing a suit that looks like the one Arcuri is wearing in the rest of the ad]. And the call was charged to Oneida County taxpayers [the only image is a black screen with white text that rapidly appears and disappears, with the word *charged* in italics]. Arcuri has denied it [image of Arcuri, with his head downcast, pointed so far toward the floor that he appears to be deeply ashamed or hiding his eyes] but the facts are there [image of the undulating woman returns lightly in the background, initially outside awareness, surrounded by what looks like white smoke as Arcuri slowly and solemnly lifts his face, at one point licking his lips, his eyes remaining closed]. Who calls a fantasy hotline and then bills taxpayers? Michael Arcuri.

FEMALE VOICE: [again in sexy voice, but this time slightly chastising]: Bad call [image remains of Arcuri juxtaposed with the exotic dancer, with no smile on his face and eyes remaining closed].

MALE ANNOUNCER: The National Republican Congressional Committee paid for and is responsible for the content of this message.

The visual images in this ad were very carefully chosen. The undulating woman was juxtaposed with what was either a video taken out of context or a photo taken while Arcuri's face was moving or changing expressions. The photo was then manipulated in space to create the impression of movement, as he appeared to throw his head back in pleasure. The image of a man's partial face in front of the keyboard activated associations of both official business and Internet porn. The face was unidentifiable, but in the context, viewers would clearly infer it to be Arcuri's. The photo of a man in a suit from the waist down was obviously meant to activate networks about a man on official business whose pants were coming off, but it was presented so rapidly that viewers wouldn't have consciously registered its meaning.

The italicization and rapid presentation of the word *charged* played on the two meanings of the word, the less frequent meaning that had just been activated by the ad (that he *charged* a call) and the more frequent meaning, particularly in an attack ad suggesting illicit behavior—against a candidate whose record as a *district attorney* the Republicans had recently run what were equally deceptive ads—that he had been *charged* with misappropriating taxpayer funds for illicit purposes. There is no other reason this word would have been italicized, and the fact that the words came and went quickly, unlike all the other text in the ad, which was stationary, suggests that its intended effects were primarily implicit (i.e., to make it vivid enough to register, but not in the context of the sentence in which it was embedded, which was its "cover").

The downcast face of Arcuri juxtaposed with narration and text reading, "Arcuri has denied it. But the facts are there," clearly indicated to voters that Arcuri was ashamed of his behavior—so ashamed that he wouldn't even show his eyes. As that image started moving, with Arcuri lifting his head to face forward but with his eyes closed, it activated two networks by virtue of the ambiguity of the body movement and his reasons for keeping his eyes closed, one implying shame and the other suggesting that he was deep in sexual fantasy. Having watched the body movement in that brief film clip of Arcuri several times, I suspect it may actually have been lifted by the ad makers from a video of Arcuri raising his head at the end of a prayer.

Like the "Harold, Call Me" ad, this one was brilliantly produced to create just the right associations. Unfortunately, the charge was manufactured out of whole cloth.[8] As described by FactCheck.org, and confirmed by multiple sources, the phone records described in the ad did indeed show a call to a fantasy phone line at 3:26 PM on January 28, 2004. But exactly a minute later, the caller redialed the same number— but with the area code corrected from *800* to *518*. The intended number was the New York State Department of Criminal Justice Services. The man who made the call was a colleague of Arcuri's, attending the same meeting of the New York State District Attorneys Association. The hotel billing charge that created the cover for the story was $1.25.

Tim Russert confronted Congressman Reynolds on the ad in late October on *Meet the Press*:

> MR. RUSSERT: Everyone admits it, and yet you put an ad on suggesting that this guy is calling sex hotlines. Is that fair?

> REP. REYNOLDS: Well, first of all, the chairman of the committee doesn't know what the IE's actually producing when it goes on, we pay for. Second, that ad is now down.

> MR. RUSSERT: You said you're responsible, that's what the banner says. You can take it down if you wanted to.

> REP. REYNOLDS: I paid for it. The committee paid for it, it was pulled down.

MR. RUSSERT: Is it, is it fair? Is it fair?

REP. REYNOLDS: Politics isn't always fair, Tim. . . . [T]he contents of both ads, we review all those.[9]

Arcuri went on to win, but so did Reynolds, in a very close race. Reynolds almost lost the race when it became clear that instead of contacting the House Ethics Committee when he learned of Mark Foley's inappropriate behavior with congressional interns, he put partisan interests before the safety of teenagers, and took no action other than, according to him, alerting "my boss," Speaker Dennis Hastert.

It is difficult to imagine how Reynolds could have won re-election if the Democrats had run a concerted campaign immediately after his indifferent admission on *Meet the Press* that he knew the facts of the case on Arcuri and ran the ad anyway, and woven together the story of a ruthless, morally defective man who let a pedophile run free in the Congress when it suited his political purposes, knowingly slandered a decent man without concern for the damage it might do both to his marriage and his reputation, and most importantly, didn't care what effects the ad would have on Arcuri's two *teenage daughters*, who had to confront a lurid story everywhere they turned raising questions about their father's alleged illicit sexual behavior—charges Reynolds *knew were untrue.*

If those actions don't define bad character, I don't know what does. And that's precisely how Democrats should have talked about it.

Democrats should replay this episode, and Reynolds' response on *Meet the Press,* in every election for the remainder of his political life. Rather than accepting the frame, "Hey, politics is dirty," they should create a very different, more appropriate, and more *personal* frame: *Imagine you were Mike Arcuri.* Imagine you were a decent man, running an honest campaign, sitting down one night watching television with your family.

Now imagine watching in horror as that ad appeared.

What would you feel? What would it do to you, your marriage, your children, and your reputation? The reality is that no matter how a message like that has been debunked, it will always leave lingering doubts. And Tom Reynolds knew that.

A person who would knowingly and premeditatedly do what Reynolds, Arcuri's opponent (Raymond Meier, who deservedly lost), and every Republican operative who researched and produced that ad did to another person has no place in American democracy. And the best way to ensure that Republicans think twice the next time they Corker or Reynolds another human being is to make a voting issue out of it—not just against Reynolds, but against any candidate who hires any producer, director, consultant, opposition researcher, or strategist who was involved in the Republican smear campaign of 2006, starting with those who used their talents to such bad ends in what was truly a "Bad Call."

The ads by Bob Casey on the one hand, and the Republican Congressional Committee against Arcuri on the other, provide useful prototypes of ethical and unethical ads. But it isn't difficult to formulate a rule of thumb about fair and ethical appeals, whether positive or negative. Aside from attacks that involve clear deception or that deliberately exploit hate and fear (to which we return in the next chapter), a good rule of thumb is that if the *real* point of an ad or other attack involves a "borderline call" the candidate made in some area of life unrelated to public service, one that is not part of a broader pattern or is distant in time and has not been repeated, or involves sex with a consenting adult, it's unfair.* Candidates or party leaders who attack their opponents outside these bounds should be hit with whatever their opponents have at their disposal, beginning with a blistering assault on their character. A candidate or party that is willing to practice the "politics of personal destruction," showing no concern about who is destroyed in the process, lacks the normal capacity for conscience that is a prerequisite to participatory democracy.

People without conscience respond to aggression, not to appeals to the conscience they don't have.

---

*The exception is when a candidate is running on sexual morality while engaging in the same kind of behavior he or she is condemning, in which case his or her behavior speaks to dishonesty and hypocrisy.

A final point about the ethics of negative campaigning deserves attention because it is rarely discussed. The *failure* to "go negative" against an incumbent whose behavior in office is deeply immoral or destructive to America's moral authority is itself an ethical failure. If voters take their cues from political leaders, and their leaders are publicly silent on issues about which they are privately outraged, they are misleading in their silence.

A prime case was the Kerry campaign's decision not to discuss Abu Ghraib. As the details of what had happened at Abu Ghraib were unfolding in the summer of 2004—during one of the greatest foreign policy disasters in American history, in which a nation that had stood for human rights rounded up and tortured not Taliban fighters in Afghanistan but citizens in the very country we were supposed to be liberating, 70 percent of whom were detained by mistake—the Kerry campaign remained silent. In this, as in virtually every other case, Kerry's advisors feared that an aggressive condemnation of the Bush administration might backfire and be spun by the Republicans as an "attack on our troops."[10] Once again, Democrats were playing checkers, instead of anticipating the other side's next move, blocking it, and mapping out the most likely moves and countermoves that would follow.

Note how easily Kerry could have blocked the likely Republican charge that an attack on Abu Ghraib was an attack on our troops, beginning with words from his own convention address:

> I know what kids go through when they are carrying an M–16 in a dangerous place, and they can't tell friend from foe. I know what they go through when they're out on patrol at night and they don't know what's coming around the next bend.

Now suppose he had continued:

> President Bush has no idea how easy it is in those kinds of circumstances for soldiers, scared and angry after they've seen a good friend blown up in front of them, to lash out in anger against the people they're there to protect. He has no idea of the

danger in which he has placed our men and women in uniform when he unilaterally declared our right to torture prisoners, giving license to any army we ever fight to declare the same right, and emboldening terrorists who don't fight by the rules of civilized nations who now sneer at what they see as our hypocrisy. He has no idea how many new terrorists he created among the teenage sons of the men who came home damaged from Abu Ghraib or who never came home at all.

Mr. Bush has no idea because he never felt a bullet whizzing over his shoulder or a piece of shrapnel lodge in his leg. He never knew what it was like to dodge a bullet because, when called to duty, he dodged the draft. Being in the National Guard is an honorable way to serve this nation. We have tens of thousands of Guardsmen fighting for our country in Afghanistan and Iraq at this very moment, and they make us proud to be Americans. But we all know what it meant in 1969 to pull strings so you could get into the National Guard during the Vietnam War. It meant somebody else got shot at in your place. And the same thing goes for his draft-dodging vice president, who not once, not twice, but *five times* had "other priorities" than to defend his nation when called for duty.

Let there be no mistake. What happened at Abu Ghraib was not the action of a few renegade soldiers. We see the same pattern at Guantánamo. We see the same pattern in Afghanistan.

This came from the top, not from the bottom. To blame it on the soldiers at the bottom of the chain of command so the civilians at the top can get off the hook is not only a moral outrage but an affront to every veteran who has ever worn the uniform of the United States of America.

And let me say to the president's Attorney General, Alberto Gonzales, who has dismissed the provisions against torture in the Geneva Conventions as "quaint" and outdated: Go ask John McCain how quaint those Conventions seem when someone isn't following them. Go ask our British comrades in arms from World War II who suffered in Japanese prison camps how quant those

Conventions are when someone isn't following them. And go ask all the Vietnam War veterans the president and vice president would have known if they'd answered their call to service how quaint those Conventions are when someone isn't following them.

So why did Kerry, a man who personally understood the stakes, choose not to make an issue of Abu Ghraib? Because his chief advisors, strategist Bob Shrum and campaign manager Mary Beth Cahill, strongly advised against it, and they had the data to back them up: what people said in focus groups.

Unfortunately, this use of focus groups represents a profound mis-understanding of how the mind works. When strategists are tempted to ask voters questions about how they should run their campaigns, they should remember a simple maxim: *don't ask, don't tell*.

As I have shown throughout this book, much of political persua-sion occurs through changes in networks that are inaccessible to con-sciousness. If you ask people conscious questions about unconscious processes, they will be happy to offer you their theories. But most of the time, those theories are wrong. And except when focus groups are per-formed by a very skillful moderator like Frank Luntz, who uses them to help identify unconscious overtones and to test alternative ways of talking about an issue,[11] they say nothing about what would happen if a candidate actually made an effort to *shape* public opinion rather than mirror it.

Ironically, Cahill and her colleagues had actually collected infor-mation on voters' unconscious networks in some of their focus groups. They just didn't know how to "read" it. In one group, they asked vot-ers to draw a picture to convey their feelings about Abu Ghraib. Voters drew a skull-and-crossbones, a hand squeezing the world out of shape, and the United States encircled by fingers pointing at it.[12] Cahill and company had used Abu Ghraib as a Rorschach (one of the first tests de-signed to assess unconscious networks), but they didn't get the picture.

So John Kerry, who had seen atrocities on both sides in Vietnam, who had testified about those atrocities, and who had spent years working with lawmakers on both sides of the aisle to bring home the remains of American soldiers in Vietnam who had been the victim of them, remained silent as the United States of America squeezed the world out of shape, encircled by pointing fingers warning that the path it was going down was poisonous.

That two Democratic presidential nominees failed to raise the "character" issue against George W. Bush, all the while letting him raise it against them, similarly represents a profound failure to understand both the necessity and ethics of negative campaigning. Attacking Bush's character would have called voters' attention to feelings they *should* have had about a man who ultimately presided over the country the same way he had presided over his life, with the same recklessness, inability to learn from his mistakes, and lack of concern for the consequences of his behavior.

Bush had led a profligate life, and the story he used to try to put that life off-limits was that he was born again at age forty. But Bush had himself discounted that principle in judging people's past actions, and demonstrated that whatever evils lurked in his soul before finding Jesus had not been exorcised, when he refused as governor of Texas, despite the impassioned pleas of even Jerry Falwell and Pat Robertson, to commute the death sentence of Karla Faye Tucker. Tucker, a convicted murderer with a childhood history that jurors might have considered to be mitigating circumstances in sentencing her had they been aware of it, had been a model prisoner for fourteen years after herself finding Jesus. Bush showed a serious character defect that would have repulsed most Americans if the Gore or Kerry campaigns had simply told them about it—and done so repeatedly—when he mocked Tucker's plea for clemency. In a candid moment with a sympathetic interviewer, Bush pursed his lips and whimpered derisively, "Please, please, don't kill me."[13] Democrats should have invoked Bush's Tucker impression every time he used the phrase "compassionate conservative," and they should have asked what kind of born-again Christian could possibly send another clearly repentant sinner to the lions.

Telling the truth about an aspect of your opponent's character that has a direct bearing on his or her capacity to lead is essential in a democracy because people vote with their emotions. If a candidate has character flaws that *should* worry voters, candidates do them a deep disservice by jamming their emotional radar.

Playing Nice

A second myth about negative appeals is that they are ineffective. This is another distinctly liberal misconception. If it were true, George W. Bush would not have won the 2004 election after spending three-fourths of his budget on attack ads—the same percentage of the electorate, by the way, that reports an antipathy to negative campaigning.[14]

Every winning campaign in the last century has featured salient attacks on the opposition.[15] Roosevelt had no trouble indicting the Republicans as sitting blithely by as people suffered through the Great Depression, and he vowed to end their "era of selfishness" that had put the interests of the rich above those of the nation. Kennedy minced no words about Richard Nixon, and Nixon ran a brutally negative campaign in 1972, describing the Democratic Party as the party of "abortion, acid, and amnesty." George W. Bush ran the two most negative presidential campaigns in recent history. Consider the ad he used to reinforce his message on Gore's character:

[Camera zooms slowly in on kitchen scene with television broadcasting speech by Al Gore] FEMALE VOICE: There's Al Gore, reinventing himself on television again. Like I'm not going to notice? [spoken sarcastically, with a half laugh in her voice] [image zooms in on Gore speaking] Who's he going to be today? [screen turns to static, with accompanying sound, to indicate that a new Gore is about to appear, which he does] The Al Gore who raises campaign money at a Buddhist temple? [video clips of Gore interacting with Buddhists] Or the one who now promises campaign finance reform? [full picture of Gore on the television set, saying, in the background, "I will fight for you!"] Really [spoken sarcastically, as screen again turns to static]. Al Gore, claiming credit for things he didn't even do [barely audible video clip of Gore doing an interview, which goes to full volume as the narrator stops speaking].

GORE: "I took the initiative, in creating the Internet."

FEMALE VOICE [interview continues, but Gore's volume decreases again, so that it is barely audible as the female narrator continues] Yeah, and I invented the remote control, too [static on television, followed by return to original scene of Gore blathering away about policy on the television in the kitchen]. Another round of this and I'll sell my television [in small boldfaced black letters in the middle of the screen: *gorewillsayanything.com*].[16]

Using Gore's own "testimony" renders the commercial particularly effective, because it makes the charges seem irrefutable. This is a technique Democratic ad makers should use uninhibitedly because it convicts an opponent with his own words. Had the Democratic Party done its job in 2004, every American would have been able to recite verbatim the following words from a 1991 National Public Radio interview by then-Defense Secretary Dick Cheney, as he described why American troops didn't march into Baghdad after defeating Saddam:

> They would get mired down inside Iraq, in a conflict that's been raging for generations, in the interest of trying to dictate who's going to govern in Iraq. That is not something that we are prepared to see American forces do. . . . For the U.S. to get involved militarily in determining the outcome of the struggle over who's going to govern in Iraq strikes me as a classic definition of a quagmire.[17]

Although Democrats can and should emulate the highly effective technique used in Bush's character ad against Gore, they should not emulate its ethics. It capitalized on principles of association in a way that reinforced an untruth. Gore never claimed to have *invented* the Internet, as charged by the Bush campaign and accepted by the media, and he didn't do it in this ad, either, although that's what most Americans remembered (and many readers probably took away from it after *just reading* the transcript—take a look at what he actually said). The ad activated the "invented the Internet" network by quoting Gore using a word, *create*, that in many contexts is a synonym of *invent*. The Gore team tried repeatedly, and unsuccessfully, to set the record straight. What they didn't realize was that what they really needed to do was to set the *emotion* straight, and the record would follow.[18]

The attacks by Bush and his surrogates on Kerry were far fiercer. Re-election campaigns generally hinge on whether people are happy or unhappy with the job performance of the incumbent. In 2004, Bush's approval ratings were hovering dangerously below 50 percent. Bush strategists knew that they needed to make the campaign "a choice, not a referendum,"[19] and to make it about the challenger, not the incumbent. So by May 2004, three months before Kerry had even officially become his party's nominee, the Bush campaign had already run an astonishing 50,000 negative ads against him throughout the country, and succeeded in defining him before he could define himself.

Confronted with a relentlessly negative campaign against him, one might imagine that Kerry would have fought back hard. But quite the opposite: Kerry's campaign literally had a rule that no one was allowed to attack the Republicans, particularly at the Democratic Convention.[20] The only Democratic campaign strategists who had actually elected a presidential candidate in thirty years, Carville and Begala, each attempted "an intervention" with the Kerry team, trying to explain to them how and why to go negative and how to avoid the politics of personal destruction while telling *some* kind of story about why voters should replace Bush and Kerry.

But Kerry's team, led by a strategist with an impressive zero-for-seven record in presidential campaigns, knew better. In the midst of a withering attack on his war hero status and an increasingly successful attempt to tell the story that Kerry was weak, effete, and feminine, they chose to stage a convention where everyone was expected to play nice. They told Bill Clinton—the most brilliant orator in the Democratic Party, who could be counted on to take just the right tone, which he did—to mute his criticism of the Bush administration. They were enraged at Jimmy Carter when he delivered an extraordinarily powerful, well-aimed attack on the Bush administration's foreign policy. And Kerry got virtually no post-convention "bump" in the polls, something previously unheard of.

Things were very different at the Republican Convention. Delegates handed out Band-Aids with purple hearts on them to mock Kerry's heroism. This should have led to a devastating offensive by Democrats against a draft-dodging president and vice president for making fun of a soldier wounded for defending his country—especially while our own men and women in uniform were fighting in Afghanistan and Iraq. A firing squad of Democrats fanning out across the networks in rapid response would have created a media event that overshadowed the rest of the convention.

The polls were clear throughout the election of 2004 that the country didn't want four more years of George W. Bush. His approval ratings hovered at dangerous levels throughout the campaign, even without any coherent attacks from the Kerry team. So why were Shrum and Cahill so convinced that it wouldn't be in Kerry's or the nation's interest for him to challenge the president on Abu Ghraib; on his extraordinary suspension of the Kyoto Treaty and the Geneva Conventions; on his decision to stay on vacation for a month after receiving a presidential daily briefing on August 6, 2001, titled "Bin Laden Determined to Attack Inside the U.S."; on his administration's cavalier dismissal of the Clinton administration's apocalyptic warning that al Qaeda would occupy more of the new president's time than any other issue and the detailed memo Richard Clark handed Condoleeza Rice on al Qaeda in January 2001 that she ignored; and on the stonewalling for two years of any investigation of the intelligence failures that led to September 11 and the Iraq War, which culminated in that dramatic moment (which the Kerry team never turned into an ad) in which Condoleeza Rice defensively disclosed the title of that memo the administration had tried to hide for fear of breaking the bubble of "George W. Bush, brave hero of September 11?" Why did Kerry's campaign decide not to "go negative" on Bush, instead arranging the sweetest, let's-play-nicest convention in American history, against one of the dirtiest, let's-play-roughest campaigns in memory?

Because of Dayton, Ohio.

Focus groups in places like Dayton told the Kerry campaign that they didn't like negativity.[21] And the Kerry team believed them[22]—

while Bush was beating the pants off Kerry with a steady stream of negativity.

Counterpunching

I had recently moved back to Georgia after twenty-five years away when Senator Max Cleland was running for re-election in 2002. What astounded me was the following sequence of events.

Cleland's opponent, Saxby Chambliss, began attacking the Vietnam veteran and triple amputee for his lack of patriotism. The orchestrated attack began in May, when Chambliss, who had received two deferments from Vietnam because of "bad knees," chided the decorated war veteran "for breaking his oath to protect and defend the Constitution."[23]

On the surface, Chambliss was attacking Cleland for a particular vote, but it was the same vote cast by the majority of Senators, including conservative Republicans, such as Bill Frist (who, by extension, must also have been a traitor). In reality, this was simply the first act of a smear campaign with all the hallmarks of Rove politics: attack your opponent on his strong suit (in this case, Cleland's war credentials) and use innuendo, whisper campaigns (about how, exactly, Cleland had lost his limbs), and misleading accusations to destroy your opponent's reputation.

The main act came in the form of an advertising campaign, interspersed with visits from the popular "war president" (who came repeatedly to Georgia at Rove's insistence, despite the fact that Chambliss was initially seen as a long shot), claiming that Cleland was "soft on terror." The most controversial (i.e., most widely watched and discussed) commercial began with images of Saddam Hussein and Osama bin Laden, accompanied by the words, "As America faces terrorists and extremist dictators, Max Cleland runs television ads *claiming* he has the courage to lead." Saddam and Osama then disappear from the screen, to be replaced by Cleland, in an obvious attempt to link them associatively. The ad then portrays Cleland as having voted eleven times against the president's proposal for the creation of a Department of Homeland Security and lying about his support for the president's antiterrorism efforts, with the phrase "but that's just not the truth" stamped in large red letters over his face.

Cleland had actually been one of the first to propose a Department of Homeland Security, against Bush's vehement opposition. Later, the president changed his mind, proposing a bill with an antilabor provision that led many Democrats, including Cleland, to vote against it—and opening them to a deceptive attack on their patriotism. The ad ends with the line, "Max Cleland *says* he has the courage to lead, but the record proves that's just misleading," with the word *misleading* stamped in large red letters over his face.

This was just the kind of attack that should lead Democrats to take the gloves off. The ad was so reprehensible that Republican Senators and Vietnam veterans Chuck Hagel and John McCain denounced it.

Although I was astounded by the draft dodger attacking the disabled war veteran on his patriotism, I was even more astounded when Cleland barely responded (until the end, when it was too late). The Cleland I had watched rise through the ranks of Georgia politics when I was a teenager would have come back with a swift, unconstrained, no-holds-barred attack, which would surely have started with some variant of, "How *dare* you, you yellow-bellied, country-club coward, accuse *me* of not loving my country. How *dare* you utter my name in the same breath with Osama bin Laden and Saddam Hussein. I have half a mind to kick your ass with the one arm I have left."

But that wasn't how Cleland responded. He seemed like he'd been muzzled.

I shook my head in astonishment, knowing that despite his having started with a twenty-point lead in the polls, he was heading for defeat. So why didn't he make the obvious response?

I understood better two years later when Republicans used exactly the same strategy against John Kerry, who responded in just the same way—and with the same results. The Democrats had kept the same consultants who were so spectacularly unsuccessful two years earlier, and they offered the same advice.

A central psychological principle in shaping voters' networks is never to let the other side create emotional associations without countering them. That means, among other things, never letting an attack linger without responding to it. Or as Carville and Begala have gracefully put it, "It's hard for your opponent to say bad things about you when your fist is in his mouth."[24]

Most people understand the Ninth Commandment: "Thou shalt not bear false witness against thy neighbor." The best response to an unfair attack is a vigorous counterpunch thrown with genuine anger that goes straight to the heart of the attacker. Particularly for Democrats, who voters tend to perceive as weak when confronted with aggression, a strong counterpunch confers the added advantage of sending the *meta-message* that this is a "different kind of Democrat," one who knows when it's time to take off the gloves.

Unfortunately, Democrats tend to respond to attacks, particularly unfair ones, with a set of strategies that virtually always fail.

The first is not to respond at all. The conscious intent of such a strategy is usually to take the high road. But a nonresponse allows the opposition to shape voters' networks with impunity, creates uncontested frames that the media readily adopt, suggests that the candidate isn't contesting the charge or has something to hide, and emboldens the person who threw the punch to follow up with another.

The second strategy is to respond to a low blow with a flurry of facts or counterarguments. This was the tack Gore took on the "serial exaggerator" charge in 2000. This response will always put a candidate on the ropes because it turns the debate into one about *the extent to which* the charges are true and erodes the candidate's credibility no matter what the eventual outcome. Candidates hit with a series of scurrilous charges may well need to answer one or two of them (preferably the weakest or most clearly dishonest), but as soon as they allow the charges to become the central focus of the exchange, they have tacitly accepted their opponent's frame—that they have something to answer to—and this will rapidly become the dominant media frame. Counterarguments or facts should always be parenthetical statements embedded in a story about the character of someone who would behave unethically in a campaign, which is a good predictor of how he or she will behave in office.

A third response is the "he knows that's not true" or "he's lying" tack. The problem with this response, like the last one, is that it turns the issue into a he-said/she-said debate that maintains the focus on whether the candidate has really done whatever he or she has been accused of doing. Once again, if you're going to say your opponent is lying, you need to establish lying as part of a broader story about your opponent's character. The response to a low blow must always convey the message that this act reflects who the opponent *is*, not just a campaign tactic.

The fourth kind of weak response, particularly to a low blow, is what Arnold Schwarzenegger might call "girlymanspeak." Senator Tom Daschle made this mistake in 2004, when Republican John Thune told him to his face on *Meet the Press* that his criticism of Bush's handling of the war in Iraq "emboldens our enemies." Like many Republicans in 2004, Thune was questioning the patriotism of his opponent. The war veteran Daschle should have come back with a withering attack, spoken directly to Thune rather than to Tim Russert, which would have guaranteed a full camera angle showing the two together, with Daschle's veins bulging in his neck and Thune leaning backwards looking weak or frightened. Had Daschle told Thune he'd had enough of chicken hawks who don't even know how to hold a gun, let alone how to salute, question the patriotism of someone who had actually *fought* for his country—and to drive the point home, egged his challenger on with, "show us, John, how you make a proper salute" (something more difficult than one might think for someone who hasn't been in the military, and a very powerful emotional message to veterans)—he would likely still be in Washington.

Daschle eventually got to the right content (mentioning, for example, that only one of the two was a veteran), but here and elsewhere, he used cautious, gentle words such as *disappointed* and *saddened*. It's fine to be saddened at a loss, but you don't express sadness or disappointment when someone slugs you. You express rage, and you start slugging back. What *is* sad is how little coaching it would have taken Daschle to avoid this mistake. But to understand why this kind of coaching should be a central task of political consultants, you have to start with the right vision of mind.

The fifth trap into which Democrats often fall is to appeal to the referees (the media), or, worse still, to the other side, to stop it and play nice. A prototypically Democratic response to grossly misleading or otherwise offensive attack ads is "that's not fair, take that down." This has three predictable, and always unwanted, consequences: it reinforces the view of Democrats as weak and woosie; it establishes the candidate who has been attacked as the supplicant to the attacker, sending a signal all humans, as primates, understand, that the candidate is *one down*[25], and it allows the other side to milk the message for all it's worth as the media replay it repeatedly while engaging in debates about its fairness, accuracy, racism, and the like, all the while allowing it to do its unconscious handiwork.

A similar problem can be seen when Democrats call for removal of some administration official who has become a lightning rod for public disapproval, such as Bush's Secretary of Defense Donald Rumsfeld. Doing so places the blame on a subordinate to the president rather than the president himself, who ultimately called the shots. This simply allows the president to jettison the offending official and weaken the associative link between himself and his failed policies. Had Democrats not waited so long to speak in unison about the failures of the Iraq War in the fall of 2006, Bush would no doubt have availed himself of this strategy and saved a dozen Republican seats in Congress.

Why is counterpunching so important?

Because failing to counterpunch costs elections.

The two most decisive moments in the 2004 election were both failures of counterpunching. The first was Kerry's silence on the "flip-flopper" charge. The only reason such a seemingly trivial attack became so powerful was that Kerry's team refused to answer it. Left unanswered, it came to define Kerry and to shape the way both voters and media analysts listened to his answers on complex questions, just as the "serial exaggerator" charge had shaped ongoing perceptions of Gore. Long before Kerry had even won his party's nomination—within forty-eight hours of his victory in the New Hampshire primary—the Bush campaign and the conservative spin machine were already using the word and defining Kerry as someone who had taken every side on every issue.[26] Kerry ultimately gave them all the ammunition they needed with his infamous statement that "I actually did vote for the $87 billion before I voted against it." That comment played thousands of times, was a primary theme of the Republican Convention, and came to define the Kerry candidacy more than any other story told by either candidate.

The flip-flopper charge was actually a familiar one. George H. W. Bush had used it against Bill Clinton, claiming that Clinton would turn the White House into the Waffle House. Nixon had used it against McGovern, in an ad called "Turnaround," that appears to have been the prototype for the highly memorable flip flopper ad run by George W. Bush against Kerry. The Nixon ad began with a photo of McGovern in profile, accompanied by the following narration: "In 1967, Senator George McGovern said he was not an advocate of unilateral withdrawal of our troops from Vietnam." The picture then rotated 180 degrees so that the viewer saw the other side of McGovern's face, conveying the message that he was literally talking out of both sides of his mouth. That this metaphor came to my mind is a good indication of the networks the ad activated. The announcer then continued, "Now, of course, he is. Last year, the senator suggested regulating marijuana along the same lines as alcohol, which means legalizing it." Once again, the photo flipped the other way: "Now he's against legalizing it, and says he always has been." The ad continued along these lines, with the "turnarounds" coming more rapidly as the ad progressed. By the end, as the photo of McGovern's "two sides" spun dizzyingly around a pole, the narrator asks, "Last year—this year. The question is, what about next year?[27]

Bush's flip-flop ad was similar, but it added the additional, largely implicit theme of Kerry as effete and privileged, by featuring him windsurfing. The ad begins as a narrator asks, "Which way would John Kerry lead?" The rest of the ad then shows him rapidly shifting back and forth in the wind to the sound of Tchaikovsky's waltz from *Swan Lake*, as the narrator describes Kerry's repeated changes in course:

NARRATOR: Kerry voted for the Iraq war [Kerry changes directions on the water] opposed it [Kerry changes direction again], supported it, [Kerry changes direction again], and now opposes it again.

The ad continues along the same lines, with its primary focus on Iraq, but then extends to domestic issues. It concludes, "John Kerry: whichever way the wind blows."

Straight from the playbook of the Gore campaign, the Kerry campaign simply let the flip-flopper charge fester for months. By April, Kerry was reportedly infuriated by it, and he wanted to strike back by showing how much Bush flip-flopped on the issues. This wouldn't have been hard to do. It can be done against anyone with a public record, and particularly against any candidate who has run toward his party's base in the primaries and then toward the center in the general election, as Bush (and most presidential candidates on both sides of the aisle) had done. Yet again bolstered by focus groups from Cahill showing that people don't like "negativity," Shrum responded at a campaign strategy meeting, "Are we really going to get into a debate about who's the biggest flip-flopper?. . . Is this what this campaign is going to be about? These attacks aren't sticking. We're ahead in the polls."[28]

The tone deafness of the Kerry campaign to the flip-flopper attack's increasing emotional resonance with the public is disturbing. But equally disturbing was the campaign's disinterest in the available science. If the debacles of the last two elections hadn't been enough evidence of the danger of letting an attack go unanswered, relevant research from political science should have been. Years earlier, political scientist Larry Bartels had published an article in a highly visible professional journal on the importance of clarity of message. Bartels found, as expected, that voters prefer candidates whose values and policies match their own preferences. But he also found that voters prefer candidates who are clear on what they believe, *even if it is not what they believe.*[29]

Kerry could easily have dispatched with the flip-flopper charge and transformed it into a potent counterattack:

President Bush is calling me a "flip-flopper," someone who changes his mind on issues. He's absolutely right: When I make a mistake or learn something new that tells me I'd better rethink my decision, I admit my mistake, figure out where to go next, and change course.

When Mr. Bush makes a mistake, he says it wasn't a mistake, blames it on somebody else, attacks whoever said it was a mistake, tries to get them arrested or blows their wife's CIA cover, and pins a medal on whoever convinced him to make it.

And the president is also right that this is an issue of character and leadership, on which the American people should cast their votes in November. A real leader doesn't make a decision, close his eyes, go full steam ahead no matter what the consequences, and attack whoever tries to get him to wake up.

That's not "staying the course." That's *pride*, and last time I looked, it was a sin.

The second decisive moment in the election of 2004 was Kerry's failure to respond to the attacks on his war record by the Swift Boat Veterans. News about the impending publication of their book, *Unfit for Command: Swift Boat Veterans Speak Out Against John Kerry,* broke on the Drudge Report the day before Kerry's acceptance speech at the Democratic Convention. The book rose to the top of the best-seller list within a week—not coincidentally, the same week Kerry was supposed to get the traditional convention "bounce" in the polls, with a convention centered on his military heroism.[30]

A week later came the first of the notorious ads. The ads were extremely well produced. The first, which appeared on August 4, was by far the most persuasive. It featured one veteran after another—all claiming to have been on the boat with John Kerry, to have served under him, to have been his commanding officer, or otherwise to have had direct knowledge of his service in Vietnam—who offered some variant of the following: "John Kerry has not been honest about what happened in Vietnam," "He is lying about his record," or "He betrayed us."[31] Particularly damning was the "testimony" of a man identified on the screen as "Louis Letson, Medical Officer, Lieutenant Commander," who stated boldly, "I know John Kerry is lying about his first Purple Heart because I treated him for that injury." The timing was not coincidental: the theme of the Democratic Convention was that Kerry was a war hero who could lead the nation in a time of war.

Unanswered, this ad would surely raise doubts on the part of anyone watching it as to whether Kerry was really who he said he was. It raised doubts in my mind, and I was a committed Kerry supporter.

The Swift Boat ads, like the Cleland ads, had all the earmarks of a classic Karl Rove smear[32]: always just one step removed from Rove (funded and produced by his colleagues, protégés, and major campaign contributors), always devastating in their impact (particularly in their immediate impact, which either disrupts momentum of the opposition or leaves lingering questions in the minds of voters), and always difficult enough to sort out at first blush that their truth or falsehood would be adjudicated, if at all, long after their damage was done.

That Kerry would have to respond, and to do so within hours after the first ad hit the airwaves, was obvious. The only question was how.

But it was not obvious to the Kerry campaign.

After watching two days of deafening silence from Kerry (which ultimately turned into two weeks), I personally sent a one-page, single-spaced memo to the Kerry campaign through a common friend, detailing why Kerry needed to respond immediately or would drop precipitously in the polls and lose the entire South. I don't know if my memo reached Kerry's top advisors, but others who had his cell phone number—including James Carville, Paul Begala, and later, Bill Clinton—did, and gave them a similar message.

I emphasized in that memo two psychological issues that made a swift display of outrage and a direct attack on the president, essential. The first was the meta-message Kerry was conveying with his silence. Bush's master narrative in the 2004 campaign was that he was a strong commander in chief, a "war president," and the right man for the job in an unrelenting battle against a relentless foe. The story he was telling about Kerry was that he was weak and indecisive in the face of aggression and could not be trusted to steward the ship of state in such uneasy times. In microcosm, Kerry's silence was confirming exactly what Bush was saying about him: that he was weak and indecisive in the face of aggression (an attack on his honor). Second, as described earlier, in the South, when a man calls you a name, questions your integrity, or attacks your honor or that of your family, to step away is an act of cowardice.

By the time Kerry responded to the Swift Boat ads, the election was over. His poll numbers plummeted, and, as predicted, he lost every state in the South. His pollster, Mark Mellman, began seeing Kerry's negatives rise immediately after the first Swift Boat ad, but Shrum didn't want to respond and Cahill was convinced that an aggressive response would only accentuate the story.[33] Oddly, they seemed unaware of classic research, known to every undergraduate who has ever taken introductory psychology, on the "sleeper effect" in advertising, in which an ad that viewers may initially judge as coming from a noncredible source has an increasing impact over time.[34] What essentially happens is that people gradually forget the source, and the message becomes absorbed into their networks. Making matters worse in this case, the credibility of the sources was not initially unclear; not until much later was it clear, for example, that the doctor who claimed he had treated Kerry was not the one who signed the medical records, and his name was nowhere in Kerry's military medical records.[35]

Kerry finally struck back, linking the ads directly to the president once the Kerry campaign had meticulously documented the trail to Bush. But not only did he strike long after the iron that had branded him turned cold, but his eventual response undermined what should have been his message: that he would respond to aggression with swift and massive retaliation. The day of the first attack, he should have launched a character assault—preferably in front of an audience of veterans—against a self-proclaimed "war president" who ran ads dishonoring a decorated war veteran while our own troops were still fighting on foreign soil. He should have angrily demanded that the president stand before the American people, with his hand squarely on the Bible, and swear before God that neither he nor Rove nor any member of his campaign had anything to do with this unprecedented wartime attack on the honor of a decorated war veteran. The Bush campaign had given him a gift: the chance to make a real story of Bush's draft evasion, and to brand Bush, not Kerry, as the fake hero, who would attack the war record of an American veteran with shrapnel still in his leg.

Instead, his campaign responded, after two weeks of silence, by putting up ads and Web site petitions pleading with the president to take it back. His campaign manager, Cahill, wrote an open letter to Bush's campaign manager, Ken Mehlman, on August 24, almost three weeks after the first ad appeared.[36] The letter impressively detailed the web of connections between the Swift Boat Veterans and the Bush campaign. (The Bush campaign's general counsel, Benjamin Ginsburg, had to resign when it turned out he'd been advising the "independent" group.) Cahill's letter concluded:

> It's time for the President to stand up and specifically condemn "Swift Boat Veterans for Truth." Not only is this a smear on John Kerry's distinguished military service; it's an insult to all veterans who've served their country. The American people want to hear an honest discussion of the issues. They're concerned about the economy and the troubling situation in Iraq. Today, as we enter week four of this smear campaign, I'm asking you to talk to the President and ask him to heed Senator McCain's call and condemn this smear. The American people deserve better.

If the letter hadn't been signed by Cahill, I would have wondered if it had been written by Rove himself. It sent virtually every message you wouldn't want to send under these circumstances. First, from a symbolic standpoint, you don't send your mother out to fight for you when another boy bullies you in the schoolyard. Kerry's response should have been man to man, and it should have been live, on the air, not in print. Second, the form and goal of the letter had a groveling, beseeching quality, which gave Bush the power to do with it what he wanted—including ignoring it, which gave him yet another chance to demonstrate that he was the more powerful primate. The letter wasn't even addressed to Bush; it was beseeching his campaign manager to beseech the president. Third, instead of making the entire incident a condemnation of the president's character, it gave Bush the opportunity to look magnanimous, if he so choose, by simply condemning the ads, now that they'd had their desired effect. Finally, it got off message, wandering into dispassionate Democratic rhetoric about how the American people want to hear debates on the issues and meandering off onto the economy and Iraq.

In his handling of the Swift Boat affair, what Kerry effectively told the American people was what he would do if America were attacked: he would wait an inordinate amount of time until he had gathered enough evidence to establish guilt beyond a reasonable doubt in a court of law, use polls and focus groups to see what kind of response Americans preferred, and then write our enemies a letter imploring them to stop their terrorist acts immediately.

Sometimes, the meta-message is the message.

Conclusion: Get There First

The last several pages have focused on how to respond to attacks. But there's one strategic principle that can sometimes head off attacks or effective appeals from the opposition before they hit: *get there first*.

In the 1940s, social psychologists began studying persuasion, including how to prevent the other side from getting the upper hand. Over time, they discovered a number of methods for increasing resistance to the opposition's message. We have known for half a century that in advertising, being the first to make a pitch renders an effort at persuasion more effective.[37] The one who gets there first has the widest latitude in shaping networks while they are most malleable (i.e., when no other dots have been firmly connected).

Psychologists discovered years ago that a related technique for reducing the power of a negative appeal from the other side is *inoculation*. Inoculation means building up "resistance" to an appeal by forewarning against it or presenting (and answering) weak arguments in favor of it before the other side can offer a stronger version.[38] Much as a vaccine builds the body's defenses through exposure to small, inert amounts of a virus, weak and easily assailable arguments supporting the other point of view prompt people to accept or spontaneously generate counterarguments that serve as emotional "antibodies."

Kerry could have prevented most of the problems that ultimately undid his campaign if he and his advisors had just followed this simple, well-researched strategy. There was no sensible alternative to inoculation on the issue of his Senate testimony of April 1971. Kerry needed to explain to the American people why he had turned against the war and why he had testified about American atrocities. Leaving an "eighteen-minute gap" in his narrative simply telegraphed to Karl Rove where Kerry's team thought he was vulnerable. Embracing this part of his history would have given him the platform he needed later to speak about Abu Ghraib and to respond to the Swift Boat Veterans, who scored some of their most powerful points with the notion that Kerry's testimony was a betrayal of his fellow soldiers.[39]

Whenever Democrats are tempted to take a "wait and see" approach, they need to remember that in politics, he who frames first usually frames best.

chapter fourteen

TERROR NETWORKS

★ ★ ★

Of Joe McCarthy it can be said that fear made him possible, partisanship was responsible for his rise, and politicians, press, and public shared the blame for failing to check his abuses, which damaged countless individuals and brought shame to the United States.

— HAYNES JOHNSON, *The Age of Anxiety*[1]

Republicans wielded terror as a weapon in the late 1940s and early 1950s during Joe McCarthy's reign of terror. They have wielded it again since 2002, when Karl Rove declared to the Republican National Committee that terror (in the guise of national security) would be the linchpin of a Republican realignment over the next several years. The primary reason the Democratic Party failed to tell an alternative story on Iraq, terrorism, or national security more broadly between September 11, 2001, and mid-September 2006 was fear: fear of being unseated, fear of being branded, and fear of being outflanked.

Unfortunately, like ambivalence, *fear leaks*. And in times of uncertain security, the last thing voters want to see in their leaders is fear. As a result, Democrats were unseated, branded, and outflanked for five years.

Fear and anger are two negative emotions that tend to polarize the electorate and paralyze Democrats. Not coincidentally, the most virulent strains of these two emotions—terror and hate—have become staples of Republican campaigns. This chapter examines the question of how to respond to campaign strategies designed to mobilize the worst in human nature, by activating hate and terror. It concludes with some thoughts on the role of courage in Democratic politics.

Where There's Fire,
Don't Wave at the Smoke

Republicans have exploited hate consistently since the 1960s, focusing on race, homosexuality, nationalism (those who "support our troops" versus those who "embolden to the enemy"), and the distinction between "true" Christians and everyone else. These targets of hate bear striking similarity to the axis of evil employed by McCarthy, and they have been used in much the same way, except this time not by a senator, who was ultimately disgraced, but by the president.[2]

In the 2006 midterm election, when blacks and gays seemed to lose some of their hate appeal, Republicans turned to immigrants to make up the difference. But recognizing that Hispanic immigrants will decide many elections in the twenty-first century, this time it was Republican ambivalence that leaked, and the effort at "immigration reform" ultimately couldn't undo the damage of Bush's war.

A single principle applies to hate appeals dressed up in religious garb, hate appeals cloaked as concerns about "law and order," terror appeals designed to frighten voters rather than to ready them for action, and last-minute "emergency" acts of Congress designed to re-elect Republicans in the name of national security: *where there's fire, don't wave at the smoke*. If you do, you just fan the flames.

Martin Luther King and Lyndon Johnson didn't make their case for "all men are created equal" by addressing the smokescreens put up by Southern politicians to stop black people from voting. They didn't argue about the pros and cons of literacy in a Democratic electorate to make a case against literary tests. They didn't argue about the utility or disutility of poll taxes in a republic. They understood that this was just the smoke, and that the real issue was the fire in the belly of those who were burning the crosses.

King talked about his dream—that one day his four little children would be judged not by the color of their skin but by the content of their character. Johnson described the scars of hatred and poverty he had seen forty years earlier on the faces of Mexican-American children. Both men went for the gut because they knew it was the gut that had to change.

What Johnson and King both intuitively understood is what colleagues and I demonstrated with brain imaging forty years later: that arguing about the rationality of rationalizations is attacking the wrong target. Rationalizations are the post hoc smoke that billows from emotional fires. In our study, only *after* partisans had come to emotionally biased judgments did we see any activation in circuits usually associated with reasoning, suggesting that they had begun to develop rationalizations for their emotional biases. You can systematically debate the fine points of these realizations, but you're wasting your time.

You don't put out a fire by waving at the smoke. You put out the fire. And if someone keeps starting those fires, you put out the arsonist.

Unfortunately, Democratic strategists have long been under the sway of both the wrong model of the mind—a dispassionate model that has led them to treat rationalizations as if they were reasons, and hence as falling within the province of rational discourse—and a paralysis born of fear. They have been afraid of their own aggression—afraid of calling hatred, bigotry, and the misuse of government through legislation designed to serve no other purpose than to re-elect Republicans what it is—and afraid that whatever they say, they will be outflanked.

This confluence of the wrong vision of mind and the wrong state of mind has led Democrats in recent years to participate repeatedly in a game whose rules were designed to circumvent American democracy for partisan advantage. The first major example was the resolution President Bush and the Republican leaders hurriedly pushed through Congress in October 2002, which gave Bush the authority to invade Iraq without any genuine congressional debate—the legislative equivalent to preapproval for an unlimited line of credit on a credit card with no expiration date and no interest.

The resolution was written of, by, and for the Republican Party. It was laced with multiple references to September 11 designed to associate the call to arms against Saddam with the war on bin Laden and, hence, both to deceive the public and to render Democrats who voted against it easier to attack as "soft on terror."

The Republicans did not hide their intention of branding any Democrat who cast a vote against that resolution or even called for debate on it as weak on terrorism, and they were ready to flood the airwaves with misleading ads that would ablate any subtlety of a principled "nay." This left Democrats who had concerns about how the United States was going to fight a war on two fronts (in Afghanistan and Iraq) and about the rationale for an elective war against Saddam Hussein with what they perceived as a Hobson's choice: to vote for an ill-defined, ill-advised blank check, or to vote against it, and likely lose the opportunity to participate in any checks on Bush's authority three months later.

There was, however, another option: To tell the truth, and to do so with the righteous indignation of someone who has the right to feel indignant.

I learned a lesson many years ago in clinical work that I teach every beginning psychologist or psychiatrist I train. There are very few things you can do that will destroy your relationship with your patients beyond repair (other than sleeping with them), but there is one: lying, even about the smallest of things.

I made that mistake once, and I never repeated it. I was still in training at the time, and a patient asked why I hadn't returned a call about some minor billing issue. Caught off guard, and feeling guilty that his phone message had slipped my mind, I said I'd tried to call but didn't get through. We had a good relationship, and although he looked at first incredulous, the issue was a trivial one, so he gave me the benefit of the doubt. But I learned an important lesson. The relationship between a clinician and patient is based on trust and honesty. Even "white lies" create an undercurrent of distance or distrust, and that undercurrent can corrode the relationship and limit your ability to help your patient.

The same is true of the relationship between leaders and the people they represent. If you're a politician and you want to maintain the trust and goodwill of your constituents over the long run, tell them the truth—about what you believe, about why you made the decision you did, or about why you are about to make a decision that may run counter to what they want to hear. Elected officials can usually repair the damage done by taking an unpopular stand if they're honest about the reasons for it and make clear that their position reflects the courage of their convictions rather than the easy way out. Lies, however, are far more likely to come back to haunt—or to require future sins of omission or commission.

Democrats who voted for the Iraq War Resolution can say, as most have, that they voted for the resolution but were then shocked by its execution, or were misled by the administration with faulty and cherry-picked intelligence. In so doing, they are telling the truth—but only about two-thirds of it.

The reality is that Democrats were playing checkers against master chess players, and their strategists were so afraid of losing all their checkers that they advised Democrats in the House and Senate to make a very bad move: to vote for a resolution they knew was not in the country's best interest. This was a fateful decision, because it tied their hands for four years, as they searched for language that could allow them to call for an end to a war that was costing thousands of American soldiers and hundreds of thousands of Iraqis their lives and limbs without admitting that what they had done had reflected bad judgment.

The alternative to capitulating would have been for the Democrats to hold a press conference, denounce the Republican ploy for what it was, and vote as a group not to vote—to make a *principled abstention*. In other words, the Democrats could have ignored the smoke, doused the fire, and doused those who had set it with their own fuel, by reframing the incendiary bill in the idiom in which it had been framed by the Republicans: patriotism.

One of the most potent ways to respond to attacks on one's character, patriotism, or faith is to use the same idiom, redefined, to turn the accuser into the accused. Doing so creates a counternarrative that activates the same emotional systems but links them to alternative networks. And even more important is to challenge the frame pre-emptively—to inoculate—rather than to remain silent and hope for the best, or to argue about the smoke after the other side has already burned down your house.

Consider, for example, if the Democrats had assembled on the steps of the Senate as the Republicans were taking their vote and of-fered a straightforward explanation for what was going on within the walls of the Congress:

> We have been asked today to sign into law a resolution allowing the president to send your sons and daughters into Iraq. Why does this resolution have such urgency? It is not about national se-curity. The president's own chief of staff, Andrew Card, told re-porters last week why suddenly the threat from Saddam Hussein looms so large, just weeks before an election: "From a marketing point of view," he brashly acknowledged, "you don't introduce new products in August."[3]
>
> America's security after September 11 is not a product line. It is our lifeline.
>
> The Republicans are demanding that we vote for this resolu-tion without discussion, without knowing whether a deployment of troops to Iraq would prevent us from finishing the job in Af-ghanistan where Osama bin Laden is still at large, and without knowing whether fighting a war on two fronts will require rein-statement of the draft.
>
> The resolution we are being asked to vote for demands that we abridge the Constitution that our founding fathers so artfully crafted, which gave Congress the sacred duty to provide oversight over the executive branch, not only in times of peace but also in times of war, when American lives are most at stake. And the rea-son we are being asked to sign this resolution now—the reason it cannot wait until the facts are more clear—is not national secu-rity. This resolution is designed for no other purpose than the partisan interests of the Republican Party.
>
> We stand here united today to tell the American people that if and when the time comes that we need to confront Saddam Hussein with military might, we Democrats stand ready to op-pose him with military might. And we will destroy him.

But we stand here today, as well, to promise the parents of this nation that we will *never* vote to send your sons and daughters off to war without first knowing the facts on the ground, and we will never send them to die without first being sure that history can be written in no other ink than their blood.

To play partisan politics with matters of war and peace, with the life and death of our brave men and women in uniform, is un-American. It is unpatriotic. It is immoral.

It is time to send the Republicans in Congress and the president a strong message, that in the post-September 11 world, we are not Democrats and Republicans. We are Americans. And Americans don't play political games with the lives of our servicemen and women.

Had the Democrats responded forcefully to the fire burning in the halls of Congress, the media would have been forced to consider an alternative frame for the Iraq War Resolution than "the party of strength versus the party of weak resolve," and the Republicans would have had a lot of explaining to do. There was no explaining away Card's candid remark. It said everything there was to be said, and Democrats should have repeated it like a mantra.

Instead, the Democrats played the hand the Republicans had dealt them, even though they knew the cards were marked. Virtually all voted to support the resolution—and with predictable results. Eight Democrats lost their seats in the House, giving the Republicans such a large majority as to render the Democrats irrelevant. The Republicans also picked up control of the Senate, giving Bush the majorities in both houses of Congress that he needed to wage any kind of war he wanted, redefining the meaning of congressional oversight.

Putting Party over Nation

In the 2004 and 2006 elections, the pattern of putting party over nation escalated, beginning with terror alerts and aging videos of terrorists pulled out of the files to distract attention every time some new piece of information damaging to the Bush administration emerged. And like a child watching a magic trick, the media shifted their attention to each "new" scare, running old footage of terrorist training camps over the banner "The War on Terror."

In late September 2006, five weeks before the midterm election, Republicans pulled their traditional "October surprise" (showing their efficiency by showcasing their new model on the last Friday of September). After their failed attempt to play the September 11 card yet again on the fifth anniversary of the attack, they had to find another way to bring terror to the fore. So they used a Supreme Court rebuke to the president's intent to hold "enemy combatants" indefinitely or try them in kangaroo courts to create a "crisis" that required immediate action.

Naturally, the matter could not wait for discussion. The vote in the Senate on a bill with wide ramifications had to be held on the final day of the legislative session before the pre-election break. Whereas initially the bill that ultimately became the Military Commissions Act had led to a chorus of public rebukes by retired generals such as former Secretary of State Colin Powell, the success of the Republican Party was apparently so important that John McCain, once known for his truth-telling, decided to settle for cosmetic changes that would allow future POWs to experience the kind of torture he himself had endured. As the "compromise" bill reached the Senate floor, Powell once again went AWOL in the face of an attack on his country and its Constitution, disappearing from the stage he could have so easily commanded.

The key provisions of the bill included the following.[4] The president can designate any foreign national, including those who are legal residents of the United States as well as those living anywhere in the world (including in their own countries), as "enemy combatants." He can detain them indefinitely without judicial review, suspend whatever provisions of the Geneva Conventions he wants to suspend at his own discretion, submit such individuals to whatever forms of coercion he prefers as long as he doesn't label it torture (subject only to his own interpretation), use coerced evidence to convict them in secret courts, and withhold from them whatever evidence he deems essential for national security as they are tried for crimes for which that evidence is used as probative. Essentially, the Republicans had managed to cross Kafka, the Gulag, and the Alien and Sedition Acts to create their own house blend of tyranny and terror.

In a blistering editorial, the *New York Times* noted that if there was ever a time for a Democratic filibuster, this was it. Yet instead, as the *Times* put it, "the Democratic leadership in the Senate seems to have misplaced its spine."

So why did the No Rights Left Behind Act pass with barely a whimper from Democrats in either the House or Senate?

Because the Republicans (this time, including the president himself) telegraphed, yet again, precisely what they would do to any Democrats who opposed it: distort their vote for political gain in the upcoming election, branding them as "soft on terrorism." Democrats had seen what had happened to Max Cleland and others who had opposed particular provisions of national security bills and were then branded as weak on national security. So Republicans put the thumbscrews on the Democrats, who promptly allowed the Republicans to pass a law legalizing thumbscrews.

That's the politics of fear.

The GOP wasted no time in painting Democrats who even called for a debate about the merits of the bill as fools or traitors who would sell our nation short on terror to save the security equivalent of the spotted owl (i.e., civil liberties). Ohio Republican House Minority Leader John Boehner expressed his consternation at the Democrats' failure to endorse the bill enthusiastically, warning, "The Democrats' irrational opposition to strong national security policies that help keep our nation secure should be of great concern to the American people."

Apparently, Democrats want to see our nation attacked.

If you can't expose the incoherence of that narrative, you are in deep trouble.

But the Democrats *were* in deep trouble. They responded in characteristic fashion—to the smoke signals. The Republicans were accusing them of nothing short of failing at the first and only task of government when national security is in jeopardy, and the Democrats either ran for cover or went for the fine print. Michigan Democratic Congressman John Conyers offered a prototypical example of a response that was factually right on point but was hand-waving at the smoke while the

Constitution burned: "Hidden in the fine print are provisions which grant the administration authority to maintain permanent records on innocent U.S. citizens, granting the administration new authority to demand personal records without court review, and terminating any and all legal challenges to unlawful wiretapping."[5]

Conyers' language, however accurate, told precisely the story the Republicans wanted to tell about their opposition, and had been telling effectively for five years: that Democrats fiddle with the fine print while the Twin Towers burn.

Democrats had actually been here before—long before 2002.

In his captivating book, *The Age of Anxiety*, Haynes Johnson[6] describes three prior moments in American history when demagogues used fear to incite hate, and hate to incite desecration of the Constitution. The first were the Alien and Sedition Acts passed under President John Adams at the beginning of our republic, prompted by threat of war with France, which led to the jailing of journalists who wrote negative stories about the president or congress. The second was the "red scare" that occurred when the Bolsheviks took power in 1917 in Russia, which ultimately led to Gestapo-like knocks at the doors of American citizens believed by the attorney general to be communist sympathizers.

The third moment, and the primary subject of Haynes' historical account, is the one he links most closely to the Republicans' use of terror since September 11: the reign of terror of Senator Joseph McCarthy in the early 1950s. The similarities are indeed striking, from the charges of disloyalty aimed at those who did not agree with him, to the use of "fear and smear" by the Republican Party to take control of Congress and the presidency (even though Eisenhower himself despised McCarthy), to the effort to brand people as "with us or against us" (first in foreign affairs and then domestically, defining people as either American or un-American), to the distinction between true Christians and everyone else, to the relentless attack on homosexuals (led, ironically, by McCarthy's chief aid and deputy grand inquisitor, Roy Cohn, who died in the mid-1980s of AIDS).

What is most instructive about the parallel between the McCarthy era and the Bush era is what happens when frightened politicians respond with appeasement to a bully with little or no capacity for empathy or remorse. Although the nation learned the dangers of appeasement in the war against Hitler, Democrats never learned the *psychological* lesson about appeasement. It is perhaps the most important lesson a boy in a schoolyard or a politician (male or female) on the steps of the Senate can learn about the dynamics of bullies, particularly those who are minimally constrained by conscience: if you back down, appease, or acquiesce to a bully, he will invariably view it as a sign of weakness, and you will have done nothing but to embolden him to increase the stakes.

If there are psychological "laws of nature," this is one of them.

When Democrats were too fearful to oppose McCarthy from the start with collective action, he knew he could destroy them. And destroy he did. It was not until McCarthy's grandiosity got the best of him and he went after Eisenhower himself that the decorated general turned president—who acted much like a Democrat, brave in war yet oddly cowardly in peace—worked behind the scenes to undo McCarthy.

There is a moral to this story: in times of terror, when someone threatens national security or the rights guaranteed in the Constitution for personal or partisan advantage in the name of nationalism, nothing short of his political destruction will stop him, and he has to be attacked using the same idiom in which he is couching his appeals to fear and hate. He has to be branded for what he is.

So suppose, instead, Democrats had produced a firestorm of their own, going straight for the Republicans on what this bill was really about—compromising security for partisan ends—and let the public wrestle with two alternative narratives about who was really protecting America and who was more worried about protecting their party.

How much more compelling a case could the Democrats have made that the Republicans had crossed the line from partisanship to *treason*? The definition of treason is putting the nation in danger—including our troops, who would now be fair game for torturers if captured—for personal gain. This is exactly what the Republicans had done, and it is exactly what the Democrats should have called it.

In failing to respond as a party to No Rights Left Behind, the Democrats failed to attend to three important political realities.

First, and most importantly, if you don't stand for anything, there's not much reason to have a party. If the *Constitution* isn't worth defending, it's hard to know what is. And if your leading strategists can't figure out how you can win by speaking the *truth* on vital matters of national security and civil liberties, get yourself new strategists.

Second, somehow in all the smoke what was lost on many in the Democratic Party was that this was simply Act II of the Iraq War Resolution. The Republicans had used precisely the same blackmail against the Democrats four years earlier almost to the day, and 3,000 Americans had died for it. Both sides were reading from exactly the same playbooks they had used in 2002. The only difference was that the Republicans had watched tapes of the game, and the Democrats hadn't. The Democrats' leadership seemed to have no memory that they had run the same "prevent" defense before, and that it hadn't prevented anything. The only thing that changed the game this time, by changing the subject, was an unexpected interception of some damning e-mails the same day that revealed that Republican Congressman Mark Foley had a fondness for male congressional pages and that the Republican leadership had chosen to huddle to protect their party even at the cost of the safety of minors in its charge.

The third political reality, to borrow the milquetoast Democratic slogan of 2006, was that "Together, we can do better." One of the most powerful political lessons of the labor movement in its heyday was that when people without power oppose those with it, they can be picked off individually. The only way to avoid becoming sitting ducks is to fire back with collective action, and that is precisely what the Democrats should have done. Or as Ben Franklin more eloquently stated the principle two centuries ago, "we must all hang together or we will most assuredly all hang separately."

In this case, there *was* a better way: the same road the Democrats should have taken when confronted with the Iraq War Resolution debacle of 2002. This time, their collective voice would have been much more powerful. And what they should have said was penned a few days later by the unelected mayor of Lake Wobegone, Garrison Keillor:

I would not send my college kid off for a semester abroad if I were you. This week, we have suspended human rights in America, and what goes around comes around. . . .

The U.S. Senate, in all its splendor and majesty, has decided that an "enemy combatant" is any non-citizen whom the president says is an enemy combatant, including your Korean greengrocer or your Swedish grandmother or your Czech au pair, and can be arrested and held for as long as authorities wish without any right of appeal to a court of law to examine the matter. If your college kid were to be arrested in Bangkok or Cairo, suspected of "crimes against the state," and held in prison, you'd assume that an American Foreign Service officer would be able to speak to your kid and arrange for a lawyer, but this may not be true anymore. Be forewarned.

The Senate also decided it's up to the president to decide whether it's OK to make these enemies stand naked in cold rooms for a couple days in blinding light and be beaten by interrogators. . . .

None of the men and women who voted for this bill has any right to speak in public about the rule of law anymore, or to take a high moral view of the Third Reich, or to wax poetic about the American Idea. Mark their names. Any institution of higher learning that grants honorary degrees to these people forfeits its honor. . . .

To paraphrase Sir Walter Scott: Mark their names and mark them well. For them, no minstrel raptures swell. High though their titles, proud their name, boundless their wealth as wish can claim, these wretched figures shall go down to the vile dust from whence they sprung, unwept, unhonored and unsung. . . .

If the government can round up someone and never be required to explain why, then it's no longer the United States of America as you and I always understood it. Our enemies have succeeded beyond their wildest dreams. They have made us become like them.[7]

Republicans were all set to portray the Democrats as too scared or misguided to know how to fight "terror." Just as planned, the following

Monday, Tuesday, and Wednesday, the president took to the road. In his first speech after the bill passed the Senate, he asserted, "If you listen closely to some of the leaders of the Democrat Party, it sounds like—it sounds like they think the best way to protect the American people is, wait until we're attacked again."[8]

The next day, he repeated the theme that Democrats want therapy for terrorists and talked about their "softer" side:

> I appreciate the fact we've got members of Congress who clearly see the enemy for what they are. You can't negotiate with these people. You cannot hope that they will go away. I like to remind people, therapy isn't going to work. The best way to deal with these folks is to bring them to justice before they hurt America again. . . . On each of these programs, the Democrats have said they share our goals. But when it comes time to vote, they consistently oppose giving our personnel the tools they need to protect us. Time and time again, the Democrats want to have it both ways. They talk tough on terror, but when the votes are counted, their softer side comes out.[9]

And the next day, he truly outdid himself:

> This bill came up—the idea of providing additional authority for the Terrorist Surveillance Program came to the House floor recently. And there was a vote, and people got to stand up and declare whether or not this program was important: 177 Democrats voted against listening in on terrorist communications; 177 of the opposition party said, you know, we don't think we ought to be listening to the conversations of terrorists.[10]

Bush could never have made such statements if he'd instead had to respond to a collective Democratic statement that called him and his party traitors for playing politics with national security, giving anyone who captured an American soldier—or an American college student abroad—the right to declare them an enemy combatant, hold them secretly and indefinitely, and torture them as long as their president called it something else since it was in their national interest.

Democrats should have fanned out all over the media with one simple sentence: *We were supposed to teach the Iraqis about democracy, not the other way around.*

That's putting out the fire, by offering a counternarrative to "the Republicans are strong on national security and the Democrats are weak."

Fortunately for the Democrats, a confluence of events took the wind out of Bush's sails, as the Foley sex scandal broke, Bob Woodward published *State of Denial* (and was prepared for the character attacks that inevitably followed), and news leaked of the National Intelligence Estimate suggesting that the Iraq War was, indeed, central to the war on terrorism, but only because it was breeding more jihadists than it was neutralizing. Bush's approval ratings on his handling of terrorism dropped below 50 percent for the first time since September 11,[11] and the steadily decreasing support for the Iraq War was dropping to historic lows.

But the laws are now on the books. And once many Democrats had broken faith with their constituents by supporting it, taking back that vote—and the laws it created—may prove very difficult.

The Trouble with Terror

As you go to the polls, remember we're at war. . . . And if you want this country to do everything in its power to protect you. . . . vote Republican.[12]

This was President Bush's final admonition to voters on the morning of the midterm election of 2006, although for the first time the terror card wasn't playing well. There hadn't been an attack on American soil in five years, Americans had begun to perceive the war in Iraq as increasing rather than decreasing the world's supply of terrorists, and the president had cried wolf a few too many times.

But the Bush team knew that if Republicans were to stand a chance, he would have to remind voters one last time of terror (and, yet again, to try to associate it with the Iraq War). Just three months earlier, the British foiled a plot to bomb several intercontinental flights to the United States by mixing liquids in the air, reminding Americans again of the terrorist threat. Within days, Bush's sagging approval numbers on his signature issue—homeland security—soared by 10 points.[13] Every time the U.S. government had announced a terrorist threat over the last five years, Bush had gotten a post-terror bounce.

Why did terror work so effectively for so long for the GOP?

Although Republicans did everything they could to maximize its effects—uttering words such as *terror*, *the war on terror*, *September 11,* and the *Twin Towers* virtually every time they opened their mouths for five years—they had some help from an unlikely ally: the human brain.

More than 250 experiments in over a dozen countries have demonstrated that reminding people of their mortality—activating networks about the fear of death—tends to tilt our brains to the right.[14] Whether the reminder comes in the form of a questionnaire asking people whether they would prefer cremation or burial, gory pictures, interviews that "incidentally" take place in front of funeral parlors, or even subliminal exposure to the words *dead* or *death*, people across the world will cling more tenaciously to the worldviews they hold dear. Except for people with strong progressive worldviews, who sometimes become more polarized toward their own ideology in response to reminders of their mortality, this generally means clinging to more "traditional" cultural values. People who are reminded of their mortality will become less tolerant toward people who differ from them in religion, more nationalistic, and harsher in the way they punish those who transgress traditional moral values.

A team of scientists led by Sheldon Solomon, Jeff Greenberg, and Tom Pyszczynski discovered the impact of what they call "mortality salience" on people's attitudes and behavior over twenty years ago, long before the current reign of terror.[15] They called their approach, presciently, "terror management theory," and it has turned out to have tremendous political implications that could not have been foreseen at the time—and that have, remarkably, failed to draw the attention of Democratic strategists.

Their initial goal was to test a theory propounded by the cultural anthropologist and social philosopher Ernest Becker (1973) in his Pulitzer Prize–winning book, *The Denial of Death*.[16] According to Becker, an unfortunate by-product of the evolution of the human intellect is that people can imagine their own death and the death of those they love. We could not live our lives staring into this existential abyss, so we develop and embrace cultural beliefs and values that give our lives meaning and symbolically allow us to transcend death. Although the prototypes of such beliefs are spiritual notions of an afterlife (e.g., heaven, reincarnation), Becker argues that everything from our quest to "make a name for ourselves" in ways sanctioned by our cultures, to our passionate attachments to political ideologies and religious beliefs, ultimately represents an escape from the reality none of us can tolerably face—that the only certainty in life is that we, and everyone we love, will die. If this discussion is beginning to make you queasy, its implications in the post–September 11 world may make you even queasier, because these natural tendencies have presented tremendous opportunities for political manipulation.

What Solomon and colleagues have done is to turn Becker's speculation into a testable hypothesis—and one that has withstood some remarkably rigorous experimental tests. In many of these studies, the researchers have put death-related networks at a heightened state of activation with a simple "death questionnaire," asking people often innocuous questions about their thoughts about death, what they think will happen to their body after they die, and so forth. They then test the impact of mortality salience on their attitudes and behavior.

In one study, the experimenters presented Christian college students with information on two people, one identified as Christian and the other as Jewish.[17] Subjects in the control condition, who were not primed with death-related thoughts, showed no preference for the Christian or the Jew. In contrast, subjects exposed to the death questionnaire evaluated the Christian more favorably. From the standpoint of terror management theory, it is perhaps no accident that during the heart of the McCarthy era, when Americans were terrified at the potential of communist invasions from without and infiltrations from within, religious books were the best sellers, and conservatives added "under God" to the pledge of allegiance.[18]

The impact of death anxiety on Christians in America is mirrored by its impact on Muslims in Iran. In a remarkable study, the investigators asked one group of Iranian undergraduate students to think about their own death, including to "Jot down, as specifically as you can, what you think will happen to you as you physically die" (the morality salience condition) and asked another group to contemplate severe dental pain (a rigorous control condition often used in these studies to arouse fear but not death anxiety).[19] They then presented them with what subjects believed were the responses of two of their fellow university students to a questionnaire about martyrdom for Islam against the United States. For example, the pro-martyrdom "student" responded to the question, "Are martyrdom attacks on the United States justified?" with "Yes. The United States represents the world power which Allah wants us to destroy." The anti-martyrdom "student" responded, ". . . human life is too valuable to be used as a means of producing change." Then the investigators asked students how interested they would be in joining the pro- and anti-martyrdom causes of the two students.

Subjects in the control condition (thinking about dental pain) tended to oppose the pro-martyrdom student's position and were uninterested in joining his cause. Yet simply being reminded of their mortality led those in the mortality salience condition to show precisely the opposite pattern, preferring the pro-martyrdom student's position and indicating a willingness to join his movement. (These data suggest, from a strictly psychological perspective, why creating anarchy and fear of death in Iraq since the fall of Baghdad could have been predicted not only to increase the number of terrorists but also to increase Sunni-Shiite tensions, as sectarians on one side or the other cling more tenaciously to their worldviews.) The investigators found, in a parallel study on the other side of the "clash of civilizations," that death anxiety led conservative (but not liberal) American undergraduates to increase overwhelmingly their support for preemptive wars, use of weapons of mass destruction, and "collateral damage" in the thousands to destroy Osama bin Laden.

Of greatest relevance to understanding American voting behavior in the post–September 11 world, Solomon, Greenberg, and Pyszczynski conducted a series of studies during the 2004 presidential election testing the effects of mortality salience on support for President Bush and his policies in Iraq.[20] In one study the investigator found that having subjects complete a death questionnaire led to dramatic increases in support for both Bush and the Iraq War. In another, subliminal presentation of reminders of September 11 or the World Trade Center increased activation of death-related thoughts and support for the president and his Iraq War policies—even among liberals.

In the most direct demonstration of the impact of terror manipulations on voting, the investigators asked young registered Northeastern voters in September who they intended to vote for, Kerry or Bush. Voters in the control condition supported Kerry by a 4 to 1 margin. Those who first filled out a death questionnaire went for Bush by a 2 to 1 margin.

During the 2004 presidential election, having successfully raised doubts about John Kerry's resolve in the face of aggression, President Bush and Vice President Cheney repeatedly issued dire warnings about terror and the danger of Democratic control of the country in a time of terror. Scarcely a minute passed during their convention, with New York City as their backdrop, without mention of terror, terrorists, the war on terror, or the events of September 11. On Election Day, the Department of Homeland Security increased the terror alert, reflecting, of course, the possibility that the terrorists might want to disrupt our elections.

The studies on terror management suggest that if these were not part of an orchestrated effort designed with knowledge of this large and public body of research, they were certainly part of a strategy that accomplished just what Solomon, Greenberg, and Pyszczynski would have predicted.

So if terror inherently tilts our brains to the right, is there anything that can be done, particularly when terror is so readily manipulated?

As with any "disease," the first and most important step in identifying an antidote is to understand it. Once again, a deep irony of our times is that the party of science, which rails against the unprecedented incursions on science by religious dogma or vested financial interests cloaked in pseudoscience (in what we teach our children about evolution, or what panels of "experts" conclude about climate change or mercury poisoning), has shown a deep disrespect for science crucial to its own survival, let alone to the values that unite those on the left.

In the wake of September 11—and in the face of a well-orchestrated Republican strategy that created a five-year reign of terror until finally it became overshadowed by the failures of the war in Iraq in November 2006—there could have been no research more important for Democrats to understand. Yet when Sheldon Solomon, one of the architects of terror management theory, managed to reach one of Kerry's chief campaign strategists to talk with him about how Kerry might counter Bush's terror offensive, Kerry's strategist had little interest in two decades of science. If something can't be said in ten seconds, he responded, it's of no use.

Conversation over.

The fact that most people reading this book will have just heard of terror management theory for the first time is a profound indictment of the Democratic Party.[21] Not only was this information essential for thinking about how to respond to the psychopolitical realities of an administration willing to manipulate terror for its own gain, but the best antidote was in print in the public domain, and Solomon and his colleagues tried to tell them about it: terror manipulations don't work if you warn people how they work. Multiple experiments have shown that you can block the effect of mortality salience on thought and behavior if you simply inoculate people by telling them about how it works.

But there are other implications of what we know about how our minds respond to terror, which Democrats should remember the next time they, inevitably, find themselves facing a terror-stricken public.

First, once again, *beware of Trojan horses*. Immediately after September 11, Bush specified his enemy—Osama bin Laden and those who supported him—and spoke about the war on terror*ism* or the war on the terror*ists*. Once he and his advisors realized the power of terror as a political tool and recognized this as an opportunity to move into Iraq, however, they broadened the term to the *war on terror*. This not only repeatedly activated terror networks—a mortality salience manipulation virtually straight out of the studies by Solomon and his colleagues—but it allowed them to conflate Osama bin Laden and Saddam Hussein.

This was a deliberate strategy. In 2004, the GOP advised its candidates to avoid using the phrase "War on Iraq" and to use instead "War on Terror."[22] It never seemed to occur to Democrats, in contrast, to put out an "All Points Bulletin" to their candidates and commentators that the words or the emotional connotations mattered at all, even after linguists had spoken to the Democratic leadership about the importance of framing and language.

Like lemmings, the Democrats started repeating the phrase "the war on terror" as often as Republicans—and they still do to this day, like Pepsi executives humming, "It's the real thing." Given that this phrase became an uncontested "truth" about the war we were fighting, it became the banner for years under telecasts by CNN and other news outlets, literally framing—visually—every image the American public saw about issues related to national security. In fact, when the White House shifted from "the war against terrorism" to "the war on terrorism" in early 2002, the media followed suit, increasingly using the new language as the White House deployed it in speeches and press releases.[23] This could never have happened if Democrats had been alert to the shift in GOP language and contested the frame.

If you let the opposition control the terms of discourse, you let them control the broadcast networks. And if you let them control the broadcast networks, they will control voters' associative networks.

By using the language of "the war on terror," Democrats allowed the Bush administration to avoid talking about its success or failure in prosecuting the *real wars* we have been fighting since September 11: the war on bin Laden, the war on al Qaeda, the war in Afghanistan, and the war in Iraq. Note that we have been unsuccessful in every one of those wars. Those are the phrases Democrats should use. When Democrats finally broke through on national security in 2006, it was when they dismantled the "terror network" of September 11 and Iraq, distinguished between Osama and Saddam, and began speaking primarily about *the war in Iraq*—the war George Bush was losing.

Second, if a Republican administration ever again produces terror alerts with suspicious timing, Democrats should call them on it. It would have been irresponsible for Democrats to make such accusations the first two or three times it happened because coincidences are always possible. But when the pattern becomes so clear that a journalist finally breaks ranks and tells it like it is (as Keith Olbermann did on MSNBC), it is time for Democrats to make the indictment and let the jurors decide in the court of public opinion.

Third, Americans need to be reminded of how great leaders have responded to threats to our country in the past so they can see when they are being manipulated. When the United States was facing the gravest threat in our history, with Adolph Hitler marching through Europe, President Roosevelt used his fireside chats to *reassure* a frightened nation, not to scare it. Juxtaposing audio clips of Roosevelt's reassuring message that Americans had nothing to fear but fear itself with Cheney and Bush's "Look out for the terrorists!" pronouncements would have made amply clear to the American public that someone was terrorizing them other than Osama or Saddam. Doing so would have begun to associate terror with Bush and the Republicans rather than with the Democrats.

Fourth, in the face of terror manipulations, as in other political situations, Democrats need to scour Republicans' words and metaphors for the networks they are activating and think about how to inhibit or turn those networks against them. Bush was fond of emasculating Democrats on matters of national security by claiming that they sought therapy instead of death for terrorists. The phrase "war on terror" actually created a perfect opportunity for turning this around. So imagine if John Kerry had declared during the 2004 election,

> We are *not* fighting a war on terror. Terror is a feeling, not an enemy. If the president wants to fight a war on feelings, I suggest he

see a therapist. As your president, I will not declare war on feelings. I will declare war on those who create those feelings."

Not only would this have attacked Bush with his own idiom (masculinity), but it would have made much more difficult the continued use of "the war on terror," with all the advantages that phrase held for Republicans.

Finally, with the Republican Party questioning the patriotism of anyone who opposed everything from illegal wiretaps to the prosecution of the Iraq War, Democrats should have looked for opportunities to turn the tables. The Valerie Plame affair gave them their best opportunity, although they never made use of it. That Karl Rove ultimately admitted giving away the name of an undercover CIA operative, and that Vice President Cheney's marked-up copy of her husband's op-ed piece exposing the misuse of intelligence data emerged after the indictment of his chief of staff (followed immediately, of course, by a terror alert), should have been devastating blows to the administration and its attempt to manufacture both fear and war. These facts should have been repeatedly juxtaposed with the president's initial statement, when the Plame affair first broke, that he would fire anyone who had anything to do with the leak. More importantly, imagine the power of their juxtaposition with the statement from a former head of the CIA, that anyone who reveals the identity of a CIA agent is "a traitor to our country."[24]

That former director was George H. W. Bush.

The next time terror comes to call, Democrats need to remember that the best ways to reduce its impact are to bring to voters' conscious awareness Republican efforts to manipulate it, to use Republicans' own words and idioms against them, and to associate terror with those who would use terror for partisan gain. When Democrats started using some of these antidotes in the late summer of 2006—for example, striking back immediately when the Bush administration tried to use the London bombings to its advantage, with rapid counterpunches from all sides on how Bush's distraction in Iraq had left us less safe at home[25]—Bush's poll numbers on both his handling of the Iraq War and his handling of terrorism dropped, and the spell of terror was ultimately broken.

Conclusion: A Different Kind of Democrat

The reader may notice that this chapter has had a somewhat different tone from those that preceded it. The tone reflects what many rank-and-file Democrats, as well as many Independents, have been feeling for some time: angry at having to choose between a party whose message they don't like (the Republicans) and another whose message they don't hear (the Democrats).

Like many Democrats, I have watched for the better part of a decade as Democratic candidates repeatedly fought the last war, using the same weapons, seemingly forgetting that *they lost the last war*. They ignored the advice of the party's best strategists and repeatedly employed strategists long on experience and short on success. They ignored scientific data of which they were aware (e.g., that was reported in the *New York Times* or *Washington Post*), cavalierly choosing instead to embark upon their own faith-based initiatives, even though their intuitions had proven consistently wrong. They failed to learn from history, including very recent history.

Although I have focused in this chapter on events since September 11, the Republicans' assault on American democracy actually began earlier, and it isn't clear that the Democratic Party has to this day figured out that *this is not your grandmother's GOP*. Had Democrats fully understood who they were dealing with in 1998 and clarified in their own minds the difference between ethical and unethical political attacks, I doubt we ever would have seen the impeachment trial of Bill Clinton. When it became clear that "special persecutor" Kenneth Starr (the term a left-leaning Luntz would no doubt have urged Democrats to use every time they referred to him) was colluding with Paula Jones' attorney in her civil suit against the president to find a way to criminalize his personal indiscretions, the Republicans had crossed the line from politics to what Clinton later called "the politics of personal destruction."

That line was a dangerous one to cross. It not only consumed the attention of the President of the United States at a time he was trying to respond to the ever-growing threat of al Qaeda, but it was used directly to interfere with his ability to strike al Qaeda, as Republican leaders publicly accused him of "wagging the dog" to distract the electorate from the Lewinsky affair. It is difficult to fathom why Democrats never used those film clips against Republicans who had made that charge, with the accompanying message, "Your Senator put partisan politics over the safety of your children"—*particularly* at a time when Republicans were running against the patriotism of Democrats. But the Starr inquisition also set a precedent for what is permissible in politics that Republicans have used ever since, because they know Democrats will not fight back.

The impeachment of Bill Clinton ultimately ran its course, and Republicans paid for it in the polls, albeit briefly. But Democratic leaders could likely have put a stop to the effort to depose a twice-elected president for a character flaw the American public already knew about and had twice determined was not relevant to his performance as president if they had sat down with their opposite numbers on the other side of the aisle and made clear that if the Republicans were going to use the nuclear option, they were doing something unprecedented in American history, and the Democrats would have no choice but to respond in kind. Had Democrats truly understood that they were dealing with a "different kind of Republican," they might have viewed the impeachment of Bill Clinton as an effort to subvert American democracy, not as a legitimate use of the checks and balances built into the Constitution, and called it that. That subversion has only expanded since 1998, and Democrats fail in their duty to protect our democracy when they accept phrases such as "dirty tricks," with its associative connotations of little boys pouring salt into someone's lemonade, and wave at the smoke as if it's just a harmless "prank" (one of the first associations most Americans have to "dirty tricks").

Democrats should have aggressively inoculated—and in so doing, set the media frame in advance—for the misleading "robocalls" and fliers Republicans have used at the end of the last three elections. Rove had used similar tactics in state politics in Texas for two decades, which had been well documented.[26] And Republicans used them liberally in 2004, when the Republican National Committee sent direct mail to voters in West Virginia and Arkansas warning them that if the Democrats got elected, they would ban the Bible.[27] In several swing states, voters received automated calls allegedly from pro-gay groups, targeted to anti-gay voters, urging them to vote for Kerry, and men dressed in unconvincing drag held up pro-gay signs while hassling voters all over the country.[28]

All the Democrats needed to say a week before every election since Rove came to town was something like, "If you get computerized calls that won't stop, calls in the middle of the night, or fliers allegedly from a Democratic candidate taking a position that anyone knows would make you angry—telling you how excited the Democratic candidate is about taking away your rifle, banning the Bible, or allowing gay people to get married in your church—send a message to the Republicans on Election Day that Republican candidates who run on values and morality but show such a deep disrespect toward both the Constitution and the Ten Commandments will get what they deserve."

Doing so would have prevented exactly what happened across the country again in 2006, as voters received repeated calls, often in the middle of the night or during major sporting events, that sounded at the beginning as if they were from the Democrat. In a Pennsylvania House race, voters received a call beginning, in a positive tone suggesting that it was from Democrat Lois Murphy, "Hello, I'm calling with information about Lois Murphy. . . . "[29] Murphy lost in a very close race, and a campaign advisor to her complained, just before the Tuesday election, that "Some of our biggest supporters have said, 'If you call me again, I'm not voting for Lois.'"[30] Exactly the same message played in dozens of close elections throughout the country, too late for the Democrats to respond effectively. When the media *did* start to report on these "dirty tricks"—a media frame that would have been impossible if Democrats had previously labeled them as *efforts to subvert American democracy* and demanded United Nations voting inspectors if the Republicans humiliated the world's oldest democracy by turning it into a Third World country—they reported them as he-said/she-said stories, with headlines beginning with phrases such as, "Democrats accuse Republicans of. . . . "

Democrats have similarly failed to call voter suppression efforts what they are—*attacks by enemies of democracy*—which have emerged in several states since the success of Jeb Bush's infamous felons list in 2000. Such efforts have sprouted like weeds precisely because Democrats have not turned them into *voting issues*. Imagine the impact of an ad showing older black people turned away from the polls, much like George H. Bush's "Revolving Door" ad, with the simple narration: "On November 7, send your Republican Congressman and Senator a message, that we are *all* God's children."

The reader will undoubtedly have observed a common denominator in many of the responses I have suggested in this chapter and the last: they are direct, and they are aggressive. The most effective candidates emanate two qualities: strength and warmth. The most charismatic presidents of the last century—Teddy Roosevelt, Franklin Roosevelt, Ronald Reagan, and Bill Clinton—all exuded both. Strength lets voters know that a leader will protect them and their families. Warmth lets them know that the candidate will be concerned for their welfare.

What we need today, to use Bill Clinton's phrase, is a "different kind of Democrat": one with *cojones*. As we have seen, you don't have to be born with them to use them. Some of the most effective, gutsy Democratic campaigners in recent years have been women, who refused to become the kind of Democrat who has repeatedly gone down in flames against aggressive GOP opponents lighting fires.

The kind of candidate who will not appeal to the American voter is the kind of candidate the Democratic Party has too often fielded or created, armed with messages crafted to *reflect* rather than to *shape* the polls. The kind of candidate who will not appeal to the American voter in the post–September 11 world is a candidate advised to takes stands that exude timidity in the face of political aggression at home for fear of being branded or outflanked. If the American people take that timidity at home as an indicator of how Democrats will respond to aggression from abroad, they are voting exactly as they should, relying on the wisdom of what Samuel Popkin has called "gut-level rationality."

It is time to stop running candidates with all the courage of their pollsters' convictions. If we present voters with bad choices, we can't blame them for making them.

chapter fifteen

CIVIL AND UNCIVIL UNIONS

★   ★   ★

Other than telling us how to live, think, marry, pray, vote, invest,
educate our children and, now, die, I think the Republicans have
done a fine job of getting government out of our personal lives.

— *PORTLAND OREGONIAN*,
Editorial Page, Sunday, June 19, 2005

In March 2005, President Bush cut short his Crawford, Texas,
vacation—something he had never done before, not even when
warned of an impending attack by Osama bin Laden in August
2001—to return to Washington to sign legislation on a matter of life
and death.[1] The bill was designed to make a federal case of a Florida
state court decision upholding multiple prior challenges to remove a
feeding tube from the arm of Terri Schiavo.

Schiavo had been brain-dead for fifteen years. When "liberal activist" Supreme Court Justice Anthony Kennedy declined to review
the case, religious extremists on the right enlisted the Republican Party
to push through "emergency legislation" to "save Terri," over the objections of her next of kin, her husband Michael. They portrayed him
as an adulterer with a motive to end his wife's life, routinely failing to
mention that he had developed this "new" relationship in the fifteen
years since his beloved wife had fallen into a terminal coma.

The issue was important enough to rouse the president from his ranch and issue a statement at 1:00 AM. It was part of the "culture of life" product line he and his party were selling their base, whose fervor had catapulted him to victory in 2004. Without examining Schiavo himself, Senator Bill Frist, a physician, took what might be described as medical license to declare Schiavo clearly responsive, contrary to the consensus of every physician who had examined her directly. "Remember, Terri is alive, Terri is not in a coma," he exhorted.[2] Scandal-ridden House Speaker, moral leader, and exterminator Tom DeLay was particularly hyperbolic about the dire need for legislation.

In the midst of the debate, however, public opinion polls revealed something surprising: nearly two-thirds of Americans disapproved of federal intervention in what they believed was a personal family matter.[3] By the time the episode was over, the percentage who believed the intervention was wrong-headed and politically inspired broke 80 percent.[4]

Why were Americans in such disagreement with their elected representatives?

Because anyone who watched the tragic video clips of Terri Schiavo could imagine *being her*. The images were hard to watch, as she moved her head and mouth in unnatural ways. The idea that the federal government should step in to override both her own expressed wishes and the decision of her next of kin, not to mention the state courts that had jurisdiction in the case and had all come to the same conclusion, was contrary to most Americans' values.

Here was the Democrats' chance to assert an *alternative moral vision*, and most importantly, to reassert the *traditional American principle* that no one's life and liberty should be governed by another person's faith. All it would have taken to seize that opportunity would have been for Democrats to ask the American people four questions: "Would *you* want to be kept alive if you were Terri Schiavo?" "Would you want the only memory of your time on earth to be the video clips repeatedly shown on television of your grotesquely smiling face and vacant stare, with your head rolling back and forth?" "Is there anyone who is more likely to know your wishes in a tragic situation like this than your spouse of many years?" and "Do you want the federal government overriding your own wishes on how you want to live or die?"

With the polls at their back, the Democrats were finally in a position to take back the high ground on values and morality, to enunciate a *progressive moral alternative*.

But they didn't.

According to a report in the *New York Times*, "Many Congressional Democrats were biting their tongues Friday as they witnessed what they considered an egregious misuse of power by Republicans."[5] Others, however, jumped on the "moral" bandwagon, standing side by side with their Republican colleagues in enthusiastically endorsing the extraordinary rendition of Terri Schiavo from her husband's care to the *700 Club*, apparently convinced that this would prove that they, too, had "values."

But these were the wrong values. They were the values of the extreme right. And if the internal polls—the moral emotions—of the Democratic leadership couldn't steer them in the right direction, all they needed to do was to look at public opinion to find wisdom in the moral emotions of their countrymen.

The House bill received the support of half the Democrats who voted on it. The Senate version passed in a voice vote with no objections. The president signed the bill into law.

And the Democratic Party remained in a politically vegetative state.

Some Democrats did stand their ground. One who understood well what was at stake, and knew how to talk about it with the American people, was then-House Minority Leader Nancy Pelosi. Pelosi made clear not only that the Republicans were abusing the powers of the Congress, but that their interpretation of values and faith was an imperious and intrusive one: "The actions of the majority in attempting to pass constitutionally dubious legislation are highly irregular and an improper use of legislative authority. . . . Michael Schiavo is faced with a devastating decision, but having been through the proper legal process, the decision for his wife's care belongs to him and to God."[6] What Pelosi was implicitly enunciating was a different value system, one centered on compassion and individual liberty rather than dogma.[7]

But the profound question is why, with roughly 60 percent of Americans supporting nothing other than the Bill of Rights (the injunction against the state-imposed intrusion of one group's sectarian religious beliefs into another person's most private and personal decisions), Democrats couldn't see their way to their own principles, and instead alternated between avoidance and acquiescence.

The Schiavo case was a battle between *two value systems, two moralities, and two visions of faith*. One vision, which is inherently antidemocratic, whether in Tupelo or Teheran, rests on assertions of the form, "I've talked to God, He has told me the answer, and I have the right to impose it on you." The other vision, which was the vision of our founders, starts with the existential paradox that to live a just and moral life, we must be firm in our moral convictions but humble in our recognition that we are not the only ones who feel certain about our faith or values.

The central point of this chapter is that Democrats need to talk about values, morality, and faith again, but not by talking like Republicans. They need to offer a counternarrative that has at its core beneficence, tolerance and humility, not hate, contempt, and dogma. Paradoxically, what progressives need to offer today is a reassertion of morality as it has been traditionally defined in America, as grounded in fairness, tolerance, empathy, and compassion, and as focused on concern for the community, for the less fortunate, and for the world we leave our children. It is the nonsectarian Judeo-Christian morality of the founding fathers, not the sectarian moralities of the lands they fled and of colonial America, which had replicated much of the religious intolerance and tyranny of the Old World and, hence, inspired the First Amendment.

Democrats have allowed Republicans to equate Christianity with a narrow and malignant strain of it that has done nothing but damage to what President Jimmy Carter, an evangelical Christian, has called *Our Endangered Values*.[8] In congressional hearings, Indiana Republican Congressman John Hostetler indignantly declared that "The long war on Christianity in America continues today on the floor of the House of Representatives," adding that this liberal jihad "continues unabated with aid and comfort to those who would eradicate any vestige of our Christian heritage being supplied by the usual suspects, the Democrats.

Like a moth to a flame, Democrats can't help themselves when it comes to denigrating and demonizing Christians."[9]

It is truly remarkable that such words—which would have seemed utterly unintelligible if Democrats hadn't allowed Republicans for years to conflate *Christian* with an extremist, authoritarian version of Christianity,[10] since most Democrats are themselves Christians—could be uttered without censure on the floor of the House of Representatives. Every time conservatives use the term *Christian* in this way, Democrats need to call them on it and remind the Methodists, Presbyterians, and Catholics who are listening that people like Hostetler do not respect their faith. Democrats need to start using the term *religious extremists* to describe those who would impose their religious beliefs on others and to distinguish them from *the rest of us*—including, most of all, from the majority of Americans who consider themselves Christians, whether progressive, moderate, or evangelical.

You wouldn't know from the language of the religious right that Jesus was preoccupied with poverty, not sex. You wouldn't know from the trumpeting by the right of school prayer that Jesus was against public displays of religion. You wouldn't know from the militant language of the right that Jesus preached peace and condemned those who would take up arms against others. You wouldn't know from the right's rhetoric on taxes that when Jesus said, "Give unto Caesar what's Caesar's," he was talking about *taxes*.

You wouldn't know these things from public discourse in America because Democrats haven't talked about them. For much of three decades, they've let the right define Jesus, in whose teachings over four-fifths of Americans believe.

In a religious nation such as ours, we can ill afford to allow the right to define faith, morality, virtue, values, and character.

In matters of morality, as in every other realm of life, what drives people are their emotions,[11] and the moral emotions of the left tend to be very different from those of the far right. University of Virginia psychologist John Haidt has distinguished several kinds of moral emotions.[12] What he and other psychologists call "self-conscious" emotions—shame, embarrassment, and especially guilt—often lead us to do the right thing even when we might want to do otherwise. "Other-suffering" emotions, such as compassion and empathy, lead us to feel for others and to try to help them. Along with what Haidt calls "other-praising" emotions, such as admiration for those who behave in ways we consider morally courageous or worthy of our respect or exaltation, these are the primary emotions that define the morality of the left.

But there is another class of moral emotions that can be a source of good or evil, what Haidt calls "other-condemning" emotions: anger, indignation, contempt, disgust, and loathing. These are the emotions to which those on the far right are most vulnerable. They are also emotions to which those in the center and center-right (e.g., evangelical Christians) are vulnerable if no one unmasks the trappings of sanctity in which they are all too frequently draped and offers an alternative moral vision grounded in compassion.

What makes this last class of moral emotions so dangerous is that those on the left tend to be afraid of them, both in others and in themselves. As a result, they fail to condemn those who stoke the fires of hatred in others, particularly when they alloy their loathing with claims to divinity. Before he made his pact with the devil, John Mc-Cain denounced the religious extremists who now run our country by proxy as "agents of intolerance" because he recognized that their agendas are driven by hate, disgust, and contempt. Since then, Mc-Cain has lost his way.

Now Democrats must find theirs.

In this chapter, I describe how and why Democrats need to make explicit what has for years been only implicit in their policy preferences—moral values—and to elicit the moral emotions these values engender, whether guilt, compassion, or anger. I begin by describing why Democrats can't afford to cede sanctity, given that a sense of the sacred is a universal aspect of human psychology and social life, and then describe, historically, how the left ceded morality and faith to the right. The chapter then turns to perhaps the central task for Democrats in the years ahead: to spell out with clarity the differences between the moral visions of the right and the left, to redefine "values issues," and to distinguish the hate- and disgust-driven fundamentalism at the heart of contemporary Republican rhetoric on morality from the compassion-based morality and faith shared by most Americans. I use the example of gay marriage to illustrate how to wed a progressive moral vision with an understanding of Americans' ambivalence toward one of the last groups toward which they can display overt prejudice.

The Sacred and the Profane

The great nineteenth-century French (but purportedly not effete) sociologist Émile Durkheim proposed a distinction that has proven central to virtually every anthropological account of culture since, between the *profane* and the *sacred*. The profane is the world in which we live our everyday lives and spend most of our time. It is the realm of the pragmatic, material, secular, commonplace, and self-interested. It is the world Jesus cast aside as of little meaning when he instructed his followers to "Render unto Caesar what is Caesar's."

The sacred is the realm of the communal, the transcendent, the moral, and the spiritual. We recognize it from the feelings of the profound and sanctified it engenders, the stylized language it employs (e.g., "Thou shalt," "And the Lord said unto him"), and the rituals it employs. These rituals take us out of our everyday existence and redefine objects, actions, or words that would be profane in any other context into profoundly meaningful (e.g., bread, wine). Across the world, the realm of the sacred can be seen in the way people hold their bodies as they sit or stand completely still, sway rhythmically, or assume postures that are, both literally and figuratively, frequently "upright."

Durkheim noted how feelings of the sacred often emerge in rituals that elicit what he called "collective effervescence," the feeling of oneness with the larger community that can occur in settings as spiritual as a religious revival or as secular as a sporting event, with cheering fans jumping to their feet and hugging strangers. What these two seemingly disparate communal experiences share—the religious revival and the football game—are two central elements: a feeling of oneness or unity with something bigger than oneself, and a shared sense of community and identification with that community and its collective symbols.

The capacity for experiencing sanctity is built into the structure of the human brain. Neurologists and psychiatrists first discovered this when they observed that a subset of patients with temporal lobe epilepsy were oddly hyper-religious. It may be no accident that religious epiphany experiences seen widely across cultures, particularly those that create an experience of rebirth, often involve experiences of paroxysm—seemingly uncontrolled, jerking bodily movements, and altered states of consciousness, two cardinal features of seizures. And perhaps it is no accident that people often describe themselves at such moments as having been *seized*, possessed, or swept up.

I learned firsthand about the innate human propensity for distinguishing the sacred and the profane from my daughter Mackenzie when she was just three years old. Attending preschool at our local Temple, with teachers who were far more orthodox than her parents, she began to learn the rituals of her family's faith, notably celebration of the Sabbath, or *Shabbat*. Her classroom had a lovely ritual, in which her teachers would pass a "Shabbat bag" each Friday to one of the children, who would take it home to his or her family. The family would celebrate the Sabbath that night, using the candles and chalices in the bag, and write about the experience on a little notepad.

As a Jew who had grown up in the heavily Christian South, I was, like many strangers in a strange land, conflicted about my religious heritage, until my late twenties (a decade after I returned to my parents' ancestral homeland, the Northeast). An index of both that conflict and its resolution occurred for me during the holiday season in 1990, when I was singing in the Ann Arbor Civic Chorus, as I had done for many years. One of the chorus members complained that all the Hanukkah songs in our annual Christmas concert (happy holidays to you, Bill O'Reilly) were wretched, typically ending with "Hanukkah—hey!"

Knowing that in a prior life I had written and performed musical comedy, that I was a somewhat lapsed Jew, and that Jews typically don't go around yelling "Hey!" to express their religious devotion, one of the members of the chorus turned to me and said, "Drew, you're sort of Jewish. Why don't *you* write something?" I didn't give it another thought until a couple of days later when an idea came to me, and I began writing fast and furious. The song debuted the next week at Chorus, as I played it for my fellow singers, and two weeks later, "Oy, to be a Goy on Christmas" was on the radio in New York, and eventually in other cities, where it occasionally plays to this day around holiday time.

Over the years, I became proud of my heritage, although like most people who had the experience as children of growing up "different," the residues of ambivalence apparently had not entirely disappeared, as the story I am about to tell reveals.

We opened the Shabbat bag and began to practice the ritual of my forefathers. Somewhat remarkable to me, the words and songs in Hebrew sprang from my tongue as I led my family in this ancient ritual. (The fact that I assumed this role reflected less the sexism that characterized ancient Judaism and characterizes all fundamentalist religions to this day than the fact that whereas I was a lapsed Jew, my wife was a *col*lapsed one, who, despite her years as a counselor at a Jewish Community Center camp in Tucson, grew up in an even more Hebraically challenged part of the country, the Southwest.)

At some point, however, what I had thought was an ethnic ambivalence of the past emerged in the present as I expressed another part of my Jewish heritage. Part way through the ceremony, I *kibitzed*—not about the ritual, mind you (as God is my witness), but I cracked some kind of joke. And in my own defense (if He is reading this), one of the things I have always appreciated about less orthodox brands of Judaism, and even of some of its orthodox variants (depending on the sense of humor of the rabbi), is the *levity* introduced in religious services, particularly weddings, much as African-American churches teach joy to their members unconsciously through the joyous music of the gospel.

In any case, my three-year-old daughter understood Durkheim but not *kibitzing*. As I broke the sanctity of the moment, Mackenzie turned to me with a seriousness and righteous indignation I had never before seen in her young face, and admonished, "Daddy, you don't *know* God, do you." Stunned and not certain I had heard her correctly, I asked her to repeat what she had asked. She said it again. My daughter, with all of three years of socialization and brain maturation, intuitively understood that I had introduced the profane into a moment of sanctity, and that it had no place there. At this point, not sure whether we had a budding fundamentalist on our hands, my wife and I felt comforted that at least we had decided against the Methodist preschool down the street.

I emphasize this distinction between the profane and the sacred because it is central to our contemporary political landscape, and to political discourse and persuasion in any country, particularly in a deeply religious nation such as ours. By staking its claims on policies, bread-and-butter issues, rationality, expertise, and expected utility, the Democratic Party has firmly established itself as the party of the profane, casting its message in the language of profanity. The Republican Party, in contrast, has cast its appeals in the language of the sacred—of the sanctity of religion, shared American symbols, and military might and right. It has even gone a step further, sanctifying the profane, turning free-market capitalism into an article of faith and anyone who wants to limit it, a blasphemer.

A party and its candidates cannot win elections if they allow the election to become a contest between the party of the profane and the party of the sacred—or if they allow the other party to define what is sacred, holy, and moral.

If you want to win elections, you can't *assume* your values. You have to *preach* them. If one side is running on values and the other side is running *from* them, it isn't hard to figure out how the electorate will start thinking, feeling, and talking about values.

How God Became a Grand Old Partisan

The history of God's conversion to Republicanism is a remarkable story, which can be traced in the speeches delivered by the major party candidates between 1960 and 1988.

Americans are a deeply religious people. Ninety percent believe in God, 84 percent believe in religious miracles, and nearly 70 percent believe in the devil.[13] The Bible has been at the top of the best-seller list in America for as long as such lists have been in existence, and it has topped the list worldwide since the invention of the printing press.[14] With those numbers, it should be clear that a party that cedes faith is tempting fate.

Until the 1980s, references to God were commonplace in the speeches of American presidents and presidential candidates of both major parties. In 1960, although John F. Kennedy was careful to make clear that his religious faith as a Catholic would not compromise his independence as a president, he referred to God liberally. Indeed, he invoked God in the first paragraph of his inaugural address: ". . . we observe today not a victory of party, but a celebration of freedom—symbolizing an end, as well as a beginning—signifying renewal, as well as change. For I have sworn before you and Almighty God the same solemn oath our forebears prescribed nearly a century and three quarters ago."[15] He closed his speech with the words, "but on this earth, His work must surely be our own."

Lyndon Johnson made four references to God in his inaugural address. In his convention speech, he promised a war on poverty, justified by scripture: "Our Party and our Nation will continue to extend the hand of affection and love to the old and the sick and the hungry. For who among us dares betray the command: 'Thou shalt open thine hands unto thy brother, to thy poor, and to thy needy in thy land.'"[16]

In responding to the violence that had killed Martin Luther King and Bobby Kennedy, Democratic nominee Hubert Humphrey spoke in deeply moving, and deeply religious, terms:

> And may we, for just one moment, in sober reflection, in serious purpose, may we just quietly and silently—each in our own way—pray for our country. And may we just share for a moment a few of those immortal words of the prayer of St. Francis of Assisi—words which I think may help heal the wounds and lift our hearts. Listen to this immortal saint: "Where there is hatred, let me sow love; where there is injury, pardon; where there is doubt, faith; where there is despair, hope; where there is darkness, light."[17]

George McGovern, often pilloried by the right as a paragon of godless liberalism, ended his convention address in the idiom of prayer: "So let us close on this note: May God grant each one of us the wisdom to cherish this good land and to meet the great challenge that beckons us home. And now is the time to meet that challenge. . . . Good night, and Godspeed to you all."

And Jimmy Carter, a deeply religious evangelical Christian, was pilloried by the press for the absence of liquor at White House events, dictated by his Southern Baptist religious beliefs, and for "lusting in his heart" (a reference to Jesus' equation of the thought with the deed).

But by 1984, Reagan had redefined faith and morality. He openly embraced the religious right and its political agenda. Kennedy and Carter had to assure the nation that their faith would not *interfere* with their governance. Humphrey was careful to insert those very important, *and very American*, words, "each in our own way," in calling the nation to silent prayer. In contrast, Reagan made his faith, and the interpretation of Scripture of a narrow and narrow-minded minority, the moral *foundation* of his presidency, on issues ranging from abortion to prayer in schools to fetal tissue transplant research (a sad and ironic twist of fate, given the hope he eliminated for himself along with millions of other victims of Alzheimer's disease).

In response, Democrats defended the traditional separation of church and state with a vengeance. This was a natural response to Reagan's attempt to tear down that wall. But what is clear in hindsight is how skillfully Reagan and the conservative movement turned liberals into God-hating "secular humanists."

Church and state had always been intertwined *to some degree* in American political culture. The Declaration of Independence declared our rights to be inalienable *because* our Creator endowed us with them. The presidential oath of office ends with the words, "so help me God" (although that addition to the oath is actually not in the constitution). Even our coins are engraved with the words, "In God We Trust." In most of the South (and in the South I knew as a child, in the 1960s and 1970s), the public school day invariably began with a prayer and the Pledge of Allegiance[18]—indelibly associating the two realms of the sacred in American life.

What liberals were objecting to was not the invocation of God to bless America but the invocation of a *particular* God, and the hegemony of the fundamentalists' interpretation of scripture that came with it. What Reagan so skillfully accomplished was a blurring of the distinction between the *generic* God of the founding fathers and the intrusion of *specific* sectarian beliefs into public policy—precisely the intrusion the founders had inveighed against.

With the benefit of hindsight, what Democrats needed to convey was not that they objected to God's presence in politics. God had been there from the start, although with a "liberal" dose of ambivalence, as the Declaration of Independence both invoked the Creator and repudiated the divine right of kings and a litany of other illiberal religious claims to authority. Democratic presidents had always found their moral inspiration in the Judeo-Christian moral tradition. On D-Day, Franklin Roosevelt uttered no words to the American public but a prayer.

What the founders, and their liberal descendants, objected to was the imposition of the religious beliefs of the few on the many.

But what emerged from the Reagan era was a polarization, reflected exquisitely in the conservative movement's framing of the issue as a conflict between those with moral values—the so-called "Moral Majority"—and the godless liberals who found themselves defending and demanding a more complete separation of church and state than had ever existed. The Moral Majority ultimately collapsed because it was not a majority: its religious leaders were extremists, and in those days, those on the left had little compunction about calling them that. But since the 1980s, as Democrats have become increasingly silent on faith (except for an occasional defensive "Amen," as in their response to the Schiavo affair), voters have increasingly come to associate God, faith, morality, values, virtue, and family with *conservative* and *Republican*, and to associate atheist, elite, and moral relativist with *liberal* and *Democrat*.

In response to the kind of religious meddling in the affairs of state that Reagan considered essential to restoring traditional values (and shoring up what became the right-wing religious base of the contemporary Republican Party), Democratic standard bearers recoiled from any mention of religion in their speeches, except to criticize its intrusion into public life. In so doing, they set themselves up for the charge of being anti-God and anti-Christian. And in fact, during the Reagan era, references to faith, and quotations and phrases from the Bible that convey the meta-message to religious voters that "this person shares my values," virtually disappeared from the public pronouncements of Democratic candidates, particularly candidates for president.

In 1984, for the first time in modern American history, the convention address of a candidate for president (Walter Mondale) was devoid of any reference to God or faith—precisely four years after Reagan had draped his presidency in right-wing religious ideology. Michael Dukakis similarly failed to invite God to the Democratic convention in 1988, except for a brief "God willing" in reference to the forthcoming birth of his grandchild. Whereas prior nominees had concluded with an invocation of God, both Mondale and Dukakis ended with some version of "thank you very much."

Although the omission may not have registered consciously with most voters, it clearly registered.[19]

Today, Democrats largely remain tongue-tied on matters of morality or faith for fear of offending "Christians," accepting a framing of morality, religious faith, and Christianity that has no basis in historical, scriptural, or electoral fact. Religious extremists on the right actually *don't* speak for most Americans who call themselves Christians. America's most prominent fundamentalist leaders—including those who have vetted every judicial nominee under the Bush administration— consider the vast majority of mainstream Christians (e.g., Methodists, Episcopalians, Roman Catholics) infidels who will face eternal damnation. And God help the Unitarians, who will no doubt burn for eternity without ever knowing what beliefs they are burning for, somewhere between Limbo and Gitmo.

Bill Clinton knew how to speak to people of faith in the language of faith and could quote scripture with the best of them. Clinton refused to accept the conservatives' framing of sanctimoniousness as sanctity. Consider this passage from his nomination speech at the 1992 Democratic Convention:

> Tonight every one of you knows deep in your heart that we are too divided. It is time to heal America.
>
> And so we must say to every American: Look beyond the stereotypes that blind us. . . . We don't have a person to waste, and yet for too long politicians have told the most of us that are doing

all right that what's really wrong with America is the rest of us—
them.

Them, the minorities. Them, the liberals. Them, the poor.
Them, the homeless. Them, the people with disabilities. Them,
the gays.

We've gotten to where we've nearly them'ed ourselves to
death. Them, and them, and them.

But this is America. There is no them. There is only us.

One nation, under God, indivisible, with liberty and justice
for all. That is our Pledge of Allegiance. . . . [20]

Clinton went straight for the fire, and in so doing he reached many
who respond to fire and brimstone but can also respond to messages of
mercy and compassion.

Agents of Intolerance

Slowly I was forced to acknowledge that every great battle that I
had joined both as a priest and as a bishop . . . was ultimately a
battle against the way the Bible had been used throughout history.
. . . Quotations from the Bible were frequently employed in the
racist battle to maintain segregation. . . . Quotations from the
Bible were also the chief source of that very patriarchal prejudice
. . . through which women were diminished. . . . My church had
filled me with a deep-seated but Bible-based religious bigotry. I
breathed it inside my congregation's life.—Episcopal Bishop John
Shelby Spong[21]

By 1986, one in four American households tuned in on Sunday
mornings to Moral Majority founder Jerry Falwell's televised ser-
mons. Today, Falwell's message is heard in all fifty states and in seventy countries around the world.[22] By 1992, 40 percent of the delegates
to the Republican Convention were members of the Christian Coalition[23]—and that was just the *first* President Bush, who, unlike his son,
was neither a born-again Christian nor someone who had their trust
(and vice versa).

By 2004, white evangelical voters constituted 36 percent of the voters who elected George W. Bush.[24] And their prayers have been answered in Washington—through weekly conference calls between their leaders and the White House and hundreds of face-to-face meetings during the entirety of the Bush presidency. This vocal and now highly influential minority has played an integral role in making, implementing, and interpreting the laws of the United States, and in vetting every judicial appointment made by the forty-third president of the United States.

With *faith*, *morality*, and *values* now firmly linked to *conservative* and *Republican* in the networks that constitute public opinion, Democrats face two tasks. The first is to redefine the religious right for what it is, to associate every Republican running for every office with the morally repugnant pronouncements of its spiritual leaders, and to elicit voters' moral emotions toward what Republicans did while they held absolute power. The second is to offer a competing moral vision, to draw out the values inherent in progressive principles and policies.

In 1992, Pat Buchanan's blistering right-wing "culture war" speech at the Republican Convention deeply alienated moderate voters. Although the words on the written page can't capture the simmering hatred, prejudice, and contempt voters heard in his intonation, they convey the polarized, Manichean worldview—the vision of the righteous engaged in a crusade against the damned and damnable—that is now the mainstream ideology of the Republican Party:

> My friends, this election is about much more than who gets what.
> It is about who we are. It is about what we believe. It is about
> what we stand for as Americans. There is a religious war going
> on in our country for the soul of America. It is a cultural war, as
> critical to the kind of nation we will one day be as was the Cold
> War itself. And in that struggle for the soul of America, Clinton
> and Clinton are on the other side, and George Bush is on our
> side.[25]

Buchanan's speech was well received on the religious right, but it was not well received in the great center of American politics, where elections are generally won and lost. It exposed an ugly underbelly to the Republican Party of 1992 that today has become its heart.

For Democrats, the lesson of Buchanan's speech should have been clear: whenever Republicans preach to the right—which they now must do to win their party's nomination, creating an extraordinary vulnerability in a nation defined by its penchant for ideological and political moderation—make sure those in the center hear them loud and clear. For most Americans, faith and morality are about love and compassion, not about dividing the country into the righteous and the damned. If Democrats convey those as the moral alternatives, they will see a Republican Party in disarray, facing in droves the kinds of defections that have already begun, as the GOP has turned from the party of Bob Dole into the party of Bob Jones.

Consider two of the most powerful religious extremists who have delivered Republicans from defeat by delivering them tens of millions of voters. These are not peripheral figures. Pat Robertson and Jerry Falwell have each spoken at two recent Republican Conventions. Their blessings are so essential to the success or failure of Republican primary candidates that John McCain, who once declared them agents of intolerance, is now their sycophant.

Americans are all familiar with the charge that the federal judiciary is packed with "judicial activists" who legislate from the bench against the values and faith of everyday Americans. But they would be surprised—and repulsed—if they knew the derivation of those terms. I was, and it is remarkable to me that as the Republicans increasingly cast their lot with Robertson, Falwell, James Dobson, and others, Democrats have never exposed their lineage.

Robertson frequently inveighs against the "judicial activism" and "legislative tyranny" that support the "gay agenda" and the "murder of millions of innocents" (abortion). But both Robertson and his language turn out to have an interesting pedigree. His father, a strident segregationist, was a Congressman and then Senator from Virginia in the middle of the twentieth century. And the younger Robertson suckled those words from the breast of bigotry in his own home. His father used *exactly the same words*—judicial activism and legislative tyranny—to describe the encroachment of the Congress and the

Supreme Court on the right to keep black people from voting and drinking from whites-only water fountains. In the 1950s, Robertson's father railed against the incursion against American and Christian values of liberals who were battling God, the natural order of things, and states' rights in their efforts to extend freedom to blacks.

Fifty years later, the rhetoric, emotion, and bigotry were the same, but it was no longer possible to declare interracial marriage the moral equivalent of bestiality. So the language stayed the same, but the target changed: gays. Robertson warned against granting "special rights" to gays (e.g., freedom from employment discrimination) because doing so would not only "destroy traditional marriage" but would legitimize similar demands "by those involved in pedophilia, bestiality, sado-masochism and even snuff films." He praised White House guards who escorted gay leaders to a meeting with the president while wearing rubber gloves and explained AIDS as "the judgment of God" on homosexuals.[26]

Jerry Falwell's history similarly implicates prejudice against people of color as the gateway drug to prejudice against homosexuals. For those addicted to hate, gays have provided a legal fix since the prohibition against open displays of racism. Always ready with the catchy slogan, in the mid-1960s, Falwell was a virulent opponent of civil rights, describing Lyndon Johnson's civil rights legislation as "civil wrong."[27] Twenty years later, in 1985, while visiting South Africa at the heart of apartheid, Falwell met with future Nobel Laureate and fellow Christian clergyman Archbishop Desmond Tutu, only to declare him "a phony" and to promise to send the message to "millions of Christians to buy Krugerrands" (the currency of the South African government).[28]

Once his preferred form of bigotry was out of favor, Falwell, like Robertson, simply changed the object of his afflictions. Gays proved particularly useful to bolster his empire after the fall of the Soviet Union in 1990. Until that time, he had intermingled messages about secular humanism in America with threats of the "godless Soviet Union" abroad, much as McCarthy had done thirty years earlier. When the Soviet Union fell, he switched to homosexuals and abortion as the "hot button" issues that could bring out the armies of the angry.[29]

He was in good company. In 1936, Heinrich Himmler, the chief of the German *Schutzstaffel (SS),* created the "Reich Central Office for the Combating of Homosexuality and Abortion."[30]

Gay baiting turned out to be very lucrative business for the two multimedia giants, a veritable goldmine of profits for prophets. Robertson and Falwell both used their extensive reach into millions of American homes to solicit hundreds of millions of dollars in donations to their ministries, media networks, and universities by frightening and enraging their flocks with tales of how gays would proselytize their children and destroy their marriages and families.*

Gays are not, however, the only objects of Robertson's and Falwell's scorn. Although gays make for good fund-raisers, the real enemy is the rest of us.

As described by evangelical minister Mel White, who worked closely with Falwell and ghostwrote books for many of the leaders of the religious right until he came to terms with his own homosexuality, when Falwell was creating the Moral Majority in the 1970s he faced a dilemma. He wanted to harness the collective might of the tens of millions of Christians (and other Americans) who had felt uneasy with the social changes of the 1960s. Yet he was theologically certain that most of that coalition—those who were not born-again Christians (i.e., the vast majority of American Christians, and of course everyone else)— were bound for hell. Ultimately, upon seeking wise spiritual counsel, he consoled himself with the recognition that at various times God, too, had used "pagans" for purposes that pleased Him.[31]

Democrats need to make sure that every American understands the contempt with which the spiritual leaders of the Republican Party hold them as "pagans." Let me repeat: these are not men at the periphery of the Republican Party. Falwell *delivered the prayer that opened the last Republican convention.* These men have instant access to the White

---

*How, exactly, gays destroy heterosexual marriages has never been clear to me. The far greater threat comes from heterosexuals, given that most people who have affairs do so with the opposite sex, so perhaps Republicans should propose a constitutional amendment against heterosexuality.

House and every Republican congressman and senator. They are selecting our judges. To the extent that they view most Americans as pagans to be manipulated to do God's bidding as they interpret it, those pagans should know it.[32]

Democrats can no longer maintain their vow of silence about Robertson, Falwell, and the other religious extremists (e.g., Focus on the Family's James Dobson) who are the spiritual leaders of the Republican Party. Every American should know these words of Reverend Robertson: "There is no such thing in the Constitution" as the separation of church and state, "It's a lie of the left, and we're not going to take it anymore." These are not the ravings of a lone extremist. They are the virtually identical to the legal theology of former Chief Justice William Rehnquist of the Supreme Court: "The 'wall of separation between church and state' is a metaphor based on bad history, a metaphor which has proved useless as a guide to judging. It should be frankly and explicitly abandoned."[33] Rehnquist seemed to believe he understood better than the framers of the Constitution what they intended, given that Thomas Jefferson used that very phrase.[34]

Every American should know how Robertson describes Christians who don't share his particular interpretation of scripture: "You say you're supposed to be nice to the Episcopalians and the Presbyterians and the Methodists and this, that, and the other thing. Nonsense. I don't have to be nice to the spirit of the Antichrist."[35] Or his definition of what it means to believe in the rights of our wives and daughters to be treated as equals under the law: "The feminist agenda is not about equal rights for women. It is about a socialist, anti-family political movement that encourages women to leave their husbands, kill their children, practice witchcraft, destroy capitalism, and become lesbians."[36] Or Falwell's words in the days immediately following the attack on the World Trade Center: "I really believe that the pagans, the abortionists, the feminists, and the gays and lesbians who are actively trying to make that an alternative lifestyle, the ACLU, People for the American Way. . . . I point the finger in their face and say, 'you helped this happen.'"[37]

These words have long been in the public record. That every American has not heard them a hundred times reflects the failure of leadership of the Democratic Party. Just as the American people were ready to hear a counternarrative on Iraq for three years before the Democrats offered them one, Americans have been ready to hear a counternarrative on faith, as was clear in the Schiavo affair. The latent associations to religious extremism are already there, if Democrats would simply activate them and offer an alternative moral vision, as evident in this soul-searching and movingly honest passage from David Kuo, who once helped lead President Bush's office of faith-based initiatives:

> When I talk to neighbors or strangers and I tell them that I try my best to follow Jesus, many look at me queerly. I've come to learn that their first thoughts about me are political ones—they figure I don't care about the environment, I support the war in Iraq, I oppose abortion, I am ambivalent about the poor, I want public schools to evangelize students, and I must hate gays and lesbians. That is what they associate with my faith. . . . Moreover, in the heat of many political moments, I have been what they feared.[38]

Ironically, it was not a Democrat but a Republican leader who took aim at the religious right just before the midterm election of 2006. Former House Majority leader Dick Armey, himself a Christian conservative, vigorously attacked "self-appointed Christian leaders" as "thugs" and "bullies" for splitting the conservative Christian movement (although he could just as easily have said the country) into two camps: those who want to "practice their faith independent of heavy-handed government" and "big government sympathizers who want to impose their version of 'righteousness' on others."[39]

It is time Democrats not only take on the fundamentalists who would impose their religious will on others but also reach out to the other "camp" Armey describes, the evangelical Christians who can be motivated by compassion just as readily than they can be motivated by anger or prejudice. In the 1820s, evangelical Christian leaders viewed slavery and the subjugation of women as sins and were activists in the cause of both the emancipation of slaves and the liberation of women.

Abraham Lincoln said that it was Harriett Beecher Stowe's novel, *Uncle Tom's Cabin*, that ultimately led him to the Emancipation Proclamation, and Stowe's father, the Reverend Lyman Beecher, was an evangelical Christian, abolitionist, and president of a seminary that enrolled an ex-slave as a student.[40]

Evangelical Christians (the term comes from *evangel*, which means spreading the "good news") are devoutly religious people who believe in the authority of the Scriptures, particularly the New Testament, and take a conservative, typically literal, interpretation of the Bible.[41] Like fundamentalist Christians, they believe that salvation lies in personal conversion, in being "born again." By virtue of their literalist interpretation of the Bible, evangelical Christians are conservative in nature, and are vulnerable to manipulation by those who selectively quote what the Episcopal Bishop John Shelby Spong has called the *Sins of Scripture*,[42] passages in the Bible that have been used to justify all manner of destruction and discrimination for two millennia (e.g., passages justifying slavery, religious crusades, and hatred of Jews). On Larry King's show, for example, the president of the Southern Baptist Convention averred that "God almighty does not hear the prayers of a Jew," a claim echoed by Falwell with almost identical words.[43] And because of their belief that only those who take Jesus as their personal savior can enter the Kingdom of God, they are equally vulnerable to splitting the world into "us" and "them," the saved and the unsaved, which is dangerous in a democracy, given the slippery slope to "those who have moral values" and "those who don't."

But unlike fundamentalists, evangelical Christians are not primarily driven by rage or loathing, and Democrats make a tremendous mistake when they fail to engage with them. Jimmy Carter spent much of his life working for the poor and homeless. And if you simply watch the face of evangelical minister Rick Warren, pastor of one of the largest mega-churches in the country and author of one of the most widely selling books in modern history, *The Purpose Driven Life*,[44] you see little of the anger, disgust, pride, and contempt that are the primary emotions expressed on the faces of Robertson and Falwell. By virtue of who they are and what they believe, evangelical Christians are readily moved by compassion.

The Reverend Billy Graham is an evangelical Christian who has ministered to tens of millions of people around the world. He infuriated fundamentalist leaders in his response to a question on homosexuality on the television show *20/20*, which illustrates the difference between the heart of an evangelical and a fundamentalist: "I think the Bible teaches that homosexuality is a sin, but the Bible also teaches that pride is a sin, jealousy is a sin, and hate is a sin, evil thoughts are a sin, and so I don't think that homosexuality should be chosen as the overwhelming sin that we are doing today." Elsewhere he added, "God loves all people whatever their ethnic or political background or their sexual orientation. . . . Christians take opposing sides on many issues. . . . Those on both sides of the issue must love each other."[45]

Democrats would do well to speak with conservative Christians in their language, making biblical allusions and using turns of phrase that let their listeners know that they *care about* their culture, values, and faith, just as they use language when speaking to New England environmentalists that makes clear that they understand and resonate with their values and concerns. Democrats would also do well to appeal to the better angels of the evangels, by posing a question religious conservatives should ask themselves every time they feel strongly about a "values issue" that has become politicized, whether abortion, homosexuality, poverty, or welfare: "Am I feeling mostly love and compassion, or am I feeling mostly disgust, contempt, or hate?" If the answer is the latter, their faith is likely being compromised by prejudice ("Whoever is angry with his brother will be liable to judgment"—Matt. 5:22).

Although there are no firm boundaries between the two, the difference between evangelical and fundamentalist Christians lies in the extent to which the latter are motivated by fear, hate, and the "other-condemning" moral emotions, particularly disgust, contempt, and loathing. No less of an authority then Jerry Falwell has described it well: "A fundamentalist is just an evangelical who is mad about something."[46]

Jimmy Carter describes what he considers the key characteristics of fundamentalist religions everywhere. They are invariably dominated by authoritarian males who consider themselves first among equals. They draw a radical distinction between themselves and everyone else, who are defined, at best, as objects of pity, and more usually, subhuman objects of scorn. They are angry and militant, often willing to resort to violence to assert the dominance of their beliefs, and view any efforts at cooperation or negotiation with others as signs of weakness. One of the ironic features of Christian fundamentalists, who avow their allegiance to the Prince of Peace, is their antagonism to any efforts to negotiate or even talk with their enemies, believing this to signal weakness.[47] Carter summarizes the central features of fundamentalism with three words: *rigidity*, *domination*, and *exclusion*.

As Karen Armstrong has written in her landmark history of fundamentalism, *The Battle for God,* fundamentalists—whether Muslim, Christian, Jewish, or of other faiths— "are convinced that they are fighting for the survival of their faith in a world that is inherently hostile to religion. They are conducting a war against secular modernity. . . . "[48] And in a sense, they are responding to something very real. The great German sociologist Max Weber described the progressive "rationalization" of the world, by which he meant that realms that were previously considered sacred and the object of theology, from the cosmos to human nature itself (e.g., whether people are gay because of genes or choice), have increasingly come under the microscope of science. The problem is that in responding to changing times, fundamentalists of all religions have been forced to mythologize the past, when even the Bible they wish to see as inerrant is filled with the prejudices of the times (e.g., condoning slavery).

Fundamentalists have many of the characteristics identified over fifty years ago by a team of researchers who fled to the United States from Nazi persecution and began studying why some people are susceptible to right-wing authoritarian ideologies. They believed, and hoped, that authoritarian personality dynamics were limited to, or especially common in, Nazi Germany—that something unique to the "German character" had produced the deadly combination of blind obedience and hatred that led many Germans to resonate with *Mein Kampf.*

Their findings took them aback, as they realized they were wrong. In their classic book, *The Authoritarian Personality,*[49] Theodore Adorno and his colleagues described a personality style characterized by a tendency to hate people who are different or downtrodden. They described a kind of person who is simmering with rage and fear, who often denies these feelings and projects all that is evil or morally contaminating onto groups such as Jews, blacks, homosexuals, or others who do not conform to rigid social stereotypes.[50]

Democrats should not worry about offending fundamentalists. Progressive values are by definition incompatible with fundamentalist ideologies, which are dominated by intolerance of differentness and moral emotions that are incompatible with progressive principles. But Democrats err if they fail to distinguish between fundamentalists, who should be the antagonists of their story, and evangelicals, whose moral emotions and sensibilities are often compatible with progressive ideology, as they were in nineteenth-century America. Evangelical Christians have turned markedly toward the right politically over the last several years in part because, until very recently,[51] no one else has been talking with them.

Although nearly 80 percent of white evangelical Christians voted for George W. Bush in 2004, many are getting increasingly uncomfortable with the assumption that their churches should be used as soliciting grounds for Republican policies or candidates, that their church membership rosters should be shipped to Republican headquarters, or that their faith should be intertwined with the Republican agenda, such as tax cuts for the rich, hatred of homosexuals, and American militarism.[52] Minnesota preacher Gregory Boyd recently told his flock, "When you put your trust in the sword, you lose the cross." His reading of scripture is far more mainstream than the reading of those who call themselves fundamentalists, who somehow come away from the New Testament with the idea that tax cuts and "shock and awe" are part and parcel of Jesus's message. Reverend Rick Warren has recently taken on AIDS in Africa as a central concern of his ministry and angered many right-wing Christian groups by inviting Barack Obama to speak at his conference on it.[53]

Resurrecting Our Moral Heritage

[O]nce in a while someone says something so remarkable that's it's worth noting, without any comment at all. Such a situation took place on March 1st in Annapolis, Maryland, where a hearing on a proposed constitutional amendment to ban gay marriage was taking place. . . . Jamie Raskin, professor of law at American University, testified as to why the amendment should not be passed. At the end of his testimony. . . . Senator Nancy Jacobs stood up and shouted: "Mr. Raskin, my Bible says marriage is only between a man and a woman. What do you have to say about that?" To which Mr. Raskin replied: "Senator, when you took your oath of office, you placed your hand on the Bible and swore to uphold the Constitution. You did not place your hand on the Constitution and swear to uphold the Bible."[54]

A progressive moral critique of the right is past due. But this critique should focus not only on the intemperate words of the moral leaders of the Republican Party but on the deeds of Republican office-holders. It should be framed as a *moral* critique, not as a matter of policy differences or a "debate on the issues." It should be framed as a debate about fundamental values and principles, and it should be designed to elicit *moral emotions*, including righteous indignation.

For the better part of six years the Republicans had complete or near-complete control over all three branches of government, and they made clear through their actions what their moral vision looks like in practice. If Democrats were to frame what the Republicans have done in moral terms, most Americans would be shocked and repulsed. Let me give a few brief examples of what I mean, in the ways I believe Democrats should frame them.

In May 2006, Republicans passed a $70 billion bill to extend tax cuts to the super rich, locking them in through 2010.[55] Just four months earlier, in the name of fiscal responsibility, they had cut $40 billion in social programs, including student loans and Medicaid.[56] When Bush had to make cuts from his tax windfall for the super rich, the first item to go was an increase in charity tax credits.[57] All the while, as the upper 1 percent were getting their windfall, the Internal Revenue Service set up a computer program to freeze and label as fraudulent tax refunds sought by 1.6 million poor people, the vast majority of which turned out to be valid.[58] These were people on the edges of subsistence who needed that refund.

The people of whom Jesus spoke most scornfully were those who were wealthy while others suffered, culminating in one of the most well-known passages from the New Testament, "It is easier for a camel to go through the eye of a needle than for a rich man to enter the kingdom of God" (Mark 10:21–25). If there is any mistaking his intent, John the Baptist made the point as clearly as it can be made: "He that hath two coats, let him impart to him that hath none; and he that hath meat, let him do likewise" (Luke 3:11). My guess is that most of the beneficiaries of the Republicans' fiscal largesse have two coats.

Jesus was called the Prince of Peace for a reason. You don't have to read much of the Bible—and certainly of the New Testament—to get the message. For example, "When a man's ways are pleasing to the Lord, he makes even his enemies live at peace with him" (Prov. 16:7), and "Blessed are the peacemakers, for they will be called sons of God" (Matt. 5:9). Yet no one could make a case that President Bush made every effort to call in the peacemakers before invading Iraq, killing 3,000 Americans and somewhere in the neighborhood of 600,000 Iraqi civilians—men, women, and children—according to the best available estimates.[59] The fact that we have no precise numbers reflects a deliberate policy by the U.S. government not to count them since doing so would be bad for public relations.

When asked about the use of negotiation to solve international problems such as Iraq, President Bush's ambassador to the United Nations, John Bolton, replied, "I don't do carrots."[60] Unfortunately, hundreds of thousands of men, women, and children, have died because of Bolton's carotene deficiency. And the link between religious zeal and military zeal is not incidental: a study of predictors of support for the Iraq War during the 2004 presidential election found that the best predictor—better than demographics such as gender, and even better than whether subjects came from "red" or "blue" states—was religious affiliation.[61] Militant religiosity kills.

The Bush administration, with the oversight of the Republican Congress, has been complicit in eliminating standards to protect the safety of the food we feed our children in compensation for the support of the fast-food and meatpacking industries.[62] The beef industry's chief lobbyist is now the chief of staff at the Agriculture Department. A former executive at the National Food Processors Association became the head of the FDA. The number of food safety inspections today is *one-tenth* the number as in the 1970s, as a result of cutbacks and staff layoffs. And the cost of this handsome payoff for industry? A recent *Consumer Reports* study found that 83 percent of the chickens for sale in supermarkets across the country are contaminated. Since the cattle industry took over the FDA, Americans should be very worried about what they are and are not being told about mad cow disease in the United States. We take a gamble every time we feed our children hamburger.

Or consider an issue at the heart of private moral decisions. Over 90 percent of women in the developed world, including the United States, use contraception, and where use of contraception is highest, abortion rates are lowest.[63] The Centers for Disease Control (CDC) found that 98 percent of American women who have had sexual intercourse have used contraceptives.

Yet President Bush appointed a doctor to be chief of family-planning programs at the Department of Health and Human Services—controlling a budget of a quarter of a billion dollars—from a "Christian pregnancy-counseling organization" whose Web site declares that "distribution of birth control is demeaning to women, degrading of human sexuality and adverse to human health and happiness"[64] and preaches sexual abstinence until marriage, opposes contraception, and refuses to distribute information on birth control at its centers. Bush similarly appointed Dr. Joseph Stanford, an opponent of contraception—even for married couples—to the FDA's Reproductive Health Drugs Advisory Committee.[65] His deputy commissioner for operations at the agency, Dr. Janet Woodcock, wrote in a memorandum that making the "morning-after pill" (called "Plan B") available over the counter, as recommended by the FDA's scientific advisors after a review of the scientific evidence, could lead to "extreme promiscuous behaviors such as the medication taking on an 'urban legend' status that would lead adolescents to form sex-based cults centered around the use of Plan B." If I heard this kind of language from a psychiatric patient, I would presume a fairly serious disturbance unless presented with evidence to the contrary. In a decision unprecedented in FDA history, the FDA not only adopted some of her language but overrode the scientific data on the safety of the medication, including evidence showing that the availability of the drug in other countries did not increase promiscuity and led to fewer abortions.[66]

After the FDA's initial decision, when President Bush's Press Secretary Scott McClellan was pressed four times by a reporter as to whether the president supported contraception, McClellan responded, "I think the president's views are very clear when it comes to building a culture of life." The reporter pressed on, "If they were clear, I wouldn't have asked." McClellan then stonewalled: "And if you want to ask those questions, that's fine. I'm just not going to dignify them with a response." A group of congressional Democrats then sent four letters to the president, asking, "Mr. President, do you support the right to use contraception?" He never responded.[67]

This is part of a dangerous pattern of behavior on the part of conservatives in office throughout the country. In the United States, at the state, local, and federal level, Republicans have been eliminating sex education programs from the schools, even though all available data show that they do not increase sexual behavior, that they reduce unwanted pregnancies, and that they reduce abortions. And where they have not eliminated sex education, they have emphasized abstinence and attempted to eliminate any mention of birth control. Yet polls show that roughly 95 percent of parents want sex education programs in the public schools that both encourage teenagers to wait until they are older to have sex *and* teach them about birth control. In the developing world, the Republicans' "see no evil" policy on contraception has not just been morally out of step with American public opinion but deadly. The Bush administration has limited or withheld aid from clinics that mention contraception or abortion, and has limited distribution of condoms in parts of Africa in which millions of people are infected with HIV daily, are dying of AIDS, and are transmitting the virus to their children through mothers' milk. By 2010, twenty million African children will be orphaned by AIDS.[68]

Democrats should be asking Republicans everywhere, in debates at every level of government, to explain their position on contraceptives. Democrats should run ads making clear that the Republican Party poses a clear and present danger to married couples who use birth control, and that they support an unprecedented governmental intrusion on the private lives of Americans in their bedrooms. Democrats should show the faces and tears of those African children infected with HIV, or whose parents have been ripped from them by the deadly epidemic, so they get the full emotional significance of putting right-wing extremist abstractions over the lives of living, breathing children, just like their own.

Democrats need to *personalize* the face of Republican immorality, hypocrisy, and indifference to suffering. They should make sure the American public understands, in a visceral way, the absence of compassion and common human decency that has become central to conservative ideology and Republican governance. Just last year, in the midst of a Republican hate campaign dressed up as immigration reform, Justice Samuel Alito refused to stay the deportation of a woman, married to an American citizen, with a nineteen-month-old child, because *twenty years ago* she lied about her immigration status when crossing the border into the United States from Mexico.[69] What is that child, who is an American citizen, and has known only one country—America—and only one family—his own—supposed to do without his mother? What moral ends could that possibly serve?

Those are the Republicans' family values.

Investigative journalist Seymour Hersh reported in May 2005 that Defense Secretary Rumsfeld had received a report that there were "800–900 Pakistani boys 13–15 years of age in custody." Human rights organizations, such as the International Red Cross and Amnesty International, have gathered considerable evidence of the torture of children *by the United States of America*, confirmed not only by Pentagon sources but by American soldiers who witnessed or participated in the abuse. Jimmy Carter tells the story of a visit by Brigadier General Janis Karpinski to an eleven-year-old detainee housed in a cell block for "high-risk prisoners." The child was weeping, and told Karpinski that "he really wanted to see his mother, could he please call his mother."[70]

Those are the Republicans' family values.

The list could go on forever. It's hard to read the Bible, and particularly the New Testament, without the uncanny sense that it was written with contemporary conservatives in mind. Consider the following words on corruption, "tort reform" that blocks people who have been victimized by egregious corporate decisions from seeking appropriate remedies, and "bankruptcy reform" that places returning National Guardsman on long tours of duty and people whose life savings have been devastated by catastrophic illness forever in debt with no hope of starting again: "For I know how many are your offenses and how great your sins. You oppress the righteous and take bribes and you deprive the poor of justice in the courts" (Amos 12); and "Do not deny justice to your poor people in their lawsuits" (Exod. 6).

You can't get much clearer as to where the Bible stood on "tort reform."

I suspect most Americans know very little about any of the decisions and policies I have just described. That isn't the fault of the Republicans. It reflects a deep moral failure of the Democratic Party that virtually every American can picture John Kerry flip-flopping in the wind but can't picture the faces of those African children, the image of that eleven-year-old "terrorist" weeping for his mother, or the possibility that the chicken they are putting on their children's plates *tonight* could infect them with dangerous bacteria.

Democrats have been scrambling to position themselves on "values issues" since the 2004 election. Perhaps the central message of this chapter is that they should not try to run as Republican look-alikes or Republican-lite on issues of faith or any other "values" issue. Doing so not only betrays the most fundamental values that have historically defined both the party and the nation, but as we have repeatedly seen, it is a strategy that virtually never succeeds at the ballot box, as voters choose the most moral candidate, not the runner-up.

The contemporary Democratic and Republican parties have two very different visions of morality and two very different visions of the relation between church and state. The Republican view of values, embodied in the party's 2004 platform, its actions in eight years of control of the executive branch and twelve years of control of Congress, and its judicial appointments, reflects a rigid, dogmatic interpretation of the Bible and a belief that the state is an instrument through which this interpretation can be imposed on those who do not share it. This view of values, and of America as a "Christian nation" (as opposed to a nation of whom the vast majority are Christians), represents a departure from two centuries of American history and a radical rejection of the pluralism and freedom of religion for which our forefathers spilled their blood. You can only believe you have the right to impose your view of when life begins on others who do not share that view if you believe your spiritual certainty gives you the right to override *their* personal faith and beliefs. At heart, this approach to church and state is as incompatible with democracy as the theocratic ideologies of the Middle East,[71] and Republicans need to be confronted with it.[72]

The progressive view of values essentially centers on the "golden rule." Its key virtues are compassion and tolerance, and it reflects the clear and simple moral dictum that we should treat others as we would want to be treated, whether or not they share our religious beliefs, gender, skin color, sexual orientation, or other characteristics, and even if we personally find some of their attitudes distasteful. It is a view that recognizes that people's faith should influence their values—their beliefs about what *should be*—but not their interpretation of data— their beliefs about what *is*. It is a view that embraces the values of the Enlightenment. Although firmly rooted in the Judeo-Christian tradition, and ultimately derived from the teachings of that tradition with its foundation in the Bible, this is a nondenominational view of public morality that can be held equally by Christians, Jews, Muslims, "secular humanists," agnostics, or atheists.

All it requires is a person of good faith, not a person of a particular faith.

These are the two views of morality, and of church and state, that comprise the contemporary "culture war." This is how Democrats should present the choice to voters so they can decide which view is more compatible with their values on moral experience.[73]

When the pollster John Zogby tracked down the meaning of the exit poll data from the 2004 presidential election showing that fully one-fifth of voters responded that "moral values" had determined their votes, he discovered something surprising: far and away, the moral values people considered most important were the Iraq War, greed, and poverty. These are Democratic "issues," but Democrats too rarely speak of them in moral terms.[74] Around the same time, the Pew Center for the People and the Press conducted a survey that similarly addressed "values issues." The survey showed that if the Democrats had made poverty a moral issue, they might well have gained considerable ground with the American public.

It wouldn't be difficult to preach a message about poverty to Americans, including those who tilt rightward, including many evangelical Christians. And it wouldn't be hard to contrast the moral visions on poverty of the right and the left in the language of values:

> They look in our inner cities and see the hardened faces of drug dealers, crack-addicted mothers, and absent fathers. We look in our inner cities and see the faces of their children, who deserve a home and a childhood. They look in the inner cities, and they see broken families. We look in the inner cities and wonder what our own children would become if they had to grow up in those broken homes. They look at our inner cities with anger and contempt, and wonder, "Why can't they act like us?" We look at our inner cities with sadness, and remember the phrase, "There but for the grace of God go I." They look at our inner cities and see their moral depravity. We look at our inner cities and see our moral responsibility.

It wouldn't be hard to make the same case in the language of faith. The theologian Jim Wallis has identified 3,000 verses in the Bible about helping the poor,[75] such as the following from the New Testament: "Don't store up treasures here on earth where they can erode or may be stolen. Store them in heaven where they will never lose their value. . . . You cannot serve two masters, God and money" (Matt. 6:19–24); "He who gives to the poor will lack nothing, but he who closes his eyes to them receives many curses" (Prov. 27); and "The righteous care about justice for the poor, but the wicked have no such concern" (Prov. 29:7).

Democrats who want to *move* voters in the South, where over 50 percent of the population is evangelical, or in much of the country, where over 80 percent espouse some religious faith, need to learn to quote scripture. Al Gore did it in his magnificent eulogy at Columbine, which could make the most devout atheist shed a tear. The fact that some readers likely bristle at the suggestion that Democrats quote scripture reflects how completely we have accepted the equation of faith and conservatism. To most Americans, the Bible is not literal truth. It is allegorical and inspirational. If you can't find a few sentiments in the Bible with which you can resonate, you're probably not looking very hard because much of it is just our own intuitive moral compass presented in the language of the sacred. If you've read Shakespeare, you may not realize how many biblical allusions to which you've been exposed. So if you're uncomfortable quoting scripture, quote Shakespeare.

When a Gay Fetus Becomes a Person

On February 24, 2004, George W. Bush held a press conference to announce the urgent need for an amendment to the Constitution to protect the institution of marriage from the hordes of gays and lesbians threatening to tear down the walls of civilization. Bush actually looked noticeably uncomfortable, suggesting, perhaps, some vestiges of a functioning conscience despite what he was about to do. The crux of his statement, spoken with a tremendous solemnity borne of flagging poll numbers against presumptive Democratic presidential nominee John Kerry (who locked up the nomination a week later), was as follows:

> In recent months . . . some activist judges and local officials have made an aggressive attempt to redefine marriage. In Massachusetts, four judges on the highest court have indicated they will order the issuance of marriage licenses to applicants of the same gender in May of this year.
>
> After more than two centuries of American jurisprudence and millennia of human experience, a few judges and local au-

thorities are presuming to change the most fundamental institution of civilization.

Their actions have created confusion on an issue that requires clarity. On a matter of such importance, the voice of the people must be heard. Activist courts have left the people with one recourse.

If we're to prevent the meaning of marriage from being changed forever, our nation must enact a constitutional amendment to protect marriage in America. Decisive and democratic action is needed because attempts to redefine marriage in a single state or city could have serious consequences throughout the country.

Bush concluded, with a disingenuousness that was mind-bending, as he deliberately unleashed a holy war against millions of his fellow citizens (including the daughter of his own vice president and the father of his chief advisor and close friend, Karl Rove),[76] "We should also conduct this difficult debate in a matter worthy of our country, without bitterness or anger. In all that lies ahead, let us match strong convictions with kindness and good will and decency."[77]

As always, Kerry's campaign let the issue fester. Shortly after Bush's speech, Kerry issued a brief statement: "All Americans should be concerned when a president who is in political trouble tries to tamper with the Constitution of the United States at the start of his re-election campaign." It was the right sentiment but delivered at the wrong volume.[78] Kerry was never heard from again on the proposed amendment except when asked, essentially assuming the stance of "Don't ask, don't tell." Emboldened by the Democrats' failure to call hate by its proper name, Republicans began using the issue—and propositions to ban gay marriage strategically placed on state ballots around the country—to mobilize their base and to cast themselves again as the party of morality and faith, with the Democrats doing nothing to "protect marriage."

The Kerry team could have turned an appeal to hate and prejudice aimed at the right into a voting issue in the center, where open displays of hate and intolerance tend not to play well. Kerry could simply have held a press conference and told the truth about what the president was doing, with his finger literally pointing at the president in moral outrage, and in precisely the same idiom the president used, the idiom of faith:

> Mr. Bush, that was one of the most *un-Christian* things I've ever seen a president of the United States do. The God I worship, and the God most Americans worship, is a God of love, not of hate, and He loves *all* his children, not just the ones you deem worthy. And He would never countenance building hatred into the sacred Constitution of the United States of America. To divide American against American for political gain, and to dress it up in the language of holiness, is as un-American as it is blasphemous.

Such a response doesn't talk about policy, plans, rights, or even Kerry's position on gay marriage. That's for another day. Instead it calls attention to the real message of Bush's proposed amendment to the Constitution: hate, prejudice, and divisiveness for partisan gain.

I use the example here of gay marriage because, for Democrats, it has proven one of the most difficult of the "values issues" as defined by the conservative movement, and because it represents the last frontier of acceptable prejudice in American life (as indexed by the fact that comics can still make jokes using stereotypes about sexual orientation). Although roughly 6 percent of men and nearly twice as many women have had homosexual encounters according to the latest Census numbers,[79] most heterosexuals harbor unconscious negative associations to gays,* and the majority in many parts of the country, particularly in Southern and rural areas, hold overtly hostile attitudes toward gays, particularly gay men.

Even on this issue, however, Americans are ambivalent, torn between a discomfort with what seems to many heterosexuals foreign,

---

*For convenience, I will use the term *gay* to include both men and women, to avoid repeating "gay men and lesbian women" or acronyms like "LGBT" that sound like a gay sandwich.

unnatural, and most of all "icky," and the value of tolerance that is central to American culture.

Poll results express this ambivalence. The lowest point from which Democrats can speak to the electorate about homosexuality is gay marriage, which nearly 60 percent of Americans oppose. But the trajectory for even that negative sentiment is downward, as acceptance of homosexuality in general has steadily increased, even during the Bush years. In 2004, the percent of Americans who reported that they "strongly oppose" gay marriage was in the low forties. Just two years later, it was in the high twenties.[80] In 1977, only 56 percent of people said gays should have equal opportunity in hiring. By 2001, that number had risen to 85 percent, and it is undoubtedly higher today.[81] The extent of change on equal opportunity is remarkably similar to the change observed between the 1940s and the early 1970s on racial discrimination in the workplace, revealing similar dynamics.

The Pew "values" poll after the 2004 election found that although Democrats ran from gays like the plague during the election, even a one-dimensional reading of poll data should have led the Kerry campaign to duke it out with the GOP because the Democrats would have won the center. Republicans, not Democrats, were out of step with public opinion, even after several months of silence on the left. Whereas only 36 percent of Republicans endorsed the statement that "Homosexuality is a way of life that should be accepted by society," the majority of Democrats (58 percent) and Independents (54 percent) agreed.[82] A 2006 Pew survey shows that attitudes toward homosexuals have liberalized considerably, with nearly half supporting gay adoption, up from slightly over one-third just seven years earlier, and with 60 percent now supporting gays serving openly in the military.[83]

Harris Polls over several years show the same trajectory.[84] In 1996, Americans disapproved of same-sex marriage by a ratio of roughly 6 to 1. By 2004, a majority still opposed it, but the ratio had dropped precipitously to 2 to 1. When asked to choose between same-sex marriage, civil unions, or neither, roughly one-third supported each position, with only 35 percent opposing both. More people than not still oppose adoption by gay couples, although by 2004, a majority supported allowing the partner of a gay or lesbian parent to adopt his or her partner's biological child.[85]

So how do we make sense of these numbers, and how can we develop a principled stand that reflects progressive values while recognizing where public opinion is?

Most Americans don't *hate* gay people, but they have a visceral discomfort with homosexuality, and they have trouble calling same-sex unions marriage. Thus, although most Americans oppose gay marriage, they don't support a Constitutional amendment against it, and they believe the government should recognize, in one way or another, long-term, monogamous same-sex relationships that may include children. Their sense of fairness leads most people to oppose discrimination against gays in the workplace as they recognize that sexual orientation has nothing to do with job performance, and after ten years of "don't ask, don't tell," the majority have grown comfortable with homosexuality even in the military, as it has clearly not confirmed the dire predictions of those who vigorously opposed any acceptance of gays in the military when Clinton first proposed it in 1993.

If we look for the high ground, three points are clear. First, Democrats should challenge Republicans everywhere on job discrimination against gays, and set them in conflict with their fundamentalist base. The vast majority of Americans believe discrimination has no place in America, and that includes discrimination against gays. Second, and related, Americans are ready to afford partner benefits and similar rights to gay couples, particularly when the issue is personalized, so they can see how the absence of such benefits affects real people and their children. Third, the majority of Americans now believe that we should have some kind of legal status for committed, long-term same-sex relationships.

So why is "marriage" such as sticking point? Marriage is a central *ritual* in American life, as it is in most cultures, and rituals are imbued with deep psychological and cultural significance. That's why gay and lesbian couples want the right to it.

But that's also why many heterosexuals, particularly those who grew up before the era of gay rights and had their attitudes shaped at a time when "openly gay" was not in our language, are uncomfortable with extending a ritual that has always united members of opposite sexes to same-sex couples. To them, it changes the meaning of the ritual, just as divorce often does, as evidenced in the less extravagant ceremonies chosen by many couples who are entering into a marriage that is not their first. Marriage also implies sex, and straight people by and large don't want to picture homosexual sex, particularly between men. (Men seem to have less trouble with lesbian sex, imagining they could be the third wheel.) A term like "civil unions" is more acceptable to most Americans in part because it is sanitized of all sexual connotations and, thus, doesn't arouse the same passions as "marriage."

Given that the low point from which progressives can speak to the American public about gay rights is gay marriage, the most obvious way to reach the progressive goal of equality is to concede the word *marriage* from the start as something better left for the states to regulate so that more liberal states can allow it and others can call gay unions by another name such as civil unions. Homosexual couples can then celebrate those unions however they see fit, appropriating whatever aspects of the ritual of marriage they want into their own wedding rituals. If and when people become comfortable with gay unions and realize that this wild and crazy "lifestyle" is not destroying Western civilization, the name can be renegotiated.

Perhaps the most powerful principle of behavior change ever discovered by clinical psychologists is *exposure*, which means exposing people to the thing they're afraid of until it is no longer threatening. Often, the most effective strategy is *graduated exposure*, in which a psychologist gradually exposes a person with a phobia (e.g., of spiders) to increasingly threatening experiences (e.g., starting with imagining a spider until the person can do so comfortably, and working up to picking one up).

Martin Luther King understood this principle in pursuing civil rights.[86] He knew that most lynchings after the Civil War were prompted by suspicion that a black man had engaged in sex with a white woman,[87] and bigots could readily activate fear and loathing in Southerners by raising the specter of interracial marriage (as Bob Corker demonstrated could still be done forty years later, as long as it was done outside of awareness). So King simply neutralized the issue by declaring, "I want to be the white man's brother, not his brother-in-law."[88] Just five years later, interracial marriage became a constitutionally protected right, and today, though some still turn their heads, the vast majority of Americans would consider limiting marriage between people of different races to be unthinkable.

A principled narrative on gay rights that integrates progressive values with an understanding of where the electorate is emotionally might look something like the following. These three simple sentences could prevent Democratic candidates in many parts of the country from the usual hemming and hawing that occurs when their own values clash with what they believe their constituents will tolerate:

> Marriage in our culture has long held both religious and legal meanings, and we respect the feelings, values, and religious beliefs of those who are uncomfortable with extending the word *marriage* to committed relationships between same-sex couples. At the same time, like all Americans, we believe we are all created equal, and that we all have the same rights to life, liberty, and the pursuit of happiness, to freedom from discrimination, and to equal protection under the law. Thus, we support the rights of couples who want to have committed relationships to have those relationships legally recognized, with all the benefits traditionally associated with marriage, but believe that each state should decide for itself what to call same-sex unions, in accordance with the values and beliefs of the people of that state.

Like the other principled stands suggested in this book, this one provides a broad framework for addressing a "values issue"—in this case, by distinguishing between the religious and legal meanings of marriage and mandating what the legal implications are, namely nondiscrimination—while giving considerable latitude to candidates, based on their own values and those of their constituents, to define the specific ways it should be applied. And like the other principled stands, it addresses the emotions and values of voters in the center who may share some attitudes with the right and some with the left, and prevents the kind of slippery slope arguments and framing by the opposition (e.g., that affording such rights to gays would affect heterosexual marriages) that often derail progressive proposals.

Conclusion:
Damning the Dispassionate River

The two visions of morality—and by extension, of faith, virtue, and character—that define the contemporary political landscape in America bring us back to the central message of this book. As progressives, we sell ourselves short, we sell our ideals short, and ultimately we sell the American people short when we fail to recognize that although ideas provide the roadmap for everything we hope to accomplish for ourselves, our families, our communities, our nation, and our world, ultimately it is our emotions that provide the fuel—and the hope—for those achievements.

The liberal philosophers of the Enlightenment used reason as a sword against those who would rule by religious dogma. But ultimately it was their *passion* for liberty, and for the liberty to take reason wherever it would go, that inspired the founding of this nation and the liberal democracies around the world, which seem as "natural" to us as the kingdoms justified by divine right did to most people at the dawn of the Enlightenment.

It is time, now, for reason, and the science it has inspired, to lead us to a better understanding of the passions that provide its sustenance, and to help those who want to lead our country in the spirit of the Enlightenment to recapture the imagination of the American people.

Behind every campaign lies a vision of mind—often implicit, rarely articulated, and generally invisible to the naked eye. Traces of that vision can be seen in everything a campaign does or doesn't do.

Two visions of mind and brain predominate in contemporary American politics. One is a dispassionate vision, which suggests that voters choose candidates by examining their positions on the issues, seeing who has the best positions on the most important issues, and calculating their relative utilities. The other, a passionate vision, suggests that voters are moved by the feelings candidates and parties elicit in them.

The dispassionate vision of the mind bears no relation to how the mind actually works. It flies in the face of everything we actually know from psychology and neuroscience about the evolution of the brain and the nature and function of emotion. It flies in the face of research in political science, which finds that the best predictors of voting behavior are emotional, not cognitive. And it flies in the face of modern American political history, in which strategists who have tried to approach voters through dispassionate, issue-oriented campaigns have routinely failed.

The dispassionate vision of mind and brain takes as axiomatic a trickle-up theory of politics, which assumes that voters start by evaluating policy positions, and that the results of these evaluations gradually trickle up into voting decisions. Yet the data from thousands of voters surveyed across multiple elections since the 1940s tell a very different story.

Voters tend to ask four questions that determine who they will vote for, which provide a hierachy of influences on their decisions about whether and how to vote: "How do I feel about the candidate's party and its principles?" "How does this candidate make me feel?" "How do I feel about this candidate's personal characteristics, particularly his or her integrity, leadership, and compassion?" and "How do I feel about this candidate's stands on issues that matter to me?"

Candidates who focus their campaigns toward the top of this hierarchy and work their way down generally win. They drink from the wellsprings of partisan feelings. They tell emotionally compelling stories about who they are and what they believe in. They "read" the emotional signals of their constituents well, and they make use of strategists who share or complement their political intelligence with intuition and science to help them express their principles, values, and positions in ways that resonate with the voters back home. They run on who they are and what they genuinely care about, and they know their constituents well enough to know where they share their values and where they don't. They can move people to tears, laughter, compassion, anger, and feelings of sanctity. They tell compelling stories. They speak at the level of principled stands. They provide emotionally compelling examples of the ways they would govern, signature issues that illustrate their principles and foster identification.

Candidates who start at the bottom of the hierarchy and work their way up generally lose. They present voters with facts and figures to support their arguments, and they trust that voters will weigh the information carefully to make informed decisions. They present laundry lists of issues and position statements showing how they would solve one problem after another. They appeal to voters' material interests and assume that rational voters will vote with their pocketbooks. If they are attacked by their opponent with emotional or inaccurate appeals, they assume that voters are rational and interested enough to ignore or refute it, and they either respond with more facts and figures or with silence.

These visions of the mind are like vast rivers, whose tributaries extend throughout the entire continent of a campaign. Each one naturally flows down certain banks but not others. When you hear a campaign operative express some version of, "We've got them beat on the issues," you know you're on the dispassionate river, and you know the candidate is going under.

It is time for those on the left to dam the dispassionate river, and to focus on navigating and channeling the emotional currents of the passionate political brain.

Pragmatically, what does that mean?

It means abandoning traditional Democratic laundry lists, with each special interest putting its "issue" in the bag, and instead telling and retelling compelling narratives of what progressives stand for and what they won't stand for.

It means recognizing the complex and conflicting networks that constitute public opinion, which can't be mapped in one dimension.

It means recognizing that most issues that matter to voters are fraught with conflicting emotions, not only between people but within people, and that the most persuasive appeals are usually those that are the most honest: that acknowledge the ambivalence, expose the limits of the extremes, and offer a principled stand that avoids any need for hedging or defensiveness.

It means recognizing the shared and unshared networks of different emotional constituencies and searching for networks that bridge them.

It means recognizing the difference between conscious and unconscious sentiments, appealing to voters' better angels, and calling hate by name.

It means recognizing that elections are won or lost in the marketplace of emotions, and that political persuasion is about managing emotions by activating the right networks.

It means selecting and nurturing candidates with the political intelligence to win, who can tell compelling stories about who they are and what they believe that will provide their fellow citizens with hope and inspiration.

It means distinguishing between ethical and unethical appeals, and gutting it out for every inch of the neural turf of the electorate, including the circuits that generate both positive and negative emotions.

It means recognizing the dangers posed by those who would demagogue hate and terror, and showing the courage to respond with compassion where appropriate and aggression where necessary.

It means reasserting the traditional American understanding of the relation between church and state, where American presidents raise their right hand and vow to protect the nation and its Constitution "so help me God," not reward the righteous and rageful who demand, in return for their campaign crusades, "so help *my* God."

But most importantly, it means that the first question a candidate should ask on any issue should always be, "In light of my values and the best available evidence, what do I believe is right?" The second question is how to close the gap between that answer and the feelings of the electorate.

The greatest leaders are those who know how to do so with wisdom and integrity.

POSTSCRIPT TO THE
PAPERBACK EDITION

★　★　★

I
t was July 2006. In the middle of writing what I thought was
going to be a brief book, I took a weekend off for an annual
family trip to Ann Arbor, Michigan. There, an old friend, a law
professor, asked me what I was up to. I told him I'd essentially put
my usual work as a clinical psychologist and researcher on the back
burner to write a book on politics and the political brain. Curious, he
asked how I'd gotten on that path and if I would send him the first
chapter.

The book, I told him, reflected two passions. I'd always had a
strong interest in politics, and over the last few years, I had occasionally
poked my head out of my research on personality disorders (some
might say a natural segue to politics) to study the role of emotion in
political decision making. That research had culminated in a study
that had garnered some popular attention, on how the partisan brain
reasons about political information. (The short answer: it doesn't.) But
my other passion was more personal. As the father of two young
daughters, I was deeply worried about the world we were leaving
them and thought that maybe it was time to use what I had learned, in
over twenty-five years as a researcher and clinician, about how the
mind and brain work to try to do something about it.

My friend emailed back to ask if he could see the rest of what I'd
written so far. A few hours later (clearly, law professors have too much
time on their hands) he wrote to see if I would mind if he forwarded the
manuscript to his friend Bob Kuttner, the co-editor of the progressive

magazine, *The American Prospect*. The following day I got a call from Bob. I don't remember much about the specifics of that conversation, other than Bob telling me as we were about to hang up, "I don't know who you are, or where you came from, but hold onto your hat, because you're going for a ride."

Two months later Bob was introducing me over lunch in a private dining room at an old Washington establishment, where I spoke for about two hours to a room filled with about fifty people. I was politically naïve enough that I didn't really comprehend the significance of the group he had assembled.

Bob had considerably more confidence in what would transpire than I did. In truth, I was expecting a lot more resistance to a message I thought many in the room might find offensive or simply wrong-headed: that Democrats and progressives had been talking to the wrong parts of the brain for the better part of four decades, and that if you want to win voters' hearts and minds, you have to start with the heart, because otherwise they aren't going to care much what's on your mind.

What I came to understand over the ensuing months was that my clinical and scientific background had provided the basis for a set of principles that many people had already intuitively understood at some level but just needed someone to make explicit. As several pollsters and strategists told me subsequently, including some who worked for failed Democratic presidential campaigns, they had often *felt* in campaign after campaign that something was amiss, that their messages weren't "getting through," but they couldn't quite put their finger on why. And many had trouble abandoning a series of deeply ingrained assumptions: that a campaign is a "debate on the issues"; that if you just lay out your best policies and plans, people will vote with their rational self-interest; that if the other side is using a wedge issue against you (stirring up fear or hatred), it's best to try to change the subject or offer a slightly more benign version of what they're proposing (to avoid being "soft" on the threat to Democratic masculinity du jour). All of those assumptions, it turns out, are wrong, and in this book, I marshal the evidence—both scientific and historical—to show why they are deadly to a political campaign.

That meeting led to dozens of others around the country. By the time the book came out in June 2007, I had already presented to the leadership of the Democratic Party and was working on a project for the Democratic Policy Committee of the United States Senate. A few weeks after the book came out, I was sitting in my sweats in a Starbucks in Atlanta, only to find President Clinton on the other end of my cell phone. Within a few months of publication of the hardcover edition, I had begun spending most of my time talking to and working with progressive leaders and elected officials all over the country about how to move from the language of think tanks to the language of dinner tables and living rooms, and had begun testing and refining the ideas in the book in the real world of campaigns.

Much as I'd like to claim some originality for the ideas in this book, the truth is that if I hadn't written it, someone else would have eventually written one with a similar message, probably from a different starting place than psychology or brain science, but articulating the same unorthodox thesis I was advancing: that elections are won and lost not primarily on "the issues" but on the values and emotions of the electorate, including the "gut feelings" that summarize much of what voters think and feel about a candidate or party. In many respects, it was an idea waiting for an author.* Candidates who win the hearts and minds of the voters are the ones who can weave together emotionally compelling stories about who they are and who their opponents are, and who can make people feel what they feel. In this view, the stories candidates tell (or fail to tell) on the stump about people they have met along the road are not just political theatre or "fluff" aimed at tugging on people's heartstrings (although they can certainly be used that way). They are illustrations of where their heart is, of what they care about, which cue voters into their emotional concerns.

---

*A handful of maverick political scientists had already, in fact, documented the importance of emotion in politics, and the linguist George Lakoff (and his Berkeley colleague, Geoff Nunberg) had written persuasively about the language of the left and its limitations. Several progressive pollsters and leaders had also been working since 2004 to put values back into progressive politics and to begin developing a more emotionally compelling progressive lexicon.

Old ways take time to change, and as I know from my experience as a psychotherapist, that time can feel glacial. But many in Washington and around the country have been listening, including those who will set the tone for future elections if they succeed. All of the major Democratic presidential candidates read the book, and all of their campaigns called for advice at various points in the campaign—some more, some less. But whatever minor influence the book may have had on this year's Democratic primary nomination process, I could not have manufactured a better set of case studies to illustrate its central thesis than what happened in the primaries on both sides of the aisle in 2008.

The real stories of the primaries and caucuses of 2008 were the rise and fall and rise again of three candidates: John McCain, Hillary Clinton, and Barack Obama. In July of 2007, when McCain's candidacy was plummeting, I wrote a piece for the *Huffington Post*, describing why McCain's campaign had turned moribund. And the same principles that explain his fall from grace explain his campaign's remarkable resurrection.

In politics, you have to tell coherent, emotionally compelling, memorable stories, particularly about who you are and what you stand for. What John McCain stood for—and what had earned him the respect of many Independents and even many Democrats who knew little about his record but liked the *story* of John McCain—was summarized by the name of his bus and his campaign theme: the Straight Talk Express.

That was his story. But many powerful voices in the Republican Party didn't like the plot, and McCain had seen them defeat him in 2000. So in 2006 he began to rewrite it. But it turned out to be impossible for McCain to bluff with an extreme right-wing hand when he didn't have a poker face and to embrace a president everyone knew he despised (because he'd looked into his eyes in the South Carolina primary in 2000 and seen his soul). No one was buying his new story because it flew directly in the face of the narrative that had made him so compelling.

Precisely when McCain made his pact with the devil is unclear, but the signs of the bargain were obvious by the spring of 2006. In March, at a straw poll of the Southern Republican Leadership Council, he

disingenuously urged those in attendance, "if any friends here are thinking about voting for me, please don't. Just write in President Bush's
name. For the next three years, with the country at war, he's our president, and the only one who must have our support today." In April, he
strained credulity even among the party faithful by calling George W.
Bush "one of the great presidents of the United States." That was the
same month he embraced Jerry Falwell, a dramatic about-face by a man
who had labeled Falwell an "agent of intolerance" just a few years earlier at a time when doing so was a sign of his straight-talking courage.
The new McCain was creating a new story, but the not one he'd hoped
for, and one that left his campaign in tatters: that he was willing to sell
his soul for a lease on 1600 Pennsylvania Avenue.

The unfolding of that new narrative was clear on *The Daily Show*,
as Jon Stewart struggled with what many in the center and the left
struggled with as they watched a man they may not have agreed with
on many issues, but nevertheless admired, lose the characteristic that
had made him seem so admirable: "You're killing me here!" Stewart
half-jokingly told McCain. "You're not freaking out on us—are you going into crazy-[conservative] base world?" McCain laughed defensively
as he defenselessly responded, "I'm afraid so." In fact, McCain had
recently voted to make Bush's tax cuts to the well-heeled permanent after having initially denounced them; supported the most draconian law
ever proposed on abortion, a South Dakota bill that would have forced
rape and incest victims to bear their rapists' babies; and expressed his
support for the teaching of "intelligent design."

In March of 2007, Adam Nagourney of the *New York Times* reported on an extraordinary moment in Iowa, when McCain was asked
a simple question while chatting on his bus with reporters: Did he
support the distribution of condoms in Africa to fight the transmission
of HIV? McCain searched for words, glanced at the ceiling, paused
awkwardly with repeated silences, asked his aides to tell him what his
position was, said he'd never thought about it before, and hoped his
physician friend, right-wing Oklahoma Senator Tom Coburn, could
help him out. When asked whether he believed sex education in the
United States should teach abstinence only (the imposition of the Bush
administration on public schools that wanted funding for sex education),

he answered after a long pause, "Ahhh. I think I support the president's policy." When a reporter followed up, asking whether he believed contraceptives help stop the spread of HIV, he answered after another long pause, "You've stumped me." An incredulous reporter followed up, leading to the only honest moment of the press conference, when McCain answered, with a defensive laugh, "Are we on the Straight Talk Express? I'm not informed enough on it. Let me find out. You know, I'm sure I've taken a position on it in the past. I have to find out what my position was. Brian, would you find out what my position is on contraception—I'm sure I'm opposed to government spending on it. I'm sure I support the president's policies on it."

McCain's response of "Are we on the Straight Talk Express?"—like his answer to Jon Stewart's question—revealed everything the American people needed to know about John McCain: He was no longer aboard his own bus.

That McCain was able to win his party's nomination reflected, in part, the years of positive associations most Americans had to him and their difficulty making sense of (and hence willingness to forget) his two-year foray into political cowardice and opportunism because it just didn't fit with the story of his extraordinary courage as a prisoner of war in Vietnam. Our brains search for order in disorder, and when a piece of information doesn't fit, people readily forget it or rationalize it away. But McCain was also the beneficiary of two pieces of simple good luck. The first, paradoxically, was that his poll numbers tumbled so rapidly when his Straight Talk Express took a sharp right off a cliff that his campaign ran out of financial fuel, and with it went the high-priced consultants who had helped him construct a story about himself that was so manifestly untrue that no one was buying it.

The second was the absence of a strong Republican field. As a Democrat, the two candidates who worried me most in watching the first Republican primary debate—because of their nonverbal behavior, their comfort in their skin, and their ability to tell a story—were Romney and Huckabee, who turned out to be the last two contenders standing before McCain clenched the nomination. But Romney, who had been twice elected governor of Massachusetts, couldn't possibly have believed most of what he was saying on the campaign trail, and he had the misfortune of having to face television clips from his years running the most liberal state in the union that belied virtually every claim he was making to Republican primary voters about himself.

From the first time I watched Huckabee, he made me nervous, because I disliked most of what he said but I liked him anyway. The fact that many pundits found his victory in Iowa unexpected, even when his poll numbers started to climb in the weeks before the caucus, reflects what happens when you're reading the wrong cues in politics. Huckabee was the most politically intelligent of the candidates on the Republican side in 2008, with a sense of humor; a genuineness that Americans craved after eight years of an administration that has made most of us wistful for the days when an honest man like, say, Richard Nixon, inhabited the White House; and a pastor's ability to deliver a sermon.

But Huckabee had two other characteristics that derailed his candidacy, one to his right and one to his left. On the right hand, he simply wasn't angry enough. One of the biggest mistakes Democrats have made is to fail to distinguish the authoritarian fundamentalists whose political emotions center on hate, disgust, and contempt, and whose moral emotions render them antagonistic to everything Democrats stand for, from the large number of evangelical Christians who can be moved by demagogues to feel those same emotions but who are more naturally drawn to messages of love, compassion, and beneficence if someone leads them to their better angels. Huckabee was a natural for the latter but anathema to the former, as evident, for example, in his stance on immigration.

To his left, Huckabee was vulnerable because of a tendency to blurt out thoughts unbefitting of a man of his intelligence, and certainly of an American president in the twenty-first century, such as his disbelief in evolution and his suggestion that we change the Constitution to fit the Bible. The latter experiment has already been tried, and as far as most of us can tell, it doesn't seem to be working all that well in Iran (different book, same concept).

These factors, plus Rudy Giuliani's decision to enter the race once it was already over (and Fred Thompson's decision to sleep through it), conspired to give McCain a second chance, and as soon as he put the wheels back on the Straight Talk Express, it started rolling again. Just how little "issues" really mattered on the Republican side could be seen in exit polls on Super Tuesday, when Republican voters in state after state—who endorsed the most draconian positions on illegal immigration—chose the newly straight-talking McCain as their man, despite his being the Republican candidate least likely to pander to the extreme right on one of the defining issues of the Republican debates. The tension for McCain for the general election is that precisely what he needs to say to bring his party's base to the polls for him is what flies in the face of his personal story and will alienate the moderates whose votes he would need to win the presidency.

On the Democratic side, 2008 was an embarrassment of riches, at least in terms of substantial candidates with the knowledge and gravitas to lead. Hillary Clinton showed herself early to have an extraordinary intellect and a firm grasp on virtually every issue confronting the nation. No reporter, no matter how motivated with a "gotcha" question, could catch her on virtually anything (except her dogged refusal to acknowledge that her Iraq War vote was a mistake). And it is difficult to imagine a candidate who better exemplifies many of the central messages of this book than Barack Obama. Although pundits tried to dissect "what Hillary did wrong," by late February of 2008, after eleven straight primary and caucus victories for Obama, Adam Nagourney of the *New York Times* asked a simple question: Is there anything Hillary Clinton could really do to defeat Barack Obama?

Our strengths and our weaknesses tend to flow from the same wells, and Hillary's commanding debate performances were emblematic of both. She made stronger appeals to voters' values than traditional Democratic campaigns, and by late January of 2008, she was a different candidate on the stump. She couldn't match the natural charisma of Obama, but after seeing what emotion could do for her in New Hampshire, she became emotionally much more "present" as a speaker and was moving away from the megaphone-like speaking style and vocal tone that had worked poorly for her on the stump and detracted from her debate performances. And her decision to bring her daughter, Chelsea, out to campaign for her—first with her and then on her own—was just what the doctor ordered, and it clearly made a difference. Chelsea was helpful in appealing to young voters, as emphasized by traditional punditry. But more importantly, Hillary's obviously loving relationship with her daughter flew in the face of the narrative with which she'd been successfully branded for so many years by the right—that she was cold, uncaring, and "unfeminine."

Yet even at her best, she seemed determined to run the kind of relentlessly issue-oriented campaign that offers a 10-point plan for every problem and that has led to the defeat of Democrats in election after election over the last thirty years—with the singular exception of her husband, who appealed instead to the American people with a charismatic style, a message of hope much closer to Obama's, and just enough policy to make clear that he was no lightweight. Although she was both tough and agile in her debate performances from the start, she failed to recognize—until her voice cracked in New Hampshire and signaled to voters that there was a person hiding inside that pantsuit—that what she needed more than anything was not another plan for another issue but a story of who she was and what she stood for, and a way to make a dent in the central story the right had branded her with since the early 1990s.

Her Christmas 2007 campaign ad in Iowa illustrated in microcosm the problems with her message—and with the message of Democratic campaigns at virtually every level of government for much of three decades. With *Carol of the Bells* playing in the background, a pair of scissors cuts through wrapping paper, and a pair of hands places gift cards on a series of presents. The camera focuses sequentially on the cards, which bear the inscriptions, "Universal Health Care," "Alternative Energy," "Bring Troops Home," and "Middle Class Tax Breaks." The candidate then appears on the couch amidst the pile of presents she's been wrapping, looks around the room for something missing, and asks herself, as the music stops momentarily for effect, "Where did I put 'Universal Pre-K'?" Suddenly, she finds it, and a big smile appears on her face as she utters the words, "Ach! Here it is!" and looks admiringly at the gift she imagines giving it to the American people. The music then resumes.

What's wrong with this picture? Everything except the music. Perhaps most centrally, it only reinforces the story Ronald Reagan told most forcefully about Democrats, which has been repeated by Republicans ever since: that they never saw a tax they didn't want to raise or a social program they didn't want to create. Here was Hillary Clinton telling the people of Iowa what she wished for them: more government programs. The problem isn't that any of those programs, taken individually, wouldn't be worthwhile or provide real solutions to real problems that would enrich millions of people's lives. The problem is that what she was offering the people of Iowa was a bag full of issues and a bag full of government solutions, with the message, "Merry Christmas!"

Campaigns aren't won with bags full of anything. They are won by candidates who can convince voters, through their words, intonation, body language, and actions that they share their values, that they understand people like them, and that they can inspire the nation or save it from dangers. Policies and plans should be *indicators* or *examples* of what candidates care about, which tell voters whether they share their values and would approach the nation's problems in sensible ways. Hillary's Christmas ad, like so many Democratic ads and campaigns, required voters to work too hard to know where her heart was, to find the yarn that tied together those seemingly disparate packages.

Contrast this with Barack Obama's message to Iowans that same Christmas. His ad began with a shot of the Obama family in front of their hearth, with a fire burning, stockings hanging above the fireplace, and a large Christmas tree in the background. Michelle and Barack Obama are sitting next to each other, her arm wrapped around his leg, and a child in each of their arms. Michelle begins, "We'd like to take a moment to thank you and your family for the warmth and the friendship that you've shown ours. . . ." Then Barack: "In this holiday season, we're reminded that the things that unite us as a people are more enduring than anything that sets us apart. . . . So from my family to yours, I approve *this* message" (turning to his older daughter, who says with a broad smile): "Merry Christmas," followed by the little one chirping, "Happy Holidays." The ad ends with the obviously proud parents joining their children with a warm smile, a picture-perfect family portrait of the Obama family in the home.

The ad had barely any "content" (other than Obama's signature theme of unity), no "issues," no policies, no plans. Yet it was remarkably effective. I've watched or shown it to audiences a dozen times, and by the end, I simply can't suppress a broad smile on my face, nor can anyone I've seen watch it. In part, that simply reflects the way our brains work: Smiles are literally contagious (when they're genuine), because they trigger neurons in our brain that not only detect emotions in others but lead us to experience directly what they are feeling.

But the ad was effective in several other ways as well. Most importantly, it fostered identification with Obama, something essential for a candidate whose race threatened to stand between him and the white Iowa populace. It conveyed a simple message: "I love my family, I love my wife, and I value families, just like you do."* It is difficult to watch the ad and not come away thinking, "You know, they're just like us (and their kids are really cute)." The ad erases their differentness from white Americans. And it adds a new dimension to Obama: an image of a strong, warm, loving father—just the kind of image that reassures voters in troubled times.

Although I do not know if this was intended, the ad also quietly conveyed something else very important about Obama: that he is Christian. That mattered for two reasons. First, Obama's Christianity breaks down another barrier between him and many white voters, particularly in the South. The ad implicitly says to the majority of Americans, "We worship the same God." Second, for a year the Obama campaign had let a story fester about him, largely on the Internet, that took many forms: that he was Islamic, that he put his hand on the Koran when taking his oath of office in the United States Senate, that he refused to say the Pledge of Allegiance, that he was trained at anti-American Islamic schools in Indonesia as a child—in a word, that he was not only Islamic

---

*The image of the handsome young man with his young family also unconsciously reinforced an association between Obama and another charismatic young Democratic president with young children in the White House who inspired the hope of the American people, John F. Kennedy. The obvious affection between Michelle and Barack Obama, who are gently touching throughout the ad, also triggers an implicit comparison with the Clintons, whose marital difficulties had been so public.

but *foreign*, not like "us." Right-wing pundits were calling him Osama Obama and B. Hussein Obama, to make the associations to terrorists as well as to everything un-American or anti-American.

This smear campaign did substantial damage. By the winter of 2008, it was impossible to attend a focus group with swing voters any-where in the United States without hearing a substantial minority describe him as Muslim or repeat with conviction the stories about the Pledge of Allegiance or his taking the oath of office with his hand on the Koran. It took nearly a year before he began to address this stealth attack directly, one of the few serious mistakes his campaign made. Unfortunately, the lore in Democratic campaign circles is that it's best not to address these kinds of attacks directly for fear of fanning the flames (just like some mental health professionals once believed that it's best not to ask depressed adolescents about suicidal thoughts for fear of "putting the idea in their heads"). As I show in this book, how-ever, for reasons that are as much neurological as political, a candidate should never allow the public to form negative associations toward him for any length of time, and certainly not a year.

The Obama campaign was, in many respects, brilliantly orches-trated, both in its ability to make its message of unity in divided times "stick" and in what political insiders call its "ground game" (e.g., getting people to the polls, understanding the complex machinery of caucuses, organizing people and events), something Obama and his lead strategist, David Axelrod, knew remarkably well how to do, with their background in community organizing. But what political pundits often forget about the Obama campaign was that it was not always electrifying, and its progress was uneven. Obama's standing in the polls was slowly but steadily slipping within a few months of the stunning speech that began his candidacy in front of the state capitol in Spring-field Illinois in January 2007. His steady decline in the polls continued through October of 2007, when Hillary Clinton broke the 50 percent mark in the national polls with Democratic voters despite a still crowded field. And as with McCain, the same principles that explain Obama's decline account for his extraordinary turnaround.

In late June 2007, I wrote a piece for the *Huffington Post,* on the day the Obama campaign announced a record-breaking fundraising quarter, called "Who Turned Out the Electricity?" I argued that if he continued to weigh down his campaign speeches and debate performances with 14-point plans to compete with the Democratic Joneses, losing his inspirational message in a morass of policies and positions instead of using his proposals as examples of where he wanted to take the country that fit his uniquely inspirational style, he would see a continued steady downward slope in the polls. Not only was the land of 14-point plans Hillary Clinton's home turf, with her encyclopedic knowledge of every issue, her years in Washington as both the most involved, accomplished First Lady in American history, and her record as a senator, but it was a no-man's land filled with the bones of fallen Democratic candidates, who had repeatedly lost to Republicans who stole the hearts of the American people while Democrats competed for their minds.

The article drew less than enthusiastic responses, given its incongruity with the news of his record-break fundraising quarter, although the donors who had been so enthusiastic about him were already beginning to express concerns privately about his lackluster debate performances and his inconsistent, sometimes professorial stump speeches. Their concern turned out to be well founded: For the next five months, his poll numbers did, in fact, drop steadily, as Clinton's fortunes climbed. In the June article, I described why I thought the campaign needed to change course:

> On the stump, Obama can be electrifying. And behind all that electricity is a first-rate intellect. But if you have electricity, the last thing you want to do is pull the circuit breaker and start explaining the fine points of transistors, electrons, and electrical engineering. Yet that's exactly what Obama has done in his recent debate performances. Whether the decision was his, his senor strategists,' or some combination of the two, he seems to have decided to check his charisma at the door, avoid the moving imagery and oratory that electrified the electorate from the first time they saw him on the national stage, and talk about issues, positions, "marginal tax rates" (as opposed, for example, to "your taxes"), and the fine print of his health care plan.

His campaign was obviously trying to put some meat on the policy bones of his positions, in part to allay concerns about his inexperience, and in part to pacify the wonk wing of the Democratic Party and the political pundits and editorial boards who had demanded from Democratic candidates for years that they obsess on precisely the level of detail that predicts failure in general elections. I concluded in June that rather than following the traditional Democratic strategy of focusing on the minutiae of policy details and rolling out plan after plan for issue after issue, "Obama would do a lot better to take a leaf out of Reagan's book than to retrace the journey of the long list of Democrats who have drowned on the dispassionate river: Let Obama be Obama."

Months later, his campaign finally did just that. At the Jefferson–Jackson Dinner in Iowa, the Obama who had been watching Hillary Clinton's stock rise for months as he sold his own stock short stepped up to the podium and electrified the audience in a way that sent shock waves through the political world—and ultimately led to his victory in Iowa and the cascade of primaries and caucuses that followed. Newspapers in cities all over the country ran headlines such as "Obama Finally Finds His Voice," and his voice grew more confident and inspiring as the months proceeded. By the time he had racked up twelve straight primary and caucus wins after Super Tuesday, Hillary Clinton had no choice but to go negative against him, because she simply couldn't out-inspire him.

Clinton's negative campaign against Obama succeeded in breaking his momentum on March 4 in the Texas and Ohio primaries, particularly when combined with a strong message about what she would do to get an ailing economy out of a second Bush's recession—a message that strongly reinforced voters' positive associations to Bill Clinton's stewardship of the economy over his eight years in the White House. But what transpired in Texas and Ohio and over the ensuing days speaks to one of the central messages of this book, and to the way Obama's strengths and weaknesses on the campaign trail, too, flowed from the same wells: You can't win an election by ceding half the brain to the other side. No one has ever won an election by harnessing only positive emotions. Franklin Roosevelt, John F. Kennedy, Ronald Reagan, and Bill Clinton were all remarkably inspirational leaders, but none of them shied away from sharply criticizing their opponents (primarily on issues of ideology, not personality), particularly in the general elections, where such criticism doesn't risk damaging their own party's chances in November and leave voters with negative associations to the attacker. Kennedy attacked the character of his opponent in the general election (Richard Nixon) because his opponent, in fact, had problems of character relevant to his fitness for the presidency, as history would bear out. Successful campaigns are campaigns that both inspire and raise concerns about the opposition. And as I argue in this book, that's exactly what they should do, because an election is a choice, not a referendum, and because positive and negative emotions both drive voting behavior, but in psychologically and neurologically distinct ways.

Obama's relentlessly positive message of rising above politics as usual left him open to attacks that tied his campaign in knots: If he attacked back, it would threaten his master narrative, that he was above the fray and intended to set a new tone in Washington; if he didn't, he would suffer the same fate as Dukakis, Gore, Kerry, and every other Democrat who refused to respond to a strong attack with a stronger counterattack. The success or failure of his campaign would hinge on whether he could stop the bleeding after Ohio and Texas and find his way to a response that would reinforce his own story—that he had come to Washington to clean it up—while reinforcing the story that had dogged Hillary Clinton for fifteen years and worried Democratic voters about her electability. It wouldn't have been difficult to craft a message that cast every attack she made as yet one more example of the divisiveness that Obama had pledged to clean up as president. As of this writing, however, this chapter in the history of the 2008 campaign is yet to be written.

But there's another lesson in the success of Hillary's attacks, one that I address throughout this book: the fact that much of what influences voters occurs outside of conscious awareness. Voters reported in exit polls on March 4 that they thought Hillary's attacks on Obama were unfair. But precisely the same voters gave her victories in two large battleground states. People can't tell you in polls and focus groups what really influences them because they don't know. Voters may have thought Hillary went over the top, but in their guts, she had sown the seeds of serious doubts about Barack Obama, and in politics, it's the gut that's ultimately decisive.

None of this is to suggest that emotion is the only factor that accounts for the rise and fall and rise again of three extraordinary politicians, or of elections more generally. For example, the media had always loved McCain and his story, and both Hillary Clinton and Barack Obama benefited from a media transfixed by the idea of a race between a black man and a woman. As a consequence, candidates such as Joe Biden, Chris Dodd, and especially John Edwards, whose performance on the stump and in debates was routinely superb, never really got a hearing.* And as the country moves into a recession while mired in a deeply unpopular war, John McCain has an enormous cross to bear, especially after taking the baton from his unpopular predecessor.

But if there's a central message in the primary campaigns of 2008, it's that whatever accounts for who became or becomes the nominee on either side has little to do with "the issues." John McCain could certainly speak with more authority on military issues as a veteran than Mitt Romney, but their policy positions were virtually identical. Hillary Clinton and Barack Obama were about as similar as two candidates could be in their voting records in the Senate. Yet in the Wisconsin primaries, for example, voters who reported in exit polls that

---

*Whether in frustration at his inability to gain traction in the polls, the tragic events of his personal life (his wife's cancer), a strategic miscalculation, or bad advice, Edwards set aside the natural optimism and capacity to inspire that almost won him the nomination four years earlier and ran a relentlessly angry populist campaign. That approach has never won a presidential election, as voters come to associate the candidate, instead of the targets of his attacks, with negative feelings. Had Edwards aimed his anger more carefully and bookended it with humor and inspiration, he might well have gained traction. But in a year dominated by the idea of an historic candidacy—a woman or an African-American at the top of the Democratic ticket—it may simply not have been enough. Edwards may, however, have had a significant impact on the election with the success of his populist message and the resonance of his attacks on corporate malfeasance—just as Ned Lamont, while losing his race for Senate against Joe Lieberman in Connecticut in 2006, taught Democrats all over the country that they could run against the Iraq War and ultimately win an unexpected landslide election.

the most important issue to them was health care—Hillary Clinton's signature issue—broke for Obama, just as militantly anti-immigrant Republicans routinely voted for McCain.

Issues—the economy, the Iraq War, energy, immigration, health care, whatever they may be—play a major role in elections. But as every presidential election since the advent of modern polling has shown, successful candidates are the ones whose personal stories, principles, ways of talking about their virtues and concerns for the nation, and personalities capture the imagination of the public (or create enough doubt about their opponent to win despite a less than compelling story of their own). Successful candidates are those who set the emotional agenda of the electorate.

ACKNOWLEDGMENTS

★　★　★

This book would not have happened without a lot of encouragement, wise counsel, help, sacrifice on the part of my family, and ignorance on my part of what I was getting myself into.

I'd first like to thank Susan Arellano, my literary agent, who helped me turn a thought into an idea and an idea into a prospectus, and then helped me find just the right publisher for it. She offered her usual superb advice and encouragement throughout the process.

I'd like to thank my editor, Clive Priddle at PublicAffairs, for both his wisdom and wisecracks throughout a project that took longer than he had hoped, and for his astute and merciless editing of a first-draft manuscript that was much longer than either of us ever imagined. I learned a great deal from his comments and suggestions along the way, and he learned never again at the beginning of a project like this to say to an author, "Do you really think it will be that short? Perhaps you'll be able to beef it up a little when you get into the writing?" He did a terrific job at finding the beef and helping me excise some of the marbling around the ribs. Many thanks also to all of those at PublicAffairs and Perseus, including Whitney Peeling and Shana Murph, who helped put this book out on a very tight schedule.

To Bob Kuttner at *The American Prospect*, and to the *Prospect* and its board, I owe a tremendous debt of gratitude. Through a somewhat serendipitous process, Bob saw an early draft of the first half of the book, read it in a day, and has gone to extraordinary lengths to introduce me all over the country to people who know how to make a difference. He has become a good friend, and he is a true friend to all those who value fairness and tolerance. And many thanks to those who have invited me into their homes to present some of these ideas or spent hours of their own time to contact hundreds of people to set up presentations and meetings in Washington, D.C., New York, and around the country even before the book was out.

Several people helped get this book started, even though they didn't know it at the time. Clint Kilts and Stephan Hamann, and our respective labs, worked together with me on the brain-scanning study with which this book begins both literally and figuratively. And thanks to many friends, old and new, at Renaissance Weekend, whose excitement about some of the ideas expressed here a little over a year ago ultimately encouraged me to write this book, and whose enthusiasm a year later helped me get through the final chapters.

I'd also like to express my thanks to Eric Russ, my wizard of the Internet, who helped track down the most obscure speeches and commercials on the Web when my Googling skills failed, and to Rachel Hershenberg, who helped get the reference list into shape.

Thanks also to Mudcat Saunders and Rebekah Bradley for their very perceptive comments on Chapter 11.

Finally, my greatest debt is to my family, who endured a very long year as Daddy cloistered himself away to write or sometimes listened with only one ear as an idea was dancing around the other. My wife Laura had to listen to more blathering than any human being should be forced to endure over the last year; two-and-a-half-year-old Sarah asked me every day for the last two months, "Daddy, are you done?"; and as soon as six-year-old Mackenzie got word that the end was in sight, she began planning out what we would be doing together the first weekend after the final manuscript was turned in with the kind of meticulous detail of a campaign manager. To all of them: Daddy's home.

NOTES

★   ★   ★

For the interested reader, we have placed complete notes, including bibliographic references and additional notes of interest to those engaged in the practice of politics or to scholars, on the Internet, at www.westenstrategies.com/PoliticalBrainNotes. Doing so allows interested readers to click on hyperlinked references and saves wear and tear on readers' spines while carrying the book around.

Below are particularly useful follow-up references for each chapter.

INTRODUCTION
Westen, D., Kilts, C., Blagov, P., Harenski, K., & Hamann, S. (2006). The neural basis of motivated reasoning: An fMRI study of emotional constraints on political judgment during the U.S. Presidential election of 2004. *Journal of Cognitive Neuroscience, 18,* 1947–1958.

CHAPTER ONE
Armstrong, J., & Moulitsas, N. (2005). *Crashing the gate: Netroots, grassroots, and the rise of people-powered politics.* White River Junction, Vermont: Chelsea Green Publishing.

CHAPTER TWO
Marcus, G. E. (2002). *The sentimental citizen: Emotion in democratic politics.* State College: Penn State Press.

CHAPTER THREE

Brader, T. (2006). *Campaigning for hearts and minds: How emotional appeals in political ads work.* Chicago: University of Chicago Press.

Morris, J. S., Oehman, A., & Dolan, R. J. (1998). Conscious and unconscious emotional learning in the human amygdala. *Nature, 393,* 467–470.

CHAPTER FOUR

Watson, D., & Tellegen, A. (1985). Toward a consensual structure of mood. *Psychological Bulletin, 98,* 219–225.

Westen, D. (1985). *Self and society: Narcissism, collectivism, and the development of morals.* New York: Cambridge University Press.

CHAPTER FIVE

Holyoak, K. J., & Thagard, P. (1997). The analogical mind. *American Psychologist, 52,* 35–44.

Kunda, Z. (1990). The case for motivated reasoning. *Psychological Bulletin, 108,* 480–498.

CHAPTER SIX

Marcus, G. E., Meuman, R., & Mackuen, M. (2000). *Affective intelligence and political judgment.* Chicago: University of Chicago Press.

Huddy, L., Sears, D. O., Jervis, R., & Slobodkin, L. B. (2003). *Oxford handbook of political psychology.* New York: Oxford University Press.

CHAPTER SEVEN

Carville, J. & Begala, P. (2006). *Take it back: Our party, our country, our future.* New York: Simon and Schuster.

Jost, J. T., Glaser, J., Kruglanski, A. W., & Sulloway, F. J. (2003). Political conservatism as motivated social cognition. *Psychological Bulletin, 129,* 339–375.

CHAPTER EIGHT

Klein, J. (2006). *Politics lost: How American democracy was trivialized by people who think you're stupid.* New York: Doubleday.

Chapter Nine

Jarding, S., & Saunders, D. (2006). *Foxes in the henhouse: How the Republicans stole the South and the Heartland and what the Democrats must do to run 'em out.* New York: Touchstone.

Chapter Ten

McClelland, D. C., Koestner, R., & Weinberger, J. (1989). How do self-attributed and implicit motives differ? *Psychological Review, 96,* 690–702.

Sears, D. O., & Henry, P. J. (2005). "Over thirty years later: A contemporary look at symbolic racism and its critics." In *Advances in experimental social psychology,* (ed.) M. P. Zanna, New York: Academic Press.

Chapter Eleven

Lakoff, G. (2004). *Don't think of an elephant! Know your values and frame the debate.* White River Junction, VT: Chelsea Green Publishing.

Luntz, F. (2007) *Words that work: It's not what you say, it's what people hear.* New York: Hyperion.

Chapter Twelve

Masters, R., & Sullivan, D. (1993). "Nonverbal behavior and leadership: Emotion and cognition in political information processing." In S. Iyengar & W.J. McGuire, (Eds.), *Explorations in political psychology.* Durham, North Carolina: Duke University Press, 150–182.

Ambady, N., & Rosenthal, R. (1993). Half a minute: predicting teacher evaluations from thin slices of nonverbal behavior and physical attractiveness. *Journal of Personality and Social Psychology, 64,* 431–441.

Chapter Thirteen

Geer, J. G. (2006). *In defense of negativity: Attack ads in presidential campaigns.* Chicago: University of Chicago Press.

Chapter Fourteen

Johnson, H. B. (2005). *The age of anxiety: McCarthyism to terrorism.* Orlando, FL: Harcourt, 460.

Pyszczynski, T., Solomon, S., & Greenberg, J. (2003). *In the wake of 9/11: The psychology of terror.* Washington, DC: American Psychological Association.

Chapter Fifteen

Cousins, N. (1958). *In God we trust: The religious beliefs and ideas of the American founding fathers.* New York: Harper & Brothers.

Kuo, D. (2006). *Tempting faith: An inside story of political seduction.* New York: Simon and Schuster.

White, M. (2006). *Religion gone bad: The hidden dangers of the Christian right.* New York: Penguin Group.

INDEX

★ ★ ★

DREW WESTEN, Ph.D., is a clinical, personality, and political psychologist and neuroscientist, and professor in the departments of Psychology and Psychiatry at Emory University. He is founder of Westen Strategies, LLC, a political and corporate consulting firm. He formerly taught at the University of Michigan, Harvard Medical School, and Boston University. Dr. Westen is the author of three books and over 150 articles. He frequently comments on political and psychological issues on radio, television, and in print, including ten years as a commentator on National Public Radio's "All Things Considered," and more recently as a political analyst on *Dan Rather Reports*. He has written for a range of popular media outlets, such as the *Washington Post*, the *New York Review of Books*, *The New Republic*, *The Huffington Post*, and *Adweek* magazine. He has advised or continues to advise or to consult a range of candidates and organizations—from presidential candidates, to major Democratic and progressive organizations, to organized labor, to international political leaders, to Fortune 500 companies. His holiday song, "Oy, to be a Goy on Christmas," still airs periodically on the radio during the holiday season. He lives with his wife and two daughters in Atlanta, GA.

PublicAffairs is a publishing house founded in 1997. It is a tribute to the standards, values, and flair of three persons who have served as mentors to countless reporters, writers, editors, and book people of all kinds, including me.

I. F. STONE, proprietor of *I. F. Stone's Weekly*, combined a commitment to the First Amendment with entrepreneurial zeal and reporting skill and became one of the great independent journalists in American history. At the age of eighty, Izzy published *The Trial of Socrates*, which was a national bestseller. He wrote the book after he taught himself ancient Greek.

BENJAMIN C. BRADLEE was for nearly thirty years the charismatic editorial leader of *The Washington Post*. It was Ben who gave the *Post* the range and courage to pursue such historic issues as Watergate. He supported his reporters with a tenacity that made them fearless and it is no accident that so many became authors of influential, best-selling books.

ROBERT L. BERNSTEIN, the chief executive of Random House for more than a quarter century, guided one of the nation's premier publishing houses. Bob was personally responsible for many books of political dissent and argument that challenged tyranny around the globe. He is also the founder and longtime chair of Human Rights Watch, one of the most respected human rights organizations in the world.

•   •   •

For fifty years, the banner of Public Affairs Press was carried by its owner Morris B. Schnapper, who published Gandhi, Nasser, Toynbee, Truman, and about 1,500 other authors. In 1983, Schnapper was described by *The Washington Post* as "a redoubtable gadfly." His legacy will endure in the books to come.

Peter Osnos, *Founder and Editor-at-Large*